Old Testament
THEOLOGY

A Thematic Approach

ROBIN ROUTLEDGE

IVP Academic

An imprint of InterVarsity Press
Downers Grove, Illinois

InterVarsity Press
P.O. Box 1400, Downers Grove, IL 60515-1426
Internet: www.ivpress.com
E-mail: email@ivpress.com

InterVarsity Press® is the book-publishing division of InterVarsity Christian Fellowship/USA®, a movement of students and faculty active on campus at hundreds of universities, colleges and schools of nursing in the United States of America, and a member movement of the International Fellowship of Evangelical Students. For information about local and regional activities, write Public Relations Dept., InterVarsity Christian Fellowship/USA, 6400 Schroeder Rd., P.O. Box 7895, Madison, WI 53707-7895, or visit the IVCF website at <www.intervarsity.org>.

ISBN 978-0-8308-2896-8

Printed in the United States of America ∞

green press *InterVarsity Press is committed to protecting the environment and to the responsible use of natural resources.*
INITIATIVE *As a member of Green Press Initiative we use recycled paper whenever possible. To learn more about the Green Press Initiative, visit <www.greenpressinitiative.org>.*

Library of Congress Cataloging-in-Publication Data
A catalog record for this book is available from the Library of Congress.

P	19	18	17	16	15	14	13	12	11	10	9	8	7	6	5	4	3	2	1
Y	25	24	23	22	21	20	19	18	17	16	15	14	13	12	11	10	09		

CONTENTS

PREFACE

There are a great many useful books on OT Theology available, with new volumes appearing regularly. Often, though, they give too much information or too little. Many are large and daunting to the ordinary student or pastor, and because of their layout, which is often determined by their approach, information may be hard to access; others take a more introductory approach and do not deal with many of the theological issues and questions the OT raises. My aim is to bridge that gap, and provide a substantial overview of the main issues in OT Theology in the main body of the text, with more detailed discussion and references for further reading in the footnotes.

The material in this book belongs in the area of biblical theology. The principal concern in biblical studies is with the text, and I have tried to maintain that priority. My purpose, though, is to look at the theological significance of the text within its wider canonical context, noting unity and coherence within the OT (and to some extent between the OT and the NT), while being aware of diversity. Due to lack of space, exegetical work is generally assumed, and references for some follow-up discussion are included. A brief outline of the relationship between exegesis and biblical theology within the overall hermeneutical task is given in the first chapter.

This book has grown out of a teaching context. Over the years, I have adapted material to meet the needs of students, and in writing I still have those students in mind. As a Christian minister, I hope too that the material here will be of benefit to others who want to take the theological content of the OT seriously, and to apply its message to the life and ministry of the church.

In recording dates, I have used the designations AD and BC rather than the more widespread CE and BCE. This decision has a theological basis. As a Christian, I believe that the coming of Jesus Christ has marked a turning point in the history of the world, and that is reflected in the transition from BC to AD. The OT has significance in its own right, but looks forward to fulfilment in Christ. In my view that forward look, and the expectation of the OT's ultimate fulfilment in Christ, is better reflected in the designation BC than in the theologically neutral BCE.

ABBREVIATIONS

AB	Anchor Bible
ABD	*Anchor Bible Dictionary*, ed. D. N. Freedman, 6 vols. (New York: Doubleday, 1992)
AnBib	Analecta biblica
ANE	Ancient Near East
ANET	*Ancient Near Eastern Texts Relating to the Old Testament*, ed. J. B. Pritchard, 3rd ed. with supplement (Princeton: Princeton University Press, 1969)
AOAT	Alter Orient and Altes Testament
AOTC	Apollos Old Testament Commentary
AV	Authorized (King James) Version
BA	*Biblical Archaeologist*
BSac	*Bibliotheca sacra*
BST	The Bible Speaks Today
BTB	*Biblical Theology Bulletin*
BZAW	Beihefte zur Zeitschrift für die alttestamentliche Wissenschaft
CBQ	*Catholic Biblical Quarterly*
ConBOT	Coniectanea biblica: Old Testament Series
DNTT	*Dictionary of New Testament Theology*, ed. Colin Brown, 3 vols. (Grand Rapids: Zondervan, 1975–8)

DOTT	*Documents from Old Testament Times*, ed. D. Winton Thomas (Edinburgh: Thomas Nelson & Sons, 1958)
EBC	*The Expositor's Bible Commentary*, ed. F. E. Gaebelein, 12 vols. (Grand Rapids: Zondervan, 1984)
EQ	*Evangelical Quarterly*
ET	English translation
ET	*Expository Times*
HSM	Harvard Semitic Monographs
HUCA	*Hebrew Union College Annual*
IBD	*The Illustrated Bible Dictionary*, ed. J. D. Douglas, N. Hillyer et al., 3 vols. (Leicester: IVP, 1980)
IDB	*The Interpreter's Dictionary of the Bible*, ed. G. A. Buttrick, 4 vols. (Nashville: Abingdon, 1962)
Int	*Interpretation*
IRT	Issues in Religion and Theology
JAOS	*Journal of the American Oriental Society*
JBL	*Journal of Biblical Literature*
JEBS	*Journal of European Baptist Studies*
JETS	*Journal of the Evangelical Theological Society*
JJS	*Journal of Jewish Studies*
JNES	*Journal of Near Eastern Studies*
JSNT	*Journal for the Study of the New Testament*
JSOT	*Journal for the Study of the Old Testament*
JSOTSup	Journal for the Study of the Old Testament, Supplement Series
JSS	*Journal of Semitic Studies*
JTS	*Journal of Theological Studies*
LXX	Septuagint
MSJ	*The Masters Seminary Journal*
NBD	*New Bible Dictionary*, ed. J. D. Douglas (London: IVP, 1962)
NCB	New Century Bible
NDBT	*The New Dictionary of Biblical Theology: Exploring the Unity and Diversity of Scripture*, ed. T. Desmond Alexander and Brian S. Rosner (Downers Grove: IVP; Leicester: IVP, 2000)
NIBCOT	New International Biblical Commentary on the Old Testament
NICOT	New International Commentary on the Old Testament
NIDOTTE	*New International Dictionary of Old Testament Theology and Exegesis*, ed. Willem A. VanGemeren, 5 vols. (Carlisle: Paternoster; Grand Rapids: Zondervan, 1996)

NIV	New International Version (1984)
NIVAC	New International Version Application Commentary
NRSV	New Revised Standard Version (1995)
NSBT	New Studies in Biblical Theology
NT	New Testament
OBT	Overtures to Biblical Theology
OTG	Old Testament Guides
OT	Old Testament
OTL	Old Testament Library
OTS	Old Testament Studies
RevExp	*Review and Expositor*
SBL	Society of Biblical Literature
SBT	Studies in Biblical Theology
SBTS	Sources for Biblical and Theological Study
SJT	*Scottish Journal of Theology*
ST	*Studia theologica*
TBC	Torch Bible Commentaries
TDNT	*Theological Dictionary of the New Testament*, ed. G. Kittel and G. Friedrich; trans. G. W. Bromiley, 10 vols. (Grand Rapids: Eerdmans, 1964–76)
TDOT	*Theological Dictionary of the Old Testament*, ed. G. Johannes Botterweck, Helmer Ringgren and Heinz-Josef Fabry, trans. John T. Willis, Geoffrey W. Bromiley, David E. Green and Douglas W. Stott, 15 vols. (Grand Rapids: Eerdmans, 1974–2006)
ThTo	*Theology Today*
TOTC	Tyndale Old Testament Commentaries
TynBul	*Tyndale Bulletin*
VT	*Vetus Testamentum*
VTSup	Supplements to Vetus Testamentum
WBC	Word Biblical Commentary
WW	*Word and World*
ZAW	*Zeitschrift für die alttestamentliche Wissenschaft*

ACKNOWLEDGMENTS

This book is the result of many years of work, and I am very grateful to those who have helped me reach this point. I want to acknowledge my particular indebtedness to Martin Selman, teacher, mentor and friend, who inspired and nurtured my love of the Old Testament. Special thanks, too, to John Rogerson, my PhD supervisor at Sheffield University, for his wisdom, guidance and encouragement. I am grateful, too, to other friends and colleagues at Mattersey Hall, the International Baptist Seminary, Prague, and Bangor University, who have also helped, supported and encouraged me along the way. Thanks, too, to the students at Mattersey Hall, past and present, whose comments and questions have kept me on my toes and helped me develop this material in a way that, I trust, will be useful to them and to others; and who have kept me focused on the real reason for all of our work: building the kingdom of God.

My thanks, too, to Philip Duce and the team at IVP for their support, and for their hard work and patience in bringing this material to publication.

And last, but by no means least, thanks to my parents; to my children, Philip and Rebekah, who have seen far less of me than they might have hoped for over the last year or so; and to my patient and long-suffering wife, and best friend, Ailsa, who is glad that someone may finally read what I have spent hours locked in my study writing – when I could have been cutting the grass!

1. APPROACHES TO OLD TESTAMENT THEOLOGY[1]

The Old Testament as Christian Scripture

The Christian Bible comprises the Old and New Testaments and, from earliest times, Christians have accepted the OT alongside the NT as canonical and normative for faith. It is impossible, here, to trace the growth and development of the OT canon. Its make-up was essentially as we know it by the NT period,

---

1. See e.g. Bernard W. Anderson, *Contours of Old Testament Theology* (Minneapolis: Fortress, 1999), pp. 1–47; Gerald Bray, *Biblical Interpretation Past and Present* (Leicester: Apollos; Downers Grove: IVP, 1996); F. F. Bruce, 'The Theology and Interpretation of the Old Testament', in G. W. Anderson (ed.), *Tradition and Interpretation: Essays by Members of the Society for Old Testament Study* (Oxford: Oxford University Press, 1979), pp. 385–416; Walter Brueggemann, *Theology of the Old Testament: Testimony, Dispute, Advocacy* (Minneapolis: Fortress, 1997), pp. 1–114; Brevard S. Childs, *Old Testament Theology in a Canonical Context* (London: SCM, 1985); *Biblical Theology of the Old and New Testaments: Theological Reflection on the Christian Bible* (London: SCM, 1992), pp. 3–106; Ronald E. Clements, *A Century of Old Testament Study* (London: Lutterworth, 1976); *Old Testament Theology: A Fresh Approach* (London: Marshall, Morgan & Scott, 1978), pp. 1–25; Gerhard F. Hasel, *Old Testament Theology: Basic Issues in the Current Debate*, 4th ed. (Grand Rapids: Eerdmans, 1991); Paul R. House, *Old Testament Theology*

though there was still debate about the acceptability of some books up to the so-called Council of Jamnia in AD 90, when some kind of a consensus about the contents of the canon appears to have been reached.[2]

'Old Testament' or 'Hebrew Bible'?

'Old Testament' is a Christian designation.[3] It is common in some circles to refer, instead, to the 'Hebrew Bible' or 'Hebrew Scriptures'. Though not strictly accurate, since some parts are in Aramaic (Ezra 4:8 – 6:18; 7:12–26; Jer.

Footnote 1 (*continued*)

(Downers Grove: IVP, 1998), pp. 11–57; Edmond Jacob, *Theology of the Old Testament* (London: Hodder & Stoughton, 1958), pp. 11–36; R. W. L. Moberly, 'Theology of the Old Testament', in David W. Baker and Bill T. Arnold (eds.), *The Face of Old Testament Studies: A Survey of Contemporary Approaches* (Leicester: Apollos; Grand Rapids: Baker, 1999), pp. 452–478; see also introductory articles in *NIDOTTE* 1:14–205.

2. After the fall of Jerusalem in AD 70, Jamnia became a centre for study of the Scriptures, including discussion about whether certain books (e.g. Esther, Ecclesiastes, Song of Solomon, Ezekiel), which were already generally accepted, should continue to have canonical status. While it is unlikely that there was an official 'Council of Jamnia', decisions taken there in AD 90 probably did result in some formalization of its content. For further discussion of the OT canon, see e.g. Norman K. Gottwald, *The Hebrew Bible: A Socio-Literary Introduction* (Philadelphia: Fortress, 1985; paperback with CD-ROM, 2002), pp. 102–114; R. K. Harrison, *Introduction to the Old Testament* (London: IVP, 1977), pp. 260–288; H. H. Rowley, *The Growth of the Old Testament* (London: Hutchinson University Library, 1950); William Sanford LaSor, David Allan Hubbard and Frederick William Bush (eds.), *Old Testament Survey: The Message, Form, and Background of the Old Testament*, 2nd ed. (Grand Rapids: Eerdmans, 1996), pp. 598–605.

3. Because 'old' might suggest out of date and no longer relevant, some prefer the designation '*first* testament'; see e.g. John Goldingay, *Old Testament Theology*, 2 vols. (Downers Grove: IVP; Milton Keynes: Paternoster, 2003–6), 1:15; see also Rolf Rendtorff, *The Canonical Hebrew Bible: A Theology of the Old Testament* (Leiden: Deo, 2005), pp. 746–749. I do not think this testament has outlived its theological usefulness; nevertheless, though not perfect, 'Old Testament' has a Scriptural basis and has been used by Christians for many centuries. For a range of views on this question, see Roger Brooks and John J. Collins (eds.), *Hebrew Bible or Old Testament: Studying the Bible in Judaism and Christianity*, Christianity and Judaism in Antiquity 5 (Notre Dame: University of Notre Dame Press, 1990).

10:11; Dan. 2:4 – 7:28),[4] this designation recognizes that before it became part of the Christian Bible, the OT was (and continues to be) Jewish Scripture, and emphasizes both the Jewish roots of the Christian faith and the fact that Christianity has not replaced Judaism.[5] Nevertheless, though certain texts are held in common by Christians and Jews, the way they are interpreted and the use made of them is different. This can be seen, for example, in the order of the books. In the (Jewish) Hebrew Bible the last book is Chronicles, which has as a key emphasis the building of the Jerusalem temple. After describing its destruction by the Babylonians, the book closes with the edict of Cyrus, which opens the way for the Jews to return and rebuild the temple (2 Chr. 36:22–23). Thus the book points to a new beginning for God's people after the exile, a new beginning linked, particularly, with the restoration of their religious life, including the birth of Judaism. The (Christian) OT ends with the prophecy of Malachi, which points to the coming of the day of the Lord that will be preceded by the return of Elijah. This opens the way for the NT focus on John the Baptist and his announcement that the kingdom of God has come in the person of Jesus Christ. With a different canonical ordering, the same Scriptures prepare their respective readers for different fulfilments.[6]

---

4. The Jewish acronym Tanak (Torah [Law], Nevi'im [Prophets], Ketuvim [Writings]) might be more accurate, though this designation also has faith content and does not allow for the different ordering of books in the OT.

5. Judaism is also a later development of the faith of the first testament, generally linked with the reforms of Ezra after the exile, which has developed over the centuries. References to the 'Jewishness' of the OT (and of the NT) can imply that Jews are in a better position to understand it than westernized Gentiles with a history of anti-Semitism. One common view, represented by David H. Stern, in his *Complete Jewish Bible* (Clarksville: Messianic Jewish Resources International, 1998), is that the whole Bible is Jewish and, because there is an essential continuity between the faith of the first testament and Judaism, Christianity needs to be set within a Jewish religious and cultural context. In my view that argument is flawed. Judaism is no less a development of the faith of the first testament than Christianity is.

6. The order of the OT is influenced by (though not identical to) the LXX, the version most commonly quoted by NT writers. The LXX groups books based on literary content: Law, History (including Chronicles), Writings/Poetry and Prophecy (including Daniel). The order and division of the Hebrew Bible seems to have been accepted during the NT period: *from . . . Abel to . . . Zechariah* (Luke 11:51) indicates a text that runs from Genesis to Chronicles (Zechariah is mentioned in 2 Chr.

This is linked with biblical theology, which has as one of its goals an appropriate relating of the Old and New Testaments.[7] How that may be achieved, and how the OT may function as an authoritative document of the Christian church is a subject of debate, and aspects of that debate are considered below. However, because it includes discussion about the relationship between the testaments, biblical theology is a Christian, rather than a Jewish, task. Jews are interested in the Tanak, but not in its function in relation to the NT. In fact theology of the first testament has also, so far, been a predominantly Christian task, with much Jewish scholarship expressing opposition to (or at least a suspicion of) doing theology.[8] Barr notes the view of Tsevat that a true Jewish theology would need to include the Talmud and the Mishnah, which are as inseparable from the Tanak for Jewish readers as the NT is from the OT for Christian readers.[9]

Footnote 6 (*continued*)

24:20–22), and reference to 'the Law of Moses, the Prophets and the Psalms' (Luke 24:44) points to the threefold division of the Tanak. This suggests that the acceptance of a different order by the church was not accidental but has theological significance. The generally accepted order of the books of the OT in the western church appears to go back to Jerome's Latin Vulgate (AD 382), which became the standard in the west.

7. For further discussion of biblical theology, see below, pp. 37–42.

8. On this discussion, see James Barr, *The Concept of Biblical Theology: An Old Testament Perspective* (London: SCM, 1999), pp. 286–311; Rendtorff, *Hebrew Bible*, pp. 740–749; Leo G. Perdue, *Reconstructing Old Testament Theology: After the Collapse of History*, OBT (Minneapolis: Fortress, 2005), pp. 183–238.

9. Brueggemann wants Christians to recognize Jews as 'co-readers', accepting that it is legitimate for one to read the OT text towards the NT while the other reads it towards the Talmud; see e.g. Walter Brueggemann, *An Introduction to the Old Testament: The Canon and Christian Imagination* (Louisville: Westminster John Knox, 2003), pp. 1–3. Rendtorff too looks for a common Jewish–Christian reading of the OT/Hebrew Bible; see e.g. Rolf Rendtorff, 'Towards a Common Jewish-Christian Reading of the Old Testament', in Brooks and Collins, *Hebrew Bible*, pp. 89–108. However, the significance of the OT cannot be separated entirely from the whole of which it is part; see Jon D. Levenson, 'Theological Consensus or Historicist Evasion? Jews and Christians in Biblical Studies', in Brooks and Collins, *Hebrew Bible*, pp. 109–145; also in Jon D. Levenson, *The Hebrew Bible, the Old Testament and Historical Criticism: Jews and Christians in Biblical Studies* (Louisville: Westminster John Knox, 1993), pp. 82–105.

Jon D. Levenson sets out his objections in the essay 'Why Jews Are not Interested in Biblical Theology',[10] and he too notes the importance of Jewish tradition, including Midrash and Talmud. Another issue is the centrality of the quest for unity in biblical theology. Levenson maintains that Judaism recognizes, and is happy to live with, tension and inner argument within the text. A third issue raised by Levenson is the emphasis in theology on belief over practice.

By contrast, Goshen-Gottstein does point to the need for Tanak theology within Jewish scholarship, analogous to (Christian) biblical theology. Perdue gives a lengthy list of Jewish scholars working in this area (including Goshen-Gottstein, Marvin Sweeney and Michael Fishbane).[11]

Another factor in the Christian view of the OT was the relationship between Christianity and Judaism in the early Christian centuries. The first Christians were Jews, and their only sacred text was the OT, which was interpreted as being fulfilled in Christ. As the church spread beyond its Jewish roots, we see a growing tension between Gentile converts and those who saw Christianity as an extension of Judaism. Opposition to Judaizing tendencies led to the OT being given a spiritual interpretation; viewing it, in effect, as a Christian book that had been misunderstood by the Jews.[12] As the gospel continued to spread among Gentiles, and the number of Jews coming into the church reduced,[13] a total separation of Christianity and Judaism became inevitable. That reduced the problem of Judaizing, but raised the question of what to do with the OT Scriptures that were not

10. In Brooks and Collins, *Hebrew Bible*, pp. 33–61.

11. Perdue, *Reconstructing*, pp. 194–225; see also Hasel, *Basic Issues*, pp. 34–38. Frymer-Kensky notes the emergence of biblical theology within Jewish scholarship as an alternative to rabbinic interpretation – opening the possibility of dialogue between biblical and rabbinic ideas; see Tikva Frymer-Kensky, 'The Emergence of Jewish Biblical Theologies', in Alice Ogden Bellis and Joel S. Kaminsky (eds.), *Jews, Christians and the Theology of the Hebrew Scriptures*, Symposium (Atlanta: SBL, 2000), pp. 109–121.

12. This is a key emphasis of the *Epistle of Barnabas* (see below, pp. 44–45).

13. One factor in the relationship between Christians and Jews seems to have been the Bar-Kochba revolt (AD 132). Bar Kochba was seen by many, including Rabbi Aqiba, as a messianic figure. Christians could not accept that and did not join the rebellion. This led to acrimony between Jews and Christians, made worse by the severity with which the Romans put down the uprising. From then on few Jews seem to have become Christians.

part of the religious heritage of those now coming into the church. Some, such as Marcion, wanted to devalue the OT in relation to the NT. Opposition to Marcion by the mainstream church resulted in the affirmation of the value of the OT for the church, though still as an essentially Christian document.

Christians see themselves as both the people of the new covenant, which was announced by the prophets and inaugurated by Jesus, and also the heirs of the promises of the Old Covenant, which find their ultimate fulfilment in Christ. Thus the OT is not simply a Jewish text that has been taken over by the church; it is part of a divine revelation that reaches completion in Jesus (e.g. Heb. 1:1–2; 2 Pet. 1:19–21). As such it is both appropriate and necessary for us to approach its study as Christians, and to recognize that the OT Scriptures have an important place in our religious heritage.[14] Implicit within this view is the conviction that the OT writers look more widely than the relationship between God and Israel. It is possible, within the OT, to discern the working out of the divine purpose to reveal God's holiness and glory throughout the whole of creation.[15] This has two aspects. It is seen in judgment on those whose proud rebellion seeks to usurp the glory that belongs to God alone. It is seen too in the salvation of those from all nations who respond to God in faith and obedience, and their acceptance alongside Israel in the coming kingdom, which includes too the redemption of the created order, and the creation of new heavens and a new earth. For Christians this purpose reaches its fulfilment in Christ. It begins, though, within the OT, and a proper understanding of God's purpose for the world and of the divine perspective on history is impossible without the OT. The universal nature of God's purpose implies, further, that the OT has a crucial relevance for our understanding of mission.[16]

The challenge of the Old Testament

For Christians, to accept the OT as part of the canon of Scripture is to recognize its divine authority. It is God's Word, and as such is authoritative and normative for the life and faith of God's people. Thus the study of the OT continues to be important for Christians. But it raises difficulties. The OT is, on the one hand, part of the Christian Bible, but, on the other, it is also a

---

14. See also B. W. Anderson, *Contours*, pp. 3–7; Brueggemann, *Theology*, pp. 733–735; Childs, *OT Theology*, pp. 8–9; *Biblical Theology* (1992), pp. 25–26, 55–69.

15. This is discussed in more detail below, pp. 311–315.

16. See 'God and the nations', below, p. 311.

document of the history and religion of Israel.[17] Its historical, cultural and religious background is different from ours; its practices and beliefs are unfamiliar, and in some cases may even be offensive. So how are we to read the OT in a way that takes it as authoritative for our faith and conduct?

Some scholars between the first and second world wars (particularly in Germany) wanted to remove the OT from the canon, and so take away its authoritative status.[18] Later liberal Protestantism does not go that far, but there is a tendency to downgrade the importance of the OT, and especially of passages that do not fit with ethical norms derived from the NT and from social conventions and what are sometimes seen as human rights issues. The OT reflects the historical development of Israel's faith, which means that some parts have more direct significance for the church than others. However, if we attach value and significance to the OT only when it agrees with the NT, or only when it fits in with modern social values, then we are denying it any real authority of its own. We need a way of viewing the OT that recognizes different levels of direct relevance to the life of the church, but also acknowledges the authoritative status of the OT as a whole.

For some, the key to unlocking the OT is found in the conversation between the risen Christ and the disciples on the road to Emmaus when, *beginning with Moses and all the Prophets, he explained to them what was said in all the Scriptures concerning himself* (Luke 24:27). The aim, then, is to find Christian, and more particularly Christological, significance in the OT.[19] In one sense,

---

17. For a discussion of the relationship between the testaments, see David L. Baker, *Two Testaments, One Bible: A Study of the Theological Relationship between the Old and New Testaments*, 2nd ed. (Leicester: Apollos, 1991).

18. Adolf von Harnack described the retention of the OT within the canon after the nineteenth century as 'the result of religious and ecclesiastical paralysis' (*Marcion: das Evangelium vom fremden Gott*, 2nd ed. [Leipzig: Hinrichs, 1924], p. 217), and Friedrich Delitzsch described the OT as 'the great deception' (*Die grosse Täuschung*, 2 vols. [Stuttgart: Deutsche Verlags-Anstalt, 1920–1]). E. Hirsch argues that the OT was retained as part of the Christian canon only as the result of a radical reinterpretation by the NT and the church, which may now be discarded (*Das Alte Testament und die Predigt des Evangeliums* [Tübingen: Mohr, 1936]); see also L. Goppelt, *Typos: The Typological Interpretation of the Old Testament in the New* (Grand Rapids: Eerdmans, 1982), pp. 2–3; also, D. L. Baker, *Two Testaments*, pp. 48–57, 84.

19. See D. L. Baker's discussion, *Two Testaments*, pp. 94–104; Baker notes the importance of the work of Wilhelm Vischer. See also Goppelt, *Typos*, pp. 1–2.

of course, all Christian theology, including OT theology, must be Christo-logical.[20] As Christians we recognize that the OT is a witness to Christ: it contains the promise of which Christ is the fulfilment, the shadow that points to Christ as its reality. And some texts may be related directly to Christ (though opinion is divided about which ones). However, it is impossible to treat the whole of the OT in that way without resorting to imaginative spiritualizing and allegorizing of some of its parts, and neglecting other parts altogether.[21] Bright notes the way some OT passages were allegorized by the Church Fathers:

> Moses seated in prayer, his arms outstretched . . . makes the sign of the cross of Christ, and it was by this sign that Amalek was overcome by Jesus (Joshua) through Moses (so Ep. Barnabas, Tertullian, Cyprian, Justin, *et al.*). So too the scarlet cord which the harlot Rahab let down from Jericho's wall . . . signifies redemption through the blood of Christ (so I Clement, Justin, Irenaeus, Origen, *et al.*), while the three [*sic*] spies (so Irenaeus) were doubtless the three persons of the Trinity; Rahab herself (so Origen) is the Church, which is made up of harlots and sinners.[22]

Allegory played an important part in giving value and relevance to the OT, particularly in the (Greek) Alexandrian school.[23] However, in Antioch, which was more Hebraic in its thought and culture, there was a growing emphasis on

---

20. According to Jacob, 'A theology of the Old Testament which is founded not on certain isolated verses, but on the Old Testament as a whole, can only be a Christology, for what was revealed under the old covenant, through a long and varied history, in events, persons and institutions, is, in Christ, gathered together and brought to perfection' (*Theology*, p. 12). This is not an argument, though, for reading Christology into the OT, but for recognizing an essential unity of theology between the OT and NT.

21. In Luke 24:27 Jesus is not suggesting, as is sometimes claimed, that we can find direct references to him in every OT text. Rather, he sets his ministry, and in particular his suffering and death, in the context of a divine purpose being worked out through the pages of the OT that finds its ultimate fulfilment in him.

22. John Bright, *The Authority of the Old Testament* (London: SCM, 1967; repr. Biblical and Theological Classics Library; Carlisle: Paternoster, 1998), p. 81.

23. Influential figures in the Alexandrian church include Clement of Alexandria (c. AD 150–215) and his more eminent pupil Origen (c. AD 185–254), and later Athanasius (c. AD 296–373).

a more literal and historical view of the OT.[24] This debate continued until the fifth century AD, when it gave way to a fourfold approach to the text (set out first by John Cassian): (1) literal/historical, (2) allegorical, (3) anagogical/spiritual, and (4) tropological/moral. Cassian relates this to the view of Jerusalem:

> Jerusalem can be taken in four senses: historically as the city of the Jews; allegorically as the Church of Christ, anagogically as the heavenly city of God . . . tropologically, as the soul of man, which is frequently subject to praise or blame from the Lord under this title.[25]

This approach was championed by Thomas Aquinas in the thirteenth century, though allegorical interpretations remained popular until the Reformation. The Reformers rejected the significance attached to allegory, and elevated the first principle, the literal/historical. Luther, for example, describes allegories as 'empty speculations and the froth . . . of the Holy Scriptures. It is the historical sense alone which supplies the true and sound doctrine.'[26]

Charles Spurgeon, the nineteenth-century Baptist preacher who founded Spurgeon's College, wanted his students to be aware of deeper meanings within a text, but also pointed to the dangers of taking the approach too far. He notes the example of the preacher who took as his text the words of the baker to Joseph in Genesis 40:16, *on my head were three baskets of bread*, and preached a sermon on the Trinity![27] Certainly, heavenly and spiritual realities may be represented by things on earth: OT sacrifices point to Christ's ultimate sacrifice; the redemption of the people of Israel in the exodus and Passover point to the believers' redemption from sin; the Song of Solomon may speak of the relationship between Christ and the church or Christ and the soul. As Christians we may look for a deeper, spiritual significance in OT passages, but does that mean an OT text has value only if it can be given a Christian interpretation? Again, this is an approach that denies to the OT any authority of its own. It results in OT texts being used as either hat-pegs for NT sermons, or

---

24. Key figures here were Theophilus (who became Bishop of Antioch around AD 169), Eusebius of Caesarea (c. AD 263–340), Theodore of Mopsuestia (c. AD 350–428) and John Chrysostom (c. AD 347–407).

25. *Conferences* 14.8.

26. Quoted by Bray, *Biblical Interpretation*, pp. 197–200 (198); see also A. Skevington Wood, *Luther's Principles of Biblical Interpretation* (London: Tyndale, 1946), p. 25.

27. C. H. Spurgeon, *Lectures to my Students* (London: Marshall, Morgan & Scott, 1976), p. 98.

illustrations with no real theological weight. There is also the danger (as, for example, with interpretations of the Song of Solomon) of spiritualizing so much that we miss the real point of what the OT is saying.

Spiritualizing or Christianizing the OT in this way, or treating it as a source of sermon illustrations or of theological proof texts, may avoid some of the difficulties, but the price is to impose meaning on it. It does not allow the OT to speak for itself. Certainly the OT points forward to the coming of Jesus, and for Christian readers is incomplete without the NT. But it is also Scripture in its own right. Its writers were moved by the Spirit of God and its pages reveal truths about God and about his dealings with his people and his world. The NT writers were rooted in these Scriptures and built on them; thus it is also true that the NT is incomplete without the OT.[28] Sometimes the message of the OT may be difficult to understand; sometimes it may be difficult to separate the message we need to hear and apply to our own lives and circumstances from its cultural and historical background. The answer to these difficulties, though, is not to impose another interpretation on the text. We need, instead, to give serious consideration to how we can remain true to the OT as Scripture: as the word of God, which continues to be normative and authoritative for the life of the church. This is one of the key challenges to confront OT Theology.

---

28. Commenting on what the OT means for the proclamation of the church, Wolff notes, 'the proposition that the Old Testament can be properly understood only in the light of the New . . . stands in need of its converse: The New Testament Christ-event can be fully understood only in the light of the Old Testament . . . no New Testament writer felt he was in a position to witness to Jesus Christ without constantly opening and quoting the Old Testament'; see Hans Walter Wolff, 'The Hermeneutics of the Old Testament', in Claus Westermann (ed.), *Essays on Old Testament Interpretation* (London: SCM, 1963), pp. 160–199 (187–188). Goldingay makes a similar comment: 'the Old Testament's insights must be seen in the light of those of the New, but only as we immediately add that it is necessary to see the New Testament's insights in light of those of the Old' (*OT Theology*, 1:21–28 [21]); see also *OT Theology*, 2:18–21. Sailhamer argues that as a Christian task, OT theology is only the first part of a biblical theology that must also include the NT, but emphasizes the need to consider the OT in its own right, claiming that 'the Old Testament not only stands on its own but the New Testament stands on its shoulders'; see John H. Sailhamer, *Introduction to Old Testament Theology: A Canonical Approach* (Grand Rapids: Zondervan, 1995), p. 23.

Old Testament theology: a brief historical overview[29]

Historical and systematic theology

Over the years scholars have approached OT Theology in several ways.[30] One emphasis is on a *systematic* or *dogmatic* approach. A systematic theology attempts to organize the central tenets of faith as a series of categories and propositions, and to collect the biblical material that relates to them. A key aim of this is to set out what the Bible says in a way that makes it accessible and relevant to the life and faith of the church, to interpret the theological principles contained within the Scriptures into principles and practice for the church, and in doing so to give some kind of order and unity to what we believe. With regard to the OT, Jacob defines this approach as 'the systematic account of the specific religious ideas which can be found throughout the OT and which form its profound unity'.[31]

This way of coming to the OT has value, and a number of helpful OT theologies adopt this methodology (including Jacob's own); but weaknesses are

---

29. See further B. W. Anderson, *Contours*, pp. 16–31; Brueggemann, *Theology*, pp. 1–60; Childs, *OT Theology*, pp. 2–17; *Biblical Theology* (1992), pp. 4–69; Clements, *Century*, pp. 118–149; Hasel, *Basic Issues*, pp. 10–27; John H. Hayes and Frederick Prussner, *Old Testament Theology: Its History and Development* (Atlanta: John Knox, 1985); House, *OT Theology*, pp. 13–52, 548–559; Elmer A. Martens, *NIDOTTE* 1:172–184; Patrick D. Miller, *Israelite Religion and Biblical Theology: Collected Essays*, JSOTSup 267 (Sheffield: Sheffield Academic Press, 2000), pp. 142–181; Ben C. Ollenburger, 'Old Testament Theology before 1933', in Ben C. Ollenburger (ed.), *Old Testament Theology: Flowering and Future*, SBTS 1 (Winona Lake: Eisenbrauns, 2004), pp. 3–11; Horst Dietrich Preuss, *Old Testament Theology*, 2 vols., OTL (Louisville: Westminster John Knox, 1995–6), 1:1–19; Sailhamer, *OT Theology*, pp. 117–175. See also Perdue, *Reconstructing*, pp. 25–75. This builds on his previous work, *The Collapse of History: Reconstructing Old Testament Theology*, OBT (Minneapolis: Fortress, 1994), in which he discusses the demise of the historical method as the dominant approach to OT theology. In this second volume Perdue describes what he sees as the current status of OT theology and discusses the relationship between biblical theology and the history of religion (*Religionsgeschichte*) approach; he also points to new approaches to OT theology – including liberation and feminist theologies.

30. Hasel notes ten methodological approaches to OT Theology (*Basic Issues*, pp. 28–114); see also House, *OT Theology*, pp. 54–57. There is some overlap between them, and the current discussion will focus only on what appear to be the most important.

31. Jacob, *Theology*, p. 11.

also apparent in some systematic approaches, and maybe inherent within the approach itself. The OT was not written as a theological document, and a systematic approach necessarily involves imposing an alien order and structure on it. While it may be right to look for coherence in the text, there is also diversity and theological development within the text, and that is not often taken into account in systematic theologies. Another problem is the tendency to be selective in quoting texts: using those that support a particular proposition, while leaving more difficult passages aside.[32] Also, and this is a particular issue for OT theology, it is common for the categories of systematic theology to be drawn from the NT or from the needs of the church. This means that discussion may focus on issues of interest to us, but not necessarily of concern to the Bible writers; as a result we may find ourselves seeking answers to questions they never thought of asking. There is also the danger that the OT may be treated as little more than a source of proof texts, with little regard for it as authoritative revelation in its own right.

Historically the church dominated dogmatic theology. Before the Reformation, the Roman Catholic Church imposed its own interpretation on the Bible, an interpretation that reinforced its own beliefs and structures.[33] The Reformation was, in part, a reaction against that: it attempted to set the interpretation of the Scriptures free from the authority of the church and, instead, to bring the church under the authority of the Scriptures.[34] After the

---

32. This is directly related to the approach. In a systematic theology that might already be several hundred pages in length it is impossible to deal, in detail, with difficult biblical texts. Inevitably, then, systematic theologies set out a more general 'overview', but leave some anomalies.

33. The Roman Catholic Church continues to set Scripture alongside Apostolic Tradition as the basis for 'the rule of faith'. In theory this gives considerable weight to Scripture; in practice, Scripture is viewed and interpreted through the lens of church tradition. In the constitution on divine revelation from the 2nd Vatican Council, *Dei verbum* (1965), which emphasizes the importance of Scripture, the church remains the final arbiter: 'all of what has been said about the way of interpreting Scripture is subject finally to the judgment of the church, which carries out the divine commission and ministry of guarding and interpreting the word of God' (3.10).

34. The Reformers embraced the idea of *sola scriptura* (an expression possibly first formulated by John Wycliffe), the belief that Scripture alone should determine matters of faith, and that the interpretation of Scripture did not depend on the teaching of the church. See Bray, *Biblical Interpretation*, pp. 191–195.

Reformation, however, it became apparent that many important passages of Scripture were unclear, and could admit several, sometimes conflicting, interpretations. This led to calls among Protestants for an orthodox interpretation of key biblical texts, and so, to some extent at least, the church took over again.

The critical approach to the Bible was a further attempt to break free from the authority of the church and church dogmatics. A key influence on thinking from the late seventeenth century onwards, which characterized the Enlightenment,[35] was *scientific rationalism*. The two main tools in the search for knowledge and truth, not only in the physical sciences but in all areas of life, were *scientific inquiry* and *reason*. Before this, the Bible had been (at least in theory) the source of knowledge and the arbiter of truth; now it became, itself, the object of critical assessment and analysis, with apparent discrepancies and inconsistencies put under the microscope. Many opposed rationalism to Christian faith, emphasizing the priority of human reason and rejecting whatever could not be explained rationally, such as the supernatural, including miracles and the idea of Scripture as supernatural revelation.[36] And among biblical scholars who did not see such a stark antithesis between rationalism and faith there was, nevertheless, a move towards 'enlightened theology', which adopted the rationalists' critical approach to the Bible.[37] The church's orthodox interpretation of Scripture was viewed as an obstacle to these new ideas, and this led, especially in the nineteenth century, to a separation between the church and biblical scholarship, which moved to the universities.[38]

---

35. This term usually refers to the intellectual movement in the late seventeenth and eighteenth centuries, which included philosophers such as Voltaire, Rousseau, Hume and Kant. Its roots, though, go back further to the work of Descartes and others. The Enlightenment provides the foundation for what became known as 'modernism'.

36. Bray, *Biblical Interpretation*, pp. 251–253.

37. One such approach, 'neology' (new word/science) was advocated by Johann Semler, in the mid-eighteenth century as an attempt to synthesize rationalism and tradition. The critical approach that characterized rationalism is also evident in the work of W. de Wette (1780–1849), who is associated with the beginnings of the modern critical approach to the OT. De Wette did not attach much historical value to the OT, though (in contrast to many rationalists) he saw its 'mythological' content as an important expression of religious ideas. See Bray, *Biblical Interpretation*, pp. 257–320.

38. Wellhausen resigned from his position of teaching ministerial students at Greifswald in 1882 because he felt his approach was not preparing them for ministry in the evangelical (Protestant) church in Germany.

The overarching belief system, or *metanarrative*,[39] governing much of the thinking of the eighteenth and nineteenth centuries was that science and reason would bring freedom from superstition, and would open the way to social and moral progress. And this led to an emphasis, particularly in the nineteenth century, on *history* and *historical development*. This had two important aspects.

First, following the scientific rationalism of the eighteenth century, together with the rapidly increasing understanding of the past through archaeological finds and advances in study of ancient languages and texts, there was the optimistic belief that the whole of history could be known: it was there to be uncovered if only we looked hard enough and in the right places.

Second, there was the belief that the world was moving on, and needed to be understood as part of a developing reality where discoveries were constantly being made, with the consequent need to revise previous ideas and opinions. As a result, it was possible to talk about absolute truth and values only within a particular historical context. Part of this was the evolutionary idea of movement from a primitive to a more scientific and sophisticated way of viewing the world,[40] and those in the nineteenth century saw themselves at the latest position in that ascent.

This led to another approach to OT theology. In a paper in 1787 Gabler distinguished *dogmatic theology* from *biblical theology*.[41] Dogmatic theology is associated with the church and church traditions, and in Gabler's view does not offer permanently valid truth, since by its very nature it is subject to change. Biblical theology is concerned with the beliefs of the Bible writers *within their historical*

---

39. The term 'metanarrative' is associated with Jean-François Lyotard, and refers to an overarching story or theory that explains and orders human knowledge and experience. The metanarrative of the Enlightenment is that human progress is achieved through scientific rationalism; Marxism also has its metanarrative, which explains life in terms of class struggle eventually leading to a socialist utopia. The Christian story, which explains the origin of the world, the present condition of the human race, and the promise of salvation and eternal life through Christ might also be seen as a metanarrative.

40. A factor in this nineteenth-century understanding of evolutionary process was Charles Darwin's *On the Origin of Species*, published in 1859. This was part of a wider view, which included social and cultural evolution.

41. J. P. Gabler, 'An Oration on the Proper Distinction between Biblical and Dogmatic Theology and the Specific Objectives of Each' (this paper is reproduced in Ollenburger, *OT Theology*, pp. 498–506).

context. Gabler emphasized the need to separate what in the biblical text was historically and culturally conditioned from what was eternally true, and so could be applied to Christians of all times,[42] and this leads to the 'appearance of biblical theology, pure and unmixed with foreign things',[43] which may then provide the proper foundation for dogmatic theology. The value of Gabler's approach is his focus on the biblical text as the basis for this 'pure' biblical theology. These disciplines, while closely related, are distinct, and their goals need to be clearly assigned. Gabler's paper was influential in the separation of dogmatic/systematic theology from biblical theology, which was seen as an essentially historical, descriptive account of the faith of the biblical writers.[44] Following Gabler, biblical theology, which may be better named *historical theology*, tended to focus on how biblical statements reflect the religious ideas of Israel at the time they were written and how those ideas developed as historical circumstances, and the needs and understanding of the people changed. The result is a series of snapshots, each giving a picture of Israel's religious life at a particular time, which could then be compared and contrasted. An important example of this is the evolutionary view, advocated by Wellhausen, that Israel's faith developed from something relatively primitive during the days of the exodus and judges into the ethical monotheism associated with the prophets.[45]

To establish the setting and significance of the biblical text, the historical theologian draws on the tools of modern scholarship, such as textual and historical criticism. He is interested in the date and authorship of the various parts of the OT, in the motivation of its writers, in the place of the texts within the development of Israel's faith. He is interested too in political and sociological factors and in the belief and practice of Israel's neighbours and how that may have influenced the Bible accounts. This results in the OT being viewed as a historical rather than a theological document, and, by focusing on what was believed at particular points of Israel's history, it sees no real unity in the OT,

---

42. Gabler distinguishes between 'those things which in the sacred books refer most immediately to their own times and to the men of those times from those pure notions which divine providence wished to be characteristic of all times and places' (Ollenburger, *OT Theology*, p. 502).

43. Ibid., p. 505.

44. Gabler recognized the need to examine the biblical material and to note points of difference and issues that were historically conditioned, but also to note points of agreement between the biblical writers, and the possibility of some kind of synthesis. It was the former that became the main focus of this area of study.

45. For further discussion, see Harrison, *Introduction*, pp. 21–24.

nor any need even to think in those terms. Indeed this approach looks for differences between the 'snapshots', in order to demonstrate theological movement. And, because in the end this is a historical, descriptive exercise, there is nothing in the developing theology presented that can be taken as authoritative and normative for the church.

Walter Eichrodt and Gerhard von Rad

The *history of religions* approach was popular until the 1920s. The two most significant contributions to OT theology in the twentieth century are part of a revival in biblical theology that reacted against the history of religions approach and against the scientific rationalism and developmental view of theological understanding that characterized it. Key concerns were to focus on the OT as a whole as revelation, and to note both its links with the NT and its relevance for the church.[46] Those reactions, though, led in different directions and reached different conclusions. Walter Eichrodt's two-volume *Theology of the Old Testament* was first published in 1933.[47] Five years later (1938) Gerhard von Rad set out the direction of his approach in his essay 'The Form Critical Problem of the Hexateuch',[48] though his *Old Testament Theology* was not published until the 1960s.[49]

---

46. Barr, *Concept*, pp. 18–26, sets out four characteristics of modern OT theology: synthesis over against historical developmentalism, the distinctiveness of the OT over against other religious texts, the search for meaning over against a superficial reading or purely critical analysis of the text, and the need to link the OT appropriately with the NT.

47. London: SCM, 1961–7.

48. In Gerhard von Rad, *The Problem of the Hexateuch and Other Essays* (Edinburgh: Oliver & Boyd, 1966), pp. 1–78; reproduced in Gerhard von Rad, *From Genesis to Chronicles: Explorations in Old Testament Theology*, Fortress Classics in Biblical Studies (Philadelphia: Augsburg Fortress, 2005), pp. 1–58.

49. Gerhard von Rad, *Old Testament Theology*, 2 vols. (Edinburgh: Oliver & Boyd, 1962–5). Samples of the approach to OT theology of a number of key scholars, including Eichrodt and von Rad, are included in Ollenburger, *OT Theology*, pp. 39–56, 92–114. For a comparison of the respective contributions of Eichrodt and von Rad, see Brueggemann, *Theology*, pp. 27–42; Ronald E. Clements, 'The Problem of Old Testament Theology', *The London Quarterly and Holborn Review* (January 1965), pp. 11–17; D. G. Spriggs, *Two Old Testament Theologies: A Comparative Evaluation of the Contributions of Eichrodt and von Rad to our Understanding of the Nature of Old Testament Theology*, SBT 2.30 (London: SCM, 1974); see also Barr, *Concept*, pp. 24–51.

Walter Eichrodt

Eichrodt offers a more systematic approach to the OT. He recognizes the need to do justice to the historical dimension of Israel's faith, but not, as had been the case with the developmental approach of historical theology, at the expense of the unity and authority of the OT. He maintains that despite variations within the historical faith of Israel, there is also an essential unity and coherence within the OT and also between the OT and the NT, which allows us to take it as normative for our faith. According to Eichrodt, the task of OT theology is to consider 'the problem of how to understand the realm of OT belief in its structural unity and how, by examining on the one hand its religious environment and on the other its essential coherence with the NT, to illuminate its profoundest meaning'.[50]

In structuring his OT Theology, Eichrodt wants to avoid schemes based on Christian dogmatics, which are foreign to the OT. Instead he sets out to use categories suggested by the OT itself; he maintains that the OT

> speaks of a revelation of the God of the People, who in his rule proves himself to be
> also the God of the World and the God of the individual. We are therefore presented
> with three principal categories, within which to study the special nature of the
> Israelite faith in God: God and the people; God and the world and God and man.[51]

And those are the headings of the three major sections of his Theology.

In the first, and largest of these, taking up the whole of the first volume, Eichrodt focuses on the idea of *covenant*, by which he means, primarily, the relationship between God and Israel established at Sinai. In his view this is the central theme that gives order and unity to the OT and around which its various religious ideas may be collected; he describes it as 'the central concept, by which to illuminate the structural unity and the unchanging basic tendency of the message of the OT. For it is in this concept that Israel's fundamental conviction of its special relationship with God is concentrated.'[52]

Eichrodt's OT theology can be criticized. By focusing as much as he does on covenant he is in danger of undervaluing other important OT themes. And by emphasizing the significance of the *Sinaitic* covenant in particular he does not give due weight to other biblical covenants, such as those with Abraham and David, which also give coherence and direction to the OT, and provide

---

50. Eichrodt, *Theology*, 1:31.

51. Ibid., 1:33.

52. Ibid., 1:13.

links with the NT. Nevertheless Eichrodt has done a great deal to open up what lies at the heart of OT theology, namely God's relationship with his people and his world, and to link the various themes within the OT to that central idea.

Another criticism is that Eichrodt's emphasis on the coherence of the OT does not do justice to historical issues and does not take sufficient account of the diversity of Israel's faith through the OT period. Eichrodt aims to work with themes and religious ideas that derive from the OT itself, and as such has confirmed OT theology as an area of study in its own right, distinct from historical theology and Christian dogmatics. However, he may be accused of dealing with them too much as abstractions separated from Israel's life and history. Nevertheless by refocusing on the theological interpretation of the OT Eichrodt achieved two important results: (1) he helped to reforge the link between the OT and Christian faith, and (2) over against the developmentalism of the historical approach, in which all theological claims are relative, he asserted that the OT is coherent, authoritative and normative. Eichrodt thus presented the OT in a way that made it, once again, relevant to the Christian church.

Since Eichrodt, other systematic approaches to OT theology have been published that follow his method of searching for the single central concept that gives unity and coherence to the message of the OT,[53] though none has enjoyed the same degree of acceptance. However, the fact that many possible themes have been put forward over the years, but without any real consensus, indicates that the search may be a fruitless one. When a particular idea or

---

53. See e.g. Barr, *Concept*, pp. 28–32, 313–316, 337–343; John Goldingay, *Approaches to Old Testament Interpretation* (Leicester: Apollos, 1990), pp. 24–29; James M. Hamilton, 'The Glory of God in Salvation through Judgment: The Centre of Biblical Theology', *TynBul* 57.1 (2006), pp. 57–84; Hasel, *Basic Issues*, pp. 139–171; Walter C. Kaiser, Jr., *Toward an Old Testament Theology* (Grand Rapids: Zondervan, 1978), pp. 20–40; Roland E. Murphy, 'Once Again – the "Center" of the Old Testament', *BTB* 31 (2001), pp. 85–89; Preuss, *OT Theology*, 1:21–23. Stephen Dempster suggests that the Davidic covenant, with its focus on Davidic dynasty, Zion and the temple, is the lens through which the canonical form of the Tanak should be viewed; see Stephen G. Dempster, 'Geography and Genealogy, Dominion and Dynasty: A Theology of the Hebrew Bible', in Scott J. Hafemann (ed.), *Biblical Theology: Retrospect and Prospect* (Leicester: Apollos; Downers Grove: IVP, 2002), pp. 66–92; *Dominion and Dynasty: A Theology of the Hebrew Bible*, NSBT 15 (Leicester: Apollos; Downers Grove: IVP, 2003).

theological theme is identified as significant in several texts, the quest for unity means that theme is then imposed on other texts, which cannot always be related to it directly. When those other texts are considered in more detail, the lack of unity becomes evident. Gerhard von Rad puts forward a different approach to OT theology.

Gerhard von Rad

Like Eichrodt, von Rad also wants to make the OT relevant to the life and faith of the church. However, while Eichrodt stresses what is fixed and constant in the faith of the OT, von Rad rejects his structural, systematic approach and the view that it is possible to discover a single theological centre to the OT, and instead emphasizes the dynamic nature of Israel's faith.

Von Rad stresses the importance of history as the principal medium of divine revelation in the OT.[54] The OT writers did not set out the contents of their faith systematically;[55] they did not abstract theological ideas into a body of doctrine about God. Instead God is revealed through what he does and through the recital of the mighty acts of God that shaped the nation. God's actions in history were remembered in confessional statements such as Deuteronomy 6:21–25, 26:5–9 and Joshua 24:2–13.[56] These summaries were gradually filled out, and other material was added to them to form the Hexateuch (Genesis to Joshua). To this was added the work of the Deuteronomists and the Chronicler, who brought their own insights and the theological demands of their own day, each building on, and elaborating and expanding, the earlier material. The key factor in this unfolding development is the conviction that God's activity in history had a contemporary relevance and was in constant need of reinterpretation to each generation in the light of later historical events and the different circumstances in which the nation found itself.[57]

As a form critic, von Rad believes it is impossible to construct an accurate picture of OT history, and certainly not one that accords with the picture given in the OT. He maintains that the stories recorded by the OT writers are not inventions: they are founded on actual events.[58] However, what appears in the

---

54. A similar approach is adopted by George E. Wright, *God who Acts: Biblical Theology as Recital* (London: SCM, 1952), pp. 12–13. See Perdue, *Collapse*, pp. 23–30 (on Wright), pp. 47–68 (on von Rad).

55. Von Rad, *OT Theology*, 1:116.

56. Ibid., 1:121–123.

57. Ibid., 1:118–119.

58. Ibid., 1:108.

OT is the end result of constant telling and retelling, and corresponds not to actual history, but *Heilsgeschichte*:[59] the story of salvation as viewed through the eyes of Israel's faith, and in which the significance of divine action is brought home to each new generation of believers:

> In what they present, the later story-tellers . . . make capital of experiences which, although they are invariably brought in on the basis of the ancient event in question, still reach forward into the story-teller's own day . . . What is historical here? Certainly some definite but very elusive particular event which stands at the primal obscure origin of the tradition in question – but what is also historical is the experience that Jaweh turns the enemy's curse into a blessing, and that he safeguards the promise in spite of all failure on the part of its recipient, etc.[60]

An elusive, but real, historical event results in a tradition modified through time to meet different theological needs. At some later date that tradition is incorporated into Israel's reconstruction of her story of salvation. According to von Rad, OT theology should focus on this *Heilsgeschichte*. Its task is to trace the way the particular stories and events have been developed, interpreted and reinterpreted in the light of changing historical situations, and to look at how the stories are used in their present form and context. This suggests that he is reviving elements of historical theology.[61] However, while historical theology resulted in ideas becoming tied to a particular period of Israel's history, and thus trapped in time, with no continuing significance, for von Rad, the message of the OT continued to be vital and relevant: it was 'living and actual for each moment that it accompanied Israel on her journey through time, interpreting itself afresh to every generation, and informing every generation what it had to do'.[62] And this process of telling and retelling of the story of salvation continues until it reaches its fulfilment in the NT:[63]

---

59. Though *Heilsgeschichte* is a significant term for von Rad, his usage of it is imprecise. The term itself goes back to J. C. K. von Hoffmann; see Clements, *Century*, p. 134; see also D. L. Baker, *Two Testaments*, pp. 145–162.

60. Von Rad, *OT Theology*, 1:110–111.

61. See Kaiser, *OT Theology*, p. 5. Von Rad, though, is critical of the history of religions approach because it does not take sufficient account of what the Old Testament actually says (*OT Theology*, 1:113–114).

62. Von Rad, *OT Theology*, 1:112.

63. Von Rad, like Eichrodt, emphasizes the unity between the Old and New Testaments. It is in the NT that the various disconnected strands in the OT are

the chief correspondence between the two Testaments does not lie primarily in the field of religious terminology, but in saving history, for in Jesus Christ we meet once again – and in a more intensified form – with that same connexion between divine word and historical acts.[64]

Von Rad's theology is radical. By focusing on the texts themselves and on the testimonies to God's action in history preserved within the texts, he attempts to do justice to the essential nature of the OT. However, von Rad too is open to criticism.

First, his view of history is ambiguous. He acknowledges a gap between actual history (as uncovered by critical scholarship) and the story of faith (history as it was reconstructed by the faith of Israel). His *Old Testament Theology* focuses on the latter: on the retelling of Israel's history, not on the history itself, thus undermining his insistence that history and event are of crucial importance to OT faith.[65]

Second, von Rad allows for considerable diversity in the way traditions of God's activity in history are reinterpreted from one generation to another, and because any theological interpretation is liable to be superseded by another, none may be seen as final. Thus the OT contains not one but several theologies, each relevant within a particular historical setting. In the end this moves us away from a theology normative for faith and (despite von Rad's own protestations) back towards a history of religions approach.

A third problem is the relationship between tradition and canonical text. In von Rad's view tradition is fluid, and should have gone on developing and adapting after the point at which OT books (particularly the Torah) were given canonical status. If von Rad is correct about the development of traditions through Israel's history, it is difficult to see how a fixed OT canon emerged, and why too the NT writers accepted that canon and set their theology against the background of the written text, rather than of the still-flowing stream of tradition.

Biblical theology
The term 'biblical theology' is ambiguous. It may refer to the theology of the biblical writers at the time of writing, and so is the same as historical

---

brought together. He discusses the relationship between the testaments at some length (*OT Theology*, 2:319–409).

64. Von Rad, *OT Theology*, 2:382.

65. Revelation comes through 'event', but the only events we have access to are reconstructions from a later period. If the original events were so important, why have they been forgotten?

theology.[66] Alternatively it may refer to theology that derives from and accords with the Bible as a whole and which has relevance to the church.[67] These two are linked. The latter requires an awareness of the theology of the OT writers in their historical contexts, but seeks to move from descriptive accounts, locked into a particular time and place, to a theology that can be related to today's world. The works of Eichrodt and von Rad are examples of a revival of interest in this understanding of biblical theology after the First World War. As we have noted, this was a reaction against the history of religions approach, and in particular to the scientific rationalism that led to an evolutionary and developmental view of religious understanding, which had undermined the theological content of the Bible, and its relevance to the church.

Brevard Childs points to the growth of the 'biblical theology movement', which was influenced by the new emphasis in European theology, but which had a particular impact in America after the Second World War.[68] Although

---

66. As we have noted, following Gabler, the term 'biblical theology' was used to describe the historical, descriptive treatment of the OT characterized in the 'history of religions' approach.

67. For a brief history of 'biblical theology', see C. Marvin Pate, J. Scott Duvall, J. Daniel Hays, E. Randolph Richards, W. Dennis Tucker, Jr., and Preben Vang, *The Story of Israel: A Biblical Theology* (Leicester: Apollos; Downers Grove: IVP, 2004), pp. 13–17; see also R. W. L. Moberley, 'How May we Speak of God? A Reconsideration of the Nature of Biblical Theology', *TynBul* 53.2 (1992), pp. 177–202; Charles H. H. Scobie, *The Ways of Our God: An Approach to Biblical Theology* (Grand Rapids: Eerdmans, 2003), pp. 3–102; 'The Challenge of Biblical Theology', *TynBul* 42.1 (1991), pp. 31–61; 'The Structure of Biblical Theology', *TynBul* 42.2 (1991), pp. 163–194; 'History of Biblical Theology', in *NDBT*, pp. 11–20. See also James Barr's critique of the methodologies used in biblical theological approaches to the OT (*Concept*).

68. See Brevard S. Childs, *Biblical Theology in Crisis* (Philadelphia: Westminster, 1970), pp. 13–87. He notes the indebtedness of the movement to Eichrodt and von Rad, but describes it as distinctively American. B. W. Anderson recognizes that biblical theology was influenced by the American debate between liberal and conservative Protestantism, but also points to European scholars such as Eichrodt and von Rad (OT) and Bultmann (NT), and maintains that this movement, and the crisis in biblical theology, was not exclusively American; see Bernard W. Anderson, 'The Crisis in Biblical Theology', *ThTo* 28.3 (1971), pp. 321–327. Perdue discusses the biblical theology movement in America (*Collapse*, pp. 19–44), though also notes that von Rad shares important features.

embracing a wide diversity of theological and methodological opinion, several points of 'consensus' indicate key emphases of biblical theology.

A central distinguishing feature of biblical theology is the desire to take seriously the theological content of the Bible as something relevant to modern life. It was recognized that while it had not failed, the historical-critical approach to the Bible, and particularly the history of religions approach to theology, had led to an overemphasis on historical analysis at the expense of theology, and there was a need to correct that balance.

Also essential in biblical theology was the recognition that history played an important part in mediating divine revelation. This challenged both the *dogmatic view*, which saw the Bible as the repository of eternal, fixed, propositional truths, and the *evolutionary view*, which saw the Bible only as the account of Israel's own developing religious understanding. The idea that it is through his action in history that God makes himself known led to an emphasis on the historical context of biblical texts and theological ideas, and so to the possibility of the development of theological understanding. It led scholars too to pay greater attention to the way the biblical writers viewed history, which combined reporting historical events with the interpretation and theological significance of those events.

Following from this was the recognition that the biblical texts needed to be interpreted on their own terms, rather than having methods of interpretation imposed on them from outside the text. Thinking in propositional terms, which had tended to dominate in western, dogmatic theology, was a Greek rather than a Hebrew characteristic. In order to understand the biblical texts the reader must take into account their particularly Hebrew style and viewpoint. Systematic theology may have a place in organizing articles of faith so that they can be applied to the church, but before we can do that we need to look at what the biblical text is actually saying.[69]

Another important element in this new theological approach was the essential unity between the Old and New Testaments. As we have noted, this was an important consideration for both Eichrodt and von Rad, though their approaches to the issue differed widely.

The 'biblical theology movement' was relatively short-lived, and Brevard Childs's book *Biblical Theology in Crisis*, published in 1970, is sometimes viewed as its obituary,[70] though many disagree with that analysis. In his book, which

---

69. This leads into areas of hermeneutical debate, which I will discuss (briefly) below.

70. In an essay written in 1990 Collins also describes biblical theology as 'a subject in decline', because, in his view, many scholars do not see theology as a goal of

began as a series of lectures, Childs notes the 'cracking of the walls' of consensus. He argues that this affected all of the points noted above. I will mention two in particular.

While it was agreed that history was an important medium of divine revelation, there was a lack of agreement about how to understand history. Von Rad distinguished between *actual* history, as discovered and confirmed by scientific analysis, and *redemption* history (*Heilsgeschichte*). The problem facing biblical theology was (and still is), what is the relationship between these two ways of understanding history?[71] Should we follow von Rad and make a distinction between them, or attempt to hold them together, as Eichrodt tried to do? Both lead to difficulties. Although archaeology and extrabiblical data are able to confirm some of the historical information in the OT, much cannot be confirmed or appears to conflict with external evidence. This raises a degree of uncertainty about the historicity of some of the biblical material, and if the message of the text is too closely linked to the accuracy of its historical context, that message is also undermined. Meanwhile those who continue to insist on the historicity of the OT are accused of ignoring the historical evidence.[72] If, on the other hand, the focus is on *Heilsgeschichte* (a history reconstructed by Israel's faith, with little or no basis in what *actually* happened), how can biblical theology claim that it is rooted in history, and that historical events play an important part in divine revelation?[73] What are the historical events that function in this way?

A second major crack in the walls of consensus relates to the unity of the Old and New Testaments. Again Eichrodt and von Rad represent the main alternatives. Eichrodt points to the structural and conceptual unity of the OT that centres on *covenant*. This focus on the relationship between God and his people also provides the essential unity with the NT. Von Rad rejects the idea

---

Footnote 70 (*continued*)

    biblical studies; see John J. Collins, *Encounters with Biblical Theology* (Minneapolis: Fortress, 2005), p. 11. However, as noted below, several important biblical theologies have been published since that date.

71. See e.g. Hasel's discussion, *Basic Issues*, pp. 115–138.

72. The question of the historicity of the OT continues to be a live issue. In my view the biblical accounts are more reliable than some critics suggest; this will be discussed further later.

73. Collins notes the contradiction in G. E. Wright's view that biblical theology involves both history as description and history as interpreted by faith (*Encounters*, pp. 13–14).

that the OT has a structural unity or a theological centre. There is a methodological unity in the building of tradition through a constant process of reinterpretation, but the outcome is a series of disconnected theological ideas. In
effect there are several theologies in the OT, and they are not always compatible. However, their forward look leans towards eventual fulfilment in the NT
and in the coming of Christ. Both of these approaches have strengths as well
as weaknesses. The greater problem, though, for those seeking consensus in
biblical theology is that they are mutually exclusive, with no middle ground
between them. Bernard Anderson suggests that 'part of the crisis in biblical
theology is that we are torn between these alternatives'.[74]

According to Childs, the failure of the consensus in biblical theology has
made it necessary to look for a new way forward. However, reports of the
death of biblical theology have been exaggerated. As a movement, enjoying a
measure of scholarly consensus, it may have lost its way, but as a means of
describing a particular approach to biblical interpretation, *which seeks to engage
with the biblical text in its own right as divine revelation, to focus on the canonical text as a
whole, and to draw out its theological content in a way that allows it to be applied to the
life and practice of the church*,[75] the term and associated ideas continue to be
applicable. Childs's own solution to the crisis, what has become known as 'the

---

74. B. W. Anderson, 'Crisis in Biblical Theology', p. 325.

75. So e.g. Steve Motyer describes biblical theology as 'that creative theological
   discipline whereby the church seeks to hear the integrated voice of the whole Bible
   addressing us today' (Steve Motyer, 'Two Bibles, One Biblical Theology', in Joel B.
   Green and Max Turner (eds.), *Between Two Horizons: Spanning New Testament Studies
   and Systematic Theology* [Grand Rapids: Eerdmans, 2000], p. 158). Barr notes the
   difficulty in providing a definition because the discussions are multifaceted and
   biblical theology is often described in contrast to other things, including dogmatic
   theology, history of religion approaches, non-theological study of the Bible,
   philosophical and natural theology and approaches that look only at the part rather
   than the whole (Barr, *Concept*, pp. 1–18). It is difficult to agree a precise definition;
   however, the statement presented here sums up its essential characteristics: (1) *It
   seeks to engage with the biblical text in its own right*, understanding it on its own terms and
   categories rather than forcing a structure on it. In my view this also includes setting
   the text (where possible) in its historical and cultural context, and considering such
   things as author's intention. (2) *It accepts the text as divine revelation.* (3) *It focuses on the
   canonical text as a whole* – looking for synthesis and coherence within the OT and in
   the relationship between the OT and the NT, while not ignoring the considerable
   diversity. Though there continues to be debate about the exact nature of the canon,

canonical approach', aims to retain key aspects of the earlier movement, especially in its attempt to see unity within the diversity of the canon of Scripture. In recent years there have been significant contributions to OT theology, which could also be classed as biblical theology, including Childs's own *Biblical Theology of the Old and New Testaments* (1991), as well as works by Horst Dietrich Preuss (1991–2; ET: 1995–6), Paul House (1998), Bernard W. Anderson (1999), John Goldingay (2003–6), Rolf Rendtorff (2001; ET: 2005), Eugene Merrill (2006) and Bruce Waltke (2006).[76]

On the continuing significance of biblical theology, we might also note the work of N. T. Wright.[77] Though primarily a NT scholar, he has attempted to provide a theological framework within which the Old and New Testaments may be seen as a unity, though again without losing sight of their diversity.[78]

Footnote 75 (*continued*)

> it is necessary to give some definition of the scope of the text, and this approach places that enterprise in the context of the faith community that has accepted it. In relation to the emphasis on the whole text, this should not be seen as precluding separate OT and NT biblical theologies, but each needs to be mindful of the other and of the appropriate relationship between them. (4) *It is concerned with the theological content of the text and its application to the life and practice of the church.* A key role of biblical theology is to explain the meaning and implication both of individual texts and of the texts in relation to one another and to the canonical whole and to allow that message to speak relevantly (and authoritatively) to believers and to the church today.

76. Eugene H. Merrill, *Everlasting Dominion: A Theology of the Old Testament* (Nashville: Broadman & Holman, 2006); Bruce K. Waltke, with C. Yu, *An Old Testament Theology: A Canonical and Thematic Approach* (Grand Rapids: Zondervan, 2006).

77. In particular, N. T. Wright, *The New Testament and the People of God* (Minneapolis: Fortress, 1992); *Jesus and the Victory of God* (Minneapolis: Fortress, 1997).

78. According to N. T. Wright, first-century (and intertestamental) Judaism felt that the nation, though in the land, was still in 'exile' waiting for God's kingdom, to bring return from exile, defeat of evil, and Yahweh's return to Zion. The OT sets out the narrative of Israel; Jesus re-enacts this narrative pattern in his ministry (e.g. Matt. 2:15, 16), and links those three expectations with his own announcement of the kingdom. However, the ways he addresses them are different from, and subversive to, the traditional Jewish narrative, e.g. in relation to the role of the Messiah. He also brings the salvation that enables his disciples, who now represent Israel, to bring blessing and salvation to the nations.

Typology[79]

In the debate about how Christians should interpret the OT, we might expect to see more emphasis placed on the exegetical and hermeneutical methods employed by Jesus and the NT writers. Is has been widely assumed, however, that the NT generally follows contemporary interpretative approaches, which were valid within a particular context, but which do not provide us with a normative methodology.[80] In part that may be true. The NT writers' treatment of the OT appears, on occasions, to have followed methods similar to those found in later rabbinic literature.[81] It needs to be emphasized, though, that

---

79. See especially the discussion in David L. Baker, 'Typology and the Christian Use of the Old Testament', *SJT* 29 (1976), pp. 137–157; *Two Testaments*, pp. 179–202; Walter Eichrodt, 'Is Typological Exegesis an Appropriate Method?', in Westermann, *Essays*, pp. 224–245; Goldingay, *Approaches*, pp. 92–115; Goppelt, *Typos*; Gerhard von Rad, 'Typological Interpretation of the Old Testament', in Westermann, *Essays*, pp. 17–39; Christopher R. Seitz, *Figured Out: Typology and Providence in Christian Scripture* (Louisville: Westminster John Knox, 2001); Hans Walter Wolff, 'Hermeneutics of the Old Testament', in Westermann, *Essays*, pp. 160–199; Christopher J. H. Wright, *Knowing Jesus through the Old Testament* (London: Marshall Pickering; Downers Grove: IVP, 1995), pp. 107–116.

80. E.g. Richard Longenecker, *Biblical Exegesis in the Apostolic Period*, 2nd ed. (Grand Rapids: Eerdmans, 1999), pp. xxxi–xxxix; cf. Peter Enns, *Inspiration and Incarnation: Evangelicals and the Problem of the Old Testament* (Grand Rapids: Baker, 2005), pp. 156–163; Grant R. Osborne, *The Hermeneutical Spiral: A Comprehensive Introduction to Biblical Interpretation*, 2nd ed. (Downers Grove: IVP, 2006), pp. 323–344.

81. Rabbinic exegesis has four main types: (1) *peshat*, the plain/literal meaning of the text; (2) *pesher*, a form of prophetic interpretation found at Qumran, but which has been applied more widely; (3) *derash/midrash*, which includes linking new laws with Scripture, explaining difficulties, apparent contradictions and the hidden meanings in texts, and relating their message to the current situation; (4) *allegory*, which takes something in the text to point to a deeper philosophical or spiritual truth. There are also rules of interpretation. Rabbi Hillel gave seven, expanded to thirteen by Rabbi Ishmael, early in the second century AD. The NT includes examples of *peshat* (Mark 7:10–13; 1 Cor. 6:16), *pesher* (Luke 4:16–24; Matt. 11:10), *midrash* (Rom. 10:6–8) and *allegory* (1 Cor. 10:1–5; Gal. 4:21–31), and there is evidence too of the application of rules of exegesis similar to those of Rabbi Hillel and Rabbi Ishmael; so e.g. in Luke 11:13 Jesus uses the principle of *qal wahomer* (the first of Rabbi Hillel's rules), which is characterized by the expression 'how much more'. See further J. T. Barrera, *The Jewish Bible and the Christian Bible: An Introduction to the*

such interpretations are very restrained when contrasted with the way OT texts are used in rabbinic Midrash, and, even when using an allegorical approach, they generally retain the historical and theological perspectives of the original texts.[82]

The NT writers offer a distinctive approach to the OT in their use of typology.[83] Following a careful study of the use of the OT in the NT, Goppelt affirms that 'typology is the method of interpreting Scripture that is predominant in the New Testament and characteristic of it'.[84] We might then ask, was this hermeneutical method appropriate only in a first-century context, or might it provide a way of looking at the relationship between the testaments today? The increasing prominence given to typological approaches within biblical theology from the second third of the twentieth century indicates that the latter may well be the case.[85]

In the past, typology was closely associated with allegory, and we have noted some of the fanciful spiritualizing of the Church Fathers (which go far beyond anything we find in the NT). The *Epistle of Barnabas*, which has been given near-canonical status, sets out to reinterpret the OT as Christian Scripture, and insists that only the spiritualized ('Christianized') meaning given to the OT text is valid, thus removing any link between the interpretation of the text and its

---

Footnote 81 (*continued*)

> *History of the Bible* (Leiden: Brill; Grand Rapids: Eerdmans, 1998); Gerald
> L. Bruns, 'Midrash and Allegory: The Beginnings of Scriptural Interpretation',
> in Robert Alter and Frank Kermode (eds.), *The Literary Guide to the Bible* (London:
> Fontana, 1997), pp. 625–646; Enns, *Inspiration*, pp. 113–165; Longenecker, *Biblical
> Exegesis*.

82. Even in the allegory in Gal. 4:21–31 the spiritual meaning adduced by Paul does not detract from the historical and theological context of the original texts; indeed it is precisely the historical relationship between Hagar and Sarah and the divine promise in regard to Isaac that provide Paul with his argument.

83. Goppelt notes that there is no evidence of typology of the kind found in the NT in the non-biblical world at the time, and within the OT and Judaism it is used principally in relation to eschatology.

84. Goppelt, *Typos*, p. 198.

85. Within OT theology there is a positive view of the use of typology by e.g. von Rad, Eichrodt and Wolff. See, however, the criticism by James Barr, 'Typology and Allegory', in *Old and New in Interpretation: A Study of the Two Testaments* (London: SCM, 1964), pp. 103–148, and the comments by Childs, *Biblical Theology* (1992), pp. 13–14.

historical and theological context.[86] The NT writers, by contrast, retain that link. Thus when Paul describes the experiences of Israel in the desert as 'types' of the experience of the church (1 Cor. 10:1–11), he does not change the original meaning or significance of the OT passages; rather, he draws parallels between saving events in the life of Israel and corresponding events in the lives of Christian believers.

Because of the way it has been used in the past (and continues to be used in some circles) the term 'typology' is open to misunderstanding; nevertheless it is biblical, and there are good reasons for its continued use,[87] if it is carefully defined. According to Baker,

> the fundamental conviction which underlies typology is that God is consistently active in the history of this world (especially in the history of his chosen people) and that as a consequence the events in this history tend to follow a consistent pattern. One event may thus be chosen as typical of another or of many others.[88]

He also offers the following definitions:

> a *type* is a biblical event, person or institution which serves as an example or pattern for other events, persons or institutions; *typology* is the study of types and the historical and theological correspondences between them; the *basis* of typology is God's consistent activity in the history of his chosen people.[89]

Typological correspondence between the Old and New Testaments operates at a general level; as Seitz observes, 'the witness of the Old Testament as Christian Scripture is fundamentally a witness to the One who raised Israel from the dead, and who, in turn, raised Jesus from the dead'.[90] There are also more particular correspondences. Things in the story of Moses parallel the ministry of Jesus. The redemption of Israel from Egypt, which includes the death of the Passover lamb, corresponds to the redemption we have through

---

86. So e.g. the epistle fancifully allegorizes the dietary laws in Lev. 11 and Deut. 14, and asserts that in them, 'Moses was taking three moral maxims and expounding them spiritually; though the Jews, with their carnal instincts, took him to be referring, literally, to foodstuffs' (*Barnabas* 10).

87. See D. L. Baker, *Two Testaments*, pp. 179–189.

88. D. L. Baker, 'Typology', p. 153.

89. D. L. Baker, *Two Testaments*, p. 195.

90. Seitz, *Figured Out*, p. 47.

Christ the Lamb's death as our Passover sacrifice, and its continued remembrance in the Passover corresponds to the Christian celebration of the Lord's Supper. Elements of the OT sacrificial system also correspond to Christ's sacrifice. There is a (negative) typological correspondence between Adam, through whom sin came into the world, and Christ, who brings righteousness and forgiveness.[91] In these last cases we also see another aspect of typology: intensification. Baker does not see this as a necessary part of typology per se; but it is a feature of moving from the OT to the NT, where the promised salvation reaches its fulfilment. The OT also provides us with 'patterns' that relate to Christian living: so, for example, Abraham's faith is 'typical' of the faith God asks of all believers, and the prayers of OT saints provide models that may instruct the praying of Christians today.

As indicated already, viewed in this way, typology is distinct from allegory. Typology, rightly understood, is concerned with general historical and theological correspondences. It does not pick up on small details (such as the attempt to link the scarlet cord let down to the spies by Rahab with redemption through Christ's blood), but focuses, instead, on the 'agreement of fundamental patterns and structures'.[92] This idea of more general analogy has led too to a comparison of narrative patterns; thus there are correspondences between the story of Israel and the story of the church, and we have noted too the view that there are correspondences between the ministry of Jesus and the narrative of Israel. Also, in contrast to allegory, typology does not attempt to cut the OT text loose from its historical and theological context, nor does it regard the 'type' as meaningful only when seen from the NT perspective: within our understanding of typology, both 'type' and 'antitype' are realities in their own right.[93] Related to this, typology does not require exact or complete correspondence. So, while there may be key analogies, for example, between Israel and the church or between Moses and Christ, we need to recognize that there are also significant differences, and so avoid forcing analogies where there are none. We should note too that the theological significance of OT persons, events and institutions is not exhausted by their typological interpretation in the NT. Typology notes relationships between texts and themes;

---

91. For a fuller discussion, see Goppelt, *Typos*.

92. Baker, 'Typology', p. 153.

93. According to Wolff, use of the OT in the NT 'does not mean superimposing on the OT text a second meaning, an allegorical one . . . Rather we are to listen to how the historical meaning of the text continues to speak in the New Testament situation' ('Hermeneutics', in Westermann, *Essays*, p. 189).

it does not, nor does it intend to, provide a definitive interpretation of the OT text.

It is also important to distinguish typology from *prophecy*. An OT 'type' is not a prophetic announcement, awaiting fulfilment. Any typological correspondence is perceived by looking backwards; it is not in general, at least so far as the author is concerned, an intentional part of the original text.[94] And that has important implications for exegesis. Exegesis of the OT should take into account language, context, background and so on, but should not give undue weight to typological links to the NT (or even to later passages in the OT). The later use made of a passage may be interesting for the history of interpretations, but this is separate from exegesis. Thus an exegesis of sacrificial texts would not be expected to consider the view of the sacrificial system in the letter to the Hebrews. Exegesis of the exodus narrative would not usually look at the way Deutero-Isaiah portrays the return from exile as a second exodus, or the way the theme is used in the NT. However, noting typological correspondences is part of the task of biblical theology, which seeks to relate texts and their theology to one another. Typology emphasizes that there is a basic correspondence between different parts of the Bible; as Baker notes, 'every part of the Bible is an expression of the consistent activity of the one God'.[95] We thus may search for, and expect to find, correspondences between different parts of the OT, and between the OT and the NT. Typology of this kind also plays a part in preaching from the OT; it allows us to discern patterns 'typical' of God's dealings with his people, which may then be applied to the life of the church.

Narrative structure

This follows from the discussion of typology. Typology looks for correspondences between structures and narrative patterns within the canonical text.

---

94. It could be argued that the typological correspondence was known by God when the original text was written and so is intentional, and the fresh insight into what the text really signifies should be taken into account in its exegesis. However, that is to misunderstand the nature of typology and its relation to exegesis. A typological correspondence recognizes, in a different context, how patterns and principles continue to apply, but it does not seek to give the original text another level of meaning (see Wolff's comment in the previous note). Consequently it does not feature in the exegesis of the original text, whose role is to examine the text in its original, historical context. Of course it is significant in the exegesis of the later text, in which the typological correspondence is made.

95. D. L. Baker, 'Typology', p. 155.

One narrative model that has been usefully applied to the Bible to identify structures in narrative and non-narrative passages is that of A. J. Greimas.[96] According to Greimas, a narrative consists of a progression of three sequences. In the *initial sequence* something has gone wrong; in the *final sequence* what was wrong is put right and order is restored; between the problem and its solution is the *topical sequence*, which contains the heart of the story. Within each sequence are six participants in the narrative (*actants*), whose relationship may be set out as follows:

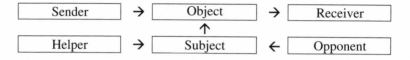

The Sender initiates the action; he determines the Object to be communicated to the Receiver, and calls the Subject to (find and) deliver it. To assist in the task the Subject has a Helper, and his mission is hindered by an Opponent. In the initial sequence the Opponent is stronger than the Subject and Helper; consequently the mission fails. The Subject needs more help, and in the topical sequence that assistance is given: the Subject becomes the Receiver of the extra Help needed to overcome the Opponent. This is delivered by another Subject, who also has a Helper and an Opponent:

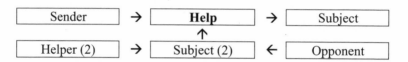

In the final sequence, with the additional Help now received, the Subject is able to overcome the Opponent and deliver the Object to the Receiver:

---

96. For more on Greimas's approach, and a bibliography, see Robin L. Routledge, 'Is There a Narrative Substructure Underlying the Book of Isaiah?', *TynBul* 55.2 (2004), pp. 183–204. Greimas developed his narrative model from an analysis of Russian folktales; however, it has also been applied to biblical texts; e.g. Rollin G. Grams, 'Narrative Dynamics in Isaiah's and Matthew's Mission Theology', *Transformation* 21.4 (2004), pp. 238–255; Richard B. Hays, *The Faith of Jesus Christ: The Narrative Substructure of Galatians 3:1–4:11*, 2nd ed. (Grand Rapids: Eerdmans, 2002); N. T. Wright, *NT People of God*, pp. 69–80; Daniel Patte, *The Religious Dimensions of Biblical Texts: Greimas' Structural Semiotics and Biblical Exegesis*, SBL Semeia Studies (Atlanta: Scholars Press, 1990).

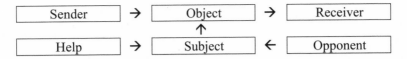

In my article 'Narrative Substructure' I have attempted to show how this model may be applied to the book of Isaiah. The book begins with a catalogue of the sin, characterized as *rebellion*, which prevents Israel from fulfilling her divine calling. This provides the beginnings of the initial sequence: God is the Sender, who has charged Israel as his servant (the Subject), with a task. What should help Israel is her divine calling and the evidence of God's activity in her history; what stands in the way is the nation's rebellion and failure to trust God.

Two further key themes in the book indicate the remaining actants. One is God's interest in and concern for the non-Israelite nations, who appear to be offered a place alongside Israel as the recipients of his salvation. The second is the revelation of God's glory. At his call Isaiah received an overwhelming revelation of divine glory, which filled the whole earth (Isa. 6:3), and it is possible to see within the book, a divine purpose to make that glory known to the nations, who do not yet recognize it (see e.g. Isa. 40:5; 43:7; 49:3; 60:1–3; 66:19). Israel features in this purpose as the one through whom that glory will be displayed.[97] This gives the following diagram:

At first, however, because of sin and rebellion, Israel's mission is unsuccessful. If the people are to be effective, they need to be restored and renewed, and this is provided in the topical sequence, where the agent of renewal is God's Servant:[98]

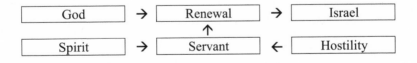

---

97. This is set out here primarily as an illustration. For more detailed discussion of the actants, see Routledge, 'Narrative Substructure'. God's purpose and the place of the nations within that purpose in the book of Isaiah and in the rest of the OT, will be discussed in chapter 10.

98. For more on God's Servant, see below, pp. 291–296.

This moves us to the final sequence, where Israel's mission is successful.

This kind of analysis helps to identify the main elements of the text, and allows us to look for recurring patterns. For example, Rollin Grams suggests that this pattern can also be discerned in the Gospel of Matthew.[99] An important question here is, can a similar narrative pattern be seen in the OT as a whole? In my view it can. I have already indicated that it is possible to discern a divine purpose in the OT, which includes the revelation and final acknowledgment of God's glory throughout the whole created order. I discuss this in more detail below.[100]

Recent approaches to Old Testament theology

Eichrodt and von Rad dominated OT Theology for much of the twentieth century. Their approaches represented the main directions for study, and the differences between them led to something of a stalemate.[101] However, the 1970s, which began with Childs's reference to the crisis in biblical theology, saw the appearance of several important OT Theologies.[102] The 1990s saw a

---

99. Grams, 'Narrative Dynamics'.

100. See below, p. 325.

101. Barr suggests that the approaches of Ludwig Köhler, *Old Testament Theology* (London: Lutterworth, 1957; repr. Cambridge: James Clarke, 2003), and of Th. C. Vriezen, *An Outline of Old Testament Theology* (Oxford: Blackwell, 1958), represent different 'types' of OT Theology from those of Eichrodt and von Rad (*Concept*, pp. 27–51). Köhler offers a systematic approach, using categories from dogmatic theology: *God, Man* and *Salvation*. Vriezen wants to go beyond Eichrodt's approach and focus more on the text of the OT and the message within the text, and less on the religion of Israel.

102. Including Walter Zimmerli, *Old Testament Theology in Outline* (Edinburgh: T. & T. Clark, 1978); Claus Westermann, *Elements of Old Testament Theology* (Atlanta: John Knox, 1982); Clements, *OT Theology*. The first edition of Hasel's *Basic Issues* was published in 1972; Walter Kaiser's *OT Theology* first appeared in 1978, and the first edition of Elmer A. Martens, *God's Design: A Focus on Old Testament Theology*, 3rd ed. (N. Richland Hills, Tex.: J. & F. Scott, 1997), was published in 1981. Some of these (with others) are discussed by Barr (*Concept*, pp. 312–329); see also Richard Schultz,

further burst of theological activity. I have already referred to the works by
Anderson, Childs, Preuss, House, Goldingay, Rendtorff and Waltke, which
appeared between 1991 and 2006; James Barr's *The Concept of Biblical Theology*
was also published in the same period, as were the two books by Leo Perdue,
The Collapse of History and *Reconstructing Old Testament Theology*, and Walter
Brueggemann's significant *Theology of the Old Testament*.[103]

Despite new moves forward in OT theology, Preuss has chosen to go back
to a more classical approach.[104] His *Old Testament Theology* follows a systematic
pattern reminiscent of Eichrodt, though instead of 'covenant' he takes as his

---

'What Is "Canonical" about a Canonical Biblical Theology?', in Hafemann, *Biblical
Theology*, pp. 83–99.

103. This list is not exhaustive. Other works that point to the growth in this area,
particularly since 1990, include Bruce C. Birch, Walter Brueggemann, Terence E.
Fretheim and David L. Petersen, *A Theological Introduction to the Old Testament*, 2nd ed.
(Nashville: Abingdon, 2005); Erhard S. Gerstenberger, *Theologies in the Old Testament*
(London: T. & T. Clark, 2002); Rolf P. Knierim, *The Task of Old Testament Theology:
Methods and Cases* (Grand Rapids: Eerdmans, 1995); Sailhamer, *OT Theology* (1995);
Ben C. Ollenburger, Elmer A. Martens and Gerhard F. Hasel (eds.), *The Flowering of
Old Testament Theology* (Winona Lake: Eisenbrauns, 1992), revised and expanded as
Ollenburger, *OT Theology: Flowering and Future* (2004). The *NIDOTTE* was
published in 1997. The fourth (revised and expanded) edition of Hasel's *Basic Issues*
was published in 1991; the second and third editions of Martens's *God's Design* were
published in 1994 and 1997 respectively, and there have been reprints of Kaiser's
Toward an OT Theology (1999) and Köhler's *OT Theology* (2003). Scobie's *Ways of Our
God* focuses particularly on biblical theology. After looking at its history and
methodology he sets out his own approach, which is to consider four themes
(God's Order, God's Servant, God's People and God's Way) in relation to the OT
under the heading Promise/Proclamation, and in relation to the NT under the
heading 'Fulfilment/Consummation'. In addition to OT theologies, several OT
introductions have been written, revised or reprinted, including Brueggemann,
Introduction to the OT (2003); John J. Collins, *Introduction to the Hebrew Bible*
(Minneapolis: Augsburg Fortress, 2004); Gottwald, *Hebrew Bible* (with CD-ROM,
2002); Tremper Longman III and Raymond B. Dillard, *An Introduction to the Old
Testament*, 2nd ed. (Leicester: Apollos; Grand Rapids: Zondervan, 2006); and R. K.
Harrison's classic *Introduction to the OT* (repr. 2000).

104. Perdue is critical of Preuss, presenting him as typical of scholars who hope 'that
new methods and their impact on theological discourse will simply disappear'
(*Reconstructing*, p. 6).

central, organizing theme God's historical activity in electing Israel.[105] He takes account of the religion of Israel, and includes a good deal that is descriptive, though he also emphasizes his desire to set out 'a structured theology of the Old Testament' rather than 'a history of Israel's religion',[106] with the hope that this could provide a basis for the larger enterprise of a biblical theology of Old and New Testaments.[107] One of Barr's criticisms is that Preuss is too descriptive and not theological enough. Also, apart from providing a wealth of background information, there is a question of how this may be related to the NT and to the life of the church.[108]

Gerstenberger looks at the OT from a historical-critical and, more particularly, a social-scientific standpoint.[109] He maintains that, rather than having a

---

105. Preuss, *OT Theology*, 1:21–26.

106. Ibid., 1:19.

107. Ibid., 1:19, 2:306–307.

108. See also Moberley's discussion of Preuss ('How May we Speak of God?', pp. 185–202).

109. Social-scientific theory looks at the faith of Israel in the light of the nation's changing social and political structures. Gerstenberger notes that 'Social structures are extraordinarily important for religion, whether this is lived out or reflected on. Consciously or unconsciously, faith relates to the institutions, roles, and balances of power in society and is also shaped by them' (*Theologies*, p. 163). And in his exploration of Israel's theologies he starts from 'the social conditions in which faith was lived out and formulated' rather than 'from the revealed word of God' (*Theologies*, p. 24). An important publication in this area is Norman K. Gottwald, *The Tribes of Yahweh: A Sociology of the Religion of Liberated Israel, 1250–1050 BCE* (Maryknoll: Orbis, 1979; repr. 1999). In a later article Gottwald sets out 'the guiding question for social science approaches to the Bible' as 'What social structures, processes, and codes are explicit or implicit in the biblical literature, in the scattered social data it contains, in the overtly political history it recounts or touches on, and in the religious beliefs and practices it attests?' ('Social Matrix and Canonical Shape', *ThTo*, 42.3 [1985], pp. 307–321 [307]). For discussion of the relationship between this approach and other biblical criticisms, see Gottwald, *Hebrew Bible*, esp. pp. 26–31. See also David J. Chalcraft (ed.), *Social-Scientific Old Testament Criticism*, Sheffield Readers (Sheffield: Sheffield Academic Press, 1997); Philip F. Esler (ed.), *Ancient Israel: The Old Testament in Its Social Context* (Minneapolis: Fortress, 2006); Perdue, *Collapse*, pp. 69–109. While providing useful insights, there is a danger in this approach that by seeing all the key movements in Israel's history as the result of sociological processes, God is reduced to a sociological construct.

theological centre, the OT is made up of diverse testimonies, conditioned by Israel's historical and social conditions. He notes, particularly, the different understandings of God as the focus of religion moves from family to village to tribal alliance to state and, finally, to the post-exilic confessional community, when the traditions of Israel's faith were collected and written down. The result is not a single theology of the OT, but several theologies in tension with one another; hence his choice of title: *Theologies in the Old Testament.* On this basis, he also challenges the canonical approach as an attempt to find coherence and unity in writings that reflect diverse theological traditions, and concludes that 'we may not read the biblical texts as a uniform norm of faith'.[110] This is reminiscent of the history of religions approach where there are no absolute truths that can be applied to the life of the church. What is relevant, for Gerstenberger, is the importance of adapting our view of God to a changing world: 'it is our task to try to engage in constant, corrective dialogue with the old witnesses; we must look for the new form and formulation of faith which is valid today'.[111]

Other recent theologies have moved away from approaches that focus on the religion of Israel to consider the theology reflected in the final form of the OT text. Significant among these is Brevard Childs's emphasis on the canon, which I discuss in more detail below. Before that, some observations about where the meaning of a text is located.

Text and meaning
In general the transmission and reception of a text involves three main links:

AUTHOR ⇒ **TEXT** ⇒ **READER**

Historical-critical approaches to the text tend to focus on the process of composition: how and why it came to be written, what was the historical and cultural context in which the pre-literary traditions circulated. This is 'the world behind the text' (the world of the author or compiler) and historical criticisms such as form, source and redaction criticism, and the more recent social-scientific criticism,[112] seek to discover as much about that world as possible. It

---

110. Gerstenberger, *Theologies*, pp. 12–17 (16).

111. Ibid., p. 279.

112. Though sometimes linked with newer literary criticisms, social-scientific theory focuses on the world behind the text.

is thought that reconstructing the world that gave rise to the text helps us to understand the text better, and in part that must be true. But there are also problems.

One is that the world reconstructed by historical criticism may bear little or no relation to the world described in the text, returning us to the issue of two versions of history. A second problem is that having supposedly discovered the world behind the text, it is this rather than the text itself that becomes the focus for theology. Having reconstructed an event, scholars are free to offer their own interpretation of it, and this may be added to or may replace the interpretation given in the text.

Another approach, *structuralism*, focuses on the text itself. It assumes that the text has to make sense to everyone who reads it, including the original reader and all subsequent generations of readers. So, the key to interpretation is the structure of the text and the interrelationship of its various elements: words, sentences and paragraphs, plot and sub-plot, characterization and so on. Similar methods are employed within narrative criticism. The aim of structuralism is to provide literature with an objective, 'scientific' method for analysing the structures of the text. More recent ('post-structural') literary approaches focus more on the interaction between text and reader, and set the text free from fixed external reference points. There is no interest in the world behind the text; rather, the text creates its own world, and readers are invited to enter and so have their own world (sometimes described as 'the world *in front of the text*') challenged and changed.[113]

The canonical approach[114]

One of the problems associated with historical-critical approaches to the OT is the loss of biblical authority. Form criticism, for example, looks at the

---

113. Thiselton follows Gadamer in talking about two horizons: of the world of the reader and of the world of the text. As the reader commits to the world of the text there is a 'fusion of horizons' (*Horizonverschmelzung*), and in that interaction between reader and text, meaning is produced. See Anthony Thiselton, *The Two Horizons: New Testament Hermeneutics and Philosophical Description* (Exeter: Paternoster, 1980); *New Horizons in Hermeneutics* (London: HarperCollins, 1992), p. 8; H. G. Gadamer, *Truth and Method*, 2nd rev. ed. (London: Sheed & Ward, 1989), pp. 302–307; Paul Ricoeur, *Interpretation Theory: Discourse and the Surplus of Meaning* (Fort Worth: Texas Christian University Press, 1976), pp. 91–92.

114. See also Childs, *OT Theology*, pp. 6–18; *Biblical Theology* (1992), pp. 70–106; John Barton, *Reading the Old Testament: Method in Biblical Study*, 2nd ed. (Louisville:

literary form of the text, and tries to discover how that form has developed from simpler oral and literary units into the more complicated structure we now see. Implicit within that approach is the idea that the original units carry more 'weight' than later additions, and the effect of describing a verse or part of a verse as an 'addition' and 'not part of the original text' is to diminish the authority of the whole text. One of the concerns of the canonical approach is to recover the authority of the biblical text as a whole.

Another problem is the relationship between exegesis and the biblical text. If the text is broken down first into literary and then possible oral sources, or into different redactional layers, the focus shifts to these fragments (or maybe to the supposed larger source they are thought to be part of) and away from exegesis of the actual text itself.

Childs argues that the proper context for the study of biblical theology is the canon of Scripture that has been received and accepted by the believing community.[115] He claims that the process of development during which the material was shaped and interpreted theologically is a vital part of the revelation, and that the final canonical construct is normative not only for the community who accepted it but for future generations of believers too. He writes:

> The shape of the biblical text reflects a history of encounter between God and Israel. The canon serves to describe this particular relationship and to define the scope of this history by establishing a beginning and end to the process. It assigns a special quality to this particular segment of human history which became normative for all successive generations of this community of faith. The significance of the final form of the biblical text is that it alone bears witness to the full history of revelation.[116]

Historical-critical methods such as source criticism and form criticism break the text up to discover sources or basic forms to which further material

---

Westminster John Knox, 1996), pp. 77–103; R. A Harrisville and W. Sundberg, *The Bible in Modern Culture: Baruch Spinoza to Brevard Childs*, 2nd ed. (Grand Rapids: Eerdmans, 2002); Hasel, *Basic Issues*, pp. 103–114; Perdue, *Collapse*, pp. 153–196.

115. A significant weakness of Childs's approach is that it is impossible to define the 'canon' objectively. There is debate over what is 'canonical', not just between Jews and Christians but among Christians – between Protestants and Catholics and even within Protestantism. For Childs the content of the canon is a matter of faith, but this limits discussion to those who hold similar views of canonicity.

116. Brevard S. Childs, *Introduction to the Old Testament as Scripture* (London: SCM, 1979), p. 77.

has been added. This approach, which looks at how the text has developed through time, is referred to as *diachronic*. An alternative is to focus on the text as we now have it, in its final form. This approach is referred to as *synchronic*. By focusing on the text as it appears in its final, canonical form, Childs adopts this *synchronic* approach. He is interested in the historical context of a text or in how redactors may have developed it where these things can be discovered, and notes that 'whatever is meant by the canon as a setting in which the Christian church reads its Scripture, it cannot imply that the original setting in which God addressed his people is irrelevant for the later generations'.[117] Nevertheless these issues are less important than the theological role of the text within the completed canonical work.

The canonical form of the text is the result of shaping by editors, who have adapted the text in the light of changing historical circumstances and theological needs. Redaction criticism seeks to identify the various layers of the text, and the theological motives of successive redactors in adapting the text. Childs recognizes the existence of these editorial layers. However, while redaction criticism is essentially diachronic, identifying the different layers and the redactors' different (sometimes competing) theological agendas, Childs is concerned with how those layers function within the canonical text. He maintains that successive redactions all contribute to the final form of the book, which has been received, and so must be interpreted, as a coherent whole.

As part of this approach, Childs claims that the study of OT theology is a Christian enterprise. Judaism and Christianity accept the same OT canon; however, as we have seen, each sets it within its own theological context and approaches it differently. Those who argue for the essential Jewishness of the OT challenge Childs on this. However, Childs is referring to the theological context of the OT, and not to its language, cultural background or interpretative traditions.

As we have also seen, a key problem facing biblical theology is the relationship between history as the account of what actually happened, and (*Heils*)*Geschichte*: history as seen through the eyes of Israel's faith. Childs resolves this tension, in common with others who adopt a final-form reading of the text, by focusing only on *Geschichte*; he maintains that 'the canonical approach views history from the perspective of Israel's faith-construal'.[118] However, as we have seen, he also attaches importance to the historical context and background of a text. By attempting to look at both the canonical and historical context of a text,

---

117. Childs, *Biblical Theology in Crisis*, p. 108.
118. Childs, *OT Theology*, p. 16.

Childs's position is ambiguous. His aim, though, is clear: he wants to free the theological meaning of the canonical text from the historical uncertainties that may surround its context, and so recover the Bible's authority.

Another important issue for Childs, and this is particularly true in relation to the literary and other postmodern approaches to the text discussed below, is his insistence on the existence of a reality behind the biblical text that needs to be distinguished from it.[119] There may be questions of how the text references the reality, but there is no doubt that such a reality exists.

Finally, in this short review, Childs does not claim that the canonical approach means that there is always a single correct way of interpreting a text. Within the development of the canonical text dissonant voices have sometimes been retained, and as those other voices are heard and evaluated by the interpreter, different interpretations will result.

Childs's method has had a significant impact on biblical theology, though he has also aroused some criticism.[120] He applies it to the text in his *Biblical Theology of the Old and New Testaments*, published in 1992. He begins by looking at 'The Discrete Witness of the Old Testament', and follows, broadly, the historical order of the Hebrew canon. He next looks at 'The Discrete Witness of the New Testament", and goes on to give two examples of 'exegesis in the context of biblical theology'. He then considers key themes as they appear in the Old and New Testaments, before concluding with comments on a holistic reading of Scripture.

Since Childs, other OT theologies have also adopted a canonical approach. Paul House agrees with Childs's emphasis on the canon, though also has reservations about his view of the relationship between Scripture and revelation and of history. In his *OT Theology* House devotes a chapter to each of the twenty-four books in the Hebrew canon. This, he argues, allows him to focus

---

119. Childs, *Biblical Theology* (1992), p. 20.

120. See e.g. Barr's fierce attack, and his conclusion that 'Childs publications in biblical theology are likely to do great harm to the subject and its prospects' (*Concept*, pp. 378–438 [438]); and the review by Walter Brueggemann, 'Against the Stream: Brevard Childs' Theology', *ThTo* 50.2 (1993), pp. 279–284. Collins is also fairly negative (*Encounters*, pp. 15–16), though that is expected since he continues to favour the historical-critical approach, which Childs questions; see also Gerstenberger, *Theologies*, pp. 12–17. For more balanced discussion, see e.g. House, *OT Theology*, pp. 43–50; Iain Provan, 'Canons to the Left of him: Brevard Childs, his Critics and the Future of Old Testament Theology', *SJT* 50.1 (1997), pp. 1–38; Schultz, 'What Is "Canonical"', in Hafemann, *Biblical Theology*, pp. 85–88.

on the unique contribution each makes to the theological content of the OT. Their unity is seen in 'canonical syntheses', which follow themes through the whole of the OT (and into the NT). House also points to the existence and worship of one God as a main focal point around which other OT themes may be centred. However, both the structure of the chapters, under the headings 'the God who . . .', and the syntheses, which help to draw OT texts together, are thematic and not based around the text.

In what is more a book about methodology than an OT Theology, John Sailhamer also advocates a canonical approach. He sets out the task of OT theology in terms of a choice between four pairs of alternatives. First, he considers whether revelation is located in the *text* or in the *event* the text refers to, and concludes in favour of the former. Text is communication between author and reader, so the primary concern must be with the words of the biblical text, and on the meaning intended by their author. This distinction is important. Event matters, but the writer's reflection on the event under the inspiration of God constitutes revelation. Thus Sailhamer accepts the view of history presented in the text; however, in accordance with his own conservative evangelical standpoint, he assumes there will be little discrepancy between this and 'what actually happened', and so finds no place to discuss different versions of 'history'. In focusing on the text, Sailhamer also wants to rule out ideals and principles that may lie behind it. Second, he argues that we need to focus on the *canonical text*, by which he means the text as we have it, taken at face value, rather than the text as reconstructed by historical criticism. He does acknowledge that the final text is the result of limited editing, and recognizes the value of research that sheds light on the historical context and culture, and so on the original intention, of the author. Again, though, there is the assumption that such research will not challenge the description of events in the text. Third, Sailhamer notes that we approach the OT not merely to describe its content, but with a faith commitment that looks for meaning and relevance. And, because the Bible is God's Word, theology should be normative. A fourth choice (about which Sailhamer appears to be ambivalent) is between focusing on diverse themes as they develop through the OT and looking for one or two themes to provide a theological centre.

Sailhamer clarifies some of the issues that need to be considered in a conservative approach to OT theology and notes important distinctions, particularly between the canonical text and historical reconstructions of either text or event. I agree with his emphasis on the importance of text as communication, and so of the need to consider the intention of the author, and also that OT theology should be both relevant and normative for the church, though Sailhamer does not explain how this works in practice. A further weakness is that he appears to adopt a relatively uncritical, literalist approach.

Rolf Rendtorff also takes a canonical approach in his *Canonical Hebrew Bible* (first published, in German, in 2001). Following von Rad, he wants to avoid imposing a foreign theological structure on the OT and to allow the biblical texts themselves to set the course for his discussion.[121] Consequently he begins by focusing on the text of the OT in the order it appears in the Hebrew canon. He adopts a narrative approach, allowing the possibility of different voices in the text. He then goes on to look at particular OT themes, which he considers in the context of the OT as a whole. In this he focuses on the variations and whether and to what extent they coincide.[122] Rendtorff does not want to reject or ignore historical criticism, but does want to reverse the emphasis, from looking first at the development of the text, to a primary interest in the text as it now is. In his view diachronic and synchronic approaches are not mutually exclusive,[123] and may in fact complement one another. However, the main focus is on the canonical text in its final form and the intention of the editor who may have brought elements from different sources together.[124] Rendtorff acknowledges Childs's influence on his approach,[125] but in my view he has linked it better with other approaches (such as diachronic and narrative) and so has applied it better to the task of OT theology.

(New) literary/narrative approaches

A central idea in the approaches of Eichrodt and von Rad is that there is a world behind the biblical text, to which the biblical text bears witness (though for von Rad it has been obscured by constant retelling and application of the story). God exists. He has revealed himself to Israel through word and deed, and the OT text makes us aware of what God has said and done. There is a reality (historical or theological) behind the written word. It is somewhat ironic that the historical-critical approach, which set out to discover the historical reality behind the text, succeeded in so undermining the historicity of the OT that it opened the way for new approaches that disregard 'actual history' altogether.

In recent years there has been a growing emphasis on the need to understand the OT from the perspective of the text alone, to set the text free from any historical 'reality' that might lie behind it. In an early example of this, David

---

121. Rendtorff, *Hebrew Bible*, p. 2.

122. Ibid., pp. 415–417.

123. See e.g. the introductory discussion of the latter prophets, ibid., pp. 161–166.

124. Ibid., pp. 717–726.

125. Ibid., p. 718.

Clines argues that we should view the Pentateuch as *narrative* or *story*.[126] He does not necessarily discount the historical approach, but argues that it is important to look at the Pentateuch as a literary whole. Historical-critical methods are unable to establish firm points of departure. Attempts to determine sources or to reconstruct the historical situation behind a text are often conjecture, and it is unwise to attempt to draw firm conclusions from one tenuous hypothesis built on another. If a text's meaning is closely bound up with historical-critical considerations, such as its historical setting or its process of development, that meaning is undermined if those things are challenged, or shown to be false. If, instead, we focus on the text as we now have it as a piece of literature, meaning is inherent within the text and the way the text is interpreted by the reader, and does not depend on uncertain background issues or on historical or scientific verifiability. Thus, according to Clines, in the case of the Pentateuch we do not have to consider whether parts of the story are believable or not; for the purpose of the story the world it describes is real. Nor do we have to answer questions about historicity; the story has significance and meaning whatever the actual historical situation.

Narrative is a dominant genre in the OT, and there is an increasing recognition that it should be studied as literature.[127] This approach is synchronic. Stories may have been built up over a period of time; nevertheless they are read and interpreted in their final form as a literary unity. Through the structure of the narrative, the use of language and literary conventions (studied under the title 'poetics') the writer (usually referred to as the *narrator*) tells the story and, like any good storyteller, seeks to involve the reader in it.[128]

---

126. David J. A. Clines, *The Theme of the Pentateuch*, JSOTSup 10 (Sheffield: JSOT Press, 1978).

127. Because source criticism was sometimes referred to as 'literary criticism', this new approach has been termed 'new literary criticism'. For examples of new literary approaches (and a discussion of what is 'no longer new'), see J. Cheryl Exum and David J. A. Clines (eds.), *The New Literary Criticism and the Hebrew Bible*, JSOTSup 143 (Sheffield: JSOT Press, 1993); see also Barton, *Reading the OT*, pp. 141–219; Perdue, *Collapse*, pp. 197–262.

128. For further discussion, see e.g. Robert Alter, *The Art of Biblical Narrative* (New York: Basic; London: Allen & Unwin, 1981); Shimon Bar-Efrat, *Narrative Art in the Bible*, JSOTSup 70 (Sheffield: JSOT Press, 2000); Adele Berlin, *Poetics and Interpretation of Biblical Narrative* (Sheffield: Almond, 1983; Winona Lake: Eisenbrauns, 1994); David M. Gunn and Danna N. Fewell, *Narrative in the Hebrew Bible*, Oxford Bible Series (Oxford: Oxford University Press, 1993); V. Philips Long, 'Reading the Bible as

This approach opens up interesting and helpful insights into the study of narrative (and non-narrative) passages. It acknowledges that story plays an important part in our understanding of ourselves and of our place in the world and was, almost certainly, more important in the world view of the OT writers. In the first volume of his *Old Testament Theology* John Goldingay wants to do justice to the OT's narrative, rather than propositional, way of doing theology, an intention reflected in its title, *Israel's Gospel*. He notes that narrative gives scope to express complex theological ideas.[129] By just telling the story, the narrator is able to include ambiguities and tensions without necessarily attempting to resolve them. The narrative form and structure of the text itself may also be theologically instructive.

However, the insistence that we as readers should focus on the text alone, and seek to cut it loose from any external points of reference, such as historical context or author's intention, is, in my opinion, flawed.[130] While it is true that those things are often uncertain, and it is unwise to make the meaning of a text dependent on speculation about them, it is equally unwise to ignore historical considerations altogether as a matter of methodological dogma. To divorce the author's intention or the immediate historical context (where these things can be found out with a reasonable measure of certainty) from the meaning of the text is to leave out a crucial piece of the interpretative jigsaw.[131] And it is not essential to a narrative approach.

Literature', in Craig C. Broyles (ed.), *Interpreting the Old Testament: A Guide for Exegesis* (Grand Rapids: Baker, 2001), pp. 85–123; Tremper Longman III, *Literary Approaches to Biblical Interpretation*, Foundations of Contemporary Interpretation 3 (Leicester: Apollos, 1987); 'Literary Approaches to Old Testament Study', in Baker and Arnold, *Face of OT Studies*, pp. 97–115; *NIDOTTE* 1:103–124; Robin L. Routledge, 'Guest or Gatecrasher: Questioning Assumptions in a Narrative Approach to the Old Testament', *JEBS* 3.3 (2003), pp. 17–28; Philip E. Satterthwaite, *NIDOTTE* 1:125–133.

129. Goldingay, *OT Theology*, 1:39–41. Goldingay's general approach in this volume offers helpful insights, though he makes some controversial assertions – not always with enough explanation or justification.

130. For a thorough discussion of where a text's meaning is located, see Kevin J. Vanhoozer, *Is There a Meaning in This Text? The Bible, the Reader and the Morality of Literary Knowledge* (Leicester: Apollos, 1998). See also Peter Cotterell, *NIDOTTE* 1:134–160; Goldingay, *OT Theology*, 1:859–883; Kevin J. Vanhoozer, *NIDOTTE* 1:15–50.

131. There are problems, though, about being too dogmatic about the intentions of the author. Often we do not know who the author is, and where we do, there is usually

Another important issue is the question of *historicity*. For many advocates of the literary/narrative approach, whether the events described by the narrative really took place or not is irrelevant. The world of the narrative is the only one we know, and within the narrative it is real: its characters are real; their actions and conversations are real. But they are real only as the characters in a novel are real. Robert Alter, one of the architects of this approach, describes OT narrative as 'historicized fiction'.[132] Alter accepts that some narratives have a broadly historical framework. Other scholars go further and argue that the history of Israel as recorded in the OT is a literary construct, with little basis in historical reality.[133]

Footnote 131 (*continued*)

> too little information about background and personality to discern his intention in writing. The fallacy that external facts about the author may be related to the meaning of the text was exposed in W. K. Wimsatt and M. Beardsley, 'The Intentional Fallacy', in *The Verbal Icon: Studies in the Meaning of Poetry* (Lexington: University of Kentucky Press, 1954); see also Meir Sternberg, *Poetics of Biblical Narrative* (Bloomington: Indiana University Press, 1987), pp. 8–9; Vanhoozer, *Meaning*, pp. 43–97. Nevertheless, if the text is to function as communication, the author's intention and the background against which he was writing must play a part. It is my contention that (to a limited extent) we can know something at least of the author's intention, not from external factors, but from the text itself, and, moreover, that the author's intention is crucial in determining meaning. See Routledge, 'Guest or Gatecrasher', pp. 22–24.

132. Alter, *Art of Biblical Narrative*, p. 41. The expression is borrowed from Schneidau, who contrasts the historical aspect of narrative in the OT, particularly in Genesis and in the story of David, with mythological forms and style evident in other ancient writings; see Herbert Schneidau, *Sacred Discontent* (Baton Rouge: State University Press, 1976), p. 215. Alter, though, uses the expression also to emphasize the fictional character of the narrative, which allows the storytellers to use creative imagination in their reporting. A particular advantage of this is that the characters in the narrative can be made to appear more real and multifaceted by including speech, and glimpses of their thought life and motivations.

133. See e.g. Philip R. Davies, *In Search of Ancient Israel*, JSOTSup 148 (Sheffield: JSOT Press, 1992); 'Whose History? Whose Israel? Whose Bible? Biblical Histories, Ancient and Modern', in Lester E. Grabbe (ed.), *Can a 'History of Israel' Be Written*, JSOTSup 245, European Seminar in Historical Methodology 1 (Sheffield: Sheffield Academic Press, 1996), pp. 104–122; Nils Peter Lemche, 'Is it Still Possible to Write a History of Ancient Israel?', in V. Philips Long (ed.), *Israel's Past in Present Research:*

By focusing primarily on the text and on the world of the text the narrative approach acknowledges that for significant parts of the OT that is all we have. This is important when it comes to OT theology. We base our view of God on the witness of the text, and must be careful not to impose external ideas on to it. But we also recognize that God exists as a theological reality outside the text: he is not merely a character in a literary construction.[134] The writers of biblical narrative want to tell their stories as effectively as possible. However, they do not have the freedom of composition sometimes claimed for them. There is a historical and theological reality that lies behind the text, to which the OT writers, using whatever literary techniques might be at their disposal, seek to bear witness.

Old Testament theology in a postmodern context

Postmodernism is difficult to define; frequently it is seen as a reaction against 'modernity', which embraces, as its metanarrative,[135] the scientific rationalism of the Enlightenment.[136] As a result there is a tendency within postmodernism

---

Essays on Ancient Israelite Historiography, SBTS 7 (Winona Lake: Eisenbrauns, 1999), pp. 391–414; Thomas L. Thompson, *The Bible in History: How Writers Create a Past* (London: Pimlico, 2000); Keith W. Whitelam, 'Recreating the History of Israel', *JSOT 35* (1986), pp. 45–70. On the other side of the argument, see John Bimson, 'Old Testament History and Sociology', in Broyles, *Interpreting the OT*, pp. 125–155; Iain Provan, 'In the Stable with the Dwarves: Testimony, Interpretation, Faith, and the History of Israel', in V. Philips Long, David W. Baker and Gordon J. Wenham (eds.), *Windows into Old Testament History* (Grand Rapids: Eerdmans, 2002), pp. 161–197; Jens B. Kofoed, 'Epistemology, Historiographical Method and the "Copenhagen School"', in Philips Long, Baker and Wenham, *Windows*, pp. 23–43. See also Iain Provan, V. Philips Long and Tremper Longman III, *A Biblical History of Israel* (Louisville: Westminster John Knox, 2003). For an overview of recent research, see V. Philips Long, 'Historiography of the Old Testament', in Baker and Arnold, *Face of OT Studies*, pp. 145–175; see also Childs, *Biblical Theology* (1992), pp. 196–207. For discussion of the relationship between history and theology, see e.g. V. Philips Long, *NIDOTTE* 1:86–102; Eugene H. Merrill, *NIDOTTE* 1:68–85.

134. See e.g. B. W. Anderson, *Contours*, pp. 56–58.

135. Jean-François Lyotard defined postmodernism in terms of its scepticism towards such universal schemes.

136. For further discussion of this in relation to the reading of the OT, see Perdue, *Reconstructing*, pp. 239–279.

to deconstruct the 'certainties' that derive from the modern era, along with the structures and institutions based on them. A key aspect of postmodernism is *pluralism*. Rather than a single unified, overarching story (metanarrative), there are several smaller and more local stories, with different, but equally valid perspectives. There is no one way of viewing the world, and, similarly, there is no single way of interpreting the Bible. This is evident within the broad sweep of the new literary criticism.

As we have seen, there are three key elements in the transmission of a text: *author–text–reader*, and three 'worlds' associated with them: (1) the world *behind* the text, (2) the world *of or within* the text and (3) the world *in front of* the text, the world of the reader. No one who reads the Bible is totally neutral, so it is important to acknowledge the world in front of the text and the part played by the reader in interpretation. This has led to 'reader-response' criticism, where a text's meaning depends solely on the context in which the passage is read and on the reader's background, social and ideological standpoint, and world view. Following this approach it is inappropriate to speak about a text having a single, legitimate meaning: it may have several meanings, conditioned by the world view of various readers, and each is equally valid. These interpretations are not arbitrary: they need to be validated by an 'interpretative community', which shares the reader's world view, preconceptions, political and cultural outlook, place in society and so on, and endorses the interpretation,[137] but none of them is the only 'right' way to interpret the text. This also allows for ideological readings of the text, including political and feminist interpretations.[138]

A key feature of post-structuralism is *deconstruction*, which reinforces the view that a text has no determinative interpretation.[139] Weaknesses in the argument, unanswered questions, gaps in the narrative, contradictions, words or ideas that may be seen from more than one point of view all emphasize the undecidability of the text, and undermine a definitive

---

137. For further discussion of interpretative communities, see e.g. Stanley Fish, *Is There a Text in This Class: The Authority of Interpretative Communities* (Cambridge, Mass.: Harvard University Press, 1980), pp. 303–371; see also David J. A. Clines, 'A World Established on Water', in Exum and Clines, *New Literary Criticism*, p. 86.

138. For a sample of literary readings, see Exum and Clines, *New Literary Criticism*; see also Perdue, *Reconstructing*, pp. 76–182. For more on feminist readings, including bibliography, see below, pp. 153–154.

139. See e.g. Vanhoozer, *Meaning*; Longman, 'Literary Approaches', in Baker and Arnold, *Face of OT Studies*, pp. 107–110.

meaning.[140] Miscall, for example, notes the ambiguity in the picture of David in 1 Samuel 17:

> David's character is undecidable. The text permits us to regard David as a pious and innocent young shepherd going to battle the Philistine because of the latter's defiance of the Lord, and as a cunning and ambitious young warrior who is aware of the effects that his defeat of Goliath will have on the assembled army.[141]

The view of David the reader adopts will depend on how he or she interacts with the text, but cannot be based with any certainty on the text alone.

A further significant trend in literary studies is to critique the ideological standpoint and world view of the writers.[142] It is usually assumed that they reinforce the ideology and values of the powerful and influential and an important reason for challenging traditional interpretations is to undermine the theological and sociopolitical institutions they shore up.

Recognizing that the text is an ideological document reflecting the beliefs and values of its writer, and that our understanding of the text is influenced by our own beliefs and values, has significant implications for OT theology. We need to evaluate the dominant theological position of the text, but also to search for and evaluate dissonant voices within the text. And our own world view and theological preconceptions will determine which voices carry the most weight, which again opens up the possibility of several different verdicts. This indeterminacy is central to the approach of Walter Brueggemann.

Walter Brueggemann[143]

In his *Theology of the Old Testament* Brueggemann gives a review of the history of the discipline, and goes on to suggest that, to move forward, OT theology

---

140. See e.g. David Miscall, *The Workings of Old Testament Narrative*, SBL Semeia Studies (Philadelphia: Fortress; Chico: Scholars Press, 1983), p. 2; Clines, 'Established on Water', in Exum and Clines, *New Literary Criticism*, pp. 83–85.

141. Miscall, *Workings*, p. 1.

142. For further discussion of the influence of ideology on the writing and interpretation of text, see e.g. David J. A. Clines, *Interested Parties, the Ideology of Writers and Readers of the Hebrew Bible*, JSOTSup 205 (Sheffield: Sheffield Academic Press, 1995); Gunn and Fewell, *Narrative*, pp. 189–205; Vanhoozer, *Meaning*, pp. 166–168.

143. See also e.g. Barr, *Concept*, pp. 541–562; Perdue, *Reconstructing*, pp. 251–255; Tim Meadowcroft, 'Method and Old Testament Theology: Barr, Brueggemann and Goldingay Considered', *TynBul* 57.1 (2006), pp. 35–56 (42–47).

needs to acknowledge its postmodern interpretative context. To achieve this he begins with the final form of the text, which he sees as Israel's testimony about God, and moves away from traditional (modernist) approaches that focus on what lies behind the text: either the historical world, or the being of God as a metaphysical reality independent of the text. For Brueggemann, the testimony is the reality: 'speech constitutes reality, and who God turns out to be in Israel depends on the utterance of the Israelites or, derivatively, the utterance of the text'.[144] Thus he criticizes Childs for wanting to affirm the existence of God as a reality behind the text. By focusing only on the text for an understanding of God, Brueggemann aims to avoid imposing preconceived ideas of God on to the text. But this raises important questions both about who God is and how we may relate to what appears to be no more than a rhetorical construct.

Focusing on Israel's testimony also allows Brueggemann to recognize the plurality of voices that can be heard within the OT.[145] He begins with *Israel's Core Testimony*: the testimony that affirms the sovereignty and faithfulness of Yahweh. This is followed by *Israel's Counter Testimony*, which focuses on the nation's experience of Yahweh's hiddenness, ambiguity (including charges of contradiction and unreliability) and negativity (such as his capacity for violence and his injustice in allowing the guilty to prosper and the innocent to suffer). Brueggemann argues that this tension is characteristic of the faith of the OT. The character of God presented in the text is open to question, review and change. There can be no settled, fixed idea of God, and even when all the evidence has been considered, the verdict is only provisional. It depends on what weight is given to the various testimonies, and that will be different for different readers:

> such an interpretative judgment is never innocent or disinterested and may be decided variously – on the basis of one's own personal need and inclination, one's particular social setting or circumstance, or one's theological nurture and tradition.[146]

This resistance to any kind of closure is, according to Brueggemann, characteristic of Jewish dialectic, and he emphasizes the Jewishness of the OT on

---

144. Brueggemann, *Theology*, p. 65; he goes on, 'the God of Old Testament theology . . . lives in, with and under the rhetorical enterprise of the text, and nowhere and in no other way' (p. 66).

145. This plurality of 'theologies' within the OT has already been noted in relation to von Rad and Gerstenberger.

146. Brueggemann, *Theology*, p. 75.

several occasions.[147] This impacts on the question of a Christian reading of the OT and on Brueggemann's understanding of the relationship between the Old and New Testaments. He does not regard the OT as a 'witness to Jesus Christ in any primary or direct sense',[148] though allows that 'an imaginative construal of the Old Testament towards Jesus is a credible act'.[149] He insists, though, that this is not a necessary movement; it must be done from the side of the NT, and it does not preclude equally valid Jewish appropriations of the OT text. He goes on to suggest that

> the task of OT theology, as a Christian enterprise, is to articulate, explicate, mobilize and make accessible and available the testimony of the Old Testament in all its polyphonic, elusive, imaginative power and to offer it to the Church for its continuing work of construal towards Jesus.[150]

Brueggemann's postmodern approach, in which there are no absolutes, suits the mood of the age. And we have to recognize that there are tensions within the OT:[151] several voices, with different emphases. One example is the different attitudes towards kingship in 1 Samuel 8 – 11;[152] another is the tension within the wisdom literature between the apparent moral certainty reflected in Proverbs, and the questions raised by Job and Ecclesiastes.[153] The picture of God in the OT is not always clear, and there is the temptation to read the OT too much in the light of the NT or of dogmatic theology. However, Brueggemann seems to go too far both in separating the Old and New Testaments, and in his view the only God we may know from the OT is the God presented through the testimony of its writers, and we should not look elsewhere. It is important to read the OT as Scripture in its own right, but if there is no clear continuity and coherence between OT and NT, or even between the God revealed in the text of the OT and the God revealed in Jesus Christ, it raises the question of why Christians should read the OT at all.

---

147. Ibid., pp. 80–84, 107–112, 733–735.

148. Ibid., p. 107.

149. Ibid., p. 732.

150. Ibid.

151. See Enns, *Inspiration*, pp. 71–112; John Goldingay, *Theological Diversity and the Authority of the Old Testament* (Grand Rapids: Eerdmans, 1987; repr. Biblical and Theological Classics Library; Carlisle: Paternoster, 1995).

152. See below, pp. 228–233.

153. See below, pp. 221–224.

John Goldingay

Like Brueggemann, John Goldingay also writes from a postmodern perspective. He has so far completed two volumes of a projected *Old Testament Theology* trilogy. As we have noted, in the first volume, *Israel's Gospel*, he emphasizes the importance of narrative in the OT,[154] and follows the narrative sequence of the canon, from creation to the exile and return, with a further section on the coming of Jesus, noting how the NT develops the OT story. In his second volume, *Israel's Faith*, he focuses on the non-narrative sections of the OT, Prophets, Wisdom and Psalms, and follows a more traditional, thematic approach. Goldingay agrees with Brueggemann on the importance of a framework that reflects the thinking of the OT itself,[155] and this leads him to want to listen to the whole of the OT. He notes the problem, in doing this, of apparently different and sometimes conflicting theological ideas, and that, again agreeing with Brueggemann, 'we cannot identify a single faith articulation in the text'.[156] He does not, though, agree with the conclusion that it is therefore impossible to construct a unified message and observes that 'Old Testament theology's task is to see what greater whole can encompass the diversity within the Old Testament'.[157] However, by also adopting a postmodern approach he is open to leave some difficult tensions unresolved. He is willing too to allow the OT to challenge the traditions of the church, and sometimes his conclusions about what a text 'says' (rather than how Christians have traditionally interpreted it) are controversial. Goldingay also discusses the relationship between the Testaments and, as we have already noted, argues that the OT should not be seen simply through NT lenses but, rather, it should provide the lens through which the NT is viewed.[158] While not wanting to interpret the OT in the light of the NT, Goldingay does (unlike Brueggemann) see the OT as the first act in a two-act drama, and thus has continued his discussion into the NT.[159]

---

154. He argues that 'the nature of the Old Testament's faith is to be a statement about God's involvement in a particular sequence of events in the world', and thus 'Old Testament theology has to be shaped by narrative' (Goldingay, *OT Theology*, 1:32). Like Rendtorff, he notes that this was much earlier perceived by von Rad.

155. Ibid., 1:19; 2:18.

156. Ibid., 1:17.

157. Ibid., 1:17; 2:17–18.

158. Above, p. 26, n. 28; see ibid., 1:21–28; 2:18–20.

159. Ibid., 1:24. As we have noted, his first volume includes a chapter on the coming of Jesus (ibid., 1:789–858), and the second volume includes a section at the end of each chapter that extends discussion of the theme into the NT.

Another important difference between Goldingay and Brueggemann is in their views of history. Brueggemann is not interested in a world behind the text: the world of the text is paramount. Goldingay also focuses on the text. He points to the uncertainties associated with historical criticism and warns against, and tries to avoid, basing 'theological exposition on any particular theory about the absolute or relative dating of the material, because we can be sure these theories will change'.[160] He also notes that in pre-modern historiography there is a merging of facts and more imaginative writing, and that divine inspiration worked within that understanding rather than in transforming the OT writers into modern historians. Nonetheless he does not discard the idea of a world behind the text. If God is known through what he has done, he must have done something. As a result, history matters (though the uncertainties remain). In this Goldingay is very much closer to Childs than to Brueggemann.

What about historical criticism?

Biblical theology, as it was understood in the mid-twentieth century, stood in an awkward relationship with history and so with historical criticism. On the one hand, there was an emphasis on God's revelation through his activity in the history of Israel; on the other, there was the belief that actual history was less significant than history viewed through the eyes of faith. Childs attempted to address this issue by focusing on the canon, and thus on Israel's perception of history as the significant factor in theology. But he also attaches importance to historical criticism – without really explaining how these two things can work together. Rendtorff argues that synchronic and diachronic approaches are not mutually exclusive and does try to show how they complement one another – though he wants to reverse the traditional method that begins with historical-critical issues.

In a recent collection of essays,[161] John Collins questions some recent approaches to the OT (including those of Childs, Barr and Brueggemann) and argues for the centrality of historical-critical methods in biblical theology. He notes the fundamental assumption 'that texts should be interpreted in their historical contexts, in the light of literary and cultural conventions of their time'.[162] While he does not set out a methodology,[163] Collins notes the value

---

160. Ibid., 1:866.

161. Collins, *Encounters*.

162. Ibid., p. 35.

163. Collins does set out some principles of historical criticism, mainly adapted from those set out by Troeltsch (ibid., pp. 12–13, 35–36). These are *Criticism*: historical

of this approach, for example, in drawing conclusions about the genre of a text – and so about the way the text should be interpreted. He is aware of the limitations of historical knowledge, and the need to adapt theories about background in the light of new discoveries and insights. But he maintains that the attempt to reconstruct the (hypothetical) world in which the text was composed, and so to imagine its significance in a real-life situation, has value in relating the text to the present situation.[164]

Collins does not answer all of the concerns about the historical-critical method. But he does provide a necessary corrective to the growing impression, in some circles, that the approach is outdated, with nothing more to offer. In my view historical criticism has real value in biblical theology – though only when balanced with other approaches, and only when it retains a clear sense of its role within the larger hermeneutical purpose, which is both to understand the text in its context and to apply it to the life of the church today.

Conclusion

In my view there is value in the canonical approach, though it is not without weaknesses. Most preachers start from the canonical text as we now have it: historical-critical questions may be of interest in the classroom or the study (and should certainly not be ignored) but not, generally, in the pulpit. This approach also gives explicit approval to the view that the whole of Scripture in its canonical form has value and authority, rather than focusing on fragments of texts or uncertain sources, and with the implicit assumption that what is later and so not 'original' is, in some way, of lesser value. From a theological and exegetical point of view this allows us to search for meaning within the whole text. Although we still need to address the question of how the canonical text of the OT may be interpreted in a way that allows it to be authoritative and normative for the life and faith of the church.

Allied to this focus on the canonical text, I recognize the importance of a narrative approach to the text and to theology; Rendtorff goes some way towards

---

Footnote 163 (*continued*)

> reconstruction is an ongoing process, offering only probabilities that need to be reviewed and adapted in the light of new evidence; *Analogy*: to understand the context of a text there is a need to draw analogies and make connections with the present: 'we can assess what is plausible in an ancient situation because we know what human beings are capable of' (ibid., p. 36); and *Autonomy*: the text needs to be interpreted free from ecclesiastical and dogmatic interference.

164. Ibid., pp. 26–27.

this and it is an important part of Goldingay's approach. I have outlined my concerns, particularly where the approach denies the relevance, and even existence, of the world behind the text, and where, by focusing, instead, on the world in front of the text, it opens up the possibility of multiple, equally valid, meanings. But I have argued too that these things are not functions of the approach per se. The narrative approach has the advantage of being text centred, inviting us to look at its structure, language and nuances, and it does greater justice than others both to the content of the OT and to the theological 'methodology' of its writers. While von Rad's view may raise questions, he is right to emphasize the importance of God's action in Israel's history. The OT writers do not, except in the briefest of terms, give a direct answer to the question 'Who is God?' They focus rather on what God does and has done, and the story of this divine activity is key to Israel's understanding of God and of what it means to be God's people. In addition a propositional approach tends to view those propositions through a particular theological and cultural filter: 'God is love' means he will do nothing *we consider* to be unloving; 'God is just' means he will do nothing *we consider* to be unjust. Thus we impose our own understanding on our view of God. These attributes of God, though, may not be abstracted from the text: their meaning must be determined not by our world view but by their narrative context, and it is from that narrative that we move to theology.[165]

Finally, we should not ignore the role of historical criticism, with all of the challenges it brings. There is a world behind the text and what we read is not just a literary construct: it arose out of a particular context. And the more we can discover about that context and about the purpose of the writer/compiler, the better we can draw from the text what we need to apply to our own lives and to the life of the Christian community of which we are part.

The authority of the Old Testament

John Bright describes the tension of ideas present within the OT:

> The Bible is at one and the same time the religious literature and the historical
> record of an ancient people; and it is the normative (canonical) document of the

---

165. A key question not clearly addressed by those who talk in terms of a metanarrative is how we move from the biblical narrative to our own story. There is still need for application and in my view that is best accomplished at the level of underlying theological principles: see the discussion below.

faith of Israel and of the Christian community which regarded itself as the true heir of Israel. Viewed as the first, it contains many things that belong to the ancient situation and cannot in any direct way serve as a model for Christians today. Viewed as the second, it is the primary record of the faith which we claim as our own and, as such, remains the court of final appeal in all discussions regarding the nature of that faith.[166]

Goldingay too argues that the OT must be seen as something that both *describes* and *prescribes* faith. It is a descriptive account of what the people of God believed and how those beliefs developed through the OT period. But it is more than a description of what God's people believed in the past: it is also normative for the faith of God's people in the present. It sets out what we should believe; it contains creedal statements, affirmations and principles vital to our faith today. Goldingay rightly suggests that any OT theology worthy of the name must bring both the *descriptive* and the *prescriptive* or *normative* together: 'the task of OT theology is to mediate between the religion of the OT and the religion we believe and practise today'.[167] For Bright, the key to interpretation is theology: 'it is precisely through its theology that the biblical word to the then and there of the ancient age speaks to us in the here and now'.[168]

The approach to the subject adopted here builds on the premise (by no means universally accepted, especially in the present postmodern, pluralistic climate) that there is an essential unity and coherence within the OT. It is more than a record of developing religious ideas and traditions, or a series of narratives through which narrators seek to present testimony and counter-testimony of what they perceive as the 'truth', and which then becomes the reality. It is *a revelation of the truth about the nature and being of the living God and about his dealings with his people and his world.* As such it contains permanently valid truth that claims authority over us.

---

166. Bright, *Authority*, p. 143.
167. Goldingay, *Approaches*, p. 23. Clements makes a similar point: 'It is in the very nature of theology to concern itself with living faith, rather than with the history of ideas . . . The latter is certainly important for theology, but it lacks the evaluative role of theology. We are, therefore, in seeking an Old Testament Theology, concerned with the theological significance which this literature possesses in the modern world' (*OT Theology*, p. 20).
168. Bright, *Authority*, p. 173.

A hermeneutical model

Before setting out a possible approach to OT interpretation, it is appropriate to note some general points about biblical hermeneutics. Grant Osborne notes four key stages in the interpretative process: exegesis, biblical theology, systematic theology (dogmatics) and homiletical theology (application).[169]

The first of these, *exegesis*, is concerned with what the text *says* in its context. In my view this includes the historical context, the world behind the text, and the intention of the author. These have a role in the exegetical task. If they are absent, the way is open for subjectivism, misinterpretation and misappropriation of OT texts. The issues are not always clear, but where insights are available, it is unwise to ignore them. It is also important to consider genre, the use of language and the narrative form and structure of the text. This does not necessarily imply a full return to historical-critical methods, for several aspects of that approach are seriously flawed. But a historical-critical analysis of the text and context should not be ruled out.

The second element in the hermeneutical model, *biblical theology*, is concerned with what the text *implies* within its canonical context, and it remains very closely related to the task of exegesis. Richard Schultz suggests that true exegesis 'involves ascertaining not only [a text's] meaning but also its message. In other words, determining the theology of a given text is an essential part of the exegetical process';[170] similarly, for Bright, 'exegesis that stops short of the theology of the text is an incomplete exegesis'.[171] This task requires us to consider the theological implications of the text. This needs to be done in the immediate context of the text (within a passage, a chapter and maybe a book)

---

169. Osborne, *Hermeneutical Spiral*, pp. 347–356. Osborne adds a fifth stage, historical theology, between biblical and systematic theology, which looks at how earlier communities understood biblical doctrine. This informs the interpretative process, though I would include it as an aspect of systematic theology. Rollin G. Grams, *Rival Versions of Theological Enquiry* (Prague: International Baptist Theological Seminary, 2005), sets out a similar fourfold model: the *descriptive* task (exegesis), the *synthetic* task (biblical theology), the *dogmatic* task and the *pragmatic* or applicatory task, based on the four tasks of ethical enquiry set out by Richard B. Hays, *The Moral Vision of the New Testament: Community, Cross, New Creation. A Contemporary Introduction to New Testament Ethics* (New York: HarperCollins, 1996).

170. Richard Schultz, *NIDOTTE*, 1:185–205 (185).

171. Bright, *Authority*, p. 171. In his 'basic proposals for doing OT theology' Hasel also notes the importance of keeping exegesis, which he sees as a historical task, and biblical theology together from the start (*Basic Issues*, pp. 194–208).

and also in the wider context of several books (e.g. the Pentateuch, the wisdom
literature or the prophets), of the Old or New Testament and of the Bible as a
whole. This involves *synthesis*: recognizing the diverse elements within biblical
texts, but also looking for what gives the Bible an essential unity and coherence. As an important part of this, we need to look more widely at the theological milieu in which the text was written and the particular idioms that may
be used to communicate to its original audience.[172] The OT is revelation, and
as such it speaks to us; it is authoritative and normative for our faith. But we
need to recognize that that revelation was first given to real people in a particular historical context. And if it was to have any meaning to them, it needed
to be expressed in language and theological categories that first audience could
relate to. Many of the situations reflected in the OT are alien to us. They are
foreign sociologically, culturally and historically, and express a world view
often very different from ours, and we need to take that into account when
we interpret the OT Scriptures. The task of biblical theology and, more
specifically in this context, the task of OT theology, is to examine the biblical
texts in order to discover what they have to say about God – so that we may
then look at how to apply them to our own day.

A key part of this is to note typological correspondences between texts as
well as recurring theological patterns within the canon. This then moves us on
to the third and fourth tasks, *systematic theology* and *homiletical theology*: relating the
theology and the typological patterns of the OT to our own setting,[173] and
then applying them to the life, faith and practice of the church.

Within those four areas, the first two might be said to look at what the text
meant in its biblical and historical context, while the latter two are concerned
with what the text *means* for the church today. This distinction emphasizes the
historical aspect of biblical theology. The text must be interpreted in context,
and we should not allow that interpretation to be subordinated to church tradition and dogmatics: 'This is what we believe, so this is what the text must say.'
Our claim is that the direction must be the other way round: that dogmatics

---

172. For an excellent discussion of reading the OT within its context and the
    implications of this for evangelicals, see Enns, *Inspiration*; see also John H. Walton,
    *Ancient Near Eastern Thought and the Old Testament: Introducing the Conceptual World of
    the Hebrew Bible* (Grand Rapids: Baker, 2006; Leicester: Apollos, 2007).

173. For Osborne this is done by building a systematic theology, which he describes as
    'the proper goal of biblical study and teaching' (*Hermeneutical Spiral*, p. 374). The
    aim is to produce a theology for our day that the church can use and apply –
    though we have noted some weaknesses in the systematic/dogmatic approach.

must be subordinated to what the text says. However, the distinction must be maintained cautiously.

As we have noted, an important feature of biblical theology is the conviction that the theological content of the Bible is relevant to the church. Thus, to look at what the text *meant* cannot be just a historical exercise, of only academic interest, as was the case in the 'history of religions' approach; the historical task (what the text meant) needs to be approached as a necessary part of discovering what the text means.[174] And it is this theological approach that provides the key to building a bridge between then and now, and giving the text relevance and authority for today's world and today's church. This approach reflects my conviction, against many within the postmodernist new literary school, that the text does have an original meaning that is relevant as we look for what the text means for us, and that background and contextual issues play a part in discerning that meaning. This may be summarized in a diagram:

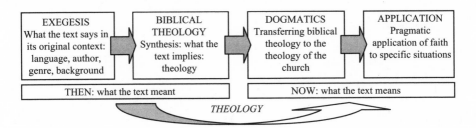

Don Carson notes that a purely linear representation does not take into account the interplay between these various tasks and, as an example, points

---

174. Wrede argued that the task of biblical theology was only a historical task, unconcerned with how the systematic theologian used its results; see William Wrede, 'The Task and Methods of New Testament Theology', in Robert Morgan (ed.), *The Nature of New Testament Theology: The Contribution of William Wrede and Adolf Schlatter*, SBT 2.25 (London: SCM, 1973), pp. 68–116. Jonathan R. Wilson, 'Theology in the Old Testament', in Broyles, *Interpreting the OT*, pp. 245–264, criticizes the 'what it meant, what it means' approach because it results in this separation between biblical scholarship and theology. His alternative 'this is that' approach seeks to draw parallels between the OT and the life of the church. But the distinction is artificial. The text still has to be interpreted in its historical and cultural context in order for us to draw appropriate parallels, and, as I have argued, the separation of biblical scholarship and theology is not inevitable.

to the influence of theology on exegesis.[175] However, he also emphasizes the importance of movement 'from exegesis right though biblical . . . theology to systematic theology. The final authority is the Scriptures, the Scriptures alone.'[176] The above diagram should not be taken to suggest that each task is wholly independent of the rest or that each task is performed in a vacuum. It is intended to emphasize the importance of beginning with the text and its meaning within its immediate and biblical context before moving to its application to the theology and practice of the church.

Underlying theological principles

An important part of biblical theology is to uncover theological principles that underlie the text, which give unity and coherence to the OT and the NT and to the Bible as a whole, and also may be applied in a different setting to the life of the church. In determining these theological truths the text (i.e. the *canonical* text) remains central. They are understood from the text, and remain closely linked with it. As we have noted, we cannot abstract some general 'guiding principles', such as love or justice, which can then be reinterpreted according to our own notion of what love and justice are. Any principle must be faithful to the text and tested against it and against the wider theology of the OT.[177] Nor is it envisaged that there will be only a few overriding ideals: in practice a text or group of texts may give rise to several fairly specific principles. So, for example, the sacrificial system in the OT could be seen to point to God's holiness and the need for his people to take the pollution of sin seriously; however, the provision of a system that provides the way for sinful human beings to approach a holy God may also emphasize his desire for relationship and his willingness to forgive – and this does not exhaust its significance. Noting these theological principles allows us to draw correspondences between the OT narrative and the narrative of our own relationship with God.

This approach affirms the importance of the canonical text as revelation. However, against Brueggemann and some others who adopt a literary

---

175. D. A. Carson, 'Unity and Diversity in the New Testament: The Possibility of Systematic Theology', in D. A. Carson and John D. Woodbridge (eds.), *Scripture and Truth* (Leicester: IVP, 1983), pp. 60–95 (91–92).

176. Ibid., p. 92.

177. It is important that the theological principles are not abstracted from OT texts and narrative so that they become an end in themselves, divorced from their OT setting. For further discussion, see below, p. 241, n. 8.

approach, it also postulates the existence of a world behind the text. In order to understand the theology of a text we need to know something of that world, and how it may have influenced the way the text is presented. Thus historical criticism has a part to play.

In his emphasis on the text as revelation Sailhamer also rules out the existence of an ideal that lies behind the text. I agree that revelation is through the text rather than through some reconstructed event in the world behind it. However, revelation is a witness to God, who does exist behind (as well as over and above) the text, and as a result it should be possible to talk about theological principles that *underlie*, and do not just *derive from*, the text: a truth that lies behind, and finds particular expression in, the biblical revelation. In this, though, the text must remain central; it is revelation, and thus a unique witness to divine reality.[178] The interrelationship of these various elements is shown in the following diagram:

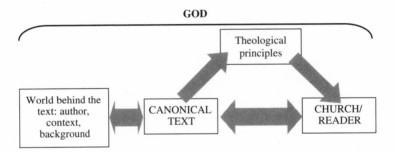

To relate this approach to our interpretation of OT texts, we need, first, to look at the passage in its original setting, if we can. We need to ask, what is the social, cultural, historical and religious background against which the passage was written? And within that setting, what was the writer or narrator seeking to convey? And, equally importantly, how would his audience have understood what he wrote? We need to look at the language and narrative structure and images used in the text. We also need to be aware of what theological language

---

178. It could be argued that if the text is only a *witness* to divine reality, then might it not be possible to access that reality in other ways, e.g. through nature or personal encounter with God or even through other sacred texts? We need to assert the importance of the canonical text as revelation: as God's chosen means of communication. This is not, of course, to undermine the further revelation through Jesus Christ, the Word of God par excellence, but there too the text remains central and takes priority over other forms of revelation.

and concepts would have been appropriate within that setting, and what limitations this might impose on the text and particularly on the view of God in the
text. The precise historical setting of the text may be a matter of debate; it may
be that texts were written *about* a particular period of Israel's history but much
later, and within a very different historical setting. I do not believe that the OT
writers reconstructed history; in my view the essence of Israel's history was preserved in traditions passed from one generation to the next. However, the later
writers use those traditions to speak also to their own generation – and it may be
this later context that has the greater influence on the interpretation of the text.

As well as challenging postmodern approaches, this also challenges attempts
to interpret the OT in too literal a way. Indeed many of the problems associated with the OT come from adopting an over-literal interpretation, which does
not look behind the text to see what it is really saying. The writers (albeit
inspired by the Spirit of God) wrote in a particular context. We recognize that
the message of Scripture is for all people at all times; nevertheless, in terms of
its language, imagery and forms of expression, it was addressed to a particular
group of people who understood those things in a particular way – a way not
always clear to those in a different context, with a different world view.

This raises the question of interpretation, and the question of *whose* interpretation? It also may be taken to imply that it is only scholars who may make
properly informed decisions about what an OT text really means – thus
making the book inaccessible to the majority of Christians. It is not my intention to reduce the accessibility of the OT; my aim is to achieve the opposite
effect. However, for those who want to take the OT seriously and to support
its authoritative status, study of the text and its background is vital. As students
of the OT grapple with difficult issues they will become better able to decide
questions of interpretation. Nor should we underestimate the role of the Spirit
of God. I do not endorse the view that we need only the Spirit to interpret
Scripture, nor do I believe that scholarship alone is enough. We need *both*: students of Scripture who are open to the Spirit and who, with the Spirit's help,
are willing to grapple with the text.

First, then, we must find out what the text says in its context. There is no
escaping the need for sound exegesis.

Second, building on that, we need to discern the underlying theological
principles. The passage may tell us about God and his relationship with his
people and his world, or about the proper response to God or the demands of
holiness and so on. Things such as the OT legal and sacrificial systems are
unfamiliar to us, but theological principles underlie those unfamiliar practices
that continue to be relevant to the life of the church. In the synthetic task, we
explore the theology of law and sacrifice as we find it in the OT.

Third, we move on to translate those theological principles into our own setting and situation, where the context and practical application may be very different. It is uncommon to sacrifice a year-old lamb as part of our regular Sunday worship! And, in a Christian context, we do not see animal sacrifice as necessary for forgiveness – the finished work of Christ on the cross has made that unnecessary. However, sacrifice of some sort is certainly in order. The sacrificial system also emphasizes the holiness, glory and transcendence of God and the need for holiness in our relationship with him. Again these are important theological principles we should not ignore.

Fourth, having made the theological link between then and now, we go on to work those principles out in practice. What kind of sacrifice is it that God requires of us in our worship and in our Christian lives? What does it mean to say we serve a holy God?

Typology plays an important part in this second task. It supplements exegesis in seeking to discern patterns in Scripture and noting the way those patterns repeat and intensify. The OT presents us with one historical reality, with its own theological significance, and OT texts need to be considered in their own right. But there are historical and theological correspondences within the OT, between the OT and the NT, and between the OT, NT and the church that need to be taken into account when we seek to recognize and apply biblical principles to the life of the church. It needs to be emphasized in this approach that the principle is not abstracted from its original narrative context – in such a way that the original context may then be discarded. While it is necessary to draw out the principle in order to apply it to a different narrative context, the original context remains in view, and any reapplication of the principle must be seen to be consistent with it.

Bright notes that the authority of the OT lies in its theology,[179] and a key challenge of OT study is to explore the biblical text and come to conclusions about both its meaning and its theological significance. To do that we need to focus on the text and on what it originally meant (so far as we can discover). We need to look at the language and images used and the ideas expressed. We need to look at what the writer intended to say and how his message would have been understood.[180] We need to be aware of the theological milieu in

---

179. Bright, *Authority*, pp. 161–251.

180. According to Sailhamer, 'the primary objective of a historical approach is to understand as accurately as possible the content of the theology of the OT as it was understood when it was first written . . . What did its original authors intend and what would the original readers have understood?' (Sailhamer, *OT Theology*, p. 177).

which it was written and how that might have influenced language and content.
We need to draw out the underlying spiritual and theological principles of the
text and the typological correspondences, and then transfer and apply them to
our own situation. And we need to do that not only for a few obvious passages
but for the whole of the OT. Then, I believe, the OT can speak to the church
today in a relevant and authoritative way.

In this book the main focus will be, primarily, on the second (synthetic) task:
biblical theology. I will seek to engage with the OT text in order to draw out its
theological content in a way that allows it to be applied, authoritatively, to the
life and practice of the church. It will not be possible to engage in detailed exegesis of the text; nevertheless what I say will be thoroughly biblical, and will
build on what I take to be sound biblical exegesis. And, while I will seek to look
at the text in its own right, which will include looking at historical issues and
theological development, I approach it as a Christian, and so accept an essential coherence and unity not only within the OT but between the OT and
the NT.

2. GOD AND THE 'GODS'

The names of God[1]

What's in a name?[2]

In the ANE a name established identity and said something about a person's character. Choosing a name mattered. So, for example, Eve was named in

1. See e.g. B. W. Anderson, *Contours*, pp. 48–55; Childs, *Biblical Theology* (1992), pp. 351–361; Clements, *OT Theology*, pp. 62–66; Frank M. Cross, '*ēl*', in *TDOT* 1:242–261; Eichrodt, *Theology*, 1:178–205; D. N. Freedman, M. P. O'Connor and Helmer Ringgren, '*YHWH*', in *TDOT* 5:500–521; Goldingay, *OT Theology*, 1:241–246, 334–340; Terence E. Fretheim, '*ēl*, '*ēlîm*, Yahweh', in *NIDOTTE* 1:400–401, 405–406; 4:1295–1300; House, *OT Theology*, pp. 92–95; Jacob, *Theology*, pp. 43–64; Preuss, *OT Theology*, 1:139–152; von Rad, *OT Theology*, 1:10–11, 179–187; Rendtorff, *Hebrew Bible*, pp. 40–43, 587–598; Helmer Ringgren, '*ĕlōhîm*', in *TDOT* 1:267–284; 5:500–512.
2. The familiar lines from Shakespeare's *Romeo and Juliet* – 'What's in a name? That which we call a rose by any other name would smell as sweet' (Act 2, Scene 2) – suggest that a name is only a label that can be changed without affecting the essential character of the thing or person that bears the name. However, even in western thought a person's name carries more significance than this. Within

accordance with the role she would fulfil as *the mother of all the living* (Gen. 3:20);[3]
Lamech named his son Noah, which sounds like the Hebrew word for
'comfort', and said, *he will comfort us in the labour and painful toil of our hands caused
by the ground the LORD has cursed* (Gen. 5:29).[4] The angel that announced the birth
of Jesus to Joseph said, *you are to give him the name Jesus* [a Greek form of *Joshua*,
meaning 'the LORD saves'] *because he will save his people from their sins* (Matt. 1:21).
God's name too reveals something of his nature and character.

In pagan religions, knowing a god's name gave access to his or her power
and could be used in a magical way to manipulate the deity. God forbids his
name to be abused in that way: *You shall not misuse the name of the LORD your God,
for the LORD will not hold anyone guiltless who misuses his name* (Exod. 20:7). He has
revealed his name not so that he may be manipulated but so that men and
women may know him and have a relationship with him. Various terms are
used in the OT to refer to God.

Elohim

The Hebrew term *'ĕlōhîm* can mean 'god' or 'gods'. It often refers to God (e.g.
Gen. 1:1; Exod. 3:6; Deut. 4:35; Isa. 40:28); sometimes it refers to the gods of
other nations (e.g. Exod. 12:12; 20:3; Josh. 24:15; Ps. 96:5; Jer. 2:28; 11:13).
'Ĕlōhîm is a plural form. One explanation of the use of the plural is that it
emphasizes majesty or intensity.[5] Clements offers another explanation. He suggests that the Israelites worshipped God at older sanctuaries where a pantheon
of gods had been worshipped before, and to emphasize that their one God
replaced *all* of the *'ĕlōhîm* formerly worshipped at the sanctuary, and to ensure

---

Footnote 2 (*continued*)

> ancient Hebrew thought names were closely tied to a person's identity and essential
> character.

3. For discussion of the relationship between Eve and the Hebrew word for 'living',
   see Victor P. Hamilton, *Genesis 1–17*, NICOT (Grand Rapids: Eerdmans, 1990),
   pp. 204–206; Gordon J. Wenham, *Genesis 1–15*, WBC 1; Milton Keynes: Word,
   1991), p. 84.

4. *Noah* is more likely related to the verb 'to rest' rather than 'to comfort'. Precise
   etymology, though, is not the point; there is almost certainly a narrative purpose in
   the words used: '[Noah's] name and its poetic etymology introduce some of the
   verbal motifs and theological themes that will dominate the next four chapters'
   (Wenham, *Genesis 1–15*, p. 128). For the purpose of this discussion, though, the
   choice of name is important and is given a particular explanation.

5. E.g. Preuss, *OT Theology*, 1:147.

that none of those other gods was worshipped alongside Yahweh, he was given that designation;[6] the use of the term thus points to Yahweh as the one God who is superior to, and replaces, all the rest.[7]

El

'Ēl is the generic term for 'god'. It sometimes refers to Israel's God (though only 199 times, while *'ĕlōhîm* is used over 2,000 times), especially in the book of Job and the Psalms. It is often compounded with other expressions, especially in the patriarchal narratives; for example, El Shaddai (*'ēl šadday*; e.g. Gen. 17:1; Exod. 6:3) traditionally translated 'God Almighty', and El Elyon (*'ēl 'elyôn*, 'God Most High'; e.g. Gen. 14:18–20). The term also describes powerless idols, which are contrasted with the true God (e.g. Isa. 44:6–23; 45:20).[8]

El is also the proper name of a chief Canaanite god,[9] which features in compound expressions similar to those found in the patriarchal narratives. This has led to speculation about the relationship between the God worshipped by the patriarchs and the gods of Canaan.[10]

Yahweh

This is the personal name of God revealed to Moses (Exod. 3:14–15; 6:3),[11] and occurs more than 6,000 times in the OT. The name consists of four consonants: Yhwh (the 'Tetragrammaton'). From an early date, it was regarded as too holy to be spoken aloud, and in public readings of the OT was read as *'ădōnāy* (my lord); this is reflected in most English translations, where the divine name is rendered 'LORD'. The (impossible) form 'Jehovah' comes from putting the vowels of *'ădōnāy* with the consonants of 'Yhwh'. The generally accepted reading is 'Yahweh', though the correct pronunciation is unknown.

---

6. Clements, *OT Theology*, pp. 63–64.

7. See also e.g. Eichrodt, *Theology*, 1:185–186.

8. In Isa. 45:20–22 the term is applied both to idols and to God: *Ignorant are those who carry about idols of wood, who pray to gods [literally 'a god', 'ēl] that cannot save . . . there is no God ['ĕlōhîm] apart from me, a righteous God ['ēl-ṣaddîq] and a Saviour; there is none but me. Turn to me and be saved, all you ends of the earth; for I am God ['ēl], and there is no other.*

9. See Frank M. Cross, *"'ēl"*, in *TDOT* 1:242–261.

10. See below.

11. See R. W. L. Moberley, *The Old Testament of the Old Testament: Patriarchal Narratives and Mosaic Yahwism*, OBT (Minneapolis: Fortress, 1992), pp. 5–35.

What does the name imply?

Although various other derivations of the name Yahweh have been put forward, the most generally accepted is the one suggested by the OT, where it is linked with the verb 'to be': *God said to Moses, 'I AM WHO I AM* ['ehyeh 'ăšer 'ehyeh]. *This is what you are to say to the Israelites: "I AM* ['ehyeh] *has sent me to you."' God also said to Moses, 'Say to the Israelites, "The LORD* [yĕhwāh] *. . . has sent me to you"'* (Exod. 3:14–15).[12] This emphasizes not only the existence of God but also his presence among his people and activity on their behalf.[13] Another important aspect of God's meeting with Moses and the revelation of the divine name is that it is presented as marking a new era in the relationship between God and his people.[14] Rather than an essentially new revelation, Goldingay takes the explanation of the divine name (which he translates 'I will be what I will be') as an assurance that the one who had been with the patriarchs would be with his people in their present situation; it emphasizes that God 'can always be something new as new situations require it'.[15] This emphasizes continuity with the faith of the patriarchs, and that God's commitment to his people and his power to act on their behalf is not limited by circumstances or location. However, while that is an important aspect of the name, it does not do full justice to the implication of Exodus 6:3, that the revelation marks a significant new departure.

---

12. See e.g. Bernard W. Anderson, *The Living World of the Old Testament*, 4th ed. (Harlow: Longman, 1988), pp. 60–63; Eichrodt, *Theology*, 1:189; Freedman, O'Connor and Ringgren, 'YHWH', in *TDOT* 5:500–521; Gottwald, *Hebrew Bible*, pp. 211–213; Moberley, *Old Testament*, pp. 21–26; Rendtorff, *Hebrew Bible*, pp. 40–43.

13. See e.g. Eichrodt, *Theology*, 1:188–191; Goldingay, *OT Theology*, 1:336–340; Kaiser, *OT Theology*, p. 107; Preuss, *OT Theology*, 1:141–142; Clements suggests that it points to God's self-existence and uniqueness (*OT Theology*, p. 63).

14. Commenting on Exod. 3:13–15, Moberley notes that 'the natural and consistent implication of the text is that it is depicting the name YHWH being given for the first time to Moses and through him to Israel. As such the story depicts a new beginning within the story of Israel, distinct from what preceded at the time of the patriarchs (*Old Testament*, p. 25). Eichrodt links this with God's presence: 'The only thing which could provide the religious basis for a new national identity was the certainty . . . that the deity was demonstrably and immediately present and active' (*Theology*, 1:190).

15. Goldingay, *OT Theology*, 1:337.

Why has God revealed his name?

Fretheim notes several aspects of this.[16] First, name-giving emphasizes distinctiveness: by revealing his name, Yahweh sets himself apart from other gods. Second, name-giving identifies a person with a community and within history. When he met with Moses, God committed himself to the people of Israel, and entered into their history. Third, revealing a name opens up the possibility of intimacy in relationship: it represents openness towards others and a willingness to make a commitment to them. By revealing his name, God has made himself accessible to those who would enter into a relationship with him. Leading on from this, name-giving entails vulnerability. As we have seen, in other religious systems, knowledge of a god's name was used in magic formulae as a means of manipulating the god's power. God, of course, may not be manipulated; however, the fact that he warns against the misuse of his name indicates that such a use might be considered a possibility and attempted in Israel too. And we know that happened in some circles. By committing to others, God risks pain if those others seek to use the relationship for their own ends. By revealing himself to his people in such an intimate way, he also leaves himself open to the pain of their rejecting him.

El, Yahweh, Moses and monotheism

Yahweh and the religion of the patriarchs[17]
The patriarchal narratives

There is debate about the date and sources of the Pentateuch. According to the traditional view, the earliest source, J, may go back to the tenth century BC, but

---

16. Fretheim, 'Yahweh', in *NIDOTTE* 4:1297.

17. See e.g. Rainer Albertz, *A History of Israelite Religion in the Old Testament Period*, 2 vols. (London: SCM; Louisville: Westminster John Knox, 1994), 1:26–103; *Israel in Exile: The History and Literature of the Sixth Century B.C.E.*, Studies in Biblical Literature 3 (Atlanta: SBL, 2003), pp. 246–271; Albrecht Alt, 'The God of the Fathers', in *Essays in Old Testament History and Religion* (Oxford: Blackwell, 1967), pp. 1–77; B. W. Anderson, *Living World*, pp. 64–66; Bill T. Arnold, 'Religion in Ancient Israel', in Baker and Arnold, *Face of OT Studies*, pp. 391–420; John Bright, *A History of Israel*, 4th ed. (Louisville: Westminster John Knox, 2000), pp. 95–102; Ronald E. Clements, *Abraham and David*, SBT 2.5 (London: SCM, 1967); Frank M. Cross, *Canaanite Myth and Hebrew Epic: Essays in the History and the Religion of Israel*

the book as a whole was not in its present form until after the exile, and reflects some of the serious theological re-evaluation that resulted from that crisis. More recently much of what was taken for granted in Pentateuchal studies has been challenged, though no new scholarly consensus has emerged. The literary approach views the patriarchal narratives as a coherent unit, but again assigns a post-exilic date to the final work. Wenham argues for an earlier date. In his view Genesis may have been in its final form before 900 BC, with J as its last major editor.[18] Even so, this still leaves a gap of several hundred years between when the patriarchal narratives were written and when the events they describe took place. This raises questions about the historicity of the narratives. Most scholars believe that the patriarchal narratives reflect the religion and theology of the (later) writers. Many consider that the stories are largely invention, possibly based on folk tales. However, historical and archaeological evidence suggests that the customs, traditions and laws associated with the patriarchal narratives are consistent with an early second-millennium date.[19] Wenham also points to religious practices within the patriarchal narratives that 'are so different from later practice that to suppose the traditions were invented in the first millennium seems unlikely'.[20] The debate will go on, and nothing can be proved. It is reasonable to conclude, though, that the patriarchal narratives are a literary unit, written by a final author (or editor) who had access to reliable traditional material enabling him to produce an accurate account, but also had some freedom to use literary and rhetorical techniques within his presentation.[21]

Footnote 17 (*continued*)

(Cambridge, Mass.: Harvard University Press, 1973; repr., 1997); William McKane, *Studies in the Patriarchal Narratives* (Edinburgh: Handsel, 1979); Moberley, *Old Testament*; Preuss, *OT Theology*, 2:3–18; Helmer Ringgren, *Israelite Religion* (London: SPCK, 1966), pp. 17–27; H. H. Rowley, *Worship in Ancient Israel* (London: SPCK, 1967), pp. 1–36; Gordon J. Wenham, 'The Religion of the Patriarchs', in Alan R. Millard and Donald J. Wiseman (eds.), *Essays on the Patriarchal Narratives* (Leicester: IVP, 1980), pp. 157–188.

18. Wenham, *Genesis 1–15*, pp. xxxv–xlv.

19. See e.g. Kenneth A. Kitchen, *Ancient Orient and Old Testament* (Downers Grove: IVP, 1966), pp. 41–56, 153–156; *On the Reliability of the Old Testament* (Grand Rapids: Eerdmans, 2003), pp. 313–372; Ringgren, *Israelite Religion*, pp. 19–26; see also Bright, *History*, pp. 77–87.

20. Wenham, 'Religion', in Millard and Wiseman, *Essays*, p. 184.

21. The suggestion that the compiler of the patriarchal narratives had some freedom in the use of sources contrasts with traditional source theory, which implies that he

El and Yahweh

In the OT the patriarchal narratives are presented as the background to the worship of Yahweh. The name of God generally linked with the patriarchs is 'El Shaddai' (Gen. 17:1; 28:3; 35:11; 43:14; 48:3; Exod. 6:3), and though in the final form of the text El Shaddai is identified with Yahweh, it has been suggested that originally they were different gods. This is an example of an attempt by historical critics to reconstruct the world behind the text, and then to base theological discussion on that world. As we have noted, 'El' was the name of the Canaanite high god, and some argue that names compounded with El had a Canaanite background, referring either to distinct gods linked with specific places in Canaan, or to local designations of the Canaanite high god. So, for example, Clements identifies El Shaddai as the local deity of the region around Hebron, whose covenant with Abraham granted him, and those claiming descent from him, entitlement to the land.[22]

Abraham also called on El Olam (*'ēl 'ōlām*, 'God eternal'; Gen. 21:33), and by accepting Melchizedek's blessing and presenting him with a tithe of his spoil (Gen. 14:18–20) he gave allegiance to El Elyon – though his use of the title *Yahweh, El Elyon, creator of heaven and earth* (Gen. 14:22), which almost exactly parallels Melchizedek's earlier words (Gen. 14:19), indicates that he identifies Melchizedek's God as his own.[23] Jacob set up a pillar to El Bethel (*'ēl-bêt-'ēl*; Gen. 31:13). In Genesis 16:13 Hagar refers to El Roi (*'ēl rŏ'î*, 'the God who sees me'), and Isaac may have been associated with this God (Gen. 24:62).

It is a common view that the Israelite tribes worshipped these gods in Canaan, and that the name 'Israel' (compounded with 'El', rather than 'Yahweh') is taken to indicate the primacy of El at the time the nation was

---

could do little more than 'cut and paste' material from the sources into the narrative without altering or adapting it – thus giving rise to 'doublets' and contradictions. Recent literary theory allows compilers a greater degree of discretion and adaptation in constructing the final narrative, so when disparate elements appear, we may assume it is deliberate, and look for reasons why; see e.g. Berlin, *Poetics*, pp. 113–121.

22. Clements, *Abraham and David*, p. 33. For further discussion of the relationship between Yahweh and El, see John Day, *Yahweh and the Gods and Goddesses of Canaan*, JSOTSup 265 (Sheffield: Sheffield Academic Press, 2000), pp. 13–41.

23. The addition of 'Yahweh' might further imply that Melchizedek's understanding of God is limited: he recognizes the true God, through creation (natural revelation), but Abraham has encountered him, also, in relationship – and that sets Israel's experience of God apart. See Goldingay, *OT Theology*, 1:242–243. For discussion of the use of the name Yahweh in Genesis, see below, pp. 92–94.

founded.[24] The stories of Abraham, Isaac and Jacob were written after the worship of Yahweh had become established in Israel, and served both to fuse these (Canaanite) El-deities into a single God, who could then be identified with Yahweh, and also to account for other religious customs, such as why certain sanctuaries were more important than others. For those who subscribe to that view, this raises the question of when the Israelite tribes began to worship Yahweh, and how this eventually took over from the worship of El.

The Kenite hypothesis

This is the suggestion that Yahweh was originally worshipped by the Kenites, a Midianite clan, and that Moses was introduced into the cult of Yahweh by his father-in-law, Jethro (Reuel), a priest of Midian (Exod. 2:15–22; 3:1).[25] It is claimed that Moses knew nothing about Yahweh before meeting Jethro in Midian and it was in that area that he had his crucial meeting with Yahweh at the burning bush. According to Albertz, when Jethro visited the Israelite camp after the exodus, he offered sacrifices and invited the Israelites to share a meal in God's presence (Exod. 18:9–12), thus confirming his priestly status. However, his words on that occasion, *now I know that the LORD is greater than all other gods* (v. 11), suggest he had been introduced to Yahweh by Moses, rather than the other way round.[26]

Albertz argues that 'Israel' already existed as a tribal alliance in Canaan before the arrival of the 'exodus group', under Joshua.[27] This alliance was

---

24. E.g. Albertz, *History*, 1:76; B. W. Anderson, *Contours*, pp. 63–64; Preuss, *OT Theology*, 1:150; see also the discussion by Mark S. Smith, *The Origins of Biblical Monotheism: Israel's Polytheistic Background and the Ugaritic Texts* (Oxford: Oxford University Press, 2001), pp. 135–148; *The Early History of God: Yahweh and the Other Deities in Ancient Israel*, 2nd ed. (Grand Rapids: Eerdmans, 2002), pp. 19–43.

25. See Köhler, *OT Theology*, pp. 44–46; Albertz, *History*, 1:51–52; Preuss, *OT Theology*, 1:143–144. Gerstenberger also argues that belief in Yahweh originated outside Israel, probably in the mountains south of Israel (maybe even east of the Gulf of Aqaba), though he suggests that any religious links with the Midianites would have been deleted by later editors (*Theologies*, pp. 138–151). Day also favours a Midianite origin (*Yahweh*, pp. 15–16); see also Smith, *Origins*, pp. 145–146.

26. Albertz recognizes that in its present (post-exilic) form the passage points to the conversion of Jethro, though he considers that it has been reworked because of the difficulty for later generations of Moses' relationship with a Midianite priest (*History*, 1:260, n. 55).

27. Albertz, *History*, 1:76–79; Preuss, also identifies 'Israel' as a group already in Palestine and worshipping El when the 'Moses group' arrived bringing the worship

formed from the lower classes of Palestinian society, mainly farmers and shepherds in the hill country, to resist the domination of the city-dwelling aristocracy. This group worshipped El, who was a symbol of their independence. When the exodus group, also made up of the lower classes and the marginalized, arrived, they joined the alliance, and their god, Yahweh, also associated with liberation, was adopted by the whole of Israel.

The God of the fathers

In his influential essay 'The God of the Fathers' Albrecht Alt tries to explain why the worship of Yahweh, which the tribes that settled in Canaan probably became acquainted with in the desert, became the central religion around which they could all unite. In particular he asks if there was anything in their religious past from which the worship of Yahweh might naturally have developed.

Alt says certain tribes worshipped the god linked with the tribe's ancestors (*the god of the fathers*) and notes that this has certain things in common with Yahwism, especially the view that God is unconnected with (and so limited to) a place, but has a relationship with his people and is involved in their history. Alt argues that the patriarchs, originally unrelated, were ancestors of separate tribes that settled in Canaan, each with its own ancestral god.[28] Over time the tribes came together and constructed a genealogy that linked their ancestors. Thus the separate 'gods of the fathers' became the single 'God of the fathers'. Alt concludes that this religion provided the ground from which the distinctive features of Yahwism could grow and become widely accepted.

The patriarchs and El

Otto Eissfeldt argues that Abraham worshipped the Semitic god El, and that the gods of Abraham, Isaac and Jacob are references to El, rather than to

---

of Yahweh (*OT Theology*, 2:7–10). This reflects the commonly held view that a relatively small number of Hebrews went into Egypt – maybe the Joseph tribes, Ephraim and Manasseh, or maybe (as Albertz suggests) the Rachel tribes, which would also include Benjamin. Over the years others may have joined them, though the overall numbers would still have remained small. When they returned to Canaan after the exodus, they were joined by the much larger number of Hebrews who had remained in Canaan. See also Bright, *History*, pp. 137–143.

28. He identifies these as 'the God (or *Shield*) of Abraham' (Gen. 15:1), 'the God (or *Fear/Kinsman*) of Isaac' (Gen. 31:42, 53) and 'the God (or *Mighty One*) of Jacob' (Gen. 49:24). However, see Preuss, *OT Theology*, 2:5–7.

Alt's tribal 'gods of the fathers'. The tribes that came from Egypt and arrived in Canaan by way of Sinai introduced the worship of Yahweh to those already in the land, and Yahweh gradually took over from El as the supreme God. According to Eissfeldt, this might explain the relatively sympathetic attitude of Yahwism towards the El cult compared with its hostility towards Baal. He suggests that Deuteronomy 32:8–9 and Psalm 82 reflect a period of Israel's history when El was still regarded as superior to Yahweh.[29]

These views recognize that the patriarchal narratives reflect theological traditions, but have little or no historical value. Alt, for example, sees no historical connection between the patriarchs and Canaan, or between the patriarchs and each other. Eissfeldt views the narratives as tribal history: they explain customs and relationships within and among tribes in terms of fictional stories about families and individuals. Cross attaches greater historical significance to the patriarchal narratives.[30] He maintains that the patriarchs worshipped the Canaanite god El, and that compounds with El are not separate deities but local designations of El. He further argues that worship of El by these names was an original part of patriarchal religion, rather than an addition to the tradition after the settlement.[31] He emphasizes the continuity between patriarchal religion and the worship of Yahweh and suggests that Yahweh may have been

29. O. Eissfeldt, 'El and Yahweh', *JSS* 1 (1956), pp. 25–37. In Deut. 32:8–9 it is *the Most High* (Elyon) who apportions the nations (v. 8) and it is argued that *the Lord* (Yahweh) is one of the (subordinate) gods to whom an allocation is made. Smith also sees this passage as a relic of earlier polytheism, where El is superior to Yahweh (*Origins*, pp. 143, 156–157). However, there is no need to see a distinction between the two. God has apportioned the nations but has retained Israel as his own possession, in order to fulfil a particular purpose. In Ps. 82:1 'God' (*ʾĕlōhîm*) is taken to refer to Yahweh, who is one of the gods in *the assembly of El*. Eissfeldt argues that this implies El's superiority. Again, though, the distinction is artificial, and in the light of v. 8 a more natural interpretation is to view Elohim (Yahweh) as the head of the divine council, and so identical with El. Smith suggests that here Yahweh is identified with El and given the role of judge of all the earth, and so recasts an earlier polytheistic theology (*Origins*, pp. 48–49, 157).

30. Cross, *Canaanite Myth*, pp. 3–75.

31. Wenham notes that 'Cross's reconstruction thus reduces the gap between theology and history in the patriarchal narratives' ('Religion of the Patriarchs', p. 170). On the other hand, McKane regards his attempt to 'read the religion of the patriarchs directly from the documentary sources' as evidence of 'critical obtuseness' (*Patriarchal Narratives*, pp. 208–209).

an epithet of El.[32] Nevertheless there are important distinctions between patriarchal and Canaanite worship.

The God of the patriarchs

One of the characteristics of patriarchal religion is in their worship of one God. This contrasts with the practice both of Abraham's ancestors and of the Canaanites. The patriarchal narratives emphasize continuity of worship: the God who appeared to Jacob at Bethel identified himself as *the God of your father Abraham and the God of Isaac* (Gen. 28:13). Abraham's ancestors in Mesopotamia were probably moon worshippers.[33] It may be possible to trace a line of faithful worshippers from Noah through Shem (Gen. 11:10–26); however, Joshua 24:2 seems to indicate that the call of Abraham represented a departure from the family's pagan worship. Wenham notes that Il (El) was a member of the Mesopotamian pantheon in the third millennium BC,[34] and thus Abraham may have been familiar with the name, and had perhaps even become a follower of El before he arrived in Canaan. It is probable that Abraham identified the God who called him in Genesis 12 with El, and that the names compounded with El refer to manifestations of that one God. However, the patriarch's understanding of, and relationship with, the God who had called him remained very personal: it was not mediated through the cult (Mesopotamian or Canaanite) but was the result of direct revelation.

Another feature of the patriarchal religion was its lack of structure and formality. Though pillars and altars were set up at various points, God was thought to accompany the patriarchs in their travels. He was the God of the family or clan, rather than of a particular locality, and in the patriarchal narratives this is expressed in the form of a covenant, made first with Abraham and renewed to subsequent generations of his family. Thus, although El Shaddai may have had links with the area around Hebron, in the patriarchal narratives he is associated, primarily, with the patriarchs themselves, introducing himself to each of them,[35] and providing continuity between them.

---

32. See also Miller, *Israelite Religion*, pp. 377–386. Day argues against this identification, pointing out that the Canaanite El and Yahweh have different characteristics (*Yahweh*, pp. 13–14).

33. Haran too was a centre of moon worship, and so would have been a natural place for Terah, Abraham's father, to settle after travelling from Ur around the Fertile Crescent.

34. Wenham, 'Religion', in Millard and Wiseman, *Essays*, p. 171.

35. God introduces himself to Abraham and Jacob as El Shaddai (Gen. 17:1; 35:11), and the name was known to Isaac, who uses it when he blesses Jacob (Gen. 28:3).

There is no indication that the patriarchs adopted Canaanite worship or offered sacrifices at already established Canaanite sanctuaries. Even if the epithets of El mentioned in Genesis were in general use by the Canaanites, it does not mean that the patriarchs subscribed to the same religious practices. As we have noted, their relationship with God was personal and their theological understanding developed within the context of that relationship, through direct revelation. The association of the God of the patriarchs, El Shaddai, with a family rather than a place, distinguished him from Canaanite El-deities, which were often local gods (or local designations of El). It is probable that the story of the testing of Abraham was, in part, polemic against the child sacrifice present in some forms of Canaanite religion.[36] When the patriarchs sacrificed, it was on altars they built themselves, and there is no mention of other worshippers or of an officiating priesthood.

Thus a strong case can be made for separating the religion of the patriarchs from Canaanite religion. That said, the patriarchs had a relatively easygoing attitude towards other El-worshippers.[37] And it remains a matter of debate and speculation just what overlap they understood there to have been between their God and the El-deities worshipped by those around them. This attitude contrasts with the exclusiveness of the Mosaic faith, and may be the consequence of a less formalized religion, where fewer lines have been drawn.

The patriarchs and Yahweh[38]

The book of Exodus indicates that the faith revealed to Moses was both continuous with the religion of the patriarchs (Exod. 3:6, 13–15) and distinct from it (Exod. 6:3). A significant difference was the revelation to Moses of the divine name, Yahweh. However, some passages use that name when referring to much earlier periods (e.g. Gen. 4:1; 5:29; 9:26; 14:22; 15:2, 7–8; 28:16). A

Footnote 35 (*continued*)

In Jacob's dream at Bethel (Luz) God describes himself as the God of Abraham and Isaac (Gen. 28:13), though in retrospect Jacob refers to God as El Shaddai (Gen. 48:3). El Shaddai is thus identified with the patriarchs themselves and any original connection with Mamre or Hebron is lost.

36. The practice of child sacrifice within El religion may account for why Abraham follows God's instructions. The outcome, though, emphasizes a clear distinction.

37. See e.g. Moberley, *Old Testament*, pp. 89–91.

38. See Moberley, *Old Testament*, pp. 36–78; Wenham, 'Religion', in Millard and Wiseman, *Essays*, pp. 177–180.

common explanation is that Exodus 6:3 belongs to a source (P) that links the revelation of the divine name exclusively with Moses, and in the patriarchal narratives refers to El Shaddai;[39] other material comes from the J source, which refers to Yahweh throughout. However, that does not explain why the final editor of the Pentateuch appears unconcerned about the inconsistency. Another explanation, aimed at harmonization, notes the close link between the name and the character of God, and suggests that *the name itself* may not have been unknown to the patriarchs, but before the revelation to Moses they were unaware of *its full significance*.[40] A similar explanation is offered by older Jewish commentators: the name was known, but not the glory associated with the name.[41]

Another explanation is that though the name Yahweh was unknown to the patriarchs, those who retold the stories recognized that the God they worshipped as Yahweh was the same God who spoke to, and was worshipped by, Abraham, Isaac and Jacob, and those before them, and so they used that name in their accounts of those earlier incidents.[42] Wenham suggests that 'the Yahwistic editor of Genesis was so convinced of the identity of Yahweh and the God who revealed himself to the patriarchs, that he not only used Yahweh in the narrative, but also more sparingly in reporting human and angelic speech'.[43]

As we have noted, there is an increased focus on narrative in the OT, and a growing acceptance (even among conservative scholars) that the narrator has some freedom in retelling a story. While not departing from the essential historical details,[44] the narrator might, nonetheless, choose not to report the *ipsissima verba* of characters in the narrative because he wants to make a particular

---

39. The name Yahweh occurs in two passages traditionally thought to be from P (Gen. 17:1; 21:1); however these are part of the narration, and are not part of direct speech.

40. See e.g. Derek Kidner, *Genesis*, TOTC (Leicester: IVP, 1967), pp. 19–20; Harrison, *Introduction*, pp. 581–582; Jacob, *Theology*, pp. 49–50; see also. A. Motyer, *The Revelation of the Divine Name* (London: Tyndale, 1959); for further discussion, see Moberley, *Old Testament*, pp. 55–67; Wenham, 'Religion', in Millard and Wiseman, *Essays*, pp. 178–180.

41. Wenham, 'Religion', in Millard and Wiseman, *Essays*, p. 178.

42. See e.g. Moberley, *Old Testament*, pp. 67–78; Wenham, *Genesis 1–15*, pp. 115–116; 'Religion', in Millard and Wiseman, *Essays*, pp. 177–183.

43. Wenham, 'Religion', in Millard and Wiseman, *Essays*, p. 183.

44. See the discussion on the historicity of biblical narrative above, pp. 62–63.

point. This recognition of the role of the narrator has changed the nature of this kind of debate. It is now less about how to explain away apparent inconsistencies in the text, and more about considering the narrative significance of the language and terminology used. In this case the narrator has a definite purpose: he uses the name Yahweh in the earlier narrative deliberately, because he wants to emphasize the continuity between patriarchal worship and the later worship of Yahweh.[45]

Monotheism[46]

Monotheism is the belief that there is only one God who is the proper object of worship *and beside him no other gods exist.* Another term, *monolatry*, means the worship of one God, but without the claim that there are no others. It is widely thought that true monotheism developed late in Israel's faith, reaching its fullest expression in Isaiah 40 – 55 (which some date in the sixth century BC).

The development of monotheism

A common view is that during the early part of its history Israel was polytheistic. The principal opposition to polytheism, in the form of a movement advocating the sole worship of Yahweh, emerged only in the ninth century BC (with prophets like Elijah); it grew and became more widely accepted during the monarchy and evolved into full monotheism during and after the exile. There are several problems with this approach.

In the first place there is little evidence of a prolonged period of polytheism in Israel. It is likely that aspects of Canaanite worship infiltrated Israelite

---

45. Goldingay comments, 'to say that people were calling on Yhwh at this stage of the story is to say that they were worshipping the one God, the God who would be active and known in Israel, known as Yhwh' (*OT Theology*, 1:157).

46. See B. W. Anderson, *Contours*, pp. 63–73; Arnold, 'Religion', in Baker and Arnold, *Face of OT Studies*, pp. 400–411; Brueggemann, *Theology*, pp. 580–581; Clements, *OT Theology*, pp. 72–77; Eichrodt, *Theology*, 1:220–227; Gerstenberger, *Theologies*, pp. 215–221, 273–281; Goldingay, *OT Theology*, 1:616–621; 2:38–40; Robert K. Gnuse, *No Other Gods: Emergent Monotheism in Israel*, JSOTSup 241 (Sheffield: Sheffield Academic Press, 1997); Jacob, *Theology*, pp. 65–67. Jon D. Levenson, *Sinai and Zion: An Entry into the Jewish Bible*, New Voices in Biblical Studies (Minneapolis: Winston, 1985), pp. 56–70; Preuss, *OT Theology*, 1:111–117; von Rad, *OT Theology*, 1:203–212; Rendtorff, *Hebrew Bible*, pp. 634–645, 667–675; Smith, *Early History*, pp. 182–199; *Origins*, pp. 149–194; Vriezen, *Outline*, pp. 175–180. For a survey of views, see Gnuse, *No Other Gods*, pp. 62–128.

worship, and continued to be practised,[47] but this was not part of Israel's official faith.

A second problem is that where the movement to a form of monotheism occurs in other contexts, it is not gradual: it comes by revolution not evolution. While it is true that Israel's faith is based on direct encounter with God, and its development might not follow patterns seen elsewhere, the evolutionary model sees the movement driven by human factors rather than divine revelation, and the lack of evidence of such development from polytheism to monotheism elsewhere is a serious weakness in the evolutionary argument.

A third issue is, why should there be such a movement? Where did the impetus for the sole worship of Yahweh come from? And why, out of all the nations in the ANE, would this have happened only in Israel? Albertz argues that it must have derived from the special bond between Yahweh and the Israelite tribal alliance following the exodus.[48] This, in turn, suggests that the roots of Israel's monotheistic faith go back to an early period of Israel's history. More recently, Stephen Cook has argued that 'biblical Yahwism', which includes the worship of Yahweh as sole god, was not a late development, but had deep roots in Israel's faith. He notes that for much of Israel's history this existed as a minority view that became dominant only within early Judaism, and that, rather than being a theological innovation, polemic against idolatry and the call to worship Yahweh alone reflects this ancient stream of tradition.[49]

---

47. We see e.g. that idolatry is rife during the period of the judges. As time went on, it is probable that unregulated provincial worship at 'high places' (which may have been at or near Canaanite sanctuaries) led to idolatrous practices being incorporated into Israelite religion. See below, pp. 182–184.

48. Albertz, *History*, 1:61–63.

49. Stephen L. Cook, *The Social Roots of Biblical Yahwism*, Studies in Biblical Literature 8 (Leiden: Brill, 2004). By 'biblical Yahwism' Cook means 'the overt religious points of view that the Bible presents and supports' (p. 1), and he identifies it with the Sinaitic, covenantal theology reflected in Deuteronomy, the Former Prophets, the Psalms of Asaph, and the prophetic books of Jeremiah, Hosea and Malachi. Though often viewed as originating in the north, Cook argues that tradition is evident in some southern circles too. This *Sinai theology* emerges at particular points, notably in the reforms of Hezekiah and particularly of Josiah; however, it became dominant only after the exile. Cook's thesis is helpful in arguing that the body of teaching reflecting Sinai tradition was not a later innovation, but goes back deep into Israel's historical faith. However, I would question whether it was as clearly definable a strand as Cook suggests, preserved by particular groups. It seems

As we have noted, according to the patriarchal narratives, the patriarchs worshipped one God, whom they probably first identified with El; though, as we have also noted, their theological understanding grew out of their relationship with God, not from involvement with the Canaanite cult, and in time clear differences emerged. Nevertheless their fairly relaxed attitude towards other El-worshippers indicates that they were monolatrous rather than monotheistic.

The worship of Yahweh, associated with Moses, was accompanied by greater exclusivism and by clear instructions to have nothing to do with the gods of other nations. The first commandment is emphatic: *You shall have no other gods before me* (Exod. 20:3).[50] This was the beginning of Israel's monotheistic faith, which appears also to be implied by Deuteronomy 4:35, 39, *you were shown these things so that you might know that the LORD is God; besides him there is no other . . . acknowledge and take to heart this day that the LORD is God in heaven above and on the earth below. There is no other.*

Earlier in that chapter the true nature of other gods is described: they are *man-made gods of wood and stone, which cannot see or hear or eat or smell* (v. 28). Many scholars argue that Deuteronomy was written at a relatively late date (in, or just before, the reign of Josiah), but it can be argued that the book, and so the beginnings of monotheism, are much earlier.[51] A form of monotheism existed in Egypt under Pharaoh Akhenaten (c. 1352–1336 BC),[52] within a century of Moses and the exodus.[53] Akhenaten, who came to the throne as Amenhotep IV, took his name from the sun disk, the *Aten*, which, he decreed, was to be worshipped as the only deity. In Egypt's polytheistic culture this was not an easy change to make, and it did not outlive the

---

Footnote 49 (*continued*)
   more likely that it represents a more general return to Israel's true, covenant faith.

50. See also e.g. House, *OT Theology*, pp. 111–113; see also, B. W. Anderson, *Living World*, pp. 107–109.

51. See Peter C. Craigie, *The Book of Deuteronomy*, NICOT (Grand Rapids: Eerdmans; London: Hodder & Stoughton, 1976), pp. 24–29; John A. Thompson, *Deuteronomy*, TOTC (Leicester: IVP, 1974), pp. 47–68.

52. These are the dates according to conventional scholarship.

53. The usually accepted date for the exodus is around 1250 BC. Some argue for an earlier date (around 1450 BC). There are arguments for both, leaving the matter uncertain. I prefer the later date, but, on either reckoning, a form of monotheism appears to have existed in the ANE under Akhenaten within a century of Moses.

Pharaoh. After his death, Akhenaten was condemned as a heretic, and Egypt reverted to polytheism. There is no evidence that the beginnings of monotheism under Moses was in any way based on what happened under Akhenaten; however, it does indicate that monotheism in Israel need not have been a late idea.[54]

It is important to bear in mind that monotheism is a theological category, and would not have meant much in the early days of Israel's religious life, when the main concern was to get to know better the God who had revealed himself to them, and to work out the practical implications of their relationship with him in daily life. Whether or not other gods existed was not an important issue; what mattered was the fact that *for Israel* there was no other God but Yahweh. He was *their* God and their dealings were to be with him alone. This may not explicitly deny the existence of other gods,[55] but it does assert they are not worth attention. Yahweh is superior to other gods: he alone is the Creator (Ps. 95:3–5); he is the God of the whole earth (Ps. 97:9); he is the God who has set Israel apart for himself (Deut. 32:8–9; Josh. 24:2–3), and the people are to worship none besides him (Exod. 20:3; Deut. 5:7). God's greatness leaves no room for competitors; this is *practical*, if not strictly *theoretical*, monotheism.[56]

Vriezen also links monotheism with Moses; he argues that

> the story of David and even the Song of Deborah are incomprehensible without the recognition of the belief in one God whose word is decisive in Israel and in the world . . . There is, therefore, nothing to stand in the way of a recognition of a

---

54. See Alan R. Millard, 'Abraham, Akhenaten, Moses and Monotheism', in Richard S. Hess, Philip E. Satterthwaite and Gordon J. Wenham (eds.), *He Swore an Oath* (Cambridge: Tyndale House, 1993), pp. 119–129.

55. The existence of other gods seems to be implied in e.g. Exod. 15:11; 18:11; Judg. 11:24; Pss 86:8; 95:3. Brueggemann suggests that the command in Exod. 20:1 'assumes a world of polytheism in which there were other possible objects of loyalty' (*Theology*, p. 183).

56. Smith objects to terms such as 'monolatry' and 'practical monotheism', arguing that Israelite religion before the exile is better characterized as recognizing a Supreme Power and lesser deities, rather than one god (*Origins*, pp. 149–150). However, other deities are relegated to such a degree that this does amount to monolatry/practical monotheism. Rendtorff argues that the non-existence of other gods is implicit in texts which refer to the inaction of alleged gods (e.g. Judg. 6:31; 1 Kgs 18:24–29); see *Hebrew Bible*, pp. 669–671.

monotheistic Yahwism given by Moses . . . though not pursued by him to its ultimate consequences.[57]

In my opinion it is reasonable to adopt the view that the roots of Israel's monotheism go back to the time of Moses and the exodus,[58] though (as Vriezen notes) its full implications were not expressed until later. The worship of Yahweh alone followed on from the patriarchal worship of the one God, El Shaddai. However, the sole worship of Yahweh was always under pressure from the influence of Canaanite religion.[59] The witness of the OT itself is that after the settlement, elements of Canaanite worship crept into Yahwism (e.g. Ps. 106:34–39; cf. Judg. 17:5; 18:30–31), and indeed there may also have been vestiges of the people's pre-Yahwistic past.[60] There was, at first, a close link between Yahweh and El, though the lack of polemic against El suggests that this did not develop into a serious problem. It may be, as Cross suggests, that there was a radical differentiation between the two at an early stage in Israel's religious history.[61] To emphasize the distinction with El, it is possible some

---

57. Vriezen, *Theology*, pp. 178–179.

58. The early chapters of Genesis might be taken to indicate that primal religion was monotheistic, though there is little to indicate how this might have degenerated into polytheism. It is possible that monotheistic worship was preserved in the line from Shem to Abraham. However, there is also evidence to suggest that Abraham came out of a polytheistic background (Josh. 24:2). There is much here that remains unclear, though whatever its primal history, the worship of one God (Yahweh) took on renewed significance from the time of the exodus onwards.

59. The idea that the early faith of Israel was essentially monotheistic (or at least monolatrous) and then came under pressure from Canaanite religion was part of an older consensus that has given way, more recently, to the evolutionary view. However, this later view has serious weaknesses.

60. It has been suggested that things such as the cultic use of bells (Exod. 28:33–35) and the regulations following childbirth (Lev. 12) may have originated as rites to keep demons at bay. However, within the worship of Yahweh, these are completely divorced from any such setting (see e.g. Eichrodt, *Theology*, 2:226). The same may be true of certain aspects of sacrifices. For example, seasoning a sacrifice with salt (Lev. 2:13; Ezek. 43:24) may reflect the pre-Yahwistic view that sacrifices were offered as food to the deity. In its Yahwistic setting, there is no suggestion that God is dependent on sacrifices for food, and the presence of salt is linked to the covenant (Lev. 2:13), though the nature of the link is unclear.

61. See Cross, *Canaanite Myth*, p. 71.

attributes and aspects of the worship of the Canaanite god Baal were incorporated into Israel's Yahwistic faith,[62] leading to the syncretism condemned by Elijah in the ninth century and by Hosea a century later.[63]

Attempts to restore true worship were made by Hezekiah and Josiah, but the effects were impermanent. It was against the background of the exile (a theological and a political crisis that brought a radical re-evaluation of Israel's faith) that it became more necessary to emphasize the attributes of Israel's God over against the gods of Babylon, and the classic expressions of true monotheism are linked with that period.[64] Though, as we have seen, this is not something new: it builds on, and draws out the implications of, ideas that go back to the time of Moses and the exodus.

Features of true monotheism
The only God
These later OT passages emphasize that God is unique: he is the only God (Isa. 43:10; 44:6; 45:5–6, 21; 46:9), and there is none to match him (Isa. 40:18, 25;

---

62. Images once associated with Baal are associated with Yahweh in some OT passages. In Isa. 27:1 Yahweh defeats Leviathan, a chaos monster defeated by Baal and described in a similar way in the Canaanite myth that describes Baal's victory over the sea god, Yam. In that same myth, Baal is referred to as 'the Rider on the Clouds', a term also used to describe Yahweh (Ps. 68:4; Isa. 19:1; cf. Dan. 7:13). It is probable that in these passages the imagery has lost its direct link with Baal but its use in this way indicates that some assimilation did take place. This assimilation may be indicated too by Israelite names compounded with Baal (e.g. 1 Chr. 8:34). See Bill T. Arnold and Bryan E. Beyer, *Readings from the Ancient Near East: Primary Sources for Old Testament Study* (Grand Rapids: Baker, 2002), p. 53; H. L. Ginsberg, 'Ugaritic Myths, Epics, and Legends', in *ANET*, pp. 129–155 (130–132); J. Gray, 'Texts from Ras Shamra', in *DOTT*, pp. 118–133 (129). For further discussion, see Day, *Yahweh*, pp. 91–127; Smith, *Early History*, pp. 80–91 . While allowing that Baal imagery significantly influenced the language of the OT, Day also notes that 'though these images lived on, everything became transformed in the light of monotheism' (p. 233).

63. By Hosea's day Baal worship was widespread and had become so confused with the worship of Yahweh that many Israelites could not tell them apart. Baal means 'lord', 'master' or 'husband', and by Hosea's day it had become a title for Yahweh.

64. Whenever Deutero-Isaiah was written, it is set against the background of the Babylonian exile, and addresses theological issues relevant to the exiles.

46:5). Other gods are described as *worthless* (Jer. 2:5, 11; 10:8; 14:22); they are *not gods* (Jer. 2:11; 5:7) but exist only as manufactured idols (Isa. 40:18–20; 44:9–20; 46:1–2; Jer. 2:26–28; 10:1–16). Isaiah uses several pictures to describe the ineffectuality of such gods. First, he notes that unless they are well made, they topple over (Isa. 40:20) and, to be on the safe side, it is better to nail them down (Isa. 41:7). Second, in an emergency the same gods to whom people bow down and pray for help have to be carried to safety by the people who worship them (Isa. 46:1–2). By contrast, God carries and sustains his people (v. 4). In another scathing attack (Isa. 44:14–17) he describes how a man divides a piece of wood into two, then uses half to make an idol and half to make the fire on which he cooks a meal. In effect those who worship idols are bowing down to firewood!

There are two important factors in emphasizing Yahweh's claim to be the one true God: he is the *Creator* and the *Lord of History*.

God as the Creator[65]

Isaiah 40:12–26 points to the distinctiveness of God by focusing on his role in creation. The chapter begins with God's promise to deliver his exiled people, and goes on to emphasize his power over the nations and their so-called gods. Yahweh alone planned and made the heavens and the earth (vv. 12–14); other gods are mere manufactured idols (vv. 18–20). The contrast between Israel's God and the idols worshipped by the Babylonians is introduced with the question *to whom then will you compare God?* (v. 18). This question is repeated in verse 25, *'To whom will you compare me? Or who is my equal?' says the Holy One*, where it introduces a section affirming God as creator and controller of the moon and stars (vv. 25–26). Polytheistic cultures like Babylon regarded heavenly bodies as gods. Here they are seen as part of creation: called into being by God and taking their place at his command within his appointed order. Yahweh, then, has no rivals: his power and authority are absolute. Elsewhere too the view of God as the Creator is decisive in distinguishing him from the gods of the nations (Isa. 45:18; Jer. 10:11–16; 51:18–19; Ps. 96:5). An important corollary of this is that creation bears witness to the one whose handiwork it is (e.g. Ps. 19:1–4; cf. Rom. 1:20).[66]

God as the Lord of history

Another decisive factor in Yahweh's claim to be the only God is his power to direct the course of history, demonstrated in the fulfilment of

---

65. The idea of God as the Creator is a central tenet of OT faith; see 'God and Creation', below, pp. 124–158.

66. See Childs, *OT Theology*, pp. 30–34; Goldingay, *OT Theology*, 2:670–671.

prophecy.[67] God alone can announce what is going to happen, and then carry it out. He has shown his people over and over again that what he says can be trusted, and he calls on the false gods to provide similar evidence. We see an example of this in Isaiah 41:21–29. The gods of the nations are challenged, *tell us what the future holds, so that we may know you are gods* (v. 23). They are unable to do so and are condemned as less than nothing and utterly worthless (vv. 24, 29).[68] Another key expression of this is in Isaiah 46:9–10:

> *I am God, and there is no other;*
> *I am God, and there is none like me.*
> *I make known the end from the beginning,*
> *from ancient times, what is still to come.*

This further emphasizes the importance of God's activity in Israel's history as a means of making himself known.[69]

The nature and being of God

The OT writers are not concerned with abstract ideas about God. He is not a subject for study and speculation, but the living One who reveals himself through his activity in the world and his encounter with his people. Their understanding of God is expressed primarily through the narrative of what God has done (through the stories in which he involves himself in the life of the people) rather than through lists of attributes and abstract propositional statements, which attempt to set out who God

---

67. In Deutero-Isaiah this issue is addressed in several 'trial' speeches, where God summons other gods to appear in court to defend their claims to divinity against the claim that he alone is God (Isa. 41:1–7, 21–29; 43:8–13; 44:6–8; 45:20–25).

68. Yahweh demonstrates the reliability of his word both through Israel's testimony to what he has done in the nation's history (e.g. Isa. 43:10–12), and in the present situation, through the previously announced appointment of Cyrus to bring deliverance to Israel (Isa. 41:26–27).

69. We have already noted the importance of history as a medium of divine revelation in relation to von Rad and G. E. Wright (above, p. 35); see also Childs, *OT Theology*, pp. 36–38; Preuss, *OT Theology*, 1:208–219.

is.[70] Nevertheless we can note certain things about the God who makes himself known in the OT.[71]

The nature of God

God is personal[72]

It is clear from the way God is often described in anthropomorphic terms that he is regarded as a personal being. God speaks, hears, sees; he has a face and hands; he is depicted *walking in the garden in the cool of the day* (Gen. 3:8); he can be angry (e.g. Num. 11:10; Ps. 78:21; Isa. 34:2) and grieved (e.g. Gen. 6:6–7; 1 Sam. 15:11; Jer. 42:10). These descriptions of God point to the way he comes to us in a down-to-earth way; this willingness to identify with us shows too his desire for relationship, and points forward, ultimately to the incarnation.

We see that God is personal too from the way the OT pictures the relationship between God and his people. So, for example, it is likened to the relationships between father and son (e.g. Exod. 4:23; Hos. 11:1–4) and between husband and bride (e.g. Jer. 2:2; 3:14; 31:32; Ezek. 16:8–14; Hos. 2:14–23). These images display the warm, tender, feeling nature of God and indicate that he can know the pain of rejection.

Eichrodt also sees a connection between the personal nature of God and the revelation of the divine Name:

> by revealing his Name God has, as it were, made himself over to them; he has opened to them a very part of his being and given them a means of access to himself . . . in

---

70. The OT contains summaries of the attributes of God (e.g. Exod. 34:6–7; Num. 14:18; Jon. 4:2), though these are brief, and need to be related to their narrative context, rather than set out as abstract theological statements.

71. See B. W. Anderson, *Contours*, pp. 56–62; Clements, *OT Theology*, pp. 58–62; Eichrodt, *Theology*, 1:206–282; Goldingay, *OT Theology*, 2:21–172; Jacob, *Theology*, pp. 73–135; Preuss, *OT Theology*, 1:239–244; Rendtorff, *Hebrew Bible*, pp. 621–634; Vriezen, *Outline*, pp. 148–198; see also John Drane, *Introducing the Old Testament*, 2nd rev. ed. (Oxford: Lion, 2000; Minneapolis: Fortress, 2001), pp. 228–252; William Dyrness, *Themes in Old Testament Theology* (Downers Grove: IVP; Carlisle: Paternoster, 1977), pp. 41–57.

72. See Köhler, *OT Theology*, pp. 22–25; Clements, *OT Theology*, pp. 58–60; Eichrodt, *Theology*, 1:211–212; Vriezen, *Outline*, pp. 171–175; Drane, *Introducing the OT*, pp. 238–243; Dyrness, *Themes*, pp. 43–44; Goldingay, *OT Theology*, 2:27–28; Preuss, *OT Theology*, 1:244–246.

the Name of the covenant God they encountered him in person and experienced his activity.[73]

God is spiritual

Though God is personal and chooses to be involved with his world, the OT emphasizes he existed before it, created it and remains above and distinct from it. An important aspect of this is that God is eternal. The OT describes the origin of the world but not the origin of God: he existed *in the beginning* (Gen. 1:1) and will outlast the creation (e.g. Pss 90:2; 93:2; Isa. 57:15). As creator and source of all things, God is of a different order of being from the natural world. We see an example of this in Isaiah 31:3, *the Egyptians are men and not God; their horses are flesh and not spirit.* The two orders of being, *flesh* (associated with *men*) and *spirit* (associated with God), are distinct from one another (cf. John 4:24). Hezekiah makes a similar distinction, between human *flesh*, represented by the Assyrian king and army, and God, whose presence guarantees the security of his people: *with him is only the arm of flesh, but with us is the LORD our God to help us and to fight our battles* (2 Chr. 32:8; cf. Hos. 11:9; see also Num. 23:19; 1 Sam. 15:29; Isa. 55:8–9). In these passages the main emphasis is on God's power over against human weakness, but the ontological distinction is also important: God's power is related to who he is.

This distinction is reflected in the prohibition of images (Exod. 20:4–5; Lev. 26:1). One reason for this prohibition is to prevent the worship of other gods in the form of idols.[74] Another is that making and worshipping images detracts from the spiritual nature of Israel's religion and from the transcendence of God. In Deuteronomy 4:15–19 the instruction not to make idols or to worship physical objects is linked with the reminder that when God appeared to Moses at Horeb, he had no form. The emphasis here is not so much on the danger of the worship of other gods (though that was ever present) but on the nature of God himself. God is above and beyond any physical representation of him.[75]

---

73. Eichrodt, *Theology*, 1:207–208.

74. This is the emphasis of Deut. 5:7–8; 29:17–18; 32:16.

75. The contrast between God and anything that can be represented by an idol is emphasized in Ps. 106:19–20, *at Horeb they made a calf and worshipped an idol cast from metal. They exchanged their Glory for an image of a bull, which eats grass* (see also Isa. 40:18–26). For further discussion, see Brueggemann, *Theology*, pp. 136–144; Clements, *OT Theology*, pp. 75–76; Eichrodt, *Theology*, 1:118–119, 215; Preuss, *OT Theology*, 1:107–111; von Rad, *OT Theology*, 1:212–219.

The idea that God is, in the very nature of his being, above and beyond the natural order and so may not be represented in physical form means that the portrayal of God in personal terms (e.g. as father or husband) is limited. These descriptions are helpful to us, to convey certain truths about God's character, but should not be pressed too far. This is also true when it comes to issues of gender. Within the ancient world there were both gods and goddesses and the chief god of a pantheon generally had a consort. So, for example, El is partnered with Asherah and Baal with Anat. The idea of Yahweh as the sole God, however, leaves no room for a female counterpart.[76] We note too that the personal images of God in the OT are predominantly male, and God is consistently referred to as 'he'. But none of this implies that God is to be viewed exclusively as male.[77] The OT was written against a cultural, religious and political background that was, essentially, patriarchal. That world view is reflected in the text, and needs to be taken into account when it comes to interpretation and theological application. But there is also female imagery, especially in the book of Isaiah. Phyllis Trible notes that the Hebrew word for 'compassion' (*raḥămîm*) comes from the root meaning 'womb' (*reḥem*), suggesting a link between God's love for his people, and a mother's love for her child (e.g. Isa. 46:3–5; 49:15; 63:7 – 64:12). She also points to other passages that suggest the metaphor of God as mother (e.g.

---

76. The close link between Yahweh and El (at least in the early days of the settlement) and the assimilation of ideas associated with Baal makes it possible that in popular religion Yahweh was thought to have a consort. The OT mentions poles (symbols of the goddess Asherah) and extrabiblical texts refer to 'Yahweh and his Asherah' (see references below). Jeremiah also refers to the worship of the Queen of Heaven (Jer. 7:18). However, even if this was popular practice, and may have been condoned by Israel's leaders, it is condemned by the OT and formed no part of Israel's official faith, contra Goldingay's suggestion that Wisdom is presented as Yahweh's consort in Prov. 8 (*OT Theology*, 2:181); see also Brueggemann, *Theology*, p. 347. For further discussion, see e.g. Albertz, *History*, 1:85–87; B. W. Anderson, *Contours*, pp. 68–69; John Day, 'Asherah in the Hebrew Bible and Northwest Semitic Literature', *JBL* 105 (1986), pp. 385–408; *Yahweh*, pp. 42–67; William G. Dever, *Recent Archaeological Discoveries and Biblical Research* (Seattle: University of Washington Press, 1990); John A. Emerton, 'New Light on Israelite Religion: The Implications of the Inscriptions from Kuntillet 'Ajrud', *ZAW* 94 (1982), pp. 2–29; see also Miller, *Israelite Religion*, pp. 197–207; Smith, *Early History*, pp. 47–54, 108–147; *Origins*, pp. 47–49, 73–74.

77. See Goldingay, *OT Theology*, 2:46–48.

Isa. 42:14; 66:13.).[78] Alongside these images are the more traditional ones of God as father, indicating that in order to understand God better it is necessary to make comparisons with characteristics of both sexes. These are, however, only comparisons: the writers use things they know and understand to talk about God, who is beyond knowledge and understanding. God is not male, nor is he male and female – he transcends sexuality.[79]

Divine characteristics
Holiness[80]
This quality, more than any other is intimately related to the nature and being of God. Jacob suggests that 'Holiness is not one divine quality among others, even the chiefest, for it expresses what is characteristic of God and corresponds precisely to his deity.'[81] God is holy because of who he is.

Holiness conveys the idea of *separation*. In the ANE, holiness was seen in terms of an impersonal, naturalistic power linked with particular sacred objects or places, though with no moral connotations. This power might be positive and beneficial, or negative and linked with danger and prohibition. The term 'holy' was rarely applied to the deity. By contrast, in the OT, holiness is focused on God (e.g. Exod. 15:11; 28:36; Lev. 10:3; 1 Sam. 2:2; Isa. 6:3; 8:13); he is the *Holy One*;[82] and places, things and people are regarded as 'holy' because of their association with him.

---

78. See Phyllis Trible, *God and the Rhetoric of Sexuality*, OBT 2 (Philadelphia: Fortress, 1978), pp. 31–71; John F. Sawyer, *The Fifth Gospel: Isaiah in the History of Christianity* (Cambridge: Cambridge University Press, 1996), pp. 198–219. Num. 11:12 and Deut. 32:18 also portray God as a mother; see further Brueggemann, *Theology*, pp. 258–259; Rendtorff, *Hebrew Bible*, pp. 618–622.

79. For a brief but helpful discussion on this, see B. W. Anderson, *Contours*, pp. 72–73.

80. See e.g. B. W. Anderson, *Contours*, pp. 39–47; Brueggemann, *Theology*, pp. 288–293; Dyrness, *Themes*, pp. 51–53; Eichrodt, *Theology*, 1:270–282; Goldingay, *OT Theology*, 2:22–24; Jacob, *Theology*, pp. 86–93; Jacobus A. Naudé, *'qdš'*, in *NIDOTTE* 3:877–887; Preuss, *OT Theology*, pp. 240–241; von Rad, *OT Theology*, 1:205–207; Rendtorff, *Hebrew Bible*, pp. 632–634; H. Seebass and C. Brown, 'Holy, etc.', in *DNTT* 2:223–228; Norman H. Snaith, *Distinctive Ideas of the Old Testament* (London: Epworth, 1953), pp. 21–50; Vriezen, *Outline*, pp. 149–162.

81. Jacob, *Theology*, p. 86.

82. The title *Holy One* or *Holy One of Israel* is a favourite designation for God in the book of Isaiah, where it occurs twenty-five times (e.g. Isa. 5:19; 10:17; 31:1; 41:14; 43:15; 54:5; 60:9).

Holiness is bound up with God's unapproachable majesty. Sinai is cordoned off because God is there (Exod. 19:23); the Most Holy Place housing the Ark, the symbol of God's presence, is separated from the rest of the tabernacle with only very limited access (Exod. 26:33–34; Lev. 16:2); even heavenly beings hide their faces in the presence of God (Isa. 6:2–3); and unauthorized attempts to penetrate the barrier of divine holiness are punished (Lev. 10:1–3; Num. 4:15–20; 2 Sam. 6:6–7). Holiness, though, is not only about separation; it is also tied to *relationship*. Restrictions and prohibitions exist not to keep God away from humankind but to provide the means and conditions by which One who is *Wholly Other* may have contact with and enter into a relationship with his people.

In the ANE, holiness had little to do with moral purity; so, for example, cult prostitutes were regarded as holy. In the OT, though, because holiness is bound up with the character of God, it is closely related to purity (e.g. Josh. 24:19; Pss 15; 24:3–4; Isa. 5:16; 6:5; Hab. 1:13). An important aspect of this is that the people who belong to God are called to be holy too: *be holy because I am holy* (Lev. 11:44–45; cf. 1 Pet. 1:16; Lev. 20:26). Holiness is closely associated with God's glory (e.g. Exod. 15:11; 29:43; Lev. 10:3; Isa. 6:3; Ezek. 28:22),[83] which may be seen as the outward manifestation of holiness.

Righteousness[84]

Righteousness has to do with right behaviour within the context of a particular relationship; According to Seebass,

> righteousness in the OT is not a matter of actions conforming to a given set of absolute legal standards, but of behaviour which is in keeping with the two-way relationship between God and man. Thus the righteousness of God appears in his God-like dealings with his people, i.e. in redemption and salvation.[85]

---

83. See e.g. Brueggemann, *Theology*, pp. 283–287, 671–672; Brevard S. Childs, *Isaiah*, OTL (Louisville: Westminster John Knox, 2001), p. 55; Eichrodt, *Theology*, 1:277; Goldingay, *OT Theology*, 2:24–26; Preuss, *Theology*, 1:167–170; Rendtorff, *Hebrew Bible*, pp. 601–602; Snaith, *Distinctive Ideas*, pp. 21–50.

84. See e.g. Brueggemann, *Theology*, pp. 130–135; Dyrness, *Themes*, pp. 53–57; Eichrodt, *Theology*, 1:239–249; Jacob, *Theology*, pp. 94–102; von Rad, *OT Theology*, 1:370–383; David Reimer, 'ṣdq', in *NIDOTTE* 3:744–769; Rendtorff, *Hebrew Bible*, pp. 630–632; Preuss, *Theology*, 1:171–179; H. Seebass and C. Brown, 'Righteousness, Justification', in *DNTT* 3:352–377 (352–358); Snaith, *Distinctive Ideas*, pp. 51–93; Vriezen, *Outline*, p. 307.

85. Seebass and Brown, 'Righteousness', in *DNTT* 3:355; cf. Eichrodt, *Theology*, 1:240.

Righteousness does have a legal and ethical dimension. It is presented as the antithesis of wickedness and evil (e.g. Exod. 23:7; Deut. 25:1; 1 Kgs 8:32; Job 35:8; Ps. 45:7; Prov. 10:2); it is used to describe weights and measures (Lev. 19:36; Deut. 25:15; Ezek. 45:10; Job 31:6), and sacrifices that accord with certain standards and regulations (Deut. 33:19; Ps. 4:5; Mal. 3:3). It is also closely related to justice. God is *upright* (righteous) *and just* (Deut. 32:4); he loves *righteousness and justice* (Ps. 33:5), and they form *the foundation of his throne* (Pss 89:14; 97:2; see also e.g. Job 37:23; Pss 9:8; 11:7; Isa. 16:5; 28:17). And, as with holiness, God wants righteousness, seen as right action in accordance with their covenant obligations, including right worship, justice and obedience to the Law, to be evident among his people (e.g. Ps. 94:15; Isa. 1:26; 33:5; Hos. 10:12; Amos 5:24).

Righteousness is also linked with God's action on behalf of his people. Brueggemann describes it as 'Yahweh's ready capacity to be present in situations of trouble and to intervene powerfully and decisively in the interest of rehabilitation, restoration, and well-being'.[86] Because of the link between righteousness and justice, the poor and oppressed could rely on the righteousness of God to uphold the justice of their cause (e.g. Pss 9:4–5; 103:6; 112:9; Isa. 11:4), and believers could trust God, in his righteousness, to protect and deliver them from their enemies (e.g. Pss 5:8; 31:1; 35:24; 71:2; 143:11). On a national level there was the confidence that God, in his righteousness, would intervene to save his covenant people, who saw themselves as the oppressed victims of the surrounding nations and so could appeal to God to uphold them. Righteousness is thus closely linked with divine deliverance; it is frequently interpreted as vindication (e.g. Pss 24:5; 35:23–27; Isa. 54:17), and, particularly in Isaiah 40 – 66, is paralleled with salvation (e.g. Isa. 45:8; 46:12–13; 51:5–8; 56:1; cf. Ps. 98:2), where it is often described as a gift from God (e.g. Isa. 54:14; 61:3, 10–11; 62:1–3; cf. Hos. 2:19).

As I have indicated, this salvation might be seen as the result of God's right action in accordance with his covenant relationship with his people; thus the mighty acts by which God delivers his people are described as righteous (e.g. Judg. 5:11; 1 Sam. 12:7; Mic. 6:5). This relationship, however, and with it the basis for God's deliverance, was jeopardized by Israel's unfaithfulness. The fact that the people continued to link God's righteousness with salvation and deliverance, despite their unrighteousness, led to righteousness being associated with the justification of the ungodly and so seen as a possible basis for forgiveness and mercy (e.g. Pss 51:14; 143:1; Mic. 7:9).[87]

---

86. Brueggemann, *Theology*, p. 130.

87. See Eichrodt, *Theology*, 1:246–247.

Love and faithfulness

Several key aspects of God's character are noted in the orthodox summary of divine attributes in Exodus 34:6, *the LORD, the LORD, the compassionate and gracious God, slow to anger and abounding in love and faithfulness.*[88] 'Compassionate' (*raḥûm*, from the same root as *raḥămîm*) includes the idea of showing mercy and, as we have seen, expresses the love of a parent for a child (Isa. 49:15; Ps. 103:13).[89] In the OT the adjective 'gracious' (*ḥannûn*) always describes God, and is usually paired with 'compassionate' (Exod. 34:6; 2 Chr. 30:9; Neh. 9:17; Pss 86:15; 103:8; 111:4; 145:8; Joel 2:13; Jon. 4:2). The noun from the same root (*ḥēn*) refers to favour or goodwill freely given to benefit another.[90]

At the heart of the relationship between God and his people is the term *ḥesed* (translated 'love' in Exod. 34:6–7).[91] This cannot be adequately conveyed in English:[92] it includes kindness and mercy, but also involves loyalty, duty and obligation. In the OT, *ḥesed* occurs predominantly in the context of relationships, especially covenant relationships, and expresses 'faithfulness and loyal conduct . . . it is an inward commitment and disposition of goodwill together with its outward expression in dutiful and compassionate action'.[93]

---

88. The formula also occurs, with slight variations, in Num. 14:18; Neh. 9:17; Pss 86:15; 103:8; Joel 2:13; Jon. 4:2. See Brueggemann, *Theology*, pp. 213–218; Preuss, *OT Theology*, 1:241–243; Rendtorff, *Hebrew Bible*, pp. 623–627.

89. See further George Michael Butterworth, '*rḥm*', in *NIDOTTE* 3:1093–1095; H. Simeon-Yofre and U. Dahmen, '*rḥm*, etc.', *TDOT* 13:437–454.

90. See further Heinz-Josef Fabry, D. N. Freedman and J. R. Lundbom, '*ḥānan*, etc.', in *TDOT* 5:22–36; Terence E. Fretheim, '*ḥnn*', in *NIDOTTE* 2:203–206.

91. See e.g. B. W. Anderson, *Contours*, pp. 60–61; David A. Baer and Robert P. Gordon, '*ḥesed*', in *NIDOTTE* 2:211–218; Gordon R. Clark, *The Word Ḥesed in the Hebrew Bible*, JSOTSup 157 (Sheffield: Sheffield Academic Press, 1993); Dyrness, *Themes*, pp. 57–60; Eichrodt, *Theology*, 1:232–239; Goldingay, *OT Theology*, 2:118–119; Jacob, *Theology*, pp. 103–107; Robin L. Routledge, '*Hesed* as Obligation: A Re-Examination', *TynBul* 46.1 (1995), pp. 188–191; Snaith, *Distinctive Ideas*, pp. 94–130; H. J. Zobel, '*ḥesed*', in *TDOT* 5:44–64; B. Britt, 'Unexpected Attachments: A Literary Approach to the Term *ḥesed* in the Hebrew Bible', *JSOT* 27.3 (2003), pp. 289–307. In the extended summary of divine attributes (Exod. 34:6–7), *ḥesed* is the only one to be mentioned twice (Brueggemann, *Theology*, p. 216).

92. Among the words and expressions used to render the term in English are 'mercy', 'kindness', 'love', 'covenant love', 'steadfast love', 'everlasting/unfailing love' and 'lovingkindness'.

93. Routledge, '*Ḥesed*', p. 186.

Ḥesed is usually associated with God, and expresses his unique, faithful love for his people.[94] It is closely linked with divine covenants. God's relationship with Israel is referred to as a 'covenant of *ḥesed*' (Deut. 7:9, 12; 1 Kgs 8:23; Neh. 1:5; 9:32; Dan. 9:4), and in several passages the terms *ḥesed* and *běrît* (covenant) occur in parallel couplets (e.g. Pss 89:28; 106:45; Isa. 54:10). This relationship is expressed in two complementary ways.

First, *ḥesed* derives from the covenant. By entering into a covenant with his people, God has bound himself to show *ḥesed* to them. This includes love, loyalty and faithfulness to his covenant promises.[95] It includes too kindness, mercy and grace that bears with, and remains committed to, his people despite their sin, and provides the basis for forgiveness and restoration.[96] This leads to the other important characteristic of God's *ḥesed*.

Second, as well as deriving from the covenant between God and his people, it also becomes the means by which that relationship continues, even though, because of the people's unfaithfulness, it might properly be terminated.[97] It thus provides the basis for restoration and the promise of a new covenant (e.g. Jer. 31:3; Hos. 2:18–20).[98]

Ḥesed overlaps in meaning with other words such as love, grace, kindness and loyalty. It is linked closely with 'faithfulness', which points to God's utter

---

94. In two-thirds of its occurrences God shows *ḥesed* to human beings. It is also used to refer to proper conduct within human relationships, including marriage, and within society (e.g. Hos. 12:6; Mic. 6:8; Zech. 7:9). Less frequently it refers to the proper response of human beings to God (e.g. Jer. 2:2; Hos. 6:4, 6).

95. E.g. in Ps. 106:45, *běrît* and *ḥesed* occur together in that order: *for their sake he [Yahweh] remembered his covenant and out of his great* ḥesed *he relented.* Here the covenant, which God has not forgotten, provides the basis for *ḥesed*.

96. The link between *ḥesed* and forgiveness is seen in Ps. 51:1, *Have mercy on me, O God, according to your* ḥesed; *according to your great compassion blot out my transgressions;* see the discussion below, pp. 195–204; see also e.g. Neh. 9:17; Ps. 40:11–12; Isa. 54:8; Lam. 3:22, 31–32; Joel 2:13.

97. E.g., in relation to the Davidic covenant, Yahweh says, *I will maintain my* ḥesed *to him and my covenant with him will never fail* (Ps. 89:28); here *ḥesed* provides the basis on which God will maintain the covenant and ensure its continuation.

98. Eichrodt comments, 'to this *ḥesed*-Yahweh, on which man can rely in every distress, it also belongs to forgive transgressions and so to ensure that the covenant relationship is not destroyed by them' (*Theology*, 2:475).

trustworthiness and reliability.[99] It is precisely because it contains so many interrelated ideas that *ḥesed* so well expresses God's response to his people: his continued faithfulness and love towards them; his commitment to act in accordance with the covenant relationship, and, in graciously bearing with their failure, his commitment to seek the continuation of the relationship in the face of all that threatens it.

Ḥesed provides the basis on which the covenant between God and his people continues. The verb *'ahăbâ* and noun *'ahăbâ*, also translated 'love',[100] might be seen as the basis for God's choice of Israel in the first place (e.g. Deut. 4:37; 10:15; Mal. 1:2).[101] This love is *unconditional* (Deut. 7:7–8) and *everlasting* (Jer. 31:3). It is likened to the love between father and child (Hos. 11:1–4) and between husband and wife (Hos. 3:1; see also Jer. 2:2).[102]

These expressions express God's grace and favour towards, his deep feelings for, and his commitment to his people.[103] When Israel turns away from God's love, he feels the pain of rejection (e.g. Hos. 11:1–4, 8–9). Sin brings *wrath* (Jer. 2 – 3; Isa. 50:1), but God's love does not, therefore, come to an end. God's punishment is part of his love; it is *educative*, intended to make his people aware of the seriousness of their sin, and to lead them back to him (e.g. Hos. 2; 6:1–3; 11:10–11; cf. Heb. 12:5–6). And it is because of his love that God is willing to redeem and rescue his people (e.g. Deut. 7:8; Pss 44:26; 103:4; Isa. 63:9; Hos. 1:7; Zeph. 3:17).

Wrath[104]

In the extended summary of divine attributes in Exodus 34:6–7 the punishment of sin stands alongside God's faithfulness and love. This highlights the

99. Goldingay, *OT Theology*, 2:119–121; Jacob, *Theology*, pp. 103–107; see further R. W. L. Moberley, "*mn*', in *NIDOTTE* 1:427–433; A. Jepsen, "*āman*, etc.', in *TDOT* 1:292–323.

100. See e.g. Brueggemann, *Theology*, pp. 414–415; Eichrodt, *Theology*, 1:250–258; P. J. J. S. Els, "*hb*', in *NIDOTTE* 1:277–299; Jacob, *Theology*, pp. 108–113; Snaith, *Distinctive Ideas*, pp. 131–142; Jan Bergman, A. O. Haldar and G. Wallis, "*āhab*, etc.', in *TDOT* 1:99–118.

101. On the distinction between *ḥesed* and *'ahăbâ*, see Snaith, *Distinctive Ideas*, pp. 94–95.

102. See Eichrodt, *Theology*, 1:251–252.

103. For an overview of different aspects of God's love for his people, see Goldingay, *OT Theology*, 2:108–132.

104. See Brueggemann, *Theology*, pp. 227–228, 293–296; Goldingay, *OT Theology*, 2:135–170, 288–290; Jacob, *Theology*, pp. 114–117; Eichrodt, *Theology*, 1:258–269; Rendtorff, *Hebrew Bible*, pp. 627–630; Vriezen, *Outline*, pp. 303–307.

possibility of God's hostility. He is described as a *jealous God* (e.g. Deut. 4:24; 6:15; 32:16), who demands the sole allegiance of his people. And his anger burns against those things and people that offend him (e.g. Exod. 4:14; 32:10–11; Num. 11:1, 33; Deut. 29:20, 24; Ps. 89:46; Isa. 30:27; Jer. 7:20). Eichrodt regards this as further evidence of the personal character of God.[105] It is not, though, a spontaneous outburst in the face of minor annoyances. In the OT divine wrath is always fully justified.[106] This was not the case with other gods, who might visit their anger on human beings arbitrarily as a result of sudden fits of pique. In the Atrahasis Epic, for example, we see how the god Enlil became annoyed because the noise made by human beings disturbed his sleep, and as a result sent a flood to wipe out the whole human race.[107] When something so relatively trivial can have such devastating consequences, it is little wonder that people felt uncertain about the favour and intentions of the gods and went to great lengths to appease them. God's wrath may be associated with his displeasure, but it is not arbitrary. It is *retribution*, punishment for sin, which is related to falling short of requirements God has made known. Thus, though there will always be an element of mystery and inscrutability surrounding divine wrath, it is also predictable (e.g. Num. 25:3; Deut. 29:25–28; Josh. 7:1; 9:20; 2 Chr. 32:25; 36:16; Ps. 78:21; Isa. 5:22–25), and may be averted by repentance and obedience (e.g. Num. 16:46; 2 Chr. 12:7, 12; 32:26; Jer. 4:4).

Divine wrath may be directed against the sin, rebellion and pride of Israel (e.g. Deut. 6:13–15; Josh. 7:1; 1 Sam. 28:18–19; Isa. 10:5–6; Amos 2:4–16), and of other nations (e.g. Isa. 10:12–19, 25–27; Amos 1:3 – 2:3; Mic. 5:15; Zeph. 3:8). It breaks out against those who threaten the sanctity and inviolability of God's nature (e.g. Lev. 10:2; Num. 1:53; Ezek. 43:8; 48:11). Wrath has too an eschatological dimension; the *Day of the LORD* will be a Day of *wrath* (e.g. Ps. 110:5; Isa. 13:9–13; Zeph. 1:15; 2:2). But there is also the confident hope that God's wrath is not the last word (e.g. Jer. 32:37; Hos. 11:9; 14:4; see also Isa. 48:9–11; Ezek. 20:8–9): it is temporary and limited (e.g. Isa. 26:20; 40:1–2; Ezek. 16:42); in contrast to his *ḥesed*, which never fails (Pss 30:5; 103:9–14; Isa. 54:7–8). So, for example, God's punishment reaches to *the third and fourth*

---

105. Eichrodt, *Theology*, 1:258.

106. Even in the controversial case of God's wrath breaking out against Uzzah (2 Sam. 6:7) a reason is given: *because of [Uzzah's] irreverent act*. David's anger may have been because he felt God had acted unjustly; or maybe because he was forced to rethink his own plans (2 Sam. 6:9–10).

107. See Arnold and Beyer, *Readings*, pp. 21–31; E. A. Speiser and A. K. Grayson, 'Akkadian Myths and Epics', in *ANET*, pp. 60–119, 501–518 (104–106).

generation, while his *ḥesed* extends to *a thousand generations* (Exod. 20:5–6; see also 34:7).

The Spirit of God[108]

The Hebrew word for 'spirit', *rûaḥ*, has to do with the movement of air. Like its NT equivalent, the Greek word *pneuma*, it may mean also 'wind' or 'breath'. It refers to the breath that gives life to human flesh, and also to human feelings and disposition.

Rûaḥ *as a powerful wind*
When *rûaḥ* refers to the wind, it is often associated with the power of the storm (e.g. 1 Kgs 18:45; 2 Kgs 3:17; Pss 55:8; 148:8; Isa. 7:2; 41:16; Ezek. 1:4; 17:10). There is also a sense of mystery and awe. The wind is an agent of Yahweh: it does his bidding (Pss 135:7; 148:8); he rides on its wings (Pss 18:10; 104:3); it heralds his coming (1 Kgs 19:11; Ezek. 1:4), and it is a symbol of his wrath and judgment (e.g. Pss 11:6; 103:16; Isa. 17:13; Jer. 4:11–12; Ezek. 13:13; Hos. 13:15; cf. Isa. 4:4). God also used the wind to cause the flood to recede (Gen. 8:1) and to part the waters of the Red Sea (Exod. 14:21; cf. 15:8, 10; see also e.g. Exod. 10:13, 19; Num. 11:31; Isa. 11:15; Jon. 1:4; 4:8).

The Spirit of the Lord
The activity of the Spirit is the activity of God
In the OT the presence and activity of the Spirit is identified with the presence and activity of God himself (e.g. Pss 51:11; 143:10; Hag. 2:4–5; Zech. 4:6). Snaith defines *the Spirit of the Lord* as 'the manifestation in human

---

108. F. Baumgärtel et al., '*pneuma*, etc.', in *TDNT* 6:332–455 (359–368); J. D. G. Dunn, 'Spirit, Holy Spirit', in *IBD* 3:1478–1483 (1478–1480); Dyrness, *Themes*, pp. 86–87; Eichrodt, *Theology*, 2:46–68; J. D. G. Dunn, E. Kamlah and C. Brown, 'Spirit, Holy Spirit', in *DNTT* 3:689–709 (689–693); Köhler, *OT Theology*, pp. 111–119, 137–142; Michael Green, *I Believe in the Holy Spirit* (London: Hodder & Stoughton, 1975), pp. 18–31; Miles V. Van Pelt, Walter C. Kaiser, Jr., and Daniel I. Block, '*rûaḥ*', in *NIDOTTE* 3:1073–1078; John Rea, *The Holy Spirit in the Bible* (London: Marshall Pickering, 1992), pp. 17–116; Preuss, *Theology*, 1:160–163; Snaith, *Distinctive Ideas*, pp. 143–158; S. Tengström and Heinz-Josef Fabry, '*rûaḥ*', in *TDOT* 13:365–402; Christopher J. H. Wright, *Knowing the Holy Spirit Through the Old Testament* (Downers Grove: IVP, 2006).

experience of the life-giving, energy creating power of God';[109] Michael Green describes the Spirit as 'God in action for the benefit of his people',[110] and, according to John Goldingay, 'talk of the activity of God's Spirit is a First Testament way of describing God's activity in the world'.[111] An important passage here is Isaiah 63:7–14. This looks back on God's blessings at the time of the exodus and the ingratitude of the people who, in spite of all God had done for them, rebelled against him. In particular it recalls Exodus 33:14, where God says to Moses, *my Presence will go with you, and I will give you rest.* In Isaiah 63 it is God's *Spirit* who is among the people (v. 11), thus linking the Spirit with the divine presence, and it is also the Spirit who gives the people rest (v. 14). In this passage too the *Holy Spirit* is paralleled with God's *glorious arm of power* (v. 12). Through the Spirit, then, God is present in the world and among his people, and through the Spirit the divine life and power is made available to human beings, enabling them to be and to do what would otherwise not be possible. We note too the parallel in Isaiah 34:16 between God's *mouth*, which announces judgment, and the work of *his Spirit*, who will carry it out.

Because the Spirit is so closely identified with God and his action in the world, the OT writers do not generally view him in personal terms, though the idea that the Spirit can be *grieved* (Isa. 63:10) does appear to be moving towards the more personal view of the Spirit that we find in the NT (cf. Eph. 4:30).

The Spirit is powerful and mysterious

As when the term is applied to the wind, the *rûaḥ* of God is also portrayed as powerful and mysterious; it is like the driving wind: strong, unseen, uncontrollable and unpredictable (e.g. Isa. 40:7; 59:19). So, in 1 Kings 18:12, Obadiah portrays the *rûaḥ-yhwh* as a whirlwind that might carry Elijah away (see also e.g. 2 Kgs 2:16; Ezek. 3:14; 11:1; 43:5), and when Samson was attacked by a lion, *the Spirit of the LORD came upon him in power so that he tore the lion apart with his bare hands* (Judg. 14:6).

The Spirit imparts life

God's *rûaḥ* plays a part in enabling physical life. In Psalm 104:29–30 it refers both to God's Spirit and to the breath that animates human flesh: *when you take away their breath* [rûaḥ], / *they die and return to the dust.* / *When you send your Spirit*

109. Snaith, *Distinctive Ideas*, p. 153.

110. Green, *Holy Spirit*, p. 30.

111. Goldingay, *OT Theology*, 1:794.

[rûaḥ], / *they are created* – suggesting a close link between them (cf. Gen. 6:17; 7:15; Job 33:4; 34:14; Isa. 57:16).[112] The Spirit also brings spiritual life, renewal and refreshment. We see this, for example, in Ezekiel 37:1–14, where God's *rûaḥ* revives the dry bones of Israel. In these verses *rûaḥ* appears with a variety of meanings: as the *wind* (v. 9), as the *breath* that brings life to lifeless flesh (vv. 5, 9–10) and also as the *spirit of God* that brings spiritual life and renewal to his people (v. 14; see also Ezek. 36:26–27; cf. 11:19; 18:31). In several passages in the OT the Spirit is also likened to the rain, bringing life and fruitfulness (e.g. Isa. 32:15; 44:3–4; Joel 2:23–29).

The Spirit of God is also linked with creation. In Genesis 1:2 the *rûaḥ* of God hovers over the primeval waters prior to God's creative activity,[113] and in Job 26:12–13 God's *rûaḥ* is instrumental in the victory over primeval chaos, which is, again, associated with creation.[114] In Psalm 33:6 the *breath* [rûaḥ] *of his mouth* parallels *the word of Yahweh*, by which the heavens were created (cf. Ps. 104:30).

The Spirit enables prophecy

As just noted, in Psalm 33:6 the *word* and the *breath* [rûaḥ] of God are parallel: *By the word of the LORD were the heavens made, / their starry host by the breath of his mouth* (cf. 2 Sam. 23:2; Prov. 1:23; Isa. 59:21). This link is seen too in the close relationship in the OT between the Spirit of God and prophecy.[115] Prophesying is a sign of the Spirit coming upon a person; for example the elders of Israel (Num. 11:25–29), Saul (1 Sam. 10:6, 10; 19:23), Saul's men (1 Sam. 19:20) and, ultimately, all people (Joel 2:28; cf. Isa. 59:21). The Spirit inspires prophets, enabling them to speak God's word (e.g. Ezek. 11:5; Mic. 3:8). In Hosea 9:7 *prophet* is parallel to *inspired man* ('*îš hārûaḥ*, 'man of the spirit'; see also Num. 24:2; 2 Sam. 23:2; 2 Chr. 15:1; 20:14; 24:20; Neh. 9:30; Isa. 48:16; Ezek. 2:2; 3:24; Zech. 7:12).

---

112. I will say more about this when we look at the role of *rûaḥ* in human personality, below, pp. 144–147.

113. *Rûaḥ 'ĕlōhîm* (Gen. 1:2) may refer to a very powerful wind (interpreting *'ĕlōhîm* as a superlative) linked with the state of chaos described in the first two clauses of the verse. More likely, *'ĕlōhîm* refers to God, giving the translation 'Spirit/wind of God'. See the discussion by Hamilton, *Genesis 1–17*, pp. 111–117; Wenham, *Genesis 1–15*, pp. 16–17.

114. See below, pp. 127–130.

115. See e.g. Johannes Lindblom, *Prophecy in Ancient Israel* (Oxford: Blackwell, 1962), pp. 174–179.

It should be noted, though, that in the pre-exilic period there seems to be a reluctance to associate the Spirit with prophecy. Few of the pre-exilic prophets attribute their inspiration to the Spirit; indeed, Amos and Jeremiah do not refer to the Spirit at all in connection with their prophecies, and prefer to attribute them to the *word* of God (e.g. Amos 3:8; Jer. 20:9; 23:18). This lack of emphasis on the Spirit may have been to distance the later prophets from the (ecstatic) ravings that characterized prophets of other religions round about Israel, and also the false prophets in Israel who may have tried to emulate them.[116]

The Spirit is associated with skill and ability

This may sometimes appear as ordinary human ability, which is nevertheless seen to come from God – as in the case of the artistic skills of Bezalel and others appointed to work on the tabernacle (Exod. 31:3–4; 35:31; cf. 28:3). It may also be seen in a much more dramatic supernatural ability, such as the extraordinary strength of Samson (e.g. Judg. 14:6; 15:14–15).

The Spirit empowers for leadership

Moses, Israel's leader, was endowed with the Spirit; when leadership responsibility was delegated to the elders of Israel, the Spirit came upon them (Num. 11:17, 25). The Spirit also came upon Israel's judges; for example Othniel (Judg. 3:9–10), Gideon (Judg. 6:34), Jephthah (Judg. 11:29) and Samson (Judg. 13:25).

The oil with which kings were anointed was also seen as an indication of the presence of God's Spirit. When Samuel anointed Saul, he promised the Spirit would come upon him (1 Sam. 10:1, 6; 11:6), and when Saul was rejected as king, the Spirit left him (1 Sam. 16:14). The link between oil and Spirit is even clearer in the case of David: *so Samuel took the horn of oil and anointed him in the presence of his brothers, and from that day on the Spirit of the LORD came upon David in power* (1 Sam. 16:13). Another significant feature of the anointing of David was that while the Spirit came on Saul and on Israel's judges only at particular times in order to equip them for particular tasks, he came upon David *from that day on* – indicating a permanent endowment.

Anointing a person as king demonstrated both God's choice and his enabling. However, while it is likely to have been assumed, there is no mention of the role of the Spirit in connection with the anointing of any of the kings of Israel and Judah after David. This omission may be intentional, pointing to the general failure of the monarchy, in contrast to the Davidic ideal. However,

---

116. For further discussion, see e.g. Dunn, 'Spirit, Holy Spirit', *IBD* 3:1480; Rea, *Holy Spirit*, pp. 76–77; Lindblom, *Prophecy*, pp. 177–178.

despite that failure, there remained the hope of the Davidic Messiah, who, like David before him, would also be anointed and permanently endowed with the Spirit (Isa. 11:1–3). The *Servant of the LORD*, sometimes identified with the Messiah,[117] is also anointed with the Spirit, both for the kingly role of establishing justice (Isa. 42:1) and for the prophetic role of proclaiming God's word (Isa. 61:1; cf. Luke 4:18).

Though there is a link between prophetic inspiration and the Spirit, this does not appear to have been linked with a formal 'anointing'. Apart from the prophetic figure in Isaiah 61:1 and a parallel between *anointed ones* and *prophets* in 1 Chronicles 16:22 (Ps. 105:15), apparently referring to the patriarchs, the only OT reference to a prophet being anointed is when Elijah is sent to anoint Elisha as his successor (1 Kgs 19:16), and there the emphasis appears to be more on his being appointed to the task than being equipped for it.

Alongside kings and (possibly) prophets, priests were also anointed (e.g. Exod. 28:41; 30:30; 40:15; Num. 3:3). The anointing with oil may again symbolize the enabling presence of God's Spirit, though that is not explicitly stated.

The Holy Spirit

This expression occurs three times in the OT (Ps. 51:11; Isa. 63:10–11), and a similar designation, 'good Spirit', appears in Nehemiah 9:20 and Psalm 143:10. Since the presence of the Spirit indicates the presence of *God*, who is holy, certain ethical demands are inevitable. So, the sin of the people grieves the Spirit (Isa. 63:10), and in Psalm 51:11 the writer is aware that his sin might cause God to remove his Spirit. The title of the Psalm attributes it to David, and though these are later additions, they do form part of the canonical text. Associating the prayer with David does give it a particular poignancy, since removing his Spirit was just what God had done with David's predecessor, Saul (1 Sam. 16:14).

A corollary of this is that under the new covenant, God will enable his people to meet the demands of his holiness by putting his Spirit within them, giving a new heart and a new ability to fulfil his Law (Ezek. 36:26–27).

The Spirit and eschatology

There is a close association, particularly in the later prophetic writings, between the Spirit and the coming era of salvation. We have seen that the

---

117. We will look more closely below at both the Messiah (pp. 280–289) and the Servant (pp. 291–296).

agents of eschatological salvation, the Messiah and the Servant, will be endowed with the Spirit (Isa. 11:1–3; 42:1; 61:1). We see too that the promise of renewed blessing and prosperity in the coming age is associated with the pouring out of the Spirit (Isa. 32:15–20; 44:3–5). In that new age the Spirit will be poured out on the whole people (Isa. 59:21; Ezek. 39:29; Joel 2:28–29; Zech. 12:10; cf. Num. 11:29), bringing the necessary inward renewal that enables a closer and more immediate relationship with God (Ezek. 36:26–27; cf. Jer. 31:31–34).

The presence of Jesus inaugurates the kingdom of God, and with the coming of this new age, we see the development of several aspects of the Spirit's role. As in the OT, the prophetic ministry in the NT is also linked with the Spirit (1 Cor. 12:10), though now it will be more widespread, reflecting the universal pouring out of the Spirit in the coming age (e.g. Joel 2:28–29; cf. Acts 2:18), and other OT roles, such as enabling and equipping for leadership, power for ministry, renewal, and the giving of new life, have NT parallels. However, there is a development in the understanding of the role and activity of the Spirit, and we need to guard against reading our view of the Spirit, based on the NT and maybe on a particular denominational emphasis, back into the OT. So, for example, one NT manifestation of the Spirit that does not feature explicitly in the OT is *speaking in different kinds of tongues* (1 Cor. 12:10).[118]

Other supernatural beings in the Old Testament[119]

Demons[120]

Though demons and evil spirits feature prominently in later Judaism, there are few references to them in the OT. Deuteronomy 32:17 links the term *šēdîm*

---

118. In his discussion of speaking in tongues Paul refers to Isa. 28:11 (1 Cor. 14:21). This is not an OT example of the spiritual manifestation, but points to the judgment reflected in the foreign tongues of (Assyrian) invaders. The people have not listened to the prophets so God will speak to them in a different way. Paul uses this analogy to indicate how 'tongues' can be a sign of judgment, leading to conviction of sin.

119. The material in this section is adapted from my article 'An Evil Spirit from the Lord', *EQ* 70.1 (1998), pp. 3–22. See also Goldingay, *OT Theology*, 2:43–58; Preuss, *Theology*, 1:256–261.

120. See e.g. Eichrodt, *Theology*, 2:223–228; Jacob, *Theology*, pp. 68–72; H. Bietenhard, 'Demon, etc.', in *DNTT* 1:449–453 (450–452); Paul D. Hanson, 'Rebellion in

(demons) with Canaanite gods. Another term, *śā'îm*, refers to goatlike idols, which in popular mythology came to be regarded as demons, and were depicted occupying deserted ruins (Lev. 17:7; 2 Chr. 11:15; Isa. 13:21; 34:14). *lîlît* (Isa. 34:14) may be an oblique reference to the night demon referred to in rabbinic folklore, who was Adam's first wife but who left him and was later associated with the abduction of newborn infants.[121]

Another possible demonic figure is *'ăzā'zēl*. On the Day of Atonement a goat was sent into the desert, *la'ăzā'zēl* (Lev. 16:8–10, 26). The traditional interpretation of this Hebrew expression is 'as a scapegoat' (so NIV; see also AV); though a more literal translation is 'to Azazel' (so NRSV), maybe referring to a demonic being sometimes identified with Azael, a fallen angel who lived in the desert (*1 Enoch* 6 – 11).[122]

In the OT there is little evidence of 'demons' having any real power to exert influence over people's lives. Some passages link idolatry with the worship of demons (Deut. 32:17; Pss 96:5; 106:37), but this is generally to emphasize the inferiority of what people accept as a substitute for Yahweh, rather than to alert them to spiritual danger. Demonic activity was limited, mainly, to the desert, where it was outside the normal experience of God's people. The need to condemn various occult practices suggests that superstitious beliefs were common in Israel, probably through the combined influence of baggage from their pre-Yahwistic past and the current practices of their neighbours. The official view was that these things should be avoided, and if they were, their impact on the lives of God's people would be minimal.

One of the few alterations to this pattern is seen in the case of the *evil spirit from the LORD*, who afflicted Saul (1 Sam. 16:14). This passage has been interpreted in various ways. On balance I take it to refer to a spiritual being, who may be hostile to God, but is nevertheless subject to God's authority and may

---

Footnote 120 (*continued*)

    Heaven, Azazel and Euhemeristic Heroes in 1 Enoch 6–11', *JBL* 96 (1977),
    pp. 195–233; George W. E. Nickelsburg, 'Apocalyptic and Myth in 1 Enoch 6–11',
    JBL 96 (1977), pp. 383–405; Preuss, *Theology*, 1:258–259.

121. See e.g. Sawyer, *Fifth Gospel*, pp. 216–219.

122. Three things are noted in favour of viewing Azazel as a demon: the contrast with
    Yahweh (one goat for Yahweh, one for Azazel); the fact that the desert was seen
    as the haunt of demons; and the identification with Azael; see Jacob Milgrom,
    Leviticus 1–16, AB 3 (New York: Doubleday, 1991), pp. 1020–1022; Gordon J.
    Wenham, *Leviticus*, NICOT (London: Hodder & Stoughton, 1979), pp. 233–235;
    see also John E. Hartley, *Leviticus 1–27*, WBC 4 (Dallas: Word, 1992), pp. 236–238.

be pressed into his service. The *lying spirit* of 1 Kings 22:22 may be viewed in a similar way. However, these instances of spirits invading humankind's domain are rare in the OT and take place only at God's command.

Angels[123]

Significant among these heavenly servants are *angels*, described by the psalmist as *mighty ones who do [Yahweh's] bidding, who obey his word* (Ps. 103:20). They perform various functions, including guarding and guiding God's people (e.g. Gen. 24:7; 48:16; Exod. 23:20; Ps. 91:11–12; Dan. 3:25). They are also instruments of divine judgment. Exodus 12:23 refers to *the destroyer* (*mašḥît*); an angel causes plague in Israel (2 Sam. 24:15–16; 1 Chr. 21:14–16); and *destroying angels* (*mal'ăkê rā'îm*) are responsible for disaster befalling Egypt (Ps. 78:49). Singled out within the general category of angelic beings are the cherubim (e.g. Gen. 3:24; Exod. 25:18–22; Isa. 37:16; Ezek. 9:3) and the seraphim (Isa. 6:2, 6). Archangels, Gabriel and Michael, are named for the first time in the book of Daniel; later writings identify others.[124]

The *angel of the* LORD is probably to be understood in a different way, as the personal representative of God, who speaks for Yahweh and is, in many cases, identified with him (e.g. Gen. 16:7–13; 22:15–18; Exod. 3:2–6; Judg. 6:11–16; Zech. 3:1–2; though note Zech. 1:12).[125]

Later Jewish writings refer to a *rebellion in heaven*. Its instigator, who fell and dragged other angels with him, is given various names: Semihazah, Azael (Azazel) or Satan.[126] Some see a possible allusion to the banishment of a heavenly being (Lucifer) from heaven in Isaiah 14:12–15, which is widely believed to contain ideas drawn from pagan mythology.[127] In the immediate

123. See further e.g. Eichrodt, *Theology*, 2:194–209; Jacob, *Theology*, pp. 68–69; H. Bietenhard and P. J. Budd, 'Angel, etc.', in *DNTT* 1:101–105 (101–102); Köhler, *OT Theology*, pp. 157–160; Preuss, *Theology*, 1:256–258; A. S. Rappoport, *Ancient Israel: Myths and Legends*, 3 vols. (London: Senate, 1995), 1:28–54; Rendtorff, *Hebrew Bible*, pp. 599–601.

124. Other archangels are Raphael, Uriel, Metatron, Sandalphon and Rediyao.

125. See Goldingay, *OT Theology*, 2:48–50; Preuss, *Theology*, 1:165–166; Rendtorff, *Hebrew Bible*, p. 600.

126. See Hanson, 'Rebellion', pp. 195–233; Nickelsburg, 'Apocalyptic', pp. 383–405. Neil Forsyth, *The Old Enemy* (Princeton: Princeton University Press, 1987), pp. 124–191.

127. See Eichrodt, *Theology*, 2:208; Ronald E. Clements, *Isaiah 1–39*, NCB (London: Marshall, Morgan & Scott, 1980), pp. 142–143; Goldingay, *OT Theology*, 2:785–787; J. A. Motyer, *The Prophecy of Isaiah* (Leicester: IVP, 1993), p. 144; John N. Oswalt, *The Book of Isaiah, 1–39*, NICOT (Grand Rapids: Eerdmans, 1986), pp. 320–321.

context the passage relates to the pride of the king of Babylon, whose desire to exalt himself against God results in his being cast down; but it may have a wider reference to an evil being who is the epitome and the inspiration of all such evil ambition (cf. Luke 10:18). Ezekiel 28:1–10 points to the downfall of the ruler [prince] of Tyre because of his boasts. Though this proud ruler claims, *I am a god* (v. 2), he will discover that he is in fact only human. In the following lament for the *king of Tyre* (28:11–19) the language takes on a different tone and makes greater use of mythological imagery. It is sometimes argued that the passage draws on Paradise myths about primal man, and his loss of perfect fellowship with God, which is now paralleled in the downfall of the king of Tyre.[128] Again, though, it may be possible to see here a reference to the fall of a once-exalted heavenly being.[129] In neither case, however, do the OT writers link this figure directly with Satan. This 'rebellion in heaven' theme is evident in myths throughout the ANE,[130] where it is frequently associated with primeval history and seeks to account for the presence of evil in the world.

Sons of God and the divine council[131]

The term *bĕnē hā'ĕlōhîm*, translated 'sons of God' or 'sons of the gods', is used on several occasions in the OT to denote supernatural beings (e.g. Deut. 32:8; Job 1:6; 2:1; 38:7).[132] Following the LXX (and the Dead Sea Scrolls), the preferred reading of Deuteronomy 32:8–9 replaces 'sons of Israel' with 'sons of God':

---

128. See Walter Eichrodt, *Ezekiel*, OTL (London: SCM, 1970), pp. 392–395; John B. Taylor, *Ezekiel*, TOTC (Leicester: IVP, 1969), pp. 196–197; John W. Wevers, *Ezekiel*, NCB (London: Marshall, Morgan & Scott), pp. 156–158.

129. Note e.g. his description in Ezek. 28:14 as a *guardian cherub*.

130. Hanson, 'Rebellion', pp. 4–6; see also e.g. Forsyth, *Old Enemy*, pp. 67–89, 124–133.

131. See G. Cooke, 'The Sons of (the) God(s)', *ZAW* 76 (1964), pp. 41–42, 22–47; Day, *Yahweh*, pp. 22–24; F. M. Cross, 'The Council of Yahweh in 2nd Isaiah', *JNES* 12 (1953), pp. 274–277; Goldingay, *OT Theology*, 2:44–46, 57–57; H. Wheeler Robinson, 'The Council of Yahweh', *JTS* 45 (1944), pp. 151–157; G. E. Wright, *The Old Testament against its Environment*, SBT 2 (London: SCM, 1950), pp. 30–41.

132. Other terms that may denote supernatural beings include 'gods' (Ps. 82:1); 'mighty ones' (Ps. 103:20); 'holy ones' (Deut. 33:2–3; Ps. 89:5–7; Isa. 13:3; Dan. 4:17); heavenly 'host' (1 Kgs 22:19; Pss 103:21; 148:2; Dan. 8:10), 'watchers' (Dan. 4:13, 23); 'princes' (Dan. 10:13, 20–21; 12:1).

> *When the Most High gave the nations their inheritance,*
>   *when he divided all mankind,*
> *he set up boundaries for the peoples*
>   *according to the number of the sons of God [see NIV n.].*
> *For the LORD's portion is his people,*
>   *Jacob his allotted inheritance.*

This suggests that while God has chosen Israel for himself, he has also appointed heavenly guardians over the other nations, an idea more fully developed in the book of Daniel (e.g. 10:13, 20–21). Similar terms in Job 1:6, 2:1 and Psalm 82:1, 6 probably refer to members of a heavenly council. The idea of a divine court presided over by the chief god of the pantheon was common in the ANE and reflects the view that the earthly order with its kings and court officials is a reflection of the heavenly realm. The OT picture, though, is distinctive. Within this council, Yahweh's authority is undisputed; other members may have a voice, but ultimately must submit to his control. Francis Andersen makes this important observation:

> the incomparable Lord has no colleagues; his attendants are shadows, scarcely persons . . . so minor is their role, so completely dominated by the incontestable sovereignty of the Lord, that no ideas of polytheism are present, even when they are called '(children of) god(s)'.[133]

A significant aspect of the divine assembly is its role with regard to prophecy. Jeremiah claims that he is set apart as a true prophet because he is admitted to the *council of the LORD* (Jer. 23:18, 22), and it is from there that he receives his message. The idea of a true prophet being granted access to the heavenly court is also found in 1 Kings 22:19–23.

Another significant feature of this council is the presence there of beings who may not generally be regarded as Yahweh's faithful servants. It may include the *sons of God* of Genesis 6:1–4, widely viewed as fallen angels,[134] and

---

133. Francis I. Andersen, *Job*, TOTC (Leicester: IVP, 1976), p. 82.

134. See e.g. Wenham, *Genesis 1–15*, pp. 139–140; Hamilton, *Genesis 1–17*, pp. 261–272; David J. A. Clines, 'The Significance of the "Sons of God" Episode (Genesis 6:1–4) in the Context of the "Primal History" (Genesis 1–11)', *JSOT* 13 (1979), pp. 34–46; Lyle Eslinger, 'A Contextual Identification of the *běnê hā'ĕlōhîm* and *běnôt hā'ādām* in Genesis 6:1–4', *JSOT* 13 (1979), pp. 65–73; Forsyth, *Old Enemy*, pp. 147–159.

also the national guardians, who are criticized for their failure to maintain justice in Psalm 82 and who appear as opponents of God in Daniel. Another being with access to the divine council is Satan.

Satan

In Job, when the *sons of God* present themselves to God, *the Satan* (*haśāṭān*), a term probably related to the Hebrew word for 'adversary' (Num. 22:22), came with them (Job 1:6; 2:1). It has been suggested that (the) Satan in this context is not an enemy of God, but appears as a kind of public prosecutor (Job 1:9–11; 2:4–5; see also Zech. 3:1),[135] whose task, like the roving secret police of the Persian Empire, was to spy on the disaffected and report disloyalty to the king.[136] Such a role, it is argued, does not presuppose an evil character; when he calls into question the piety of Job (1:9–11; 2:4–5) or accuses the high priest, Joshua (Zech. 3:1), he is only doing his duty. It has also been suggested that the 'watchers' (Dan. 4:13, 23) assisted (the) Satan in this role of keeping an eye on human affairs.

The view of Satan develops through the OT. We see this in the parallel accounts of David's census. In 2 Samuel 24:1 God incites David to number the people; in 1 Chronicles 21:1, it is Satan (now a proper name) who does it. The first passage reflects the theological principle that God is sovereign and everything, good or bad, is ultimately attributable to him. By the time Chronicles was written (in the fourth century BC) the idea had developed of a definite supernatural being opposed to God, to whom evil could be attributed; though there is never the suggestion that Satan is God's equal.

We see something of this development in the intertestamental book of *Jubilees*. In the midrash on Exodus 14:8 (*Jubilees* 48.12–18) the hardening of Pharaoh's heart, originally described as the work of Yahweh, is attributed to the demonic figure Mastema (also called Belial) who, in this later work, has replaced Semihazah and Azael as leader of the angelic rebellion and is also identified with Satan (*Jubilees* 10.11). Mastema is also responsible for the demand that Abraham sacrifice Isaac (*Jubilees* 7:15 – 18:19) and for the attack on Moses (Exod. 4:24; cf. *Jubilees* 48.1–3). In these later writings Satan's evil character and enmity against God are also more pronounced. He is still the accuser of men, but is also linked with the serpent that tempted Eve (Wisdom

---

135. See e.g. Eichrodt, *Theology*, 2:205–209; Goldingay, *OT Theology*, 2:54–55; Jacob, *Theology*, pp. 70–72; H. Bietenhard, C. Brown and J. Stafford Wright, 'Satan, etc.', in *DNTT* 3:468–477 (468–472); Preuss, *Theology*, 1:259–261.

136. See e.g. Naftali H. Tur-Sinai, *The Book of Job* (Jerusalem: Kiryath-Sepher, 1957).

of Solomon 2.24), whose aim is to disrupt the relationship between God and Israel and to separate humankind from God.

In the prologue to Job it is difficult to regard the Satan as one of God's loyal servants. He appears as the enemy of God's people, resorting to insinuation to accuse Job and pursuing enthusiastically his task of persecution. In Zechariah 3:2 God's words to Satan are hardly those of one addressing a servant only doing his duty. Even at this stage Satan's hostility is recognized; the later understanding enlarges on a characteristic already present. Jacob, for example, suggests that

> the identification of the serpent with Satan which is stated for the first time in the Wisdom of Solomon (2:24) and which passed into the New Testament (Rom. 16.20; Rev. 12.9 and 20.2) only draws the final consequences of what the story-teller in Genesis had already glimpsed.[137]

We have noted already that, according to later Jewish traditions, Satan (under various names) was the leader of a heavenly rebellion against God, and was cast out of heaven. In some literature he is given the name Sammael and is presented as first among the seraphim and the greatest of God's created beings, but with ambitions to take God's place. Some of these later developments are evident in the NT. So far as the OT is concerned, though, there are few clear references, and the picture is therefore sketchy.

---

137. Jacob, *Theology*, p. 282. Goldingay seems to say something similar: 'the adversary is not an embodiment of evil, but a being subordinate to God who is used by God to "test" his servants (including Jesus)' (*OT Theology*, 1:796–797); however, he suggests this testing was done from 'malicious motives' (1:133), and sees (the) Satan alongside the Snake, the Dragon and the Devil as figures emphasizing 'different aspects of the reality of evil' (1:134).

3. GOD AND CREATION

Origins[1]

Ideas of creation in the ancient Near East
Other creation accounts
The Genesis accounts of creation and the flood have points of contact with the primeval histories of Israel's neighbours, though in general, differences far

---

1. See Bernard W. Anderson, *From Creation to New Creation: Old Testament Perspectives*, OBT (Minneapolis: Fortress, 1994); *Contours*, pp. 87–97; Brueggemann, *Theology*, pp. 528–551; Childs, *Biblical Theology* (1992), pp. 384–412; Drane, *Introducing the OT*, 253–266; Dyrness, *Themes*, pp. 62–73; Eichrodt, *Theology*, 2:93–117; Terence E. Fretheim, *God and World in the Old Testament: A Relational Theology of Creation* (Nashville: Abingdon, 2005); Goldingay, *OT Theology*, 1:42–130; Richard S. Hess and David T. Tsumura (eds.), *I Studied Inscriptions From Before the Flood*, SBTS 4 (Winona Lake: Eisenbrauns, 1994); House, *OT Theology*, pp. 58–64; Jacob, *Theology*, pp. 136–150; Kaiser, *OT Theology*, pp. 71–77; A. S. Kapelrud, 'The Mythical Features of Genesis 1', *VT* 24 (1974), pp. 178–186; George A. F. Knight, *A Christian Theology of the Old Testament* (London: SCM, 1959), pp. 107–118; *Theology in Pictures* (Edinburgh: Handsel, 1981); Köhler, *OT Theology*, pp. 85–88; Preuss, *OT Theology*, 1:226–239; von Rad, *OT Theology*, 1:136–153; John W. Rogerson, 'Creation and Origin Stories', in

outweigh similarities. One text, the Babylonian Epic of Creation, which takes its name from its first two words, *Enuma Elish*, 'when on high', is claimed to have close parallels with Genesis and is sometimes referred to as 'the Babylonian Genesis'. It describes the victory of Marduk, the city god of Babylon, over Apsu and Tiamat (who represent the waters of primeval chaos) and Marduk's installation as king among the gods. After killing Tiamat, Marduk divided her body to form heaven and earth, and from the blood of her consort and the commander of Tiamat's armies, Kingu, he created human beings to do the work of the gods and so allow the gods to live at ease.[2] We have already noted the Atrahasis Epic, which is concerned mainly with a universal flood. It does not describe the creation of the world, but does include a detailed account of the creation of human beings. An underclass of gods responsible for work on earth went on strike. To resolve the problem, the ringleader of the rebellion was killed, and from his blood, mixed with clay, seven pairs of human beings were created – again to do the work and so to free the gods from labour. It is a common view that the idea of God as creator found in Genesis and Deutero-Isaiah arose during the exile and was influenced by these Mesopotamian creation stories. Gunkel, in common with many at the end of the nineteenth and beginning of the twentieth centuries, regarded the Genesis account as little more than a Judaized version of *Enuma Elish*,[3] though that

---

Philip R. Davies and John W. Rogerson, *The Old Testament World*, 2nd ed. (London: T. & T. Clarke; Louisville: Westminster John Knox, 2005), pp. 111–123; Claus Westermann, *Creation* (London: SPCK, 1974); Walton, *ANE Thought*; David Wilkinson, *The Message of Creation: Encountering the Lord of the Universe*, BST (Leicester: IVP, 2002); Ellen Van Wolde, *Stories of the Beginning: Genesis 1–11 and Other Creation Stories* (London: SCM, 1996).

2. See Arnold and Beyer, *Readings*, pp. 31–50; Speiser and Grayson, 'Akkadian Myths', in *ANET*, pp. 60–119, 501–518 (60–72, 501–503); J. V. Kinnier Wilson, 'The Epic of Creation', in *DOTT*, pp. 3–16.

3. Hermann Gunkel, 'The Influence of Babylonian Mythology upon the Biblical Creation Story', in Bernard W. Anderson (ed.), *Creation in the Old Testament*, IRT 6 (London: SPCK, 1984), pp. 25–52; *Schöpfung und Chaos in Urzeit und Endzeit* (Göttingen: Vandenhoeck & Ruprecht, 1895), trans. K. William Whitney, Jr., as *Creation and Chaos in the Primeval Era and the Eschaton: A Religio-Historical Study of Genesis 1 and Revelation 12* (Grand Rapids: Eerdmans, 2006); however, see e.g. Drane, *Introducing the OT*, pp. 261–263; Eichrodt, *Theology*, 2:113–117; Enns, *Inspiration*, pp. 23–29, 39–41; Wilson, 'Epic of Creation', in *DOTT*, p. 14; Kenneth A. Kitchen, *The Bible in its World* (Downers Grove: IVP, 1977), pp. 26–27; W. G. Lambert,

view is not widespread today. More recently scholars have recognized links with Canaanite/Ugaritic myths.

The exile was a formative time in the development of Israel's theology. The destruction of Jerusalem and the temple, and exile from the land, led to a serious evaluation of the nation's relationship with God, and to questions of how to maintain that relationship within a hostile, polytheistic culture. This is reflected in the theology of creation. It is a common view that the P source (which includes Gen. 1) is post-exilic and focuses on creation to emphasize the power and majesty of God over against the gods of Babylon. If so, the biblical account should be seen not as dependent on Babylonian myths but as polemic against them. Where there is similar language and even deliberate allusions, the purpose is to emphasize the superiority of Israel's God. He, not the Babylonian chaos monsters, existed first, and he called the universe into being. This emphasis would also serve to reassure the people that God has final authority in the history of his people.

As we have noted, there are questions about the dating of sources of the Pentateuch. There is also a growing recognition that mythological imagery in the OT has closer links with Ugarit than with Mesopotamia. There may be allusions to Mesopotamian myths, but these myths were probably known throughout the ANE well before the exile. Whenever it was written, though, the biblical account of creation, emphasizing God's priority and power over against that of other gods, would have taken on a new significance during the exile. We see this renewed emphasis too in Isaiah 40 – 55. At a time when God's people saw little of his activity in history, they focused, instead, on his power over nature, and on the fact that the God who created heaven and earth could give his people a new beginning (e.g. Isa. 40).

Myth in the Old Testament[4]
What is 'myth'?
Childs notes two basic definitions of myth. For one he quotes Gunkel, 'Myths

---

Footnote 3 (*continued*)
> 'A New Look at the Babylonian Background of Genesis', *JTS* 16 (1965), pp. 285–
> 300; E. Leach, *Genesis as Myth and Other Essays* (London: Cape, 1969), pp. 7–23;
> Alan R. Millard, 'A New Babylonian "Genesis" Story', *TynBul* 18 (1967), pp. 3–18;
> Walton, *ANE Thought*, pp. 43–83, 179–199.

4. See further e.g. Bernard W. Anderson, *Creation versus Chaos: The Re-Interpretation of Mythical Symbolism in the Bible* (New York: Association Press, 1967), pp. 11–42; Brevard S. Childs, *Myth and Reality in the Old Testament* (London: SCM, 1960); Drane,

are . . . stories about gods.'[5] The second, broader definition, considers myths to be stories that reflect an early stage of humankind's intellectual development and attempt to attribute events and phenomena that cannot be explained within that pre-scientific world view to supernatural intervention by gods or other beings. Thus myths are not simply fiction; they convey a basic truth: they are reflections on what has taken place, through which people express their view of the world and their understanding of reality.

Viewed in this way, parts of the OT may be described as myth, though the term needs to be used with caution. As I have emphasized, the biblical material was written in a way that was intelligible to its first audience. As God's Word, the Scriptures have continuing relevance for every generation, including our own. However, they originated at particular points in history, addressed to particular people and situations, and it was necessary to present the truths they contain in ways appropriate to the understanding and world view of those who first received their message. Since mythological language and imagery were common currency at the time, it is unsurprising that the OT writers would employ them in their writings. This is not to suggest that they simply borrowed them or that they subscribed to the religious views behind them – and the imagery has often been transformed so as to be a polemic against other religious views. However, this was a useful way of presenting truths that could not easily be expressed in other ways at the time.

Chaoskampf[6]

The term *Chaoskampf* refers to the common depiction of creation as a battle between the creator god and the powers of chaos, usually represented by the

---

Introducing the OT, pp. 260–266; Dyrness, *Themes*, pp. 68–73; Enns, *Inspiration*, pp. 39–41, 49–56; Robert S. Fyall, *Now my Eyes Have Seen you: Images of Creation in the Book of Job*, NSBT 12 (Leicester: Apollos; Downers Grove: IVP, 2002), pp. 26–28; Knight, *Theology in Pictures*, pp. xi–xiii; Walton, *ANE Thought*, pp. 43–44; Claus Westermann, 'Biblical Reflection on Creator–Creation', in B. W. Anderson, *Creation in the OT*, pp. 90–101; *Creation*, pp. 12–15.

5. Childs, *Myth*, p. 15.

6. See B. W. Anderson, *Creation versus Chaos; Creation to New Creation*, pp. 20–22, 34–38, 75–80, 195–198; Brueggemann, *Theology*, pp. 147, 656–657; John Day, *God's Conflict with the Dragon and the Sea: Echoes of a Canaanite Myth* (Cambridge: Cambridge University Press, 1985); *Yahweh*, pp. 98–107; Drane, *Introducing the OT*, pp. 260–261; William J. Dumbrell, *The Faith of Israel: A Theological Survey of the Old Testament*, 2nd ed. (Grand Rapids: Baker; Leicester: Apollos, 2002), pp. 14–15; Fretheim, *God and World*, pp. 43–46; Fyall, *Now my Eyes*, pp. 83–100, 157–174; Gerstenberger, *Theologies*,

primeval waters and the monsters that rise from them. *Chaoskampf* is a characteristic theme of the Babylonian creation epic, *Enuma Elish*, and there are elements of it in the Ugaritic myth that describes the victory of Baal over the sea god, Yam,[7] though this is not strictly a creation myth. A version of this motif may be found in the OT. Some passages refer to Leviathan, a chaos monster defeated by Baal (e.g. Ps. 74:14; Isa. 27:1), and Rahab (e.g. Job 26:12; Isa. 51:9), who may be another such monster. There are also references to *tannîn*, a more general term for 'sea monster' or 'dragon' (e.g. Ps. 74:13; Isa. 27:1). Gunkel suggested that 'the deep' (*tĕhôm*) in Genesis 1:2 is a reference to the Babylonian Tiamat. However, though the terms may have a common root, there is no direct link between them, and any suggestion of dependence is ill-founded:[8] in fact there is no immediate indication of the *Chaoskampf* motif in Genesis 1. Even so, the use of cognate terms indicates a narrative correspondence: the reference to *tĕhôm* and to dividing the waters is likely to have brought the Babylonian myth to mind, though in its present context this would have been, primarily, to highlight theological differences.

Although the mythological language and imagery found in some OT passages may have had wide circulation in the ANE, the OT writers use it in a

---

Footnote 6 (*continued*)

pp. 242–244; Goldingay, *OT Theology*, 1:79–82; 2:718–730; Gunkel, 'Babylonian Mythology', in B. W. Anderson, *Creation in the OT*, pp. 35–44; *Creation and Chaos*; Dennis J. McCarthy, 'Creation Motifs in Ancient Hebrew Poetry', in B. W. Anderson, *Creation in the OT*, pp. 74–89; Jon D. Levenson, *Creation and the Persistence of Evil: The Jewish Drama of Divine Omnipotence* (Princeton: Princeton University Press, 1994); Preuss, *Theology*, 1:235–236; Rendtorff, *Hebrew Bible*, pp. 418–426. For a contrasting view, see also David T. Tsumura, *The Earth and the Waters in Genesis 1 and 2: A Linguistic Investigation*, JSOTSup 83 (Sheffield: Sheffield Academic Press, 1989), revised and expanded in David T. Tsumura, *Creation and Destruction: A Reappraisal of the Chaoskampf Theory in the Old Testament* (Winona Lake: Eisenbrauns, 2005); see also Rebecca S. Watson, *Chaos Uncreated: A Reassessment of the Theme of "Chaos" in the Hebrew Bible*, BZAW 341 (Berlin: de Gruyter, 2005).

7. Arnold and Beyer, *Readings*, pp. 50–62; Ginsberg, 'Ugaritic Myths', in *ANET*, pp. 129–155; Gray, 'Texts from Ras Shamrah', in *DOTT*, pp. 129–133.

8. Tsumura's detailed linguistic study rightly rules out any idea that *tĕhôm* is a depersonalized or demythologized form of Tiamat, and that its use in Gen. 1 implies any kind of dependence on *Enuma Elish* (*Creation and Destruction*, pp. 36–57).

distinctive way.[9] The imagery is removed from its original (pagan) setting and given new meaning and significance. Rather than depicting rival gods fighting for power, the OT emphasizes that there is only one God who is the Lord of heaven and earth. And where the *Chaoskampf* motif appears in this context, it is concerned, primarily, not with God's initial victory in a cosmic pre-creation battle but with his ongoing power over creation and his ongoing presence in the world.[10] Thus mythological imagery may express God's power over nature (e.g. Ps. 93:1–4). It may also be reapplied to the events of Israel's history. The surging waters are often taken to symbolize the Red Sea, dried up to make a way for Israel to cross (e.g. Pss 74:12–17; 77:16–19; Isa. 51:9–10). In Psalm 46 the roaring seas quelled in the creation myth (vv. 2–3) are identified with threatening nations subdued before God (v. 6).

Elsewhere too sea monsters symbolize Israel's historical enemies. Because of the close link between *Chaoskampf* and the parting of the Red Sea at the exodus, Egypt is most frequently portrayed in this way. It is represented by Leviathan (Ps. 74:14), by Rahab (Ps. 87:4; Isa. 30:7; 51:9) and by *tannîn* (Ezek. 29:3–5; 32:2–8). This last term is also applied to Babylon (Jer. 51:34). Leviathan in Isaiah 27:1 may represent a particular enemy, but is probably to be seen more generally as human power in opposition to God, which will finally be overthrown. God's victory over the monsters of Chaos at creation is thus brought into the present. Chaos and disorder still threaten to disrupt God's purposes;[11] monsters, in the form of oppressive nations or of idolatry and unbelief still threaten the life and faith of God's people, but they too will be defeated. And in the vision of the future this motif is remythologized and given an apocalyptic setting: the primordial battle that resulted in creation and the defeat of rebellious and chaotic elements will be repeated in the eschatological overthrow of evil and the promise of the arrival of a new creation (e.g. Isa. 24:21–23; 27:1). This way of looking at the future in terms of the past is sometimes known as *Urzeit wird Endzeit* (primal history becomes the end time); the end of time is therefore a reflection of what happened at the

---

9. This distinctive use indicates that OT writers in no way accepted the substance of ANE myths; nevertheless it is likely that the language is intended to recall some of the elements of the *Chaoskampf* myth. The idea was used to highlight aspects of God's activity in the world by OT writers who also emphasized differences between their theology and world view and that of their contemporaries in the ANE.

10. Rendtorff, *Hebrew Bible*, pp. 420–421.

11. See below, pp. 133–136.

beginning.[12] Mythological imagery thus enables the OT writers to show God's victory in creation as a past event, a present reality and a future hope.

Ancient Near Eastern cosmology

Another area of comparison between the OT and the ANE is in the cosmology they present. There is a temptation in some circles to try to fit the description of the cosmos in Genesis into a modern scientific setting. It is likely, though, that the OT writers' understanding of issues such as creation and the flood has much in common with their contemporaries in Ugarit and Mesopotamia, which is why there may be similarities in the way the stories are told.

In OT cosmology the earth is surrounded by sky, a solid expanse that holds back the waters above it (Gen. 1:6–7). There are also the waters under the earth (Gen. 7:11). The sun, moon and stars are set in the sky (Gen. 1:14–18). Several passages also refer to the foundations of the earth (e.g. 2 Sam. 22:16; Pss 82:5; 102:25; 104:5; Prov. 8:29; Isa. 24:18; 48:13; 51:13, 16; Zech. 12:1), and the place of the dead, Sheol (šĕʾōl),[13] was thought to be located somewhere in the depths of the earth (Job 11:8; Ps. 86:13; Prov. 9:18; Amos 9:2). The general picture was similar in other parts of the ANE. In Babylon there were three heavens and three levels of earth. In Egypt the sky was sometimes represented by the goddess Nut arching over the earth, and sometimes by a cow.

Interpreting Genesis 1 – 11 theologically?

Some take the stories in Genesis 1 – 11 of the creation, the fall,[14] the flood, the Tower of Babel and so on to refer to literal, historical events. And, of course, none of these things is beyond God's power. However, important though the question of historicity may be,[15] that is not central to these

---

12. This term is associated with Gunkel (*Creation and Chaos*); see also B. W. Anderson, *Creation versus Chaos*, pp. 114–115; *Creation to New Creation*, pp. 34–38, 196–198; Day, *Yahweh*, pp. 105–107.

13. For further discussion of Sheol, see below, pp. 304–306.

14. By this term we refer to the sin of Adam and Eve and the judgment that followed (Gen. 3). The question of whether 'fall' is an appropriate term is discussed below, pp. 154–156.

15. I have voiced, already, opposition to an ahistorical view of OT narrative (above, pp. 62–63). A text that purports to be reporting history should be assumed to have a degree of historical veracity. However, the genre of Gen. 1 – 11 is different; it does not attempt to set events within a historical setting (as e.g. the patriarchal narratives do), and instead refers back to an indefinable past age (e.g. Gen. 1:1; 2:4; 6:1, 4; 11:1).

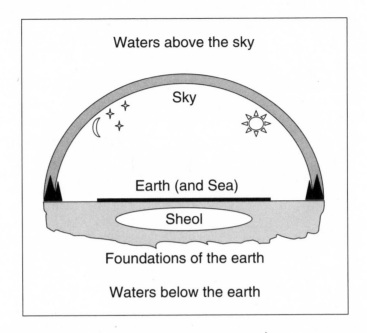

chapters; the main issue here is their theological significance. Genesis 1 – 11 is 'primeval history' or 'prehistory'. It is concerned with beginnings: the origin of the world, and also the origin of things that play an important part in the lives of human beings, such as sin, death, marriage, conflict (between husband and wife, within families and communities and between nations), the nature of God and his relationship with human beings, judgment, forgiveness and covenant. The OT believers are confronted with the same world as their counterparts in Babylon and Ugarit. They are also aware of the mythologies of surrounding nations, in which those nations seek to account for the world as they see it, though from a very different perspective; and they present their own explanation of the way things are, an explanation that puts God at the centre. That is not to suggest that this is a human attempt to explain origins. It continues to be divine revelation, but revelation given in a form that would make most sense to those who received it, rather than necessarily appealing to modern standards of scientific and historical enquiry.[16] Genesis 1 – 11 also describes the ever-deepening decline into sin,

---

16. We have already noted the discussion of this by Enns, *Inspiration*, pp. 39–41, 49–56; see also Goldingay, *OT Theology*, 1:876–883.

and so prepares for the story of salvation, and the call of Abraham in Genesis 12.

Features of the biblical account of creation
God's transcendence
Other creation accounts display religion that is polytheistic and naturalistic. Natural forces and elements in the physical world are identified with gods who emerge from the primordial chaos. In contrast the Bible depicts only one God, who exists independently of the world and who calls it into being. In the OT, even when similar language and imagery is used, natural forces are not deified. It is possible that the description of the sun in Psalm 19:4–6 reflects ANE myths about the sun god. However, the psalmist has radically changed their character. The sun is not a separate god but a part of God's handiwork: he has made it, he assigns it its place and it fulfils the very physical function of providing heat and light.[17] As we have already noted, God's creative activity is a key distinction that sets him apart from other so-called gods of the nations.

God's immanence
As its creator, the world belongs to God (e.g. Pss 24:1–2; 95:4–5). He has not set it up with its physical laws in place and left it to continue alone. He continues to take care of it: he orders the seasons (Gen. 8:22), provides water and makes grass grow (Ps. 104:13–14), sends lightning, wind and rain (Jer. 10:13; 51:16), brings out the stars (Isa. 40:26; Job 38 – 39) and sustains life (Job 34:14–15; Ps. 104:29). The prosperity and blessings of the land are attributed to God's ongoing activity (e.g. Deut. 28:1–14; Ps. 65:9–13; Hos. 2:8–9); when he withdraws his presence, the blessings fail (e.g. Deut. 28:15–63). In Isaiah 40 – 66 God's creative power is a source of his people's confidence: the God of nature is also the God of history who can be relied upon for deliverance (Isa. 40:21–31; 42:5–6; 43:1; 45:11–13; 48:12–15; 51:9–16; 65:17–25; see also e.g. Pss 74:12–23; 136). God's creative power and continuing activity, bringing order out of chaos, light out of darkness and life out of death, gives hope to his people.

God is also involved in the affairs of individuals and nations to bring his purposes to fulfilment (e.g. Isa. 46:10; Dan. 4:35). This may take place by direct intervention, through miracles, where the laws of nature are temporarily suspended, and also indirectly, by influencing the course of historical events

---

17. See Goldingay, *OT Theology*, 1:91.

and moving them towards their divinely appointed goal, but without any obvious intervention. This idea of providence as, what Eichrodt terms, 'God's guiding of human destinies',[18] will be considered in more detail below, when we look at God and the nations.

Creation by God's word

The OT sometimes describes God as a potter moulding clay (e.g. Job 10:9; Isa. 45:9; Jer. 18:6–7), but this is usually in connection not with the creation of the world but with the fashioning of its peoples, and especially Israel. The creation itself is generally attributed to God's 'word' (e.g. Gen. 1:6–7, 9, 11, 14–15; Pss 33:6, 9; 148:5–6; cf. Isa. 55:11). This further emphasizes God's transcendent power. There are parallels between creation by God's word and the role of Wisdom in creation in Proverbs 8:22–31.

Creation and chaos

In other creation myths the heavens and earth are formed out of chaos. As we have noted, in the Babylonian myth *Enuma Elish* they are formed from the body of the defeated Tiamat, sometimes related to the Hebrew word *tĕhôm* (deep) in Genesis 1:2. This may allude to *Enuma Elish*, reinforcing the idea of a pre-creation state of chaos. The description of the earth as 'formless and empty' (*tōhû wābōhû*) is also taken to suggest a primeval chaos from which the universe was made. Linked with this is debate about the translation of Genesis 1:1 and its relation to verse 2.[19] The traditional view is that what was *formless and empty* (v. 2) was the result of God's initial act of creation (v. 1),[20] which brought matter into being out of nothing, and this was then transformed by further creative acts. Other translations take verse 2 to describe the state of the universe *before* God began to create;[21] and this may be taken to imply that chaotic matter existed before the work of creation began. There is, though, still considerable support for the traditional view.[22]

---

18. Eichrodt, *Theology*, 2:168.

19. See e.g. Wenham, *Genesis 1–15*, pp. 11–13.

20. This is reflected in the NIV translation: *In the beginning God created the heavens and the earth. Now the earth was formless and empty.*

21. For example, the NRSV translates Gen. 1:1–2 as *in the beginning when God created the heavens and the earth, the earth was a formless void.*

22. Some identify a gap between Gen. 1:1 and 1:2, and suggest that following the creation described in Gen. 1:1, Satan's rebellion took place. As the result of that catastrophic event the earth *became formless and empty* (Gen. 1:2), necessitating its

The idea that God created the universe out of nothing is also implied by passages that point to God calling everything into existence (e.g. Ps. 148:5; Prov. 8:22–27) and those that emphasize his pre-existence (e.g. Ps. 90:2; cf. Heb. 11:3). If the heavens and earth were created from something else, then matter must be, in some sense, eternal. The OT writers refute that. God did not create the universe from the body of a dead monster (as in *Enuma Elish*), or put into order matter that was already there. Only God is eternal; everything else comes from him.[23]

But that raises a further important question. If God did create out of nothing, why begin with something *formless and empty*? It seems strange that God would create chaos, or anything resembling it.[24] The reason is theological.

Footnote 22 (*continued*)

recreation. However, though popularized by the Scofield Bible, such a view has little to commend it. The translation 'became' is difficult to justify, and why would such a significant event be left to the reader's speculation? It also seems unlikely that God would declare his creation *very good* (Gen. 1:31) if Satan and fallen angels were already active within it. For further discussion, see Hamilton, *Genesis, 1–17*, pp. 115–117.

23. Rendtorff argues that God has responsibility for all that happens in the world, including the creation of chaos (*Hebrew Bible*, p. 425).

24. Tsumura argues that the Hebrew expression *tōhû wābōhû* does not point to a state of chaos (*Creation*, pp. 9–35). Elsewhere in the OT *tōhû* refers only to something empty, and *bōhû?* (which only appears in the OT in combination with *tōhû*) reinforces that meaning. However, *tōhû* in the OT rarely has a neutral meaning. It is the desert, or trackless wasteland, which is threatening as well as empty (Deut. 32:10; Job 6:18; 12:24). It describes a scene of desolation following divine judgment (Isa. 24:10; 34:11; 40:23) and the desolate state of Judah in exile (Isa. 45:18; Jer. 4:23 – where the same expression as in Gen. 1:2, *tōhû wābōhû* occurs). It describes the empty words of the unrighteous (Isa. 29:21; 59:4) and the worthlessness of idols (Isa. 40:17; 41:29; 44:9). It may be interpreted neutrally in Job 26:7, *He spreads out the northern skies over empty space* (*tōhû*), though this is followed by what appears to be a clear example of the *Chaoskampf* motif (vv. 10–13). Tsumura's conclusion that the world in Gen. 1:2 is only uninhabited and not yet productive (*Creation*, pp. 33–35) does not take sufficient account of the negative associations of *tōhû wābōhû*, and while I accept that 'chaos' may not be an ideal term to describe this early stage in creation (particularly if it is too closely linked with ANE pre-creation myths), it does have value in pointing to an undesirable state that only God's power can transform, and to which, without God's continuing activity, the world may revert.

The verses set two ideas alongside one another. The first is that, over against the ideas found in Ugaritic and Babylonian creation myths, the created order is the work of God alone. That is the significance of Genesis 1:1, which is the setting for all that follows. God made it. The second is that we see in the act of creation a process in which God brings order out of chaos. The chaos of Genesis 1:2 points to a world without God's transforming power. The rest of the chapter shows that power at work: transforming what is formless and empty into something God can declare to be *very good*. This portrays chaos, rather than 'unbeing', as the opposite of creation,[25] and allows the possibility that sin and the rejection of God's purposes for the world can open the way for the world to revert to chaos once again.[26] We see something of that in the rest of Genesis 1 – 11, and especially in the flood.[27] The story of the flood indicates that chaos has not been removed from creation; rather it is held back, and may be allowed to return as a result of human sin.[28] So Jeremiah

------

25. Rendtorff, *Hebrew Bible*, pp. 418–419.

26. See e.g. Brueggemann, *Theology*, pp. 534–551; Childs, *OT Theology*, pp. 221–224; von Rad, *OT Theology*, 1:143–144.

27. Clines notes possible thematic patterns running through Gen. 1–11. In the 'Creation–Uncreation–Recreation' theme the flood is at the centre: 'creation', the separation of dry land from the waters, is followed by 'uncreation', where that separation is reversed (Gen. 7:11–12; cf. 1:6–10), and by 'recreation', the receding of the waters and the separation again of dry land from the waters above and below the earth (Gen. 8:1–2); see Clines, *Theme*, pp. 73–76); see also B. W. Anderson, *Contours*, p. 94; *Creation to New Creation*, pp. 34–36; Fretheim, *God and World*, pp. 79–83.

28. See B. W. Anderson, *Creation to New Creation*, pp. 35–37; Brueggemann, *Theology*, pp. 200–201, 534–543; P. C. Craigie, P. H. Kelley and J. F. Drinkard, Jr., *Jeremiah 1–25*, WBC 26 (Dallas: Word, 1991), pp. 80–82, 112; Fretheim, *God and World*, pp. 81–82. In his seminal work *Creation*, Levenson sets out the view that, after God's primordial victory, chaos (which he sees as pre-existent evil) is controlled, but not eliminated. This, he argues, explains the presence of evil in the world, and the appeal to God's victory is a call to reduce the gap between the affirmation of God's sovereignty and the apparent triumph of evil. Chaos, though, is not the final word, and God's victory will be reaffirmed, finally, in the eschatological future. While I agree with the model of chaos held in check by God, I disagree with the (dualistic) view that chaos represents primordial evil. It points, rather, to an undesirable state, created by God, which may re-emerge as a result of sin. Levenson also limits the application of the myth to prehistory and eschatology; it does not point to God's

likens the judgment coming on Israel to a return to pre-creation chaos: to an earth *formless and empty* (Jer. 4:23; cf. Gen. 1:2). Isaiah 24 points to the devastation of the earth caused by breaking the *everlasting covenant* (v. 5), again probably a reference to the covenant with Noah, and goes on to describe cosmic instability (vv. 18b–20), including the opening of the floodgates of heaven, which directly echoes the language of the flood (Gen. 7:11; 8:2), and the shaking of the earth's foundations (cf. Ps. 82:5). Zephaniah 1:2–4 also points to a disaster that echoes the destruction of the flood (Gen. 6:7) and represents the reversal of creation.[29] We have seen too how Israel's historical enemies are sometimes depicted as chaos monsters, suggesting that national disasters such as the Egyptian captivity and the Babylonian exile were viewed as a return to a state of chaos. But though sin might lead to God withdrawing his hand, and so to the re-emergence of chaos, there is the confident hope that the God who once defeated the monsters of the deep and brought order out of chaos is able to do so again, and that he will restore his people. And of course that principle also applies to everyday things in the lives of God's people. God is still in the business of bringing order out of chaos and light out of darkness.

Creation and redemption[30]

In several passages God's mighty acts in creation are recounted alongside his saving acts in history (e.g. Pss 33; 136; 148). This link between creation and

Footnote 28 (*continued*)

    continued action in history. I have argued that by historicizing God's victory, the writers of the OT relate it to immediate crises, and not just eschatological hope.

29. See Goldingay, *OT Theology*, 2:307–308; O. Palmer Robertson, *The Books of Nahum, Habakkuk and Zephaniah*, NICOT (Grand Rapids: Eerdmans, 1991), pp. 257–260. Robert Murray, *The Cosmic Covenant: Biblical Themes of Justice and Peace and the Integrity of Creation* (London: Sheed & Ward, 1992), describes Isa. 24 as 'the undoing of creation and its order' (p. 19).

30. See C. Stuhlmueller, *Creative Redemption in Deutero-Isaiah*, AnBib 43 (Rome: Biblical Institute, 1970); S. Lee, *Creation and Redemption in Isaiah 40–55* (Hong Kong: Alliance Bible Seminary, 1995); see also B. W. Anderson, *Living World*, pp. 479–485; Brueggemann, *Theology*, p. 147; Goldingay, *OT Theology*, 1:288–290, 363–365; Gerhard von Rad, 'The Theological Problem of the Old Testament Doctrine of Creation', in B. W. Anderson, *Creation in the OT*, pp. 53–64 (= *Problem of the Hexateuch*, pp. 131–143; = *Genesis to Chronicles*, pp. 177–186); *OT Theology*, 1:137–139; Preuss, *OT Theology*, 2:235–239.

redemption is particularly evident in Isaiah 40 – 55, where the idea of God as creator emphasizes his power to fulfil his promise to save his people.

Von Rad notes the importance of the creation motif in encouraging faith: the God who created the world out of chaos has the power to deliver Israel from the chaos of exile and re-establish her in her own land.[31] Von Rad notes the close relationship in Isaiah 51:9–11 between God's power in creation and his deliverance of his people in the exodus. The *road in the depths of the sea so that the redeemed might cross over* (Isa. 51:10b) refers to the exodus; while references to the *waters of the great deep* and to *Rahab* (v. 9) allude to God's victory over the waters of chaos at creation. Thus the creation and exodus are brought together as one act in God's redemptive purpose. In Isaiah 45:18 we are told that God did not create the world to be *empty* (*tōhû*; cf. Gen. 1:2), but made it to be *inhabited*. God's purpose for ruined Jerusalem is the same (Isa. 44:26), and the way this is expressed, as a word of command, is reminiscent of God's creative word in Genesis 1. In Isaiah 44:27 there is a further reference to God drying up the waters of the deep (see also Isa. 50:2). This again brings exodus and creation traditions together: the idea that in redemption God raises his people out of chaos.[32]

Its close link with creation also indicates that the exodus may be seen as the creative act by which God's people were brought into being. By relating this to the deliverance from Babylon, that deliverance is also portrayed as a creative act, which will result in the recreation and renewal of Israel. According to Stuhlmueller, God's word in Deutero-Isaiah has this kind of creative power for the life of the exiled nation.[33] However, Israel does not live in isolation.

---

31. In von Rad's view Deutero-Isaiah is not concerned with a doctrine of creation in its own right but uses older traditions to emphasize God's power to redeem his people: 'Yahweh the Creator, who raised up the world out of chaos, does not leave Jerusalem in chaos; he who dried up the elemental waters will also raise up Jerusalem anew' ('Theological Problem', in B. W. Anderson, *Creation in the OT*, p. 57); cf. Goldingay, *OT Theology*, 1:79.

32. D. M. Gunn, 'Deutero-Isaiah and the Flood', *JBL* 94 (1975), pp. 493–508, relates these passages to the flood, and notes that in the light of Isa. 54:9 such allusions might be expected. However, as we have seen, the drying up of the waters after the flood is itself viewed as a recreation, indicating the same general idea.

33. Stuhlmueller notes that Deutero-Isaiah begins and ends with the theme of the powerful, life-giving word of God (Isa. 40:1–11; 55:10–11; see also e.g. 41:4, 17–20; 43:1–7; 44:24–28); the fulfilment of that divine word will result in a new creation, in which Israel is renewed and re-established (*Creative Redemption*, pp. 169–170).

Recreating Israel's world involves others, including Cyrus and the surrounding nations. This leads to the assertion that God is not only Israel's Maker but also the Creator of all the earth, and this, in turn, enables the prophet to look forward also to the final redemption and recreation not only of Israel but of the whole world. This has important implications for the idea of mission to the non-Israelite nations in the OT.[34]

The close link between creation and redemption, however, allows us not only to see Israel's redemption as a creative act but also to view the act of creation itself as a salvific act in which God rescues the cosmos from chaos (e.g. Ps. 74:12–17).[35] This is related to the Noahic covenant, which, as we have seen, further expresses God's desire to preserve the world from chaos, and whose implicit redemptive significance is confirmed explicitly by Isaiah 54:9–10, where it provides the pattern for God's activity as the Redeemer of his people from exile. This points to a divine commitment to the redemption of the whole of the created order, and this, again, has significant implications for the OT view of world mission.

Man and woman

The creation of human beings[36]
Humankind was made from the dust (Gen. 2:7; see also 3:19; Job 10:9; Ps. 104:29; Eccl. 3:20), indicating oneness with the rest of God's creation. As flesh, human beings share an order of being with creation distinct from God (Isa. 31:3). However, they are also distinct from the rest of the created order, and have a special place within it. Human beings are described as having the *breath*

---

34. See below, p. 332.

35. Goldingay maintains that 'God acted as glorious deliverer at the Beginning' (*OT Theology*, 1:67), and goes on to quote Knierim, who sees a 'Creation . . . as the first in a chain of salvific actions'; see Knierim, *Task of OT Theology*, pp. 209–213 (209–210). Goldingay takes a similar position in his second volume: he notes the oneness of God's activity in creation and liberation, and describes Creation as 'an act of liberation' (*OT Theology*, 2:160).

36. See e.g. Brueggemann, *Theology*, pp. 450–452; Dyrness, *Themes*, pp. 79–84; Eichrodt, *Theology*, 2:118–131; House, *OT Theology*, pp. 59–63; Goldingay, *OT Theology*, 1:98–117; 2:517–527; Jacob, *Theology*, pp. 151–182; Köhler, *OT Theology*, pp. 131–135; Vriezen, *Outline*, pp. 143–147; Walton, *ANE Thought*, pp. 203–215; Westermann, *Creation*, pp. 47–60, 70–88.

of life, which, as we have seen, is given by God; but that same expression is used in relation to other living creatures (Gen. 1:30; 6:17). What is more decisive in emphasizing the distinctiveness of human beings is that they are made *in the image of God* (Gen. 1:26–27).[37]

Made 'in the image of God'[38]

The Bible does not explain what this expression means, and though many suggestions have been offered, most are, as Hamilton observes, 'based on subjective inferences rather than objective exegesis'.[39]

The most usual use of the term 'image' (*ṣelem*) suggests physical resemblance, and the expression 'in the image of God' has been taken to imply that human beings in some sense 'look like God'. However, we have already noted that there is a fundamental, ontological distinction between God and the created order and that it is impossible to make a physical representation of God. Such an interpretation, then, is highly unlikely, and this may be reflected in the use of the more abstract term 'likeness' (*dĕmût*).[40]

---

37. Other creation accounts also distinguish human beings from the rest of creation by including a divine element. In the Atrahasis Epic, as in Genesis, there is a combination of earthly and divine elements: the blood of a god (We-ila) mixed with clay. In *Enuma Elish* Ea creates human beings from the blood of Kingu. In some Egyptian cosmogonies human beings are formed from the tears of Ra or Atum; in others, only from clay (see further Walton, *ANE Thought*, pp. 205–210). However, differences between these and the OT account far outweigh similarities.

38. See also Phyllis A. Bird, 'Male and Female he Created Them', in Hess and Tsumura, *Inscriptions*, pp. 329–361; Gerald Bray, 'The Significance of God's Image in Man', *TynBul* 42.2 (1991), pp. 195–225; Brueggemann, *Theology*, pp. 451–452; Childs, *Biblical Theology* (1992), pp. 567–569; David J. A. Clines, 'The Image of God in Man', *TynBul* 19 (1968), pp. 53–103; Gerstenberger, *Theologies*, pp. 286–287; Goldingay, *OT Theology*, 1:102–103; 2:517–520; Hamilton, *Genesis 1–17*, pp. 134–137; G. A. Jónsson, *The Image of God: Genesis 1:26–28 in a Century of Old Testament Study*, ConBOT 26 (Stockholm: Almqvist & Wiksell, 1988); Preuss, *Theology*, 2:114–117; Rendtorff, *Hebrew Bible*, pp. 426–429; Trible, *Rhetoric of Sexuality*, pp. 12–21, 94–105; Wenham, *Genesis 1–15*, pp. 29–32; Westermann, *Creation*, pp. 55–60; *Genesis 1–11* (London: SPCK, 1984; Minneapolis: Fortress, 1994), pp. 149–158; Wilkinson, *Message of Creation*, pp. 31–45.

39. Hamilton, *Genesis 1–17*, p. 137.

40. Goldingay emphasizes the concrete and visible force of the terms 'image' and 'likeness', and suggests the OT 'presupposes a correspondence between God and

Although we may not arrive at a precise understanding of the expression 'made in the image of God', several important things may be implied by it, which can be said to separate human beings from other living creatures.

Human beings share spiritual characteristics with God

While unlikely to denote physical resemblance, the expression may indicate that human beings, as distinct from the rest of creation, share certain spiritual qualities with God. These will include things like personality, intelligence and free will. However, because there is little objective basis for deciding which characteristics and qualities are intended, any list will be subjective and will reflect the theological agenda of its compiler.[41]

Human beings are made for relationship with God

The expression may indicate a special relationship between humankind and God. Westermann suggests, 'The meaning is that mankind is created so that something can happen between God and man. Mankind is created to stand before God.'[42] Human beings are made by God and for God and may find their full meaning only in relationship with him.

Human beings are given authority to rule on behalf of God

This aspect of being made in the image of God is the one most clearly related to the biblical text. Genesis 1:26 expresses two parallel ideas: *Let us make man in our image* and, *let them rule . . . over all the creatures that move along the ground* (see also Gen. 2:19–20; Ps. 8:3–8). Being made in God's image is closely linked with having authority to rule. This idea is reflected elsewhere in the ANE, where the expression 'the image of god' might be applied to kings, as the earthly representatives of the deity. God has created human beings with the authority and responsibility to rule over his world on his behalf.

Footnote 40 (*continued*)

    humanity in its bodiliness as well as its inner nature' (*OT Theology*, 1:103). However, this is challenged by other passages that reflect on the distinction between God and human beings. See Hamilton, *Genesis 1–17*, pp. 135–136; Rendtorff, *Hebrew Bible*, pp. 426–427; Preuss, *Theology*, 2:115–116; Wenham, *Genesis 1–15*, pp. 29–30.

41. Goldingay is probably right when he suggests that people who want to emphasize the value of particular human characteristics, e.g. the capacity for rational thought or ethical reflection, identify these things with what it means to be made in God's image (*OT Theology*, 1:102).

42. Westermann, *Creation*, p. 56.

Human beings are made to reflect the glory of God

Linked with this special calling, the psalmist describes humankind as *a little lower than the heavenly beings and crowned . . . with glory and honour* (Ps. 8:5). God made human beings as the pinnacle of his creative work and has given them a unique place within the natural order. This contrasts sharply with myths such as the Atrahasis Epic and *Enuma Elish*, where people are created as little more than the slaves of the gods.[43] In the OT humankind is made in the image of God, to reflect the glory of God within his world, and human beings are thus conferred with a wholly different dignity and status.

The uniqueness of human relationships

Another aspect of humankind's uniqueness is the special relationship between persons. No companion from the rest of the created order could be found to provide the fulfilment possible only through relationships with other human beings, and especially within marriage (Gen. 2:20–24).

The reference to human beings being created *male and female* (1:27) is significant. I will discuss later the way the OT portrays the respective roles of men and women. For the moment, we can note the following. First, both sexes are made in God's image. Second, it is only in relation with one another that God's purpose to fill and subdue the earth, which, as we have seen, is associated with being made in the divine image, will be fulfilled. Third, the relationship is harmonious: there is no sense of a hierarchy, with male superior to female. Trible argues that there is also no sense of priority or superiority in Genesis 2:21–24, and maintains that the differentiation between the sexes came only with the creation of woman; from one 'earth creature', God created two sexual beings.[44] This suggestion is interesting,[45] though within the context of the narrative, which is written from a patriarchal viewpoint, we are probably to understand that Adam was created as a male and Eve as his (female) consort. Nevertheless the emphasis of this section of the narrative would appear to be

---

43. So, in the Atrahasis Epic, the god Anu says, 'create humanity, let him bear the yoke . . . let man bear the toil of the gods', and, after human beings have been created, the goddess Mami announces to the other assembled gods, 'I have removed your heavy work, I have imposed your toil on humankind' , and *Enuma Elish* tells how Ea, after creating humankind, 'imposed the service and let free the gods . . . imposed upon it the service of the gods' (Arnold and Beyer, *Readings*, pp. 24, 43).

44. Trible, *God and the Rhetoric of Sexuality*, pp. 94–105; see also Rendtorff, *Hebrew Bible*, p. 427.

45. However, see Childs, *OT Theology*, pp. 189–191.

the origin and interdependence of the sexes: without a female counterpart, Adam's maleness would have no meaning.

Human beings and the environment[46]

In Genesis 1:28 human beings are told to increase in number, subdue the earth and rule over every living creature. The relationship between human beings and the environment is a big issue today. When Genesis was written, the impact of daily life on the environment was minimal and the issues were less important. Nevertheless, ruling over the earth, which we have taken to be a key aspect of being made in God's image and therefore a key aspect of what it means to be distinctively human, implies responsible stewardship (Gen. 2:15), not selfish exploitation. As God's representatives, human beings will share his concern for his creation. We also see human beings in a relationship with creation: Adam names the animals (Gen. 2:19–20); they eat the same food (Gen. 1:29–30); initially, there is no killing, though that relationship was altered by the fall, and there is a marked contrast in the provision for food between Genesis 1:29 and 9:3.

Complementary creation accounts

Source critics regard Genesis 1:1 – 2:4a and 2:4b–25 as variant accounts of creation, attributed to P and J respectively. It is better to see them, however, as complementary accounts, each with its own style and distinctive emphasis, which focus on different aspects of the creation story and express different aspects of God. The division between these accounts is usually made in 2:4. The first part of the verse (*this is the account of the heavens and the earth*) concludes the first account, and the second part (*when the LORD God made the earth and the heavens*) introduces the second. However, the verse has a chiastic structure,[47] which links the two parts and indicates that the two creation accounts have been placed side by side for a purpose. The chiasm also alerts us to the different

---

46. See also e.g. Childs, *Biblical Theology* (1992), pp. 409–411; W. Houston, "'And Let them Have Dominion . . .'" Biblical Views of Man in Relation to the Environmental Crisis', *Studia biblica 1978 – 1:Papers on the Old Testament and Related Themes*, JSOTSup 11 (Sheffield: JSOT Press, 1978), pp. 161–184; Lawrence A. Turner, *Announcements of Plot in Genesis*, JSOTSup 96 (Sheffield: Sheffield Academic Press, 1990), pp. 21–49; B. W. Anderson, *Creation to New Creation*, pp. 111–150.

47. 'Chiasm' refers to the repetition of words and/or ideas that occur in the first part of a text in the second part, but with the order reversed. In Gen. 2:4 this is seen in the reversal of the elements 'the heavens' and 'the earth'.

emphases of the accounts. The first is concerned with *the heavens and the earth* (see also Gen. 1:1; 2:1) and focuses on the cosmic dimensions of God's creative work. The second refers to *the earth and the heavens*, pointing to God's interest in and relationship with the earth.

The first account emphasizes God's transcendence as he calls the cosmos into being by his word, and its climax is the creation of humankind, who are given dominion over the world. If this account came to prominence during the exile, the focus on God as creator would emphasize his superiority to other gods and his power to give his chosen people a new start. The creation of humankind and the institution of the Sabbath reflect the special place God's people have within the divine purpose.

The second account is much more down to earth. It focuses on the creation of human beings, and describes God's intimate involvement with them. He forms them, like a potter moulding clay; he breathes life into them; he finds a companion for Adam, because it is not good for him to be alone; he plants a garden and places Adam and Eve in it; he walks with them in the cool of the day. This account goes on to describe how the perfect relationship with God was spoilt by human rebellion and sin (Gen. 3:1–24). By setting the fall in this context, the writer is making an important theological point: sin is not just rebellion against God's authority (although it is that) but is also a rejection of the intimate, caring relationship God created human beings for.

Human personality[48]

The OT writers do not set out to give a comprehensive description of the human make-up, and it is likely that the understanding was not static. However, there are four main elements that constitute human personality.

Nepeš

Nepeš is often associated with the inner life of a person: it is the seat of deep needs (e.g. Job 7:11; Pss 119:28; 143:6) and of feelings and desires (e.g. Deut. 6:5; Ps. 42:1; Prov. 13:4). It is also frequently linked with a person's relationship

---

48. See e.g. Brueggemann, *Theology*, pp. 452–454; Childs, *OT Theology*, pp. 196–203; *Biblical Theology* (1992), pp. 571–573; Dyrness, *Themes*, pp. 84–96; Eichrodt, *Theology*, 2:131–150; Goldingay, *OT Theology*, 2:548–564; Köhler, *OT Theology*, pp. 135–152; Preuss, *Theology*, pp. 109–114; John W. Rogerson, *Anthropology and the Old Testament*, The Biblical Seminar 1 (Sheffield: JSOT Press, 1984); Snaith, *Distinctive Ideas*, pp. 141–153; Walton, *ANE Thought*, pp. 203–215; Hans Walter Wolff, *Anthropology of the Old Testament* (Philadelphia: Fortress, 1974).

with God (e.g. Pss 25:1; 57:1; Isa. 61:10), and especially the longing for God and his salvation (e.g. Pss 35:3, 9; 42:1–2; 63:1, 5, 8; 84:2; Isa. 26:9). This has led to *nepeš* being translated 'soul', which may be misleading. Christians view the 'soul' as an inward element of human personality, albeit the element that makes us who we are. As such it is distinct from, and will survive the death of, the body. In the OT *nepeš* cannot be separated from the rest of the person, including the body. For example, in Psalm 84:2, *My soul* [nepeš] *yearns, even faints, / for the courts of the LORD; / my heart and my flesh cry out / for the living God, nepeš* is paralleled with 'my heart and my flesh', and refers to the psalmist's entire being, including the physical. *Nepeš* embraces the whole person, and in some passages 'my soul' can simply mean 'I' or 'me' (e.g. Ps. 7:2). Thus *nepeš* is not something human beings *possess*; it is what they *are*. It is in that sense that the term is used in Genesis 2:7, *the LORD God formed the man from the dust of the ground and breathed into his nostrils the breath of life, and the man became a living being* [nepeš].[49]

Rûaḥ *(breath / spirit)*

We have seen that *rûaḥ* may refer to the *breath* that animates lifeless human flesh.[50] It may also denote human disposition and feelings. *Grief* (Gen. 26:35) is, literally, 'grief of spirit'; to be *troubled* is to be 'pained in spirit' (1 Sam. 1:15). When the Queen of Sheba saw Solomon's court (1 Kgs 10:5), she was *overwhelmed* (NIV); literally 'there was no more *rûaḥ* in her' (see also NRSV). Snaith suggests that in such cases what is felt takes over the person to the exclusion of all other feelings; thus *rûaḥ* is the impulse that governs a person's life and controls his or her behaviour.[51] So, in his conversation with Job, Elihu says:

> I am full of words,
>   and the rûaḥ within me compels me;
> inside I am like bottled-up wine,
>   like new wineskins ready to burst.
> (Job 32:18–19)

---

49. For further discussion of *nepeš*, see e.g. Daniel C. Fredericks, '*nepeš*', in *NIDOTTE* 3:133–134; H. Seebass, '*nepeš*', in *TDOT* 9:497–519; cf. Nobuyoshi Kiuchi, *Leviticus*, AOTC (Nottingham: Apollos; Downers Grove: IVP, 2007), pp. 34–36. In my view Kiuchi's portrayal of the human *nepeš* in Leviticus is too influenced by Christian theology.

50. Above, pp. 113–114; this aspect of *rûaḥ* will be discussed further below.

51. Snaith describes *rûaḥ* as the 'controlling power in man' (*Distinctive Ideas*, p. 148).

Jacob's *rûaḥ* (and so his whole personality) was *revived* by the news that Joseph was alive (Gen. 45:27; cf. Judg. 15:19). The psalmist speaks about the need for a *steadfast* or *right* rûaḥ (Ps. 51:10), by which he means a whole disposition that shows itself in action pleasing to God; Caleb had a *different* rûaḥ (Num. 14:24), which resulted in his following God wholeheartedly. By contrast, unfaithful Israel is *wayward in* rûaḥ (Isa. 29:24), resulting in a lifestyle displeasing to God.

Lēb *(heart)*

According to Dyrness, the heart 'lay at the deepest level of feelings and registered the most profound responses to life'.[52] When used in a figurative sense in the OT, the *heart* is the seat of the will rather than (as often in our way of thinking) of the emotions. A person whose heart is hardened is not open to reason (e.g. Exod. 7:22); people need hearts that understand (e.g. Deut. 29:4; 1 Kgs 3:9; Isa. 6:10; 42:25); the discerning heart seeks knowledge (Prov. 15:14). The heart is also associated with a person's response to God (e.g. 1 Sam. 12:20; Ps. 119:36; Jer. 3:10; 31:33), and ultimately, therefore, needs to be renewed (e.g. Jer. 4:4; Ezek. 11:19–20; 18:31; 36:26). In Ezekiel's prophecy this new *heart* is closely linked with a new *spirit*; both imply a transformation that will enable a new understanding of God and a new desire and ability to obey him.

Bāśār *(flesh)*

This generally refers to physical, bodily existence. The word may refer to meat, often the meat of sacrifices (e.g. Exod. 12:8; Lev. 7:15). It also denotes the human body (e.g. Lev. 16:24, 26; Ezek. 10:12). In the physical union between husband and wife the two become *one flesh* (Gen. 2:24), and members of a person's family are described as being of that person's *flesh* (e.g. Gen. 29:14; Lev. 25:49; Judg. 9:2). The OT does not suggest that the flesh is inherently evil. It is sometimes presented positively. For example, God's promise to replace his people's heart of stone with a heart of flesh (Ezek. 11:19) indicates that flesh, as it was created to be, is receptive to God and responsive to his will. However, the OT does point to the frailty and impermanence of human flesh, especially when contrasted with the strength and eternity of God (e.g. 2 Chr. 32:7–8; Ps. 78:39; Isa. 40:6–8; Jer. 17:5). We have also noted the distinction in Isaiah 31:3 between *flesh*, associated with humankind, and *spirit (rûaḥ)*, associated with God (see also Gen. 6:3).

---

52. Dyrness, *Themes*, p. 89; see e.g. Pss 25:17; 61:2; Jer. 4:19.

Body, soul and spirit

We have noted the significance of *rûaḥ* as the breath that gives life to human flesh (see e.g. Job 33:4; 34:14–15; Ps. 104:29–30; Isa. 42:5; 57:16; Ezek. 37:9–10). We have also drawn attention to Genesis 2:7, where the *nepeš*, the essential living person, comprises a body, made from the dust, animated by divine breath. The Hebrew word for 'breath' here is *nĕšāmâ*, rather than *rûaḥ*; however, in this context the meaning of the two terms overlaps,[53] and in similar expressions elsewhere *rûaḥ* is used.[54] Consequently we may suggest the (somewhat oversimplified) equation, *bāśār* + *rûaḥ* = *nepeš*, to indicate the relationship between the terms. This emphasizes, further, that the term *nepeš* refers not to one element of human personality, but to what human beings are. We also need to be clear about the part played by *rûaḥ*. The *rûaḥ* that gives life to flesh is not an intrinsic part of human personality: it is not the possession of human beings. It comes from God and continues to belong to God (e.g. Job 12:10; 33:4; Isa. 57:16; Zech. 12:1), and when God withdraws it, life ends and the body returns to the dust (Job 34:14–15; Pss 104:29; 146:4; Eccl. 12:7).

In this we see that the OT does not view human personality as *tripartite* (body, soul and spirit), or even *bipartite* (flesh and spirit); in the OT human personality is a unity. Because of the *rûaḥ* breathed into human beings by God there is an important spiritual dimension,[55] but when the *rûaḥ* returns to God, the result is the death of the whole person. There is the idea in the OT that after death a 'shadow' of the person survives in Sheol; though again, this must not be confused with the Christian view of the 'soul'. I will have more to say about this later when we consider death and the afterlife.[56]

There are points where the meanings of *rûaḥ*, *nepeš* and *lēb* overlap. *Rûaḥ* is sometimes linked with *nepeš* (e.g. Job 7:11; 12:10; Isa. 26:9). *Rûaḥ* and *lēb* often

---

53. *Nĕšāmâ* also refers to God's breath, and to the breath that gives life to human beings, and occurs in parallel with *rûaḥ* in Job 27:3; 32:8; 33:4; 34:14; Isa. 42:5; 57:16. See further H. Lamberty-Zielinski, '*nĕšāmâ*', in *TDOT* 10:65–70. *Nĕšāmâ* occurs less frequently than, and its semantic range is broadly covered by this aspect of, *rûaḥ*; Eichrodt suggests that it may be a poetic synonym for *rûaḥ* (*Theology*, 2:142).

54. The expression *breath of life* occurs with *nĕšāmâ* in Gen. 2:7 and with *rûaḥ* in Gen. 6:17; 7:15.

55. As we have seen, the idea that there is something of the divine in human beings is common to other ANE cosmogonies.

56. Below, p. 304.

appear in parallel couplets (e.g. Deut. 2:30; Ps. 51:10, 17; Prov. 17:22; Isa. 57:15), indicating a close relationship between them. *Lēb* is also associated with *nepeš*, particularly in the formula *with all your heart and with all your soul*, which occurs twenty times in the OT (e.g. Deut. 4:29; 6:5; Josh. 23:14; 2 Kgs 23:25). Nevertheless, though their circles of meaning intersect, each of the three terms also has distinctive elements.

The origin and spread of sin[57]

God's command

Human beings were created as the pinnacle of God's very good creation: made for relationship with God, made to rule over the earth on God's behalf and made to reflect the glory of their Creator. The question of whether they would fulfil this role was raised by the introduction of a divine command: *You are free to eat from any tree in the garden; but you must not eat from the tree of the knowledge of good and evil* . . . (Gen. 2:16–17).

The reason for the command

This command gave human beings an opportunity to play an active part in their relationship with God. It gave a choice: obey God's word and maintain the relationship, or disobey and reject the relationship. This shows that God wants a relationship with human beings that is entered into freely. It also emphasizes that a key element within that relationship is obedience. God cares for us, is committed to us and wants to have fellowship with us; but this is not a relationship of equals. The proper response of human beings to God is to obey him. We see this in the covenant at Sinai. The link between covenant and Law indicates that living in relationship with God and fulfilling his purposes in the world requires obedience. We see it too in the distinction in Deuteronomy 30:15–20 between *obedience*, which leads to blessing and life (seen in terms of prosperity and relationship with God in the land), and *disobedience*, which leads to death (seen in terms of the withdrawal of divine blessings and eventual expulsion from the land).

---

57. See e.g. Childs, *Biblical Theology* (1992), pp. 119–121, 569–571; *OT Theology*, pp. 222–226; Dyrness, *Themes*, pp. 99–110; Eichrodt, *Theology*, 2:380–443; Goldingay, *OT Theology*, 1:131–192; 2:254–310; House, *OT Theology*, pp. 67–71; Köhler, *OT Theology*, pp. 201–211; Bruce Milne, 'Sin', in *IBD* 3:1456–1459; Preuss, *Theology*, pp. 170–184; von Rad, *OT Theology*, 1:154–165; Westermann, *Creation*, pp. 89–112.

The divine command also makes a statement about human behaviour. Human beings are not free agents: they need to accept, and act within, defined limits in order to maintain relationships within the community and their relationship with God.

The 'knowledge of good and evil'

The precise meaning of this expression is unclear. It could mean, simply, being able to distinguish between right and wrong. However, that would imply that before eating the fruit Adam and Eve did not know the difference and so were not morally responsible and could not properly be held accountable for their disobedience. The expression might refer, instead, to *the experiential knowledge of good and evil*. Before they sinned, they may have been aware of what was right and wrong, but the distinction was not yet part of their experience. The knowledge of what it was to sin came only when they chose evil, disobeyed God, and ate the forbidden fruit.

Another possibility, which may fit better with the context of the verse, is that the phrase points to the means by which human beings might attempt to take control of their own destiny. By eating the fruit they would come to possess for themselves the knowledge of what was beneficial or harmful,[58] and so could break free from dependence upon God and on his word. The idea that eating the fruit of the tree corresponds, in some way, to taking God's place, is in line with the serpent's temptation: *you will be like God* (Gen. 3:5).

Temptation and fall (Gen. 3:1–7)

The serpent

Temptation comes via a snake. In later Judaism and in the NT the serpent is identified with Satan; the earliest text to do this is Wisdom of Solomon 2.24 (*through the devil's envy death entered the world*), which dates from the start of the Christian era. In the mythology of the ANE, chaos monsters are sometimes depicted as serpents (e.g. Leviathan); serpents are also linked with wisdom, and there are elements of both of those things here. The association with chaos may be significant in this context. God has created the world out of chaos, but, as we have already seen, continued order in creation depends on God, and there remains the threat that sin and rebellion open the way for chaos to return (as with the flood). By tempting Eve away from reliance on God, the

---

58. See e.g. Gerhard von Rad, *Genesis*, OTL (London: SCM, 1972), p. 89; Westermann, *Creation*, p. 93.

snake/serpent represents that possibility. The narrative also indicates an ongoing conflict between the serpent and the seed of the woman (3:15).[59] This is reflected in the constant temptation for human beings to seek to be like God, to take control of their own destiny and so allow the world to fall back into chaos. The formulation *he will strike your head and you will strike his heel* (NRSV) does not necessarily indicate a decisive outcome,[60] though it does suggest the serpent will come off worse. And, since it is set in the context of God's judgment on the serpent, we can assume it is intended to suggest an outcome in favour of Eve's descendants.[61]

There is also a parallel (of sorts) in the Gilgamesh Epic, where a serpent prevents Gilgamesh from eating a plant that will give him immortality.[62] This is not to suggest that the writer of Genesis copied the story: significant differences rule that out. But it is possible that he used popular imagery to make his point.

---

59. According to Wenham, 'the imperfect verb is iterative. It implies repeated attacks by both sides to injure the other' (*Genesis 1–15*, p. 80). One way of interpreting this passage is as aetiology; it explains the hostility between human beings and snakes. However, the context appears to require a deeper theological significance.

60. The NIV translation *he will crush your head and you will strike his heel* implies that the serpent is dealt a fatal blow. However 'crush' and 'strike' translate the same Hebrew verb (NRSV, NIV mg.), giving the sense that each strikes at the other. The Vulgate also translates the verbs differently, possibly influenced by a messianic interpretation of the text. See further Hamilton, *Genesis 1–17*, pp. 197–200; Wenham, *Genesis 1–15*, pp. 80–81. See also T. Desmond Alexander, 'Messianic Ideology in the Book of Genesis', in Philip E. Satterthwaite, Richard S. Hess and Gordon J. Wenham (eds.), *The Lord's Anointed: Interpretation of Old Testament Messianic Texts* (Carlisle: Paternoster, 1995), pp. 19–39 (27–32).

61. The term *zera'* (seed) may refer to 'descendants' collectively, or to a single descendent. The pronoun *hû'* (he) is often taken to suggest the latter; however as a pronoun it agrees with its antecedent, *zera'*, a masculine singular noun; whether it should be translated 'he', 'it' (because Hebrew has no neuter) or 'they' depends on the interpretation of *zera'*. Traditionally Gen. 3:15 is taken to refer to Christ's victory over Satan, and several Jewish writings (including the LXX, the Palestinian targums and the Onkelos targum) also appear to relate it to the Messiah's victory over Satan. That is possible. But, even if it does not specifically refer to a single descendant of the woman who will crush the serpent's head, it does point to a victory on behalf of the human race, which we know was won, finally, by Christ.

62. Speiser and Grayson, 'Akkadian Myths', in *ANET*, p. 96.

In Genesis 3:1 the snake is described as 'crafty' or 'shrewd' (*'ārûm*). This may have the sense of wise or sensible, but may also mean cunning or wily. It sounds like the word for 'naked' (*'ārûm*) used in Genesis 2:25, a poetic device that links the creation account with the account of the fall.

The nature of temptation

The serpent first raises a question in Eve's mind: *did God really say?* (Gen. 3:1). Her response shows that she may already be feeling dissatisfied and disaffected. So, she emphasizes the prohibition rather than the abundant provision: she omits the word 'any' (v. 2) and exaggerates the command: *you shall not eat of it – or touch it* (v. 3; cf. 2:17).[63] That gives the serpent a foothold. It proceeds to challenge outright what God has said, *you will not surely die* (v. 4), it questions God's motives in giving the command, and finally makes what is an almost irresistible offer: *when you eat of it . . . you will be like God* (v. 5). This desire to be like God, and even to take his place, is at the heart of temptation and sin (Isa. 14:12–15).[64]

Divine judgment[65]

Guilt

The first expression of guilt is subjective: Adam and Eve feel ashamed (Gen. 3:7–10) in the presence of God (see also Isa. 6:5). This continues the play on the similar sounding words 'naked' and 'shrewd', and introduces an irony: they want to be 'wise', and discover instead they are 'naked'. But guilt is also

---

63. The original instruction was given to Adam, and we may assume Eve heard the instruction from him (rather than directly from God). It is possible the narrator wants to imply that Adam did not trust his partner to act responsibly and so put an additional 'fence' around the commandment. It seems more likely, though, that the repetition, with variation, is intended to indicate something about Eve's attitude to God.

64. Significantly, when Paul describes Christ's attitude in Phil. 2:6–7a, it is just the opposite of this: *who, being in very nature God, did not consider equality with God something to be grasped, but made himself nothing.*

65. See also John Goldingay, 'Postmodernising Eve & Adam (Can I have my Apricot as Well as Eating it?)', in Philip R. Davies (ed.), *The World of Genesis: Persons, Places, Perspectives* (Sheffield: Sheffield Academic Press, 1998), pp. 50–59; Alan J. Hauser, 'Gen. 2–3: The Theme of Intimacy and Alienation', in Hess and Tsumura, *Inscriptions*, pp. 383–398; R. W. L. Moberly, 'Did the Serpent Get it Right?', *JTS*, NS 39 (1988), pp. 1–27.

objective (e.g. Exod. 34:7; Lev. 4:13; 5:17; Num. 14:18). Eichrodt describes it as 'liability to punishment at the hands of God'.[66] Sin brings guilt before God, the divine judge, even where there is no subjective awareness of it. Note too that the OT recognizes that all sin is ultimately against God (Ps. 51:4; see also e.g. Lev. 5:19; 6:2).

Punishment

In other ANE religions punishment was the reaction of an offended god and, because of the variable character (and emotional instability) of the gods, this could be arbitrary. As we have seen, in the Atrahasis Epic the flood is sent to wipe out the human race because their noise disturbs Enlil's sleep: 'Enlil heard their noise and addressed the great gods. The noise of humankind has become too intense for me, with their uproar I am deprived of sleep.'[67] This is in striking contrast to the reason for God's judgment given in Genesis 6:5–6, *The LORD saw how great man's wickedness on the earth had become, and that every inclination of the thoughts of his heart was only evil all the time. The LORD was grieved that he had made man on the earth, and his heart was filled with pain.* In the OT, divine punishment is linked with divine wrath but, as we have already seen, that wrath is never arbitrary pique, and usually comes only after a long period of grace in which people are encouraged to repent.[68]

In Genesis 3 one consequence of sin is death. Access to the Tree of Life is denied (Gen. 3:22–24) and human beings will return to the dust from which they came (Gen. 3:19). This appears to follow God's threat in Genesis 2:17, *when you eat of [the fruit] you will surely die.* This is traditionally taken to refer to *physical death*: as a result of sin, death entered the world and human beings became mortal. There may also be a link between sin and the shortening of the span of human life in Genesis 6:3.[69] However, Genesis 2:17 suggests

---

66. Eichrodt, *Theology*, 2:413; see also Goldingay, *OT Theology*, 2:573–574; Preuss, *Theology*, 2:170–177.

67. See Arnold and Beyer, *Readings*, p. 26; Millard, 'Babylonian "Genesis"', p. 11.

68. It is possible that the 'noise' in the Atrahasis Epic is a euphemism for sin; in *Enuma Elish* it is the noise of the younger gods that provokes Apsu (Arnold and Beyer, *Readings*, p. 32). It is still the case, though, that the flood is prompted by Enlil's capricious and irrational anger; we see this further in Ea's challenge to Enlil: 'How could you, unreasoning, bring on the deluge?' (Arnold and Beyer, *Readings*, p. 69).

69. This verse is open to several interpretations; at face value, though, it appears to have more to do with limiting the amount of damage human beings can do during their time on earth than with punishing their misdeeds.

immediate retribution,[70] while Adam went on to live to the ripe old age of 930!
The fact that the threat was not carried out immediately undermines its seriousness if it refers to physical death alone. And for those who first read this
story, living to such a great age would not indicate divine judgment. It may be
better, therefore, to understand death in Genesis 2:17 primarily in terms of
separation from God. In the OT, physical death also has a spiritual dimension:
it brings relationship with God to an end. Similarly life is more than mere existence: it is also about continuing to enjoy the blessings of God's presence
(Deut. 30:15–16, 19–20). The real threat and the real punishment here is expulsion from the garden, and with it exclusion from the blessings of being in
God's presence. A result of this is that human beings may no longer eat from
the Tree of Life, so death, here, certainly includes mortality;[71] but it is more
than that. The reference to returning to the dust again indicates mortality, but
also reminds human beings of where they came from, and what they are
without God. They sought a life independent of him, and, as a result, would
go back to what they had been without him.

God's purpose for humankind

In Genesis 1:28 God's purpose for humankind is expressed in a threefold
instruction: increase in number, subdue the earth and rule over every living
creature.[72] Lawrence Turner sees this as one of several passages in Genesis that
announce important themes in the ensuing narrative and indicate how the
reader might expect the plot to develop.[73] Significantly all three elements are
undermined by the fall and the consequent judgment announced in Genesis
3:14–19. As a result of God's judgment, the means of increasing in number,
childbirth, is made difficult and painful (v. 16); it will also be painful and

---

70. The NIV when (Gen. 2:17) translates běyôm ('in the day': see NRSV).

71. We assume from the story that immortality required continued eating from the
    Tree of Life, and this corresponds to the need for a continuing relationship with
    God, as symbolized by life in the Garden.

72. Goldingay sees this as a sharing of God's work with human beings, who 'continue
    the task of subduing and ordering the earth . . . It is now humanity's task to bring
    in the rule of God over the created world' (OT Theology, 2:523).

73. Turner, Announcements. In Turner's view the primeval history is introduced by Gen.
    1:28; the plot of the Abraham story is announced in Gen. 12:1–3; themes that will
    be developed in the story of Jacob are announced in Gen. 25:23 and 27:27–29,
    39–40; finally the story of Jacob's family, which focuses largely on Joseph, is
    introduced by Gen. 35:5–11.

difficult to work the land (v. 17), and dominion over the animals, already undermined by the fact that the serpent deceived the first human pair, is replaced with conflict (v. 15).

After the fall, these things are further undermined. The imperative to increase in number is complicated by murder (Gen. 4:8, 23–24). There is another complication in Genesis 6:1–3. This is a difficult text, but indicates that when people did begin to multiply, the result was negative. Problems associated with subduing the earth are even greater. Outside Eden, agriculture will be difficult. Cain began as a farmer, but his sin led to further difficulties (Gen. 4:11–12). And when we come to the story of the flood, this seems to suggest that, far from humankind subduing the earth, the earth has subdued humankind.

Putting Eve in her place[74]

All literature, including the OT, reflects something of the cultural and ideological values of its writers: people write in the context of the world they know. Their writing may also serve a particular agenda. It is argued that the OT reflects (and seeks to maintain) the values and concerns of a patriarchal society, and that is what we see in Genesis 2 – 3, which could be read as an

---

74. See e.g. Childs, *OT Theology*, pp. 188–195; David J. A. Clines, 'What Does Eve Do to Help? and Other Irredeemably Androcentric Orientations in Genesis 1–3', in *What Does Eve Do to Help? And Other Readerly Questions to the Old Testament*, JSOTSup 94 (Sheffield: JSOT Press, 1990), pp. 25–48; Danna Nolan Fewell, 'Reading the Bible Ideologically: Feminist Criticism', in Steven L. McKenzie and Stephen R. Haynes (eds.), *To Each Its Own Meaning: An Introduction to Biblical Criticisms and Their Application*, rev. ed. (Louisville: Westminster John Knox, 1995), pp. 268–282; Goldingay, *OT Theology*, 1:105–109; Gunn and Fewell, *Narrative*, pp. 194–205; Carol Meyers, *Discovering Eve: Ancient Israelite Women in Context* (New York: Oxford University Press, 1988), pp. 72–121; Trible, *Rhetoric of Sexuality*, pp. 72–143. On feminist criticism, see also e.g. Alice Bach, 'Good to the Last Drop: Viewing the Sotah (Numbers 5.11–31) as the Glass Half Full and Wondering How to View it Half Full', in Exum and Clines, *New Literary Criticism*, pp. 26–54; Alice Ogden Bellis, *Helpmates, Harlots and Heroes: Women's Stories in the Hebrew Bible* (Louisville: Westminster John Knox, 1994); Phyllis A. Bird, *Missing Persons and Mistaken Identities: Women and Gender in Ancient Israel*, OBT (Philadelphia: Fortress, 1997); Eryl W. Davies, *The Dissenting Reader: Feminist Approaches to the Hebrew Bible* (Aldershot: Ashgate, 2003); Phyllis A. Trible, *Texts of Terror: Literary-Feminist Readings of Biblical Narratives*, OBT (Minneapolis: Augsburg Fortress, 1984).

explanation of why women should be kept in subjection to men.[75] Eve was created after Adam; Adam named her, signifying his authority over her; she was the one responsible for giving way to temptation and for the disobedience that led to expulsion from the garden. So far as her role in life is concerned, she is Adam's helper; as her name ('mother of all the living') indicates,[76] her role is to bear children, the one thing Adam cannot do alone.

Phyllis Trible takes a more positive view: she argues that Eve is presented as decisive and assertive, while Adam is passive. Certainly it is Eve who converses with the snake, disobeys God and leads Adam into temptation. On the other hand, Adam seems willing to be led and offers no resistance, and there is no indication in the narrative that Eve employed any kind of deception to draw Adam into her sin. In these chapters of Genesis Eve is much more fully characterized than Adam. We are given an insight into Eve's inner tensions, her growing dissatisfaction with life in the garden and her desire for knowledge, while the character of Adam seems flat by comparison. It is unlikely the passage is intended to challenge patriarchal ideology; but nor does it offer outright support. The difference in characterization is significant. The idea of a weak, passive, irresponsible male in a text that might be expected to assert male dominance is a contradiction, and raises doubts about the man's suitability for the status assigned to him. Eve did not subvert Adam; rather, both failed to fulfil the role for which God created them.

The 'fall' of humankind

According to the traditional Christian interpretation, the sin of the first human pair had a devastating and permanent impact on the whole of humanity.[77] Adam stood as the representative head of the human race, and the guilt and consequences of his sin thus affect every member of the race after

---

75. E.g. Deborah W. Rooke, 'Feminist Criticism of the Old Testament: Why Bother?', *Feminist Theology* 15.2 (2007), pp. 160–174. Rooke sees this passage as 'primarily intended to enforce a patriarchal world-order' (p. 171), and the response to Eve represents the 'knee-jerk reaction of patriarchy when its authority is challenged' (p. 170).

76. See the discussion of Eve's name, above, pp. 81–82.

77. This is also reflected in Jewish texts, e.g. 2 Esdras 7.118, *O Adam, what have you done? For though it was you who sinned, the fall was not yours alone, but ours also who are your descendants.* Though rabbinic literature appears to attach more significance to the 'sons of God' episode in Gen. 6:1–4 when discussing the problem of sin and evil in the world (e.g. *1 Enoch* 6–10).

him.[78] Some, however, question this interpretation, arguing that the text does not imply such an all-embracing significance and that the rest of the OT does not presume it or link the presence of sin in the world with a primeval 'fall'.[79] We need to be wary of reading more into the text than it actually says. However, though the term 'fall' may not be used,[80] the effect of sin described in Genesis 3:14–19, on human beings and on the order of creation, does indicate a far-reaching and continuing significance. This is reinforced by the reference to Eve as *the mother of all the living* that immediately follows (Gen. 3:20), suggesting that the entire human race must now live with the consequences of her and Adam's sin. We have noted too how this judgment threatens God's purpose in creating human beings (announced in Gen. 1:28) and so points to the serious impact of sin on creation itself. The position of Genesis 3 within the primeval history also indicates its significance. The nature of the sin as a desire to be like God and so break free from dependence on him is fundamental to the decline that begins here and culminates in the rebellion against God by the tower builders at Babel (Gen. 11:1–9).[81] As such it gives a theological explanation for the problems of everyday human existence. The OT writers acknowledge the pervasiveness of sin within human nature (e.g. Ps. 51:5; Jer. 17:9; cf. Gen. 6:5; 8:21; Job 14:4; 15:14; Ps. 58:3). House notes that after Genesis 3, no human being avoids sin: it affects every person in every generation,[82] and it seems probable that, in its position at the start of the canon, the story of Adam and Eve's disobedience is intended to explain why this is.

Goldingay questions the appropriateness of the term 'fall', but does allow its usefulness,

> in its assertion that at the beginning of the human story something happened that brought about a once-for-all negative change to humanity's situation . . . The first

---

78. This is seen in the NT; e.g. Rom. 5:12, 14–19; 1 Cor. 15:22.

79. See e.g. Köhler, *OT Theology*, pp. 178–181; Westermann, *Creation*, p. 89.

80. There are no specific references to the 'fall' of the human race linked with Gen. 3 in either Testament. Paul speaks of sin causing human beings to *fall short of the glory of God* (Rom. 3:23), and while that failure may be evident also in Gen. 3, there is no direct link. Paul does, though, attribute the entrance of sin into the world to Adam's disobedience (Rom. 5:12–17).

81. See below. Clines notes the possibility that these two incidents form an inclusio: 'with the final episode in the story of human sin repeating and balancing the first' (Clines, *Theme*, p. 70).

82. House, *OT Theology*, p. 67.

human beings acted in a way that had decisive implications for everyone who would come after, who would not be able to undo what they had done.[83]

Eichrodt is less critical of the traditional terminology: he suggests Genesis 3 does indeed point to

> a decisive event, by which God's plan for Man in his creation was frustrated and human history came to be branded with the stamp of enmity towards God. *This event has the character of a 'Fall', that is of a falling out of the line of the development willed by God,* and, as the subsequent narrative shows, exerts a determining influence on the spiritual attitude of all men.[84]

The spread of sin

Genesis 4 – 11 catalogues a quickening decline into sin. Disobedience in Genesis 3 becomes murder in Genesis 4. And within the space of a few generations, what Cain does in secret and tries to hide (Gen. 4:8–9), Lamech openly acknowledges, and even makes an occasion for boasting (Gen. 4:23–24). This culminates in God's tragic conclusion about the state of humankind (Gen. 6:5–6), and his decision to send the flood.[85] After the flood God blesses Noah (Gen. 9:1–3). This is similar to the blessing in Genesis 1:28, though there are significant differences. The first imperative is unchanged, *Be fruitful and increase in number and fill the earth* (9:1), though the difficulty of carrying it out has increased. The second command, to subdue the earth, is entirely missing, suggesting that the task has by now become impossible. The idea of humankind ruling over the animal kingdom is still there (9:2–3) but the relationship has now become one of fear, with permission given to kill animals for

---

83. Goldingay, *OT Theology*, 1:144–148 (145). Fretheim also questions the use of the term 'fall' in relation to Gen. 3, though suggests that this began the process by which sin became 'universal and inescapable'; see Terence E. Fretheim, *The Pentateuch* (Nashville: Abingdon, 1996), p. 77.

84. Eichrodt, *Theology*, 2:406. Childs too prefers to retain 'fall' terminology (*Biblical Theology* [1992], pp. 570–571).

85. The 'sons of God, daughters of men' episode in Gen. 6:1–4 is often thought to be linked to the flood, though the nature of the link (and the meaning of the passage) is unclear. One possibility is that it emphasizes the extent of sin and disorder (chaos?) in the world seen in the crossing of the boundary between the human and the divine. This is seen in Gen. 3; it is there to some extent in Gen. 11, and it may be evident also in Gen. 6:1–4.

food.[86] As we have noted, Genesis 1:28 may be seen as an announcement, alerting the reader to what will be important issues in the unfolding plot.[87] The substantial modifications in Genesis 9:1–3 prompt us to look back over the text and note how and why changes have taken place – in this case largely as a result of the fall.

After the flood humankind's moral decay continues, and in Genesis 11 we see further rebellion against God at Babel. The people want to *make a name for themselves* (Gen. 11:4); they want to take control of their own destiny – a hubris echoing that of Adam and Eve, who also wanted to be like God and to break free from dependence on him (Gen. 3:5). At Babel, though, the sin that began in the garden may be seen to be more fully grown, into the arrogant desire not only to become independent of God but to displace him: to take his place as lord of creation and of history, and, by human labour and ingenuity, even to gain access to heaven itself.[88] The decision to build the tower is also related to not wanting to be *scattered over the face of the whole earth* (Gen. 11:4), suggesting resistance to God's purpose for humankind to fill the earth. Such pride and defiance may not go unpunished, and so God's judgment falls again, scattering the people and confusing their language.[89]

---

86. There is evidence of a changing relationship before this: Abel killed some of his flock to offer a sacrifice (4:4), and after the flood had subsided, Noah also killed animals and birds as sacrifices. The significant difference after the flood is that animals may be killed for food as well as sacrifice, thus pointing to the potential for even greater slaughter (cf. Gen. 10:8–9).

87. Above, pp. 152–153.

88. A *tower that reaches to the heavens* (Gen. 11:4) may refer to a vast tower that will stand as a monument to human achievement. 'Heavens' though may refer to God's dwelling place, and building such a tower may represent an attempt to make an assault on God (cf. Isa. 14:13–14), or at least to gain access to a domain that belongs to God alone, and so further break down the barriers between the human and the divine. There is irony in Gen. 11:4, where God comes *down* to see what they are doing!

89. While it may be argued that the sin at Babel has the characteristics of, and so could be seen to repeat and even intensify, the sin in Gen. 3, can it be seen as the climax of the decline into sin in Gen. 1 – 11 rather than, say, the flood? Certainly the flood is central to the Creation–Uncreation–Recreation theme, which points to its significance, and we have also noted its importance in relation to God's commitment to the world, and his intention never to allow the waters of chaos to return. However, as Clines notes, the negative impact of the flood was not as

Divine grace

However, even against the backcloth of this long and inexorable decline into sin, God's grace is evident in the expressions of mercy that accompany the curses and judgments in Genesis 3 – 11. Adam and Eve are expelled from Eden, but not before God has clothed them (3:21); Cain is made a wanderer, but is given a mark of divine protection (4:15); despite the global destruction of the flood, Noah and his family are saved, and the confusion of tongues at Babel is followed by the genealogy of Shem (11:10–26), which links the primal history to the patriarchs, and introduces the promise of restoration through Abraham.

The call of Abraham in Genesis 12 marks a significant turning point: it opens the way for the nations, on whom God's judgment has just fallen, ultimately to receive his blessing.

Footnote 89 (*continued*)

> lasting as the judgment at Babel (Clines, *Theme*, p. 70). The flood itself affected only the generation alive at the time, and afterwards the human race continued through Noah and his family. In contrast, the confusion of tongues at Babel has resulted in a permanent division within the human race. Clines also notes that in Gen. 10 (in anticipation of the events at Babel) different groups are referred to as 'nations' (*gôyîm*) rather than 'people' ('*am*; Gen. 11:6), which implies a kinship that has been broken.

4. GOD AND HIS PEOPLE (1): ELECTION AND COVENANT[1]

The idea of covenant in the Old Testament[2]

The OT view of God is of one who has made himself known. He has shown himself to humankind in general, but has also entered into a unique

---

1. B. W. Anderson, *Contours*, pp. 74–105, 137–164; Brueggemann, *Theology*, pp. 415–434, 578–599; Childs, *Biblical Theology* (1992), 413–428; *OT Theology*, pp. 155–174; Clements, *OT Theology*, 77–103; Drane, *Introducing the OT*, pp. 47–57; Dyrness, *Themes*, pp. 113–141; Eichrodt, *Theology*, 1:36–97; Goldingay, *OT Theology*, 1:173–175, 181–183 (Noahic covenant), 193–251 (Abrahamic covenant), 369–385 (Sinaitic covenant), 559–560 (Davidic covenant), 713–715 (new covenant); 2:182–209; House, *OT Theology*, pp. 71–76, 109–118, 169–172; Jacob, *Theology*, pp. 201–223; Kaiser, *OT Theology*, pp. 100–121; Köhler, *OT Theology*, pp. 59–84; Elmer A. Martens, 'The People of God', in Scott J. Hafemann and Paul R. House (eds.), *Central Themes in Biblical Theology: Mapping Unity in Diversity* (Leicester: Apollos; Grand Rapids: Baker, 2007), pp. 225–253; Preuss, *OT Theology*, 1:27–28; von Rad, *OT Theology*, 1:129–135; Rendtorff, *Hebrew Bible*, pp. 432–456.
2. For a recent overview of scholarship, see Scott Hahn, 'Covenant in the Old and New Testaments', *Currents in Biblical Research* 3 (2005), pp. 263–292; see also Ronald E. Clements, *Prophecy and Covenant*, SBT 43 (London: SCM, 1965); *Abraham and*

relationship with one people in particular: the nation of Israel. This relationship, of vital significance to the life of Israel, was expressed in the form of a *covenant (běrît)*. As we have seen, Eichrodt attaches great importance to this idea and makes it the point of departure for his *OT Theology*: 'the concept in which Israelite thought gave definite expression to the binding of the people to God and by means of which they established firmly from the start the particularity of their knowledge of him was the Covenant'.[3]

How old is the idea of covenant?

Many modern scholars claim that the idea of covenant developed late in Israel's history. It is often associated with the 'Deuteronomic movement',[4]

Footnote 2 (*continued*)

> *David*; John Bright, *Covenant and Promise* (London: SCM, 1977); William J. Dumbrell, *Covenant and Creation: A Theology of the Old Testament Covenants* (Exeter: Paternoster, 1984; repr. Biblical and Theological Classics Library; Carlisle: Paternoster, 1997); Scott J. Hafemann, 'The Covenant Relationship', in Hafemann and House, *Central Themes*, pp. 20–65; Kitchen, *Ancient Orient*, pp. 90–102; *Reliability*, pp. 283–294; Meredith G. Kline, *Treaty of the Great King* (Grand Rapids: Eerdmans, 1963); Levenson, *Sinai and Zion*; Dennis J. McCarthy, *Treaty and Covenant* (Rome: Pontifical Biblical Institute, 1963); *Old Testament Covenant* (Oxford: Blackwell, 1972); Thomas Edward McComiskey, *The Covenants of Promise* (Nottingham: IVP, 1985); J. Gordon McConville, '*běrît*', in *NIDOTTE* 1:747–755; George E. Mendenhall, 'Covenant', in *IDB* 1:714–723; E. W. Nicholson, *God and his People: Covenant and Theology in the Old Testament* (Oxford: Oxford University Press, 1986); O. Palmer Robertson, *Christ of the Covenants* (Phillipsburg: P. & R., 1980); Moshe Weinfeld, '*běrît*', in *TDOT* 2:253–279; 'The Covenant of Grant in the Ancient Near East', *JAOS* 90 (1970), pp. 184–203; P. R. Williamson, 'Covenant', in *NDBT*, pp. 419–429; *Sealed with an Oath: Covenant in God's Unfolding Purpose*, NSBT 23 (Leicester: Apollos; Downers Grove: IVP Academic, 2007).

3. Eichrodt, *Theology*, 1:36.

4. B. W. Anderson notes a distinction between the terms 'Deuteronomic' and 'Deuteronomistic' (*Living World*, p. 183). The former relates to the content of the book of Deuteronomy, and so also (as here) to movements, etc. that promote or take direction from Deuteronomy; the latter is usually used in connection with the historical books Joshua to 2 Kings, thought to be influenced by Deuteronomic ideas, the so-called Deuteronomistic History (see below, pp. 261–263).

which dates from the seventh century BC.[5] However, covenants in the form of international treaties were well known in the fourteenth/thirteenth centuries BC. In an article published in 1954 Mendenhall noted significant parallels between the Sinaitic covenant and second-millennium Hittite vassal treaties, where a king made a treaty with a subject power, offering protection in return for loyalty and obedience.[6] These parallels have strengthened the arguments in favour of an early dating of Deuteronomy.

The ANE treaties included an *introduction* or *preamble*, which identified the speaker ('These are the words of . . .'; cf. Exod. 20:1; Deut. 1:1–5; Josh. 24:2); a *historical prologue*, which described the events leading up to the treaty and listed some of what the suzerain had already done for the vassal (cf. Exod. 20:2; Deut. 1:6–3:29; Josh. 24:2–13); and a statement of the requirements and obligations placed upon the vassal (cf. Exod. 20:3–17; 21 – 23; Deut. 4 – 26; Josh. 24:14–25). There was often also a *document clause*, with instructions for depositing a copy of the covenant in the vassal's sanctuary and, possibly, for its public reading or renewal (cf. Deut. 27:1–26; Josh. 24:26). There would also be a call for the gods of the participating nations to act as *witnesses* to guarantee the treaty (cf. Exod. 24:4; Deut. 30:19; 31:19; 32:1–43; Josh. 24:25–28), and a list of *blessings or curses* that resulted from compliance or non-compliance with its terms (cf. Deut. 28 – 30). Comparisons are also made with ninth–seventh century BC Assyrian treaties, which are taken to support the later date, though Kitchen's analysis shows a much closer correspondence to the earlier treaty

---

5. As noted above (p. 95, n. 49), Cook argues for the existence of a stream of Sinaitic theology, which includes the idea of covenant, from earliest times in Israel. He accepts that Deuteronomy was written in the seventh century BC, but it reflects earlier Sinaitic traditions; see Cook, *Social Roots*, pp. 23–28, 58.

6. George E. Mendenhall, 'Covenant Forms in Israelite Tradition', *BA* 17.3 (1954), pp. 49–76; reprinted in *Law and Covenant in Israel and the Ancient Near East* (Pittsburgh: The Biblical Colloquium, 1955). See also e.g. Craigie, *Deuteronomy*, pp. 22–24; Drane, *Introducing the OT*, pp. 55–56; Dyrness, *Themes*, pp. 14–116; House, *OT Theology*, pp. 171–172; Kitchen, *Ancient Orient*, pp. 92–94; *Reliability*, pp. 283–312; Levenson, *Sinai and Zion*, pp. 23–56; Thompson, *Deuteronomy*, pp. 14–21.

7. Kitchen, *Reliability*, p. 288. Assyrian treaties do not include a historical prologue and though there are curses, there are no blessings. Parallels have been noted between the curses in Deut. 28 and the 'Vassal Treaties of Esarhaddon', the Assyrian king who succeeded Sennacherib; see Moshe Weinfeld, *Deuteronomy and the Deuteronomic School* (Oxford: Clarendon, 1972), and the discussion by J. Gordon McConville,

forms,[7] and he takes this to affirm 'that the Sinai covenant really was instituted and renewed in the thirteenth century BC'.[8] Craigie argues that though they may not prove an early date for the Deuteronomy and covenant concept, they do support it, and he notes that this form of covenant was particularly appropriate at the time of the exodus. Israel was freed from Egypt to become the willing vassal of a new (divine) overlord. Craigie observes, 'the form of the book and the religious significance of that form make it not unreasonable to assume that the book comes from the time of Moses or shortly thereafter'.[9]

Hittite suzerainty treaties, then, indicate that the covenant concept has a long history. Scholars have also noted a resemblance between the OT civil law and other collections of laws in the ANE.[10] Bright points further to the history of Israel itself, and suggests that 'it is difficult to understand early Israel in any other way than as a tribal league, or confederation, formed in covenant with Yahweh and under the rule of Yahweh'.[11] He goes on to assert that

> we may believe with some confidence that Israel did in fact come into being as a
> sacral confederation formed in covenant with Yahweh, and that this covenant
> followed broadly the pattern of those international suzerainty treaties that are known
> to us from texts of the second millennium BC.[12]

Cook takes issue with this, maintaining that Israel's national life could not have been founded on covenant alone, but required underlying bonds of kinship. Nevertheless he argues in favour of an early dating for the covenant idea, which brought cultural practices and social institutions under Yahweh's authority.[13]

Footnote 7 (*continued*)

Deuteronomy, AOTC (Leicester: Apollos; Downers Grove: IVP, 2002), pp. 23–24, 402–403. McConville notes Steymans's view that the Deuteronomy text is taken from a section of the Assyrian document. Arguments for direct dependence are weak, though, and McConville concludes that the case is not proven.

8. Kitchen, *Ancient Orient*, p. 99.

9. Craigie, *Deuteronomy*, p. 28.

10. The Hammurabi Law Code (eighteenth century BC) includes similar legislation, including what to do if a bull gores a person to death (cf. Exod. 21:28–30) and the eye-for-an-eye, tooth-for-a-tooth dictum (Exod. 21:24); see Arnold and Beyer, *Readings*, pp. 113–114.

11. Bright, *Covenant*, p. 35.

12. Ibid., p. 43.

13. Cook, *Social Roots*, pp. 23–24, 158–159.

Eichrodt also supports the idea that the covenant concept arose early in Israel's history: he maintains that 'the safest starting point for the critical examination of Israel's relationship with God is still the plain impression given by the OT itself that Moses, taking over a concept of long standing in secular life, based his worship of Yahweh on a covenant agreement'.[14]

What is a covenant?

Covenants were a common feature of life in the ANE, and played an important part in business, politics and family life, as well as in religion. A covenant was not just an agreement or contract; it was a solemn bond established between two or more parties (usually on the basis of a promise or pledge) and involved a firm commitment to the relationship established by the covenant and to its obligations.[15] Making a covenant was a serious matter. It might be accompanied by sacrifice (e.g. Gen. 15:9–10; Jer. 34:18–19) or a covenant meal (e.g. Gen. 26:30; 31:54),[16] or be confirmed by a solemn oath (e.g. Gen. 21:31; 26:31; Josh. 9:15; 2 Kgs 11:4; Neh. 10:28–29), which, even though extracted by deception, was regarded as irrevocable (e.g. Josh. 9:15; cf. Num. 30:2; Ezek. 17:15–16).

Běrît is applied to treaties between national powers: either an alliance between equals (e.g. Gen. 14:13; 21:27, 32) or the conditions for peace and protection imposed by a greater power upon a lesser (e.g. Josh. 9:11; 1 Sam. 11:1–2; 1 Kgs 15:19–20; Ezek. 17:13–19). In each case the relationship involves mutual obligation. *Běrît* also describes the relationship between a king and his subjects (e.g. 2 Sam. 3:21; 5:3; 2 Kgs 11:17; Jer. 34:8). Each had a part to play in the successful functioning of society, and a ruler should be as aware of his obligation to the people as they of their duty to him.

An important use of *běrît* is in connection with marriage (e.g. Prov. 2:17; Mal. 2:14).[17] When married, a husband and wife enter into a covenant

---

14. Eichrodt, *Theology*, 1:37.

15. The Hebrew word *běrît* is sometimes linked with the Akkadian *biritu* (fetter), suggesting the binding nature of the settlement. It has been suggested that *běrît* originally involved a one-sided obligation, a solemn promise or a condition imposed on someone else, and developed into a mutually conditioned agreement.

16. The usual Hebrew expression for covenant inception is, literally, 'to cut a covenant' (*kārat běrît*). This may be linked with the practice of cutting an animal in half and walking between the pieces, or with cutting food as part of a covenant meal.

17. See further Gordon P. Hugenburger, *Marriage as a Covenant: Biblical Law and Ethics as Developed from Malachi*, Biblical Studies Library (Grand Rapids: Baker, 1998).

relationship that involves total commitment to one another (Gen. 2:24), in which each accepts the obligations and responsibilities their relationship imposes on them both. The covenant between God and Israel is often likened to the bond between husband and wife (e.g. Isa. 54:5; Jer. 2:2; 3:14, 20; 31:32; Hos. 2:7, 16).

Divine covenants

There are several divine covenants in the OT. The first reference to *běrît* is in connection with the covenant with Noah (Gen. 6:18; cf. 9:8–16). This has as its heart God's commitment to his world and expresses his intention to restore what has been spoilt by the fall. Some discussions also refer to a covenant with Adam,[18] though it may be more appropriate to talk about a covenant implicit within the act of creation itself, a 'covenant with creation',[19] which is then *confirmed* in the Noahic covenant.[20] Other divine covenants include those with

---

18. Traditional covenant theology notes a 'covenant of works' between God and Adam, offering life as a reward for obedience. Adam's disobedience made necessary the 'covenant of grace', which offers life and salvation through faith in Christ. This emphasizes God's demand for obedience, humankind's inability to meet that demand, and the need for God's gracious provision of salvation. However, there is little scriptural support for the idea of Adam's probation. In the Genesis account sin leads to the loss of blessings already received: life in the garden, knowing the presence of God, sharing his rest and eating the fruit of the Tree of Life (the idea that they had not eaten from this tree prior to the fall is implausible). Hos. 6:7 is often quoted in this connection: *like Adam they have broken the covenant – they were unfaithful to me there.* Many commentators prefer to translate, 'at Adam . . .', referring to the place mentioned in Josh. 3:16, though the precise nature of the transgression there is unclear. See further Dumbrell, *Covenant*, pp. 44–46; McComiskey, *Covenants*, pp. 213–221.

19. See Dumbrell, *Faith*, p. 26; Goldingay, *OT Theology*, 1:91–93; Murray, *Cosmic Covenant*; Robertson, *Christ of the Covenants*, pp. 67–87; Walter F. Vogels, *God's Universal Covenant* (Ottawa: University of Ottawa Press, 1979). For further discussion of a universal covenant and its relationship to the Noahic covenant, see below, p. 321.

20. In Gen. 6:18 the usual expression *kārat běrît is* is replaced with *hēqîm běrît*, which generally refers to the confirmation of a covenant already established (e.g. Gen. 9:9, 11, 17; 17:2, 19, 21; Exod. 6:4; Lev. 26:9; Deut. 8:18). It has been argued that P uses *hēqîm běrît* for covenant inception in Gen. 6:18 (and also in Gen. 17, which might then point to a second covenant with Abraham). See Dumbrell, *Faith*,

Abraham, with Israel at Sinai, with Israel's priests, and with David. We will look at the covenants with Israel's priests and with David when we discuss priesthood and kingship, respectively. For the moment we will focus on God's covenant with Abraham and the covenant made at Sinai.

The covenant with Abraham

The second covenant, and the first to refer to God's election of a people through whom God's purpose of redemption would begin to be fulfilled, is with Abraham. The promises to Abraham are spread through several sections of the Genesis narrative. In Genesis 12:2–3 God declares:

> *I will make you into a great nation*
> *and I will bless you;*
> *I will make your name great,*
> *and you will be a blessing.*
> *I will bless those who bless you,*
> *and whoever curses you I will curse;*
> *and all peoples on earth*
> *will be blessed through you.*

God's unconditional promise that Abraham will have many offspring and that his descendants will occupy the land of Canaan is confirmed in a covenant (Gen. 15).[21] There is further reference to a covenant between God and Abraham in Genesis 17:7, *I will establish my covenant as an everlasting covenant between me and you and your descendants after you for the generations to come, to be your God and the God of your descendants after you*, though this is conditional upon Abraham's obedience (v. 1), and particularly on the observance of the rite of circumcision (vv. 10–14).[22] Finally, after testing Abraham's obedience, God confirms his promises with an oath (Gen. 22:16–18; see also 26:3–5).

---

pp. 25–26; *Covenant*, pp. 24–26, 32; Wenham, *Genesis 1–15*, p. 175; cf. Brueggemann, *Theology*, p. 418.

21. The promissory nature of this covenant has led to it being compared to the royal land grant kings in the ANE might make to loyal subjects; see e.g. Weinfeld, 'Covenant of Grant'; Wenham, *Genesis 1–15*, p. 333.

22. According to source critics, Gen. 15 and 17 are the accounts by J and P respectively of God's covenant with Abraham. I have already pointed out problems with the assumptions of source criticism. Also, differences between the content of, and the

God's promises to Abraham

The Abrahamic covenant includes four key promises. First, God promises that Abraham, at the time childless, will become the father of a great nation (Gen. 12:2), with descendants outnumbering the stars in the sky (Gen. 15:5) and the grains of sand on the seashore (Gen. 22:17), and that the promises and blessings of the covenant will be extended to those descendants and confirmed to successive generations (Gen. 17:19; see also Exod. 2:24). Second, as part of this, God promises to give the land of Canaan to the nation descended from Abraham (Gen. 17:8; see also 12:7; 15:18). The third promise, and the central feature of the covenant relationship, is the divine promise *I will be their God* (Gen. 17:8). The covenant with Noah suggested a general relationship between God and the whole of creation; here, through Abraham, God promises something more. He has chosen this man and this nation to belong to him in a way others do not. It is this continuing relationship with God that accounts for the conditional element in Genesis 17. All who are in covenant relationship with God are expected to live in a way that pleases him. For Abraham in particular, as the father of this people, his exemplary faith must be worked out in exemplary obedience (see Heb. 11:8, 17; Jas 2:21–23).

These three promises were of great significance for the people of Israel in understanding their relationship with God, their special calling and their

---

Footnote 22 (*continued*)

conditions attached to, the covenants described in those chapters make it unlikely that they refer to the same transaction. Those differences have led some to view them as separate (though complementary) covenants; see e.g. T. Desmond Alexander, 'Abraham Reassessed Theologically: The Abraham Narrative and the New Testament Understanding of Justification by Faith', in Hess, Satterthwaite and Wenham, *He Swore an Oath*, pp. 8–28 (14–18); Paul R. Williamson, *Abraham, Israel and the Nations: The Patriarchal Promise and its Covenantal Development in Genesis*, JSOTSup 315 (Sheffield: Sheffield Academic Press, 2000). Others maintain that the 'covenant of circumcision' (Gen. 17) reaffirms the earlier covenant, though expands it both in range and in the conditions attached; see e.g. Joyce G. Baldwin, *Genesis 12–50*, BST (Leicester: IVP, 1986), p. 62; Hamilton, *Genesis 1–17*, p. 459; Kidner, *Genesis*, p. 128; Gordon J. Wenham, *Genesis 16–50*, WBC 2 (Dallas: Word, 1994), pp. 16–19. Whether or not they refer to technically distinct covenants, these passages (and others in the Abraham narrative) present complementary and developing aspects of the relationship between God and Abraham (and his descendants). Consequently this discussion will subsume them all under the general heading 'Abrahamic Covenant'.

attitude to the land. The fourth lifts the covenant out of what might be seen as a purely nationalistic context, and promises universal blessing: *all peoples on earth will be blessed through you* (Gen. 12:3).[23] God promises to bless Abraham so that he and the nation that come from him will in turn be the means by which divine blessing will extend to the whole world. That blessing flows from Abraham's covenant relationship with God, and to share the blessing, the nations must also be brought to share the relationship. Thus the extension of divine blessing anticipates also the extension of the covenant relationship with God to all peoples. The relationship between God and creation may have been broken by sin, but God's commitment to his world, embodied in the earlier covenant with Noah, opens the way for a renewed relationship with God and the blessings associated with it to be established.

The significance of circumcision[24]

An intrinsic part of the Abrahamic covenant is *circumcision*. It is described as the sign of the covenant (Gen. 17:11). In the earlier covenant with Noah the rainbow is described in a similar way: *it will be the sign of the covenant between me and the earth* (Gen. 9:13). In the context of the Sinaitic covenant the Sabbath is also referred to as a *sign* (Exod. 31:13, 16–17). These signs function in different ways. The rainbow is a sign to God (Gen. 9:16), linked with his promise to maintain the order of creation, and not to allow the waters of chaos to return and engulf the world. The Sabbath is a sign to God's people: it points to their special calling, which includes the need to obey God's law, but also suggests that a key aspect of the nation's distinctiveness was to set time aside from regular labour to worship God. Circumcision was, primarily, a mark of belonging to God. It was a sign of the grace by which God chooses and sets his seal on the covenant people he has called to be his own. It also points to the obedience to God that living in covenant relationship with him requires. From infancy, God's people bore this sign that marked them out as belonging to God

---

23. There is some discussion about the precise meaning of the Hebrew expression in this verse. It seems best to take the verb either in a passive (so NIV) or middle sense ('all peoples . . . will find a blessing'). For further discussion, see e.g. Wenham, *Genesis 1–15*, pp. 277–278; Christopher J. H. Wright, *The Mission of God: Unlocking the Bible's Grand Narrative* (Downers Grove: IVP; Leicester: IVP, 2006), pp. 252–254; see also Goldingay, *OT Theology*, 1:213–214; Goldingay suggests that Abraham will become 'a means of other people's blessing . . . as all peoples pray to be blessed as Israel is blessed' (2:205–206).

24. See e.g. Goldingay, *OT Theology*, 1:201–203; Wenham, *Genesis 16–50*, pp. 23–24.

in a special way. They were in turn required to reflect that calling in the way they conducted their lives and to let the outward sign become the mark of inward consecration (e.g. Deut. 10:16; 30:6; Jer. 4:4; cf. Rom. 2:28–29).

Is it thus not inconsistent to say that the Abrahamic covenant is a unilateral act of God's grace, devised, initiated and executed by God, but that it also puts an obligation on those who would inherit the blessings of the covenant to live in accordance with its requirements? Rather than being incompatible, these two things are inseparable: God, in his sovereign grace, has entered into a relationship with Abraham and through him with the people of Israel. While the people can do nothing to earn or merit inclusion within God's covenant people, having been included, they are obliged to seek to live as members of it. The intimacy of their relationship with God must be allowed to affect every part of their lives. This is something that will be even more evident when we come to look at the covenant at Sinai.

But why this particular sign? What is the relationship between circumcision and the covenant with Abraham? Why a sign only applicable to the male population? Did women not have the same assurance of belonging? And why a sign that appears to be closely associated with male sexuality? One possibility is that it indicates the need for discipline in male sexual activity. God's aim is to call into being a distinctive people who will be used by him to bring blessing to the world, and that has implications for family and community life. The birth of children and the biological increase of the community is clearly a very important part of the fulfilment of that purpose; but for the community to retain its distinctiveness, that increase needs to take place in a proper way.[25] With regard to the female members of the community, the OT does not call for, or even suggest, female circumcision as the equivalent of male circumcision. If there is an equivalent, it is probably in giving birth.[26] The link between the sign of the

---

25. It may be significant that the passage on circumcision is placed immediately between the account of Abraham's attempt to move God's purposes along by having a child with Hagar and the promise that Sarai/Sarah will have a son. Any link is speculative, but if circumcision indicates the need for sexual discipline for God's purposes to be fulfilled, it is very appropriate at this point in the narrative, where Abraham's own situation is an example of the problems caused by seeking progeny outside God's plan.

26. This does not, of course, take account of female members of the community who do not have children, and this to some extent reflects the patriarchal nature of the community. We know though that there was a social stigma attached to those women who remained childless.

covenant and procreation does indicate that the raising up of a people is at the heart of God's covenant with Abraham. Occupation of the land is important,[27] but not central in the way that belonging to a special and distinctive people appears to be. And that is what we also see in the Sinaitic covenant.

The Sinaitic covenant

Continuity with the Abrahamic covenant

God promised Abraham that he would be the father of a great nation, which would live in its own land, and whose people would share the close relationship with God that Abraham had known. During Israel's slavery in Egypt God did not forget that covenant, and, in accordance with it, brought the Israelites out of Egypt and promised to lead them to the land of Canaan (Exod. 3:16–17; 6:2–8).

At Sinai God made a covenant relationship with those who came out of Egypt. This is often taken to mark the birth of the nation, and represents, in part, the fulfilment of the promise that Abraham would become the father of a great nation, and the blessings promised to him would extend to his descendants. The second promise concerned the land of Canaan and, though the people had not yet received their inheritance, possession of the Promised Land featured prominently in the events surrounding the exodus. The third promise to Abraham, which lay at the heart of the covenant relationship, was the declaration *I will be their God* (Gen. 17:8). This finds expression in the Sinaitic covenant in the similar statement *I will take you as my own people, and I will be your God* (Exod. 6:7).[28] The final promise, of universal blessing through Abraham's descendants, is seen in Israel's call to be a nation of priests, who will make God known to the nations and will bring the nations to God.

Election

The uniqueness of election

We have noted that, because of the significance of the relationship between God and Israel established by this covenant, the events at Sinai are often

---

27. See below, pp. 241–242.
28. For further discussion, see Rolf Rendtorff, *The Covenant Formula: An Exegetical and Theological Investigation*, OTS (Edinburgh: T. & T. Clark, 1998); cf. Preuss, *OT Theology*, 1:76–77.

regarded as marking the birth of Israel as a nation. However, nationhood alone does not guarantee receipt of the blessings, and so we see the covenant relationship, together with its demand for obedience, renewed to successive generations. Just before his death, Moses assembled the people on the plains of Moab and exhorted them to renew their commitment to the God who had called and delivered them, and was now about to bring them into the Promised Land (Deut. 29). Here the basic relationship established by the Sinaitic covenant, of Israel as a people belonging to God, is renewed to a generation absent from Sinai (Horeb), or too young to respond to the covenant's demands (vv. 12–13), and is widened further still to incorporate those of future generations who will also accept its obligations (vv. 15, 29).[29] Entry into the covenant relationship between God and his people remains, ever, a contemporary issue, calling for renewed commitment and rededication.

The Sinaitic covenant is also likened to a marriage bond, and the early days in the desert became idealized as the honeymoon period of the relationship between Israel and her divine husband; so, in Jeremiah 2:2 God says:

> *I remember the devotion of your youth,*
> *how as a bride you loved me*
> *and followed me through the desert,*
> *through a land not sown.*

(See also e.g. Isa. 54:5; Jer. 3:14; 31:32; Ezek. 16:8; Hos. 2:16–17.) This way of portraying the covenant relationship gives scope for the love, compassion, tenderness and intimacy that are also part of God's commitment to his people. This is seen, especially, in the prophecy of Hosea, where God's relationship with Israel is mirrored in the prophet's relationship with his unfaithful wife. Through his own pain Hosea is given a glimpse of the heart of God, and of God's desire to win back his bride (Hos. 2:14–15). God's tender feelings for his people and the pain of rejection are evident too in Hosea 11, where the relationship is likened to that between father and son.

In bringing her into this covenant relationship with himself, God singled out Israel from among the nations (Exod. 19:5–6). Israel is unique, set apart from other peoples as God's own 'treasured possession'. The word used here, *sĕgullâ*, occurs elsewhere to denote the personal treasure of a king (1 Chr. 29:3; Eccl. 2:8). We have already noted the special choice of Israel indicated by Deuteronomy 32:8–9. This one nation has been chosen and set apart by

---

29. See Levenson, *Sinai and Zion*, pp. 80–86.

God to enjoy an intimacy with him that other nations do not yet know. Even so, the whole world belongs to God. He owns it all, rules over it all and has a purpose for it all. Israel is called out as God's special, but not his sole, possession, and Israel's role within the divine plan is one that will involve every nation.

The basis of election

As we have noted, the election of Israel was a partial fulfilment of God's promises to Abraham. God's gracious commitment to those earlier promises, expressed even more strongly in the form of an oath (Gen. 24:7; 50:24–25; Exod. 13:11; cf. Heb. 6:17), formed the basis of the divine choice. The idea of election as a gift is clearly seen in Deuteronomy 7:7–8, *The LORD did not set his affection on you and choose you because you were more numerous than other peoples, for you were the fewest of all peoples. But it was because the LORD loved you and kept the oath he swore to your forefathers that he brought you out with a mighty hand and redeemed you from the land of slavery, from the power of Pharaoh, king of Egypt.*

Here, as in earlier covenants, we see God taking the initiative. He chose Israel, redeemed the nation from bondage in Egypt and, in a profound act of sovereign grace, took this people to be his own, committing himself to them. The people were chosen and saved by grace. Such communion with God, however, makes inevitable demands, and the response of the people was to be obedience to the Law: *we will do everything the LORD has said* (Exod. 19:8).

This element of Law has led to the claim that the Sinaitic covenant was fundamentally different from the covenant with Abraham, which is seen, primarily, as a covenant of promise depending ultimately on God for its fulfilment and not on the response of the people. The covenant with Noah is also seen as a covenant of unconditional promise, as is the later covenant with David. In my view covenants have to do with relationship, so there is always a conditional element. For Noah, it is obedience to the command to build the ark and then go inside, and there may also be a conditional element in Genesis 9:5–6, which prohibits the shedding of blood. In the covenant with Abraham we have noted the importance of his obedience, and the role of circumcision. Some covenants, such as the Abrahamic and Davidic, contain unconditional elements; but those to whom the promises are addressed may still cut themselves off from the blessing through disobedience. The promises and their ultimate fulfilment are sure, but people can choose whether or not to be part of them. The Abrahamic covenant made demands consistent with continued relationship with God – and those who would receive the blessings of God's promise were those willing to submit to his will. The same is true of the covenant at Sinai and the demands of the Law.

The purpose of election

The character of Israel's special calling is seen in the two expressions *kingdom of priests* and *holy nation*. *Holy*, here, means 'set apart, consecrated to God's own use'. Israel was to be set apart for service to God. The nature of this service is seen in the former expression, *kingdom of priests* (or *royal priesthood*). The priest in Israel was an intermediary, representing God to the people, and the people to God. He was consecrated in the service of God, and granted special access into the divine presence. There he offered sacrifices, both for himself and on behalf of the people, and presented to God the prayers and petitions of the nation. He also brought God's word to the people. The priest was a man of the Law (Torah), who passed on and interpreted God's teaching. This twofold role, of teaching the Law and offering sacrifices on behalf of the people, is seen in the blessing of Levi:

> *He teaches your precepts to Jacob*
> *and your law to Israel.*
> *He offers incense before you*
> *and whole burnt offerings on your altar.*
> (Deut. 33:10)

As a priestly kingdom, Israel too was set apart. Israel was taken from the nations to be an intermediary: to be God's representative to the nations and to stand before God on their behalf. Israel was called to bring the nations closer to God and, by sharing the light of God's revelation and the good news of his salvation, to bring God closer to the nations.[30] Israel's role in this was to be mainly passive. They were called to be holy and distinctive: a people among whom God's presence would be seen, and to whom other nations would be drawn – seeking to share Israel's relationship with God. The effectiveness of Israel's witness depended on her distinctiveness. And that continues to be true

---

30. Alec Motyer, *The Message of Exodus*, BST (Leicester: IVP, 2005), questions whether Exod. 19:6 points to Israel as an intermediary, arguing that the main emphasis is on access to God (p. 199, esp. n. 8). However, that access is granted in order to fulfil a mediatoral role, and for Israel that must be in relation to the nations. Goldingay notes that Israel's priests were not *missionaries* (*OT Theology*, 2:503; see also 1:374). Nevertheless they had a responsibility to the people, which is reflected in Israel's responsibility to the nations. See Brueggemann, *Theology*, pp. 430–434; C. J. H. Wright, *Mission*, pp. 332–333; see also Daniel Block, 'The Privilege of Calling: The Mosaic Paradigm for Missions (Deut. 26:16–19)', *BSac* 162 (2005), pp. 387–405.

in the life of the church today. Several passages refer to nations being drawn to God's people (e.g. Isa. 60:1–3; Zech. 8:23), though Ezekiel also notes that unfaithfulness and disobedience led to the converse: God's name being *profaned among the nations* (Ezek. 36:20–21).

The Law[31]

Following the Sinaitic covenant, the instrument through which God would fulfil his promise to bring blessing to the world was enlarged from an individual and his family to a nation. God would reveal himself to the world through Israel's life as a community. To fulfil this calling, though, Israel needed to know what it meant to live as the covenant people of God. So, alongside the covenant that set Israel apart as his people, God gave the Law. The Law gave the people the opportunity to respond to God in loving obedience. It was also a restraint: it gave guidance and instruction in godly living and served as a means by which the distinctive character of the people, and with it the effectiveness of their witness, might be preserved. Seen in this way the Law was regarded positively. It was revelation from God, setting out the path of life in fellowship with him, and was something in which the OT saints could take delight (e.g. Ps. 19:7–11).

Two further things about the Law need to be mentioned, particularly in a day when its relevance for the church is sometimes dismissed.

First, the Law was not given as a means by which people could attempt to earn their salvation. The basis of Israel's election is God's grace. Redemption from Egypt depended on the people's response to God's offer of salvation, and had nothing to do with the Law (though their response did involve obedience). The Law came later as a basis not for *becoming* God's people but for *living as* God's people. At the same time we need to recognize that, though this offers an important corrective to the idea that the Law is a basis for salvation, in the OT being and doing cannot be separated. This is true when it comes to God's character. In answer to questions about the nature and character of God, the OT points to what God does: the divine action in history. The same is true of God's people: identity and action are inseparable. Those brought into covenant relationship with God must reflect that in their actions – and those unwilling to do so may be cut off from the people (e.g. Gen. 17:14; Exod. 31:14; Num. 15:30).[32]

---

31. See also e.g. B. W. Anderson, *Contours*, pp. 253–259; Brueggemann, *Theology*, pp. 198–201; Childs, *OT Theology*, pp. 51–57; Goldingay, *OT Theology*, 1:371–373; Preuss, *OT Theology*, 1:84–87; von Rad, *Theology*, 1:190–203.
32. For further discussion of this expression, see below, pp. 196–197.

Second, rather than being a set of regulations, the Law expresses the character of God and his will for his people. Those who bear God's name are called to reflect that in their lives (see also Eph. 4:1; see also Matt. 5:16; 1 Pet. 2:12). Through the covenant, Israel was called into fellowship with a holy God, and as a consequence was called to be holy too. A key expression of this is Leviticus 20:26, *You are to be holy to me because I, the LORD, am holy, and I have set you apart from the nations to be my own* (see also Lev. 19:2; 21:8; cf. 1 Pet. 1:15–16). The Law reveals something of God's holy character, and shows his people how they can be more like him.[33]

---

33. For further discussion, see below, pp. 242–245.

5. GOD AND HIS PEOPLE (2): WORSHIP AND SACRIFICE[1]

Places of worship

Dyrness defines the cult as 'the form of Israel's response to the revelation of God', through which 'God prescribed for Israel what was to be the visible expression of their faith'.[2] In Israel the regularized system of worship provided the setting in which the temporal and the infinite could meet, and so gave the means by which God's people could draw near and worship him.

---

1. See e.g. B. W. Anderson, *Contours*, pp. 106–134; Brueggemann, *Theology*, pp. 650–679; Childs, *OT Theology*, pp. 145–174; Clements, *OT Theology*, pp. 40–66; Drane, *Introducing the OT*, pp. 306–337; Dyrness, *Themes*, pp. 142–159; Eichrodt, *Theology*, 1:98–177; Jacob, *Theology*, pp. 233–279, 294–295; Kaiser, *OT Theology*, pp. 116–118; Köhler, *OT Theology*, pp. 181–198; Preuss, *OT Theology*, 2:209–252; Rendtorff, *Hebrew Bible*, pp. 509–544; Ringgren, *Israelite Religion*, pp. 151–219; H. Wheeler Robinson, *Religious Ideas of the Old Testament*, Studies in Theology (London: Duckworth, 1913), pp. 130–158; Roland de Vaux, *Ancient Israel: Its Life and Institutions* (London: Darton, Longman & Todd, 1961; repr. Grand Rapids: Eerdmans; Livonia: Dove, 1997), pp. 271–517.
2. Dyrness, *Themes*, p. 143.

The OT writers recognize that God dwells in heaven, which they envisage as above the earth. He comes *down* to see what is happening at Babel and at Sodom (Gen. 11:5; 18:21); Jacob saw a stairway to heaven, with God standing above it (Gen. 28:12–13); at the dedication of the temple Solomon noted that *the heavens, even the highest heaven, cannot contain you* (1 Kgs 8:27); Isaiah describes God as sitting *above the circle of the earth* (40:22; see also e.g. Exod. 19:11; 20:22; Deut. 4:36; 26:15; Pss 2:4; 18:9; Isa. 31:4). But the God of heaven also makes his dwelling among his people, and, under certain conditions, in particular those prescribed by the cult, they may approach and meet him.

Encounters with God could take place anywhere, though places associated with a special revelation from God were often regarded as holy and took on a particular significance within Israel's worship (Gen. 12:6–7; 13:14–18; 35:6–7).

Places of worship in patriarchal times[3]
Various altars are associated with the patriarchs: at Bethel (Gen. 12:8; 35:6–7), Shechem (Gen. 12:6–7), Mamre (Gen. 13:18), Beersheba (Gen. 26:23–25) and Moriah (Gen. 22:9). We have already noted the suggestion that some of these had a prehistory as sites of Canaanite worship, and that the patriarchs worshipped the gods already associated with the shrine. References to sacred trees (e.g. Gen. 12:6; 21:33; 35:4) have also been taken to reflect elements of Canaanite worship. However, as we have also observed, the patriarchs worshipped individually on altars they built, and there is no mention, at any of the shrines, of an officiating priesthood. This suggests that even if shrines had Canaanite links, the patriarchs did not join in with Canaanite cultic practices or worship Canaanite gods.

The tabernacle[4]
God's intention to establish his presence among his people is closely associated with the exodus and the Sinaitic covenant (e.g. Exod. 29:45–46). The people were aware of God's presence on Sinai (Exod. 24:15–18), but he is not limited

---

3. E.g. de Vaux, *Ancient Israel*, pp. 289–293; Rowley, *Worship*, pp. 1–36.

4. See e.g. B. W. Anderson, *Contours*, pp. 106–115; Richard E. Averbeck, '*miškān*', in *NIDOTTE* 2:1130–1134; Brueggemann, *Theology*, pp. 662–664; Drane, *Introducing the OT*, pp. 310–312; D. W. Gooding, 'Tabernacle', in *IBD* 3:1506–1511; Goldingay, *OT Theology*, 1:385–401; House, *OT Theology*, pp. 118–120; Preuss, *OT Theology*, 1:253–256; Rendtorff, *Hebrew Bible*, pp. 512–518; Rowley, *Worship*, pp. 37–57; de Vaux, *Ancient Israel*, pp. 294–302.

to one place, and the tabernacle enabled them to know God continuing to dwell among them, even after leaving Sinai. The purpose of the tabernacle is made clear in Exodus 25:8, *have them make a sanctuary for me, and I will dwell among them.*

Prior to the building of the tabernacle, there was a much simpler 'tent' erected outside the camp, known as the 'tent of meeting', where Moses consulted God (Exod. 33:7–11), but which was not permanently associated with the divine presence. The tabernacle was significantly different: it was constructed at the centre of the Israelite camp and represented God's abiding presence among his people.[5] At its centre was the Most Holy Place, which housed the Ark of the Covenant (Exod. 25:10–22). This was a wooden chest overlaid with gold, containing the stone tablets of the Law (Exod. 25:16); its cover, overshadowed by the wings of gold cherubim, may have been seen as

---

5. Some think that Exod. 33:7–11 (E) describes the original structure in the desert; while the tabernacle (P) is an idealized structure combining it with the more elaborate construction of Solomon's temple; see e.g. J. P. Hyatt, *Exodus*, NCB (London: Marshall, Morgan & Scott, 1971), pp. 258–64, 271–72, 314–15. If the intention is to imply continuity between desert traditions and the temple, the inclusion of Exod. 33:7–11 is strange, since it emphasizes difference. More likely, the reference here to the earlier 'tent' is intended to indicate that the construction of the tabernacle points to something new in the relationship between God and the people following the Sinaitic covenant. The name 'tent of meeting' is retained in references to the tabernacle, suggesting that what had been associated with the former structure was now incorporated into the new dwelling place of God among his people. Von Rad wonders whether the 'tent of meeting' derives from a separate, maybe southern, tradition; see Gerhard von Rad, *Studies in Deuteronomy*, SBT 9 (London: SCM, 1953), pp. 42–44. Cook also links this 'tent of meeting/assembly' with a separate stream of tradition – in his case Sinai tradition (preserved in E). He argues that the tent, situated outside the camp, was associated with the council of elders, which was the administrative instrument of a wider 'assembly of Yahweh'. This operated alongside the Levites' tabernacle, which was within the camp (Cook, *Social Roots*, pp. 221–230). There are close links between the assembly of elders and the 'tent of meeting', where they gathered to allot the tribal divisions of the land (e.g. Josh. 18:1–10; 19:51) and to install leaders (Deut. 31:14). Linking the 'tent of meeting' with the tabernacle/temple would be a way of incorporating what was at first a decentralized structure into the state machinery. Viewed less cynically, it may represent an attempt to demonstrate how older structures were preserved within the developing life of Israel as a nation.

God's throne (e.g. 1 Sam. 4:4; 2 Sam. 6:2; 2 Kgs 19:15).[6] The purpose of the tabernacle's elaborate construction was to separate the holy from the profane and so to provide the conditions that would allow a holy God to dwell among his people. Through the cult and its rituals, people who would otherwise be excluded from God's presence, or risked being struck down for approaching him, could have access to him.

This idea that God dwelt *among his people* was very different from the common view that gods were associated with particular places and that their power was restricted to that domain. It was, though, a constant temptation for Israel to limit God in that way and, once in Canaan, to adopt the worship of the Canaanite gods associated with the new land.

Sanctuaries in Canaan[7]

After the settlement, several sanctuaries became centres of worship, including Bethel, Gilgal, Mizpah, Ramah, Shechem, Shiloh and Gibeon. In Deuteronomy 12 Moses gives instructions to worship at a *single* sanctuary: *the place the LORD your God shall choose as a dwelling for his Name* (v. 11). Many scholars argue that this reflects the centralization of worship in the Jerusalem temple, particularly during the reign of Josiah.[8] It is possible that Moses could have envisaged a central sanctuary, though after the separation of the tribes in Canaan this would have been increasingly difficult. Another possibility is that Deuteronomy 12 intends to make a distinction between the place of worship appointed by God, and the many Canaanite sanctuaries at which the people might be tempted to worship. The scattering of the tribes throughout Canaan made it difficult to maintain order in the religious life of the nation; the existence of a central shrine that could in some way oversee the worship of the nation was seen as a corrective to spiritual anarchy (Deut. 12:8).

---

6. Eichrodt agrees with the description of the Ark as 'the unoccupied throne of deity' (*Theology*, 1:108); see also Gordon J. Wenham, *Numbers*, TOTC (Leicester: IVP, 1981), pp. 66–67. There is the suggestion too that the Ark/temple is God's footstool (Ps. 132:7). For further discussion of the Ark, see Brueggemann, *Theology*, pp. 665–666; Goldingay, *OT Theology*, 1:398–399; Stephen T. Hague, ''ārôn', in *NIDOTTE* 1:500–510; Preuss, *OT Theology*, 1:253–254; Rendtorff, *Hebrew Bible*, pp. 513–518; Hans-Jürgen Zobel, ''ārôn', in *TDOT* 1:363–374.

7. See Drane, *Introducing the OT*, pp. 312–313; House, *OT Theology*, pp. 182–184; Rowley, *Worship*, pp. 57–70; Thompson, *Deuteronomy*, pp. 35–42; de Vaux, *Ancient Israel*, pp. 302–311, 330–344.

8. See e.g. Albertz, *History*, 1:128, 206–209.

In the early days of the settlement in Canaan there were several centres for worship, though the main sanctuary is likely to be the one that housed the Ark of the Covenant. The Ark was situated at Gilgal (Josh. 4:19–20; 5:9–10; 7:6; cf. Hos. 12:11), Shechem (Josh. 8:30–33; 24:1) and Bethel (Judg. 20:18, 26–28; 21:2). Later, Shiloh became prominent, with first the tent of meeting (Josh. 18:1) and then a more substantial structure described as a 'temple' (1 Sam. 1:9; 3:3), though there were still sanctuaries at Bethel, Mizpah and Gilgal (1 Sam. 7:16). The tribes gathered at Shiloh for an annual festival (Judg. 21:19), probably the Feast of Tabernacles. After the Ark was captured by the Philistines, Gibeon became *the most important high place* (1 Kgs 3:4–5), and the tabernacle was set up there (1 Chr. 16:39; 21:29; 2 Chr. 1:3). Even after the establishment of a permanent central sanctuary by David and Solomon in Jerusalem, worship at other sites continued. In time these local shrines or 'high places' became associated with idolatry, though they were still used for worship during the period of the monarchy, and only Hezekiah and Josiah made serious attempts to remove them (e.g. 2 Kgs 18:4, 22; 23:8, 13).

As we have noted, Moses pointed to the need for a centralized system of worship to guard against a religious free-for-all (Deut. 12:8). In the book of Judges similar language is used to point to the need for a more central political authority, focused on the person of the king, to guard against moral anarchy (e.g. Judg. 17:6; 21:25). It seems likely that the similarity of the formula is deliberate, and indicates the close link between God's presence among his people and the continuance of their relationship with him, and the installation of the earthly monarch. Both of these came together under David, who established Jerusalem as both the religious and the political capital of the nation.

The temple[9]

The Jerusalem temple, planned and prepared for by David and built by Solomon, played a central role in Israelite religion. Like the tabernacle, it was

---

9. See e.g. B. W. Anderson, *Living World*, pp. 238–239; *Contours*, pp. 195–208; Brueggemann, *Theology*, pp. 654–662; Drane, *Introducing the OT*, pp. 314–315; William J. Dumbrell, '*hêkāl*', in *NIDOTTE* 1:1026–1031; Goldingay, *OT Theology*, 1: 562–572; 2:237–252, 372–376; 2:245–249; John M. Monson, 'The Temple of Solomon: Heart of Jerusalem', in Richard S. Hess and Gordon J. Wenham (eds.), *Zion, City of our God* (Grand Rapids: Eerdmans, 1999), pp. 1–22; A. R. Millard and R. J. McKelvey, 'Temple', in *IBD* 3:1522–1532 (1522–1525); Preuss, *OT Theology*, 1:250–253; Rendtorff, *Hebrew Bible*, pp. 518–521; Rowley, *Worship*, pp. 71–110; de Vaux, *Ancient Israel*, pp. 312–330; see also G. K. Beale, *The Temple and the Church's*

associated with God's presence among his people. At its dedication it was filled with the cloud of glory symbolizing God's presence (1 Kgs 8:10–11; cf. Exod. 40:34–35) and it was regarded as God's dwelling place (e.g. 1 Kgs 8:13; 2 Kgs 19:14; Pss 27:4; 76:2; 132:13–14). Zion, the hill on which the temple stood, was sometimes equated with the temple and so, also, with the presence of God. In figurative language, reflecting both ancient traditions that depict the deity occupying mountains (as the nearest things to heaven) and also its future prominence, Zion is described as *the mountain of the LORD* (Isa. 2:2; cf. Mic. 4:1; see also e.g. Pss 43:3; 48:1; 68:16). However, just as the cloud of glory filled the temple, Ezekiel describes how the sin of the people could cause that glory to depart (Ezek. 10:3–4, 18–19; 11:23), though he also points to its eventual return (Ezek. 43:4–5). Significantly, a vital task for the returning exiles was to rebuild the temple in order to ensure the blessings associated with God's presence (Hag. 1:9; see also Zech. 2:10–13; 8:3). The emphasis on the temple suggests that God might be thought to be present in a particular place, and that people might come to that place in order to approach him; there was, nevertheless, the recognition too that he could not be confined there (1 Kgs 8:27; cf. Isa. 40:22).

The temple was also associated with the Davidic dynasty (e.g. 2 Chr. 6:5–6) and with *Zion tradition*, which depicts Zion (which came to represent the whole city of Jerusalem) as God's throne (e.g. Pss 46; 47; 74) and so, also, a symbol of Israel's election. The divine choice of Israel, David and Zion included the promise of protection from the nation's enemies (e.g. Isa. 37:35), which was demonstrated in the miraculous deliverance from Sennacherib in 701 BC (2 Kgs 18:17 – 19:37).[10]

The priesthood[11]

Priests and Levites
According to the OT writers, the priesthood in Israel was formalized in connection with the tabernacle. An earlier reference to priests (Exod. 19:22, 24)

Footnote 9 (*continued*)

    Mission: A Biblical Theology of the Dwelling Place of God, NSBT 17 (Leicester: Apollos; Downers Grove: IVP, 2004); Ronald E. Clements, *God and Temple* (Oxford: Blackwell, 1965). For discussion of the relationship between the temple/tabernacle and the Sabbath and the order of creation, see below, pp. 322–324.

10. For more on Zion Tradition, see below, pp. 276–277.

11. See e.g. Brueggemann, *Theology*, pp. 664–665; Childs, *OT Theology*, pp. 145–154; Drane, *Introducing the OT*, pp. 334–336; Eichrodt, *Theology*, 1:402–415; Goldingay,

may refer to the elders of Israel or the heads of households, who were responsible for the first Passover sacrifices. It is also possible that the *young Israelite men* who offered sacrifices in Exodus 24:5 are the firstborn, who, following the Passover, were consecrated to God and may have had a priestly role. Later their place was taken by the Levites (Num. 3:12, 45).

The special place of the Levites is linked with their zeal in rallying to Moses after Israel's sin of worshipping the golden calf (Exod. 32:26–29; Deut. 10:8). The OT refers to a *covenant* with the Levites (Neh. 13:29; Jer. 33:21; Mal. 2:8). The institution of this covenant is not mentioned, but the setting apart of the Levites may have been expressed formally in that way. There is also mention of *a covenant of lasting priesthood* made with Aaron's grandson Phinehas and his descendants (Num. 25:10–13), though this probably relates to the office of high priest. Both covenants emphasize God's promise to preserve a faithful priesthood in Israel.

Numbers 3:6–10 sets out the special place of Aaron and his descendants: only they could serve as priests in the tabernacle (Num. 3:10). Aaron's leading role was embodied in his appointment as *high priest*, a hereditary office (Lev. 16:32) passed on first through Aaron's son Eleazar (Num. 20:26, 28; 25:10–13; Deut. 10:6) and later through Zadok (Ezek. 40:46; see also 1 Chr. 6:3–8). Other Levites assisted Aaron (Num. 3:6–9), especially by looking after the tabernacle (Num. 1:50–53). In return for this work, and because their consecration to God meant they did not receive an entitlement of land (e.g. Num. 18:24; Josh. 14:4), other than forty-eight cities allocated to them (Num. 35; Josh. 21), the Levites were supported by the nation's tithes (Num. 18:21–24).

Wellhausen offers a reconstruction of the historical relationship between priests and Levites.[12] He begins with the regulations set out in Ezekiel 44:6–16, which criticizes the Levites, and allows only Zadokites to serve as priests. This restriction appears to be something new, and Wellhausen concludes that the similar regulations in Numbers could not have been in existence at that time. Thus the distinction between priest and Levite was a late idea, and references to Aaron and his descendants were introduced at this later date to link the priesthood with the Mosaic period. In Wellhausen's view the true character of Israel's early worship was much less elaborate than Numbers 3:6–10 (P)

OT Theology, 2:249–251, 491–504; House, *OT Theology*, pp. 133–135; D. A. Hubbard, 'Priests and Levites', in *IBD* 3:1266–1273; Jacob, *Theology*, pp. 246–250; P. Jenson, 'Priests and Levites', in *NIDOTTE* 4:1066–1067; Preuss, *OT Theology*, 2:52–66; Ringgren, *Israelite Religion*, pp. 204–212; Rowley, *Worship*, pp. 96–103; de Vaux, *Ancient Israel*, pp. 345–405; Vriezen, *Outline*, pp. 263–269.

12. For discussion of Wellhausen's view, see e.g. Miller, *Israelite Religion*, pp. 182–196.

implies. The first Passover lambs were killed by heads of families, and this simple approach continued into the period of the settlement. So, for example, at Shiloh the young Samuel slept beside the Ark (1 Sam. 3:3), apparently contrary to the (later) regulations in Leviticus 16.

According to Wellhausen, the hereditary priesthood began with David's appointment of Zadok.[13] Establishing Jerusalem as the nation's capital led also to the centralization of worship, and this, together with the building of the temple, led to a two-tier system among the Levites: those who served at the Jerusalem temple came to greater prominence, while at the other end of the scale were those who continued to minister at local shrines – which became associated with idolatry. When Josiah abolished the high places as part of his religious reforms, the Levites serving there came to Jerusalem to look for work. The book of Deuteronomy, usually dated during Josiah's reign, supports the centralization of the cult in Jerusalem, but also insists on the right of dispossessed provincial Levites to serve alongside the Jerusalem priesthood (e.g. Deut. 18:6–7).[14]

By the time of Ezekiel, this assimilation had become a serious problem, and there was a need to distinguish the Zadokites, the long-standing Jerusalem

---

13. Abiathar also served as priest under David. After the massacre of his family by Saul at Nob, he fled to join David (1 Sam. 22:20). His support for David before he became king may have led to his seniority over Zadok, who also served as priest under David. After Abiathar supported Adonijah's claim to succeed David, Solomon replaced him with Zadok (1 Kgs 2:35). Abiathar appears to have been a descendant of Eli (1 Kgs 2:27) and Cook suggests that Abiathar represented the Levites, while Zadok represented the Aaronides – and David preserved the balance between the older Sinai traditions, linked with the Levites, and the new state institutions, centred on Jerusalem and the Aaronic priesthood. By dismissing Abiathar, Solomon disenfranchised the Levites, and moved towards greater centralization of the Jerusalem cult (*Social Roots*, pp. 147–149).

14. Von Rad maintains that Deuteronomy was written by Levites from the Judean countryside, who adapted and applied older tribal traditions, from before the establishment of the monarchy, to the current (seventh century BC) setting (*Studies in Deuteronomy*, pp. 60–73). He suggests that these traditions were preserved among the 'people of the land', which he takes to be 'the free, property-owning, full citizens of Judah' (p. 63). The Levites were the spokesmen for this group, and condemned the syncretism in Jerusalem. Cook also notes the significance of the 'people of the land' in preserving Sinai traditions, though argues that the spokesmen of this group were elders of the rural communities, who may have shared the role with Levites (*Social Roots*, pp. 213–214).

priesthood, from the Levites who had come in from outside and brought idolatrous practices with them. Ezekiel's solution was to allow the Levites to serve in the temple but not in the sanctuary (Ezek. 44:10–16). The regulations in P, which allow all the descendants of Aaron, not just the Zadokites, to serve as priests, may be a compromise solution.[15] To justify the distinction between Aaronic priests and Levites and to give greater authority to the priesthood, stories about the beginnings of the priesthood were written into the history of the wilderness period. It was also necessary to construct a genealogy linking Zadok with Aaron (e.g. 1 Chr. 6:3–8).

It is unnecessary, however, to regard the distinction between priests and Levites as a late idea. Numbers 3:6–10 can be related to the wilderness period, and at that time the distinction could be maintained. After the settlement it was no longer practical to have one central point to which everyone could come, and worship was conducted at many different local sites. It may be that in the main centres of worship only priests could minister in the sanctuary (*before God*) but in rural areas, where there might be a shortage of priests, a Levite was better than nothing. So Micah was glad to install a Levite as priest (Judg. 17:10–13), and the same Levite, Jonathan (a grandson of Moses), was appointed as priest by the Danites (Judg. 18:19–31). Under such circumstances the prohibition on Levites might have been relaxed, in practice if not officially. It is easy to see from the attitude of Aaron's great nephew, willing to serve at a shrine with idols, how the unsupervised and unaccountable ministry of Levites could fall into error.[16]

During the monarchy the ideal was for Aaronic priests to be assisted by Levites (e.g. 1 Chr. 6:48–49; 23:28–32). Even in Jerusalem, though, a shortage of consecrated priests might make it necessary for Levites to take on priestly duties (2 Chr. 29:34), and it is likely that in outlying districts Levites might have ministered regularly in this way. Two things brought Levites to Jerusalem: Jeroboam's appointment of non-Levitical priests to serve in the northern sanctuaries (which would have antagonized the Levites, as well as robbing many of them of employment [2 Chr. 11:13–15]),[17] and the abolition of the high places by Josiah (2 Kgs 23:8–9). Deuteronomy 18:6–7 (which does not have to be dated as late as the time of Josiah) may anticipate these movements, and gives Levites from the

---

15. See Rowley, *Worship*, pp. 100–101; de Vaux, *Ancient Israel*, pp. 365–366.

16. This challenges the view that traditions maintained by the Levites represented pure Yahwism that was corrupted by the move to centralization.

17. This did not amount to a total ban on Levitical priests, since Dan appears to have been served by descendants of Jonathan, the grandson of Moses, until the exile (Judg. 18:30).

provinces the right not to serve as priests at the central sanctuary (see also 2 Kgs 23:9) but to serve on equal terms with other Levites already serving there. By Ezekiel's time the distinctions seem to have been relaxed, leading to a corruption of temple worship. His prohibition is essentially a return to the instructions in Numbers 3:10; though, since the problem was thought to have been caused by those who came from outside, only those who had served in the temple from the start (the Zadokites) were allowed to continue as priests in the sanctuary.

The role of the priest in Israel

Apart from service in the sanctuary, the roles of *priest* and *Levite* are similar, and so will be considered together. This role is indicated in the blessing of Levi:

> *He teaches your precepts to Jacob*
> *and your law to Israel.*
> *He offers incense before you*
> *and whole burnt offerings on your altar.*
> (Deut. 33:10)

Giving instruction

The priest represented God before the people, and they consulted him to know God's will (e.g. Num. 27:21; 1 Sam. 14:36, 41–42; 28:6). To assist in this he had the Urim and Thummim (Exod. 28:30; Num. 27:21; Deut. 33:8). The OT does not explain what these were, or how they were consulted; they may have been a kind of dice, or possibly flat stones corresponding to 'yes' and 'no'.[18] In the description of the high priest's garments, the Urim and Thummim were kept in the *breastpiece*, a pouch attached to the *ephod* (Exod. 28:30; Lev. 8:8; cf. Prov. 16:33).

The Levites were entrusted by Moses with the Torah (Deut. 31:9). A clear statement of the priestly responsibility to give instruction in the Law is in Malachi 2:6–7, *True instruction was in his mouth and nothing false was found on his lips . . . the lips of a priest ought to preserve knowledge, and from his mouth men should seek instruction – because he is the messenger of the LORD Almighty* (see also e.g. 2 Chr. 35:3; Neh. 8:7–9; Jer. 18:18; Ezek. 7:26; Hag. 2:11).

As part of this responsibility, priests had a judicial role (e.g. Deut. 17:8–12; 19:17; 2 Chr. 19:8–11); they declared what was clean and unclean (e.g. Lev. 14:48, 57; Deut. 24:8), and pronounced divine blessing (e.g. Num. 6:23–27; Deut. 10:8; 2 Chr. 30:27).

---

18. See e.g. Cornelis Van Dam, '*ûrîm*', in *NIDOTTE* 1:329–331; J. A. Motyer, 'Urim and Thummim', in *IBD* 3:1612–1614.

Offering sacrifices

The priest also represented the people before God (e.g. Num. 3:12, 41; 8:16–17). An important part of his role was to offer sacrifices on behalf of the people. Usually the worshipper killed the victim himself, unless he was ceremonially impure (2 Chr. 30:17; Ezek. 44:11), and then the priest sprinkled its blood on the altar (e.g. Lev. 1:5, 11; 2 Chr. 29:22–24). Offering sacrifices for sin was significant in preserving the holiness of God's people, and to fulfil this role, the priest too needed to be in a state of consecration to God (e.g. Exod. 28:41; 1 Chr. 15:14; 2 Chr. 5:11; 29:34).

Other duties

The Levites were responsible for sanctuaries, and especially for the Ark of the Covenant, which contained the tablets of the Torah and was the symbol of God's presence among his people (e.g. 1 Chr. 15:2, 12–15; see also e.g. Deut. 31:24–26; 2 Sam. 15:24; 1 Kgs 8:3–4). In the Jerusalem temple the Levites' duties included serving as gatekeepers, guarding the purity of the sanctuary (1 Chr. 9:19–20, 22–27; 15:23–24; 2 Chr. 23:6; cf. Num. 1:53) and, as singers and musicians, leading the people in worship (e.g. 1 Chr. 6:31–32; 15:16, 27; 25:1–31; 2 Chr. 20:21–22; Neh. 12:45).

Religious festivals[19]

Spring feasts

Passover/unleavened bread[20]

Passover was celebrated on the evening of 14 Nisan (Abib),[21] and looked back to Israel's deliverance from Egypt. It was one of three 'pilgrim feasts', where

---

19. See e.g. Albertz, *History*, 1:88–91; Childs, *OT Theology*, pp. 162–163; Drane, *Introducing the OT*, pp. 328–332; Dyrness, *Themes*, pp. 148–151; Eichrodt, *Theology*, 1:119–133; Mitch and Zhava Glaser, *The Fall Feasts of Israel* (Chicago: Moody, 1987); House, *OT Theology*, pp. 146–147; Preuss, *OT Theology*, pp. 224–235; Rendtorff, *Hebrew Bible*, pp. 535–542; Ringgren, *Israelite Religion*, pp. 185–200; Rowley, *Worship*, pp. 87–94; Hayyim Schauss, *The Jewish Festivals* (London: Jewish Chronicle Publications, 1986); de Vaux, *Ancient Israel*, pp. 468–474, 484–517.

20. Exod. 12; Lev. 23:4–8; Deut. 16:1–8; 2 Kgs 23:21. See also Robin L. Routledge, 'Passover and Last Supper', *TynBul* 53.2 (2002), pp. 203–221.

21. Abib is the Palestinian month name (e.g. Exod. 13:4; Deut. 16:1); after the exile, the Babylonian name, Nisan, was used (e.g. Esth. 3:7).

people were encouraged to gather at a central shrine. Passover was followed immediately by the Feast of Unleavened Bread, which marked the start of the barley harvest (see Lev. 23:9–14; Deut. 16:9). Both festivals may have their roots in much earlier spring festivals linked with the pastoral and agricultural year respectively, which were reinterpreted in the light of the exodus. The first sheaf of corn was presented during the Feast of Unleavened Bread *on the day after the Sabbath* (Lev. 23:9–14), though it is unclear whether that is the weekly Sabbath or the first day of Unleavened Bread.

Feast of Weeks[22]

This is the second pilgrim feast. It celebrates the end of the grain harvest and was held seven weeks, that is fifty days,[23] after the presentation of the first sheaf (Lev. 23:15–16).[24] In later Jewish tradition the feast came to mark the anniversary of the Sinai covenant.[25]

Autumn feasts

Day of Atonement (Lev. 16)

This was celebrated on the tenth day of the seventh month (Tishri). It was a day of national repentance on which the high priest offered sacrifices for sin. A distinctive element of this ritual was the choice by lots of two goats: one *for*

---

22. Exod. 34:22; Lev. 23:15–21; Num. 28:26–31.

23. The name 'Pentecost' comes from the Greek, *pentēkostos*, 'fiftieth'.

24. In later years uncertainty about how to interpret *the day after the Sabbath* (Lev. 23:15) led to disagreement between Pharisees and Sadducees over the date of Pentecost. The Sadducees celebrated Pentecost on a Sunday, and, since the Sadducees controlled the temple, this was probably the official view in the NT period. The Pharisees celebrated the festival seven weeks after 16 Nisan, and after the destruction of the temple in AD 70 this became the official date.

25. See e.g. Schauss, *Jewish Festivals*, p. 89. This helps explain how the coming of the Spirit at Pentecost fulfils the OT festival. Passover symbolizes redemption; the covenant at Sinai marks the birth of the nation. For us, redemption is won by Christ, our Passover Lamb; the coming of the Spirit marks the birth of the church. There is a link too between the giving of the Law, which revealed God's will for his people and was a means of preserving their distinctiveness, and the coming of the Spirit through whom God's law is written on our hearts, and who enables us to live as God's people. There may also be a parallel between the three thousand killed after the incident with the Golden Calf (Exod. 32:28) and the three thousand saved on the Day of Pentecost (Acts 2:41).

the LORD and one *for/to Azazel* (*la'ăzā'zēl*; Lev. 16:8). The first was then sacrificed as a purification offering (v. 9). Later in the ceremony the high priest laid his hands on the second goat and symbolically transferred to it the sin and rebellion of the nation. The goat was then taken away and released in *a solitary place* (literally 'a land of cutting off') in the desert (v. 22), taking Israel's sins with it. As we have already noted, Azazel may be the name of a desert demon,[26] though this should not be seen as a sacrifice or gift made to Azazel, but rather as sending sin back to where it came from. It is possible that 'cutting off' refers to the death of the goat in the desert (according to the Mishnah, it was pushed over a precipice), and it has been suggested that *la'ăzā'zēl* should be interpreted 'for destruction' or 'to the precipice'.[27] Whatever the precise meaning of the Hebrew terms, the significance of the ceremony is clear, and the goat being led away to a deserted region was a clear illustration of the removal of sin.

Feast of Tabernacles[28]

This was Israel's third pilgrim feast, and began on 15 Tishri. It was a harvest festival, celebrating the ingathering of the fruit and was an occasion to rejoice in God's provision (Lev. 23:40; Deut. 16:14); the rabbis described it as 'the season of our joy'.[29] As with Passover and Unleavened Bread, the agricultural roots of the festival may be ancient, but like them it was also linked with deliverance from Egypt and, during the eight days of the feast, the people lived in temporary shelters to recall their days in tents in the wilderness. The importance of this festival is seen in the fact that it was sometimes referred to simply as 'the feast' (Ps. 81:3; Ezek. 45:25).[30]

---

26. See above, p. 118.
27. See the discussion by Wenham, *Leviticus*, pp. 233–235.
28. Lev. 23:34–43; Deut. 16:13–16; Neh. 8:14–17; Zech. 14:16–19.
29. The joyfulness of the celebration is seen too in relation to a later custom, which became an important part of the festival, the drawing of water. Each day of the festival, water was collected from the pool of Siloam and, in a joyful procession, was brought into the temple through the Water Gate and poured out on the altar. Describing the celebrations associated with the water-drawing ceremony, the Mishnah observes, 'Anyone who has not seen the rejoicing of *bet hashshoebah* [the place of water drawing] in his life has never seen rejoicing' (*Sukkah* 5.1; J. Neusner, *The Mishnah: A New Translation* [New Haven: Yale University Press, 1988], p. 288). The Talmud links this with the anticipation of the pouring out of the Holy Spirit, and Jesus speaks about the Holy Spirit in this context (John 7:37–39).
30. See also e.g. Judg. 21:19; 1 Sam. 1:3, 21; 1 Kgs 8:2; 2 Chr. 7:8.

Sacrifice[31]

Theories of sacrifice

Eichrodt notes that a key element in primitive sacrifice was the belief that the
deity depended on the offerings for food. The OT practice of cooking
offerings and using salt may be vestiges of this idea, but the writers never view
sacrifice in this way. God does not need food, and is not dependent upon
human beings (e.g. Ps. 50:8–15). Sacrifices may also be seen as a gift to the deity.
In a pre-scientific world, natural forces were often viewed as gods, and people
tried to win their favour by offering gifts. These were intended to exalt a god
thought worthy of praise, to pacify an angry god, or to induce the aid of a
reluctant god – and since the intention was to please and influence the god, the
offering must be of value. In the OT, sacrifices are gifts to God and are meant
to please him; they are not bribes to pacify him or enlist his help, but are
expressions of praise: they acknowledge his glory and power, and are offered
not to overcome his reluctance but in recognition of what he has done in the
past, and of the need to depend on him for the present and the future. The
OT strongly resists any idea that sacrificial rites or religious formulae can be
used to manipulate God.

A significant aspect of sacrifice is to bring cleansing and atonement.
Cleansing is important, and religious systems include elaborate ceremonies for
cleansing, purification and consecration. In the OT, blood is closely associated
with ritual purity, including cleansing from the uncleanness caused by disease
(e.g. Lev. 14:1–7) or sin (e.g. Exod. 30:10; Lev. 16:11, 15–16, 27; 2 Chr. 29:24).

---

31. See e.g. B. W. Anderson, *Contours*, pp. 116–121; Gary A. Anderson, 'Sacrifice and
    Sacrificial Offerings: Old Testament', in *ABD* 5:870–886; Richard E. Averbeck,
    'Offerings and Sacrifices', in *NIDOTTE* 4:996–1022; Brueggemann, *Theology*,
    pp. 666–668; C. Brown et al., 'Sacrifice, etc.', in *DNTT* 3:415–438 (418–428);
    Childs, *Biblical Theology* (1992), pp. 503–508; *OT Theology*, pp. 168–171; Drane,
    Introducing the OT, pp. 321–328; Dyrness, *Themes*, pp. 153–159; Eichrodt, *Theology*,
    1:141–172; Goldingay, *OT Theology*, 1:416–417; Hartley, *Leviticus 1–27*, pp. lxvii–lxxii,
    1–102; House, *OT Theology*, pp. 128–133, 137–141; Jacob, *Theology*, pp. 268–269, 294–
    296; Milgrom, *Leviticus 1–16*, pp. 133–489; Preuss, *OT Theology*, 2:238–245; Rendtorff,
    Hebrew Bible, pp. 526–534; Vriezen, *Outline*, pp. 286–293; Ringgren, *Israelite Religion*,
    pp. 166–178 (esp. pp. 451–456); John Rogerson, 'Sacrifices and Psalms', in Davies
    and Rogerson, *OT World*, pp. 151–165; Rowley, *Worship*, pp. 113–143; R. J.
    Thompson and R. T. Beckwith, 'Sacrifice and Offering', in *IBD* 3:1358–1368 (1358–
    1366); de Vaux, *Ancient Israel*, pp. 415–456; Wenham, *Leviticus*, pp. 25–29, 47–135.

Most sacrifices in the OT contain some element of atonement. In the case of sin, atonement has also to do with turning away divine wrath (propitiation). Some argue that God does not need to be appeased in order to show goodwill to human beings – on the contrary, in sovereign grace he has acted unilaterally to provide the means by which human sin can be dealt with.[32] But that is to misunderstand God's wrath, which exists alongside his grace. Wrath is linked with righteous judgment on sin, and reconciliation is only possible when divine justice is satisfied. That requires repentance and obedience and, in so far as sacrifices are expressions of that, they may be said to turn away God's wrath and avert the judgment sin deserves.

How the death of an animal provides cleansing and reconciliation is not explicitly stated in the OT. It may include the idea of making reparation to God for offending against him. Offering of a sacrifice also implies awareness of sin and of the need to be put right with God. Another important idea is that the sacrifice, in some sense, takes the place of the worshipper.[33]

Types of sacrifice
Sacrifices in the OT can be divided into three broad categories.[34]

Gift offerings
These were offered as tribute, in acknowledgment that everything comes from God (e.g. 1 Chr. 29:14). They included offerings of *first fruits* and the regulations about the firstborn. Gift offerings were also offered in thanksgiving for blessings received. This element was present in the harvest offerings, which were both a recognition that the fruit of the land (and the land itself) belonged to God, and a celebration of its ingathering. A common term for such an offering is *minhâ* (Gen. 32:13; Judg. 3:15; 1 Sam. 26:19; 2 Sam. 8:2). This sometimes refers to the *grain* offering (e.g. Lev. 2; 6:14; 7:9–10) but is sometimes used more generally (e.g. Gen. 4:3–5; Num. 16:15; 1 Sam. 2:17; 1 Chr. 16:29; Isa. 1:13; Mal. 3:3).[35]

---

32. So e.g. B. W. Anderson, *Contours*, pp. 120–121.

33. See further below, pp. 194–195.

34. See e.g. Drane, *Introducing the OT*, pp. 323–328; Jacob, *Theology*, p. 268; Preuss, *OT Theology*, 1:238; de Vaux, *Ancient Israel*, pp. 451–454.

35. See further Richard E. Averbeck, '*minhâ*', in *NIDOTTE* 2:978–990; Heinz-Josef Fabry and Moshe Weinfeld, '*minhâ*', in *TDOT* 8:407–421; Hartley, *Leviticus*, pp. 29–30; Kiuchi, *Leviticus*, pp. 65–75; Milgrom, *Leviticus 1–16*, pp. 195–202; Wenham, *Leviticus*, pp. 67–73.

Also associated with this kind of sacrifice is the *'ōlâ*, usually translated 'burnt offering'.[36] Such offerings were burned whole on the altar (e.g. Exod. 29:15–18; Lev. 1:13; 9:12–14). Animals used for burnt offerings were bulls, goats, sheep or pigeons. These were usually perfect males; the most common were year-old male lambs. And they were often accompanied by grain offerings (Lev. 23:10–13; Num. 28:3–6). Burning may have been seen as a way of transferring the sacrifice from the physical to the spiritual world: the smoke rising symbolized it 'going up' to God. It may be too that by being burned completely, the *'ōlâ* represented an irrevocable gift, a sacrifice from which no one but God could benefit, and that made it acceptable and pleasing to him.

Burnt offerings were the most common sacrifices. They, and their accompanying grain offerings, were offered twice daily in the sanctuary (Num. 28:3–4). Leviticus 1:3–13 describes how individuals brought burnt offerings. The worshipper brought an unblemished male animal from the flock to the sanctuary. He laid his hand on its head to indicate that it was offered on his behalf and that its acceptance signified his acceptance.[37] Then he killed, skinned and cut it into pieces. The priests took the blood and sprinkled it around the altar, and burned the pieces of the sacrifice on the altar.[38]

Fellowship/communion offerings

The Hebrew for this kind of offering is *šĕlāmîm*. It is often translated 'fellowship offering', based on the nature of the meal that accompanied the sacrifice. The translation 'peace offering' connects *šĕlāmîm* with *šālôm* (peace). This offering is described in Leviticus 3. The form is similar to that for the burnt offering, though in this case God, the priest and the worshipper all shared in the animal. God's part was burned on the altar, the priest received the breast and right leg (Lev. 7:31–34), and the rest was eaten by the worshipper and his family (Lev. 7:15–16; Deut. 12:7). Animals permitted for these sacrifices were

---

36. The word 'holocaust' comes from this term.

37. There is discussion about whether Lev. 1:3b refers to the acceptance of the offering or the worshipper; see Milgrom, *Leviticus 1–16*, p. 153; Hartley, *Leviticus*, p. 55; Wenham, *Leviticus*, p. 55. However, these two are indissolubly linked; the aim of offering an acceptable sacrifice is to secure the acceptance of the worshipper.

38. See further Richard E. Averbeck, "'ōlâ', in *NIDOTTE* 3:405–415; Hartley, *Leviticus*, pp. 17–18; Diether Kellermann, "'ōlâ/'ôlâ', in *TDOT* 11:96–113; Kiuchi, *Leviticus*, pp. 51–65; Milgrom, *Leviticus 1–16*, pp. 172–177; James W. Watts, "'Ōlāh: The Rhetoric of Burnt Offerings', *VT* 56.01 (2006), pp. 125–137; Wenham, *Leviticus*, pp. 51–66.

the same as for burnt offerings, except birds – which were not big enough to provide meat for a fellowship meal.

Leviticus 7:12–16 notes three kinds of fellowship offering, with slightly different rules: *thank-offerings* (v. 12; see also 2 Chr. 29:31; Pss 50:14; 116:17); *votive offerings*, made in fulfilment of a vow (v. 16; see also Pss 50:14; 56:12; 116:17–18); and *freewill offerings* (v. 16; see also Exod. 35:29; Deut. 16:10; Ezra 1:4; Ps. 54:6). *Šĕlāmîm* were also associated with the covenant (Exod. 24:5; Deut. 27:7; Josh. 8:30–31; 2 Sam. 6:17–18; 1 Kgs 8:63–64) and probably included both thanksgiving to God and the renewal of covenant vows.[39]

Sacrifices for sin

A key term when considering sacrifices for sin is 'atonement', which may indicate cleansing or purification, or the payment of a ransom.[40] The burnt offering played a major role in making atonement for sin (e.g. Lev. 1:4; Num. 15:22–26; 2 Sam. 24:25; Job 1:5; 42:8), and turning away God's wrath (Gen. 8:20–21; 2 Chr. 29:7–8).[41] Two further offerings that also seek to overcome the separation between human beings and God caused by sin are the *purification offering* (*ḥaṭṭā't*), often referred to as the *sin offering*,[42] and the *reparation* or *guilt offering* (*'āšām*).

The purification offering

The purification offering was offered to make atonement for sin, and to purify the sanctuary. It was offered at some festivals (e.g. Num. 28:11 – 29:38), though,

---

39. See further Richard E. Averbeck, '*šelem*', in *NIDOTTE* 4:135–143; Hartley, *Leviticus*, pp. 37–39; Kiuchi, *Leviticus*, pp. 75–85; Milgrom, *Leviticus 1–16*, pp. 217–225; Wenham, *Leviticus*, pp. 78–84.

40. The Hebrew term *kipper* (make atonement) is a piel form of the verb. It may be linked with the Akkadian *kuppuru*, and so mean 'purify, cleanse'; the Hebrew, *kōper*, from the same root, refers to a ransom paid for a life (e.g. Exod. 21:30; 30:12; Ps. 49:8; Isa. 43:3), and possibly both ideas are present in the idea of atonement; see further Richard E. Averbeck, '*kpr*', in *NIDOTTE* 2:689–710; Kiuchi, *Leviticus*, pp. 56–57; Milgrom, *Leviticus 1–16*, pp. 1079–1084; Wenham, *Leviticus*, p. 28; however, cf. Hartley, *Leviticus*, pp. 64–66 (63).

41. See Kiuchi, *Leviticus*, pp. 60–61; Milgrom, *Leviticus 1–16*, p. 175; Wenham, *Leviticus*, pp. 57–63.

42. Although associated with atonement for sin, this offering has much more to do with purification, e.g. after childbirth (Lev. 12:6–7), which results in ceremonial uncleanness, but is not sinful. See Hartley, *Leviticus*, p. 55; Milgrom, *Leviticus 1–16*, pp. 253–254; Wenham, *Leviticus*, pp. 88–89; cf. Kiuchi, *Leviticus*, pp. 90–91.

usually, it was brought by individuals who had committed inadvertent sins (Lev. 4:2–3, 13–14, 22, 27), or who had become ceremonially unclean (e.g. Lev. 5:1–6; 12:1–7). Acts of wilful defiance could not be atoned for in this way (Num. 15:27–31).

The purification and burnt offerings have some features in common, suggesting key elements in sacrificial atonement, but the rituals also had important distinctive elements. What set the purification offering apart was that the victim's blood was used to purify the sanctuary. In the case of the sin of a leader or individual, blood was smeared on the horns of the altar (Lev. 4:25, 34); for a priest or for the whole community, a bull was sacrificed and its blood was taken into the sanctuary. Some was sprinkled in front of the curtain separating off the Ark (Lev. 4:6, 17) and some was smeared on the horns of the incense altar (Lev. 4:7, 18). These were the only sacrifices, other than on the Day of Atonement, where part of the victim was taken inside the sanctuary. The rest of the blood was poured away at the base of the altar outside the sanctuary. Brown suggests that 'the sacrifice absorbed the impurity',[43] and this explains why it was necessary to destroy or scour the vessels used (Lev. 6:28), and, when the blood had been taken into the sanctuary, to destroy the carcass of the animal outside the camp (Lev. 4:11–12, 21; 6:30).

This indicates that sin not only defiles people but also pollutes God's sanctuary. God is holy and cannot live in the midst of sin; so if people are to continue to know his presence among them, there must be purification – by blood.[44] The fact that the instructions about cleansing the sanctuary vary according to the person or group that has committed the sin suggests there were different degrees of pollution. While all sin is treated seriously, generally individual sins had less of an impact on the religious life of the nation than the sin of the whole people – unless that individual was a priest. In the case of the sin of the whole nation or of those charged with maintaining the spiritual life of the nation, the pollution goes much deeper, and to remedy it, the blood must be taken further into the sanctuary.

The different animals used in the sacrifice may also indicate the differing degrees of pollution. A bull was sacrificed to make atonement for the priests. Leviticus 4:3 indicates that a bull was also sacrificed to atone for the sin of the community; though in other passages the prescribed animal is a male goat (Lev. 9:15; 16:5; Num. 15:24; 2 Chr. 29:21; Ezra 6:17; Ezek. 43:22–27). To atone for the sin of a leader, the sacrifice is also a male goat (Lev. 4:23; Num. 7). The

---

43. Brown et al., 'Sacrifice', in *DNTT* 3:419.

44. This idea is expressed in the NT; e.g. Heb. 9:22; 1 Pet. 1:2; 1 John 1:7; Rev. 7:14.

sacrifice offered for the sin of individual members of the community is a female goat (Lev. 4:28; Num. 15:27) or lamb (Lev. 4:32; Num. 6:14). This graduated scale appears to link the seriousness of the sin with the value of the sacrifice. In the case of individuals who could not afford a goat or lamb, birds (Lev. 5:7) or even grain (Lev. 5:11) could be offered instead.[45]

The instructions regarding the purification offering emphasize that the sins committed are inadvertent and the perpetrator may be unaware of having committed them. On the Day of Atonement, the language is different. On that occasion atonement is made *for the uncleanness and rebellion of the Israelites, whatever their sins have been* (Lev. 16:16), indicating that deliberate sins are included. In order to purify the sanctuary from this greater degree of pollution, the blood of the sacrifice was taken further into the sanctuary, right into the Most Holy Place, and sprinkled on and in front of the Ark (Lev. 16:15–17). As we have seen, the ritual of the Day of Atonement also portrays the offences of the nation being transferred on to a goat, which carries them away into the desert (Lev. 16:21–22).

The Day of Atonement dealt with the sin of the nation as a whole, and its purpose was, primarily, to purify the sanctuary so that God's holy presence could continue to dwell among the people. For this to happen, and for the people to survive God's judgment, there was provision for corporate forgiveness – even of deliberate defiance. There appears to be no corresponding atonement for the deliberate sins of individuals.

The reparation offering

This was offered to make reparation for certain offences. It was similar to the *fellowship offering*, though in this case only a ram or year-old male lamb could be offered, and the part of the animal not burned on the altar was kept and eaten by the priests. The reparation offering was also accompanied by a fine (Lev. 5:14–16; Num. 5:5–8). This offering is described as *a penalty* (Lev. 5:15), and includes the idea of making restitution to God, as well as to others against whom sins have been committed.[46]

---

45. See further Richard E. Averbeck, '*ḥaṭṭā'*', in *NIDOTTE* 2:93–103; Hartley, *Leviticus*, pp. 55–57; Wenham, *Leviticus*, pp. 86–103; cf. Kiuchi, *Leviticus*, pp. 85–109.

46. See further Richard E. Averbeck, '*'āšām*', in *NIDOTTE* 1:557–566; Hartley, *Leviticus*, pp. 76–80; Diether Kellermann and J. B. Payne, ''*āšām*, etc.', in *TDOT* 1:429–437; Kiuchi, *Leviticus*, pp. 109–119; Wenham, *Leviticus*, pp. 104–112.

Sacrifice and forgiveness

The significance of sacrifice

An important common factor in the purification and the burnt offerings is that the worshipper laid (or 'pressed') his hand on the animal before killing it. In the case of the burnt offering, this is explained: *he is to lay his hand on the head of the burnt offering, and it will be accepted on his behalf to make atonement for him* (Lev. 1:4). This suggests some kind of substitution. By putting his hand on the animal's head, the worshipper identified himself with the sacrifice, which was then killed in his place. One way of understanding this is as an act of surrender: through the sacrifice the worshipper offered his own life up to God. Another possibility is that the sacrifice was offered as a ransom: the victim died instead of the worshipper. In this case the sacrifice would have the effect of turning away God's punishment. The idea that it gave up a *soothing aroma* (Lev. 1:9) also suggests turning away wrath and attracting God's favour to the one who offered it.[47] Pressing a hand on the victim may also indicate the symbolic transference of sin, as in the case of the goat *for Azazel* on the Day of Atonement (Lev. 16:21–22).[48] Laying (both) hands on this animal is linked with

---

47. 'Soothing aroma' is probably a better translation than *pleasing aroma* (as NIV, NRSV). The expression is usually linked with the burnt offering (Gen. 8:21; Exod. 29:18; Lev. 1:9, 13, 17), maybe because only the aroma remained and, in the form of smoke, was seen going up to God, though it might apply to other sacrifices offered by fire (Num. 15:3). This does not suggest that God needs to be calmed down. Before Noah sacrificed burnt offerings (Gen. 8:21), God had remembered him and ended the flood. Noah's sacrifices were a grateful response for deliverance, not an attempt to soothe divine pique. Wenham notes that though the offering did not change God's attitude towards Noah, it does have significance for the rest of humanity. The reason for the flood was the evil inclination of the human heart (Gen. 6:5), and that has not changed (Gen. 8:21). Following Noah's sacrifice, though, God promises not to add to the curse already placed on the ground, and not again to destroy all living creatures. In a way this prefigures the sacrificial system, where sacrifices are offered to turn away God's wrath from the sinful community. Again this is a response to rightly offered sacrifices, rather than because of divine intoxication with their aroma, and when obedience is lacking, God will not respond (Lev. 26:31); see further Wenham, *Genesis 1–15*, pp. 189–191.

48. See Wenham, *Leviticus*, pp. 62–63. Hartley notes that both hands are laid on the scapegoat, which becomes defiled and so is sent away; if the burnt offering was similarly defiled, it could not be burnt on the altar (*Leviticus*, pp. 20–21); see also Averbeck, "*'ōlâ*", in *NIDOTTE* 3:412; Eichrodt, *Theology*, 1:165–166; Milgrom, *Leviticus*

confession (Lev. 16:21), and confession is also specifically mentioned in relation to the purification offering (Lev. 5:5), which may have been accompanied
by some statement of penitence. An appropriate point for this would be when
the worshipper put his hand on the animal's head prior to killing it. This indicates that, however mechanistic the ritual of sacrifice became, a significant
interior aspect was present from the beginning.

A second common factor is the shedding of blood. The various sacrifices
fulfilled different roles, and that accounts for differences in the animals offered
and the way the blood was used. However, despite the different emphases, it is
clear that shedding blood plays an important part in dealing with the separation from God caused by sin. This is best explained by the idea of substitu-
tionary atonement: shedding blood signifies death, and the death of the
animal, on behalf of the sinner or sinful community, opens the way for cleansing and forgiveness, and for God's continued presence among his people.

Ḥesed *and forgiveness*

The sacrificial system offered a partial solution to forgiveness and the
maintenance of a relationship with God in the face of human sin. But it was
only partial: not all sins could be atoned for in this way. In general the burnt
offerings and the purification offerings covered only unintentional sins. The
annual Day of Atonement made provision for the deliberate sins of the nation;
but there was no similar provision for individuals. Some deliberate sin directed
against the property of others may have been covered by the reparation
offering, which was accompanied by compensation for the wronged party.[49]

1–16, pp. 150–152. Sin may be thought of as being 'transferred' in the sense that the
sin of the worshipper necessitates the death of the sacrifice, though this is not *penal*
substitution, where guilt is also transferred and the sacrificial victim is regarded as
being punished in place of the sinner. There may be a suggestion of this in Isa. 53:5,
where the punishment the people deserve falls on the Servant. John N. Oswalt, *The
Book of Isaiah 40–66*, NICOT (Grand Rapids: Eerdmans, 1997), views this as penal
substitution, satisfying divine justice (p. 388). Another interpretation, more in line with
the idea of the Servant as a guilt/reparation offering (Isa. 53:10), is that the people's
punishment falls on the Servant in the sense that his death has turned away the
punishment they deserve. See below, pp. 295–296; see also Frank S. Thielman, 'The
Atonement', in Hafemann and House, *Central Themes*, pp. 102–127.

49. Offences for which a guilt offering was required include deceiving, lying and
cheating (Lev. 6:1–7); these are unlikely to be inadvertent, yet when the sinner
offers the sacrifice and pays the fine, atonement is made and the sinner is
accounted forgiven (Lev. 6:7).

But wilful defiance of the laws that touched the nature and character of God himself could not be atoned for through sacrifice, and resulted in the offender being *cut off from his people* (e.g. (Num. 15:30–31). This penalty is probably to be linked with God's direct activity. The community may also be required to take appropriate action; however, if it fails to act, God will still carry out his threat.[50]

The nature of the threat is unclear. It may be premature death, judgment beyond the grave by being denied the proper burial that would enable continued fellowship with ancestors, or being denied descendants. It is more natural, though, to take it to refer to severing the sinner's link with the community.[51]

---

50. On some occasions this is explicit: *I will set my face against that person . . . and will cut him off from his people* (Lev. 17:10; cf. 20:3, 5–6; Ezek. 14:8). The NIV translation 'he *must* be cut off from his people' (Exod. 30:33, 38; 31:14; Lev. 7:20–21, 25–27; 17:4, 9–10; 18:29; 19:8, 20:17–18; 22:3; 23:29; Num. 9:13; 15:30–31) implies that action is expected from the community; however, the niphal, *nikrat*, is better translated 'he *will* be cut off' (Gen. 17:14; cf. NRSV), which may be a warning of divine action, rather than instruction to the people. It is likely that there would be some provision within the legal system; so in Num. 15:32–36, the Sabbath-breaker is taken outside the camp and stoned to death (cf. Lev. 23:29), and in Lev. 20:3, sacrificing children to the god Molech, which results in God cutting the offender off from his people, also calls for the death penalty. In neither case, though, is the community action described as doing the 'cutting off' – that seems to remain God's prerogative, and if the community does not carry out its judicial responsibility, God will take action against the guilty party and any others who condone his actions (Lev. 20:5). It is possible that 'cutting off' was generally effected by death (e.g. Jer. 9:21), and in the legal material is sometimes associated with execution (Exod. 31:14; Lev. 20:2–3). However, the link is made specific on only a relatively few occasions. Where the expression occurs in other passages, it is frequently linked with failed inheritance (e.g. 1 Sam. 2:33; 24:21; cf. 1 Kgs 2:4; 8:25), including the failure to inherit divine blessings (e.g. 1 Kgs 9:7; Ps. 37:9, 22, 28, 34, 38). For further discussion of the expression, see Eryl W. Davies, *Numbers*, NCB (Grand Rapids: Eerdmans; London: Marshall Pickering, 1995), pp. 83–84; Milgrom, *Leviticus*, pp. 457–460; Kiuchi, *Leviticus, passim*; Wenham, *Leviticus*, pp. 241–243.

51. Similar expressions refer to offenders being cut off from the community (Num. 19:20) and from Israel (Exod. 12:15, 19; Num. 19:13). This may result in formal expulsion from the nation (von Rad, *Theology*, 1:264, n. 182; Kiuchi, *Leviticus*, p. 34; however, cf. Milgrom, *Leviticus*, pp. 457–458), but cannot be limited to it, since excommunication would require judicial action and God's threat to cut guilty parties off from the people may be carried out without the cooperation of the judiciary.

Genesis 17:14 suggests a link between being cut off from the people and moving outside the boundaries of the covenant.[52] It seems reasonable, therefore, to take the expression to indicate that under certain circumstances, God will act to put a guilty party outside the covenant's protection. The Sinaitic covenant provided safeguards for the nation as a whole in their relationship with God; this included turning away divine wrath by offering appropriate sacrifices, and providing a worship environment in which sinful human beings could approach and meet with a holy God. In some cases those safeguards might be withdrawn. Certain offences put the sinner beyond the scope of the covenant, and so beyond the provision of sacrifices valid only to those who are within the covenant.[53]

For those whose sin has put them beyond the reach of the sacrificial system, forgiveness is still possible by direct appeal to God's *hesed*. God has committed himself to show *hesed* to his people because of the covenant he has entered into with them. Sacrifice is set within that context: offerings are brought in accordance with the requirements of the covenant, and God's response, also in faithfulness to the covenant, is to forgive. Offering sacrifices is thus not opposed to *hesed*. The sacrificial system, along with every other aspect of the covenant, is effective precisely because of God's *hesed*: because of his loving, faithful commitment to his covenant people. But *hesed* also expresses God's ongoing love for his people when they have broken the covenant, and is the basis for restoration, leading, ultimately, to the promise of a new covenant.[54] In this case *hesed* comes close in meaning to 'grace', and provides the basis of appeal for those whose sin has put them outside the provisions of the covenant.

Such appeals are particularly prominent in the Psalms (e.g. Pss 25:7; 130:7).

---

52. In Gen. 17:14 *[he] will be cut off from his people* is in apposition to *he has broken my covenant*, indicating a level of equivalence between the two expressions. Breaking the covenant might thus be seen, not as one more offence that results in being cut off from the people (the particular offence here is the failure to be circumcised), but the general category into which all of the offences deserving of that particular punishment are incorporated.

53. This is not necessarily the same as formal excommunication; it relates, rather, to how offenders stand in God's sight. They might still take part in worship, but sacrifices would not be accepted and so would be ineffective in securing forgiveness. The ineffectuality of inappropriately offered sacrifices is not an uncommon idea in the OT.

54. This aspect of *hesed* is discussed above, pp. 109–110.

An important example is in Psalm 51:1, where the psalmist, who has committed the kind of serious, deliberate sin that would put him outside the provision
of the sacrificial system,[55] prays:

> *Have mercy on me, O God,*
> *according to your ḥesed;*
> *according to your great compassion*
> *blot out my transgressions.*

In this situation the offender has stepped beyond the normal covenantal provisions for forgiveness and might expect, rightly, to be cut off from his
people.[56] So he pleads, on the basis of divine *ḥesed*, that he will not be cast from
God's presence (v. 11a). The strength of this language, *save me from bloodguilt* (v.
14), *Do not cast me from your presence / or take your Holy Spirit from me* (v. 11), indicates the real possibility of separation from God. That may also be suggested
by verses 18–19, which, when read as part of a canonical whole, seem to point
to a time after the appeal to God's *ḥesed* has been heard, when the psalmist may
again join in the worship of the believing community, which includes bringing
righteous sacrifices and whole burnt offerings. This implies that those sacrifices are not
presently being offered, and suggests a breach in fellowship that needs to be
restored.

Sacrifice, then, is limited within the boundaries of the covenant, and is
unable to help those who step outside those boundaries. By contrast, God's
ḥesed, which operates largely within the mutual relationship established by the
covenant, is also able to reach out to those beyond its limits, and, by a miracle
of grace, offer the forgiveness that allows them to be drawn back into a
restored relationship with God.

---

55. The title of the psalm links it with David's adultery with Bathsheba. Though not
    part of the original Hebrew text, titles are part of the canonical text and are an
    early guide to the context in which the psalms were understood. It seems,
    therefore, reasonable to assume that the basis of appeal and the hope of
    forgiveness are relevant to someone who, like David, is guilty of a serious,
    deliberate sin.

56. The expression is not used specifically in connection with adultery and
    murder, though it is applied to those guilty of shedding blood (Lev. 17:4), and
    this may be linked with the reference to *bloodguilt* in Ps. 51:14; cf. Num.
    35:30–34.

Is the appeal to God's ḥesed enough?

In Psalm 51 the psalmist not only appeals to God's *ḥesed* but also appears to take a negative view of sacrifice:

> *You do not delight in sacrifice, or I would bring it;*
> > *you do not take pleasure in burnt offerings.*
> *The sacrifices of God are a broken spirit;*
> > *a broken and contrite heart,*
> > *O God, you will not despise.*
> (Ps. 51:16–17)

Some take this to imply a total repudiation of animal sacrifices and claim support for this from the pre-exilic prophets, who also appear to reject sacrifice in favour of a right interior attitude (e.g. Isa. 1:11–17; Jer. 6:20; Hos. 6:6; Amos 5:21–24; Mic. 6:6–8). A better way of interpreting this negative language is that it is relative. It condemns not sacrifice itself but the idea that the ritual act alone is a sufficient response to God, and emphasizes that sacrifice has meaning only when accompanied by, and subordinated to, a right interior attitude.[57] The prophet Samuel, who was certainly not against sacrifice, says something similar when he criticizes Saul's disobedience:

> *Does the LORD delight in burnt offerings and sacrifices*
> > *as much as in obeying the voice of the LORD?*
> *To obey is better than sacrifice,*
> > *and to heed is better than the fat of rams.*
> (1 Sam. 15:22)

Significantly, sacrifices still have a place after the return from exile (e.g. Ezra 3:1–6; Neh. 12:43; Mal. 1:6–9) and even within the prophetic vision of the kingdom of God (Jer. 33:18; Ezek. 40:38–43; 46; Zech. 14:20–21; Mal. 1:11),[58] indicating that the OT writers did not envisage the end of the sacrificial system.

---

57. The prophets condemn *all* religious practice that has been corrupted by a long-term exposure to the worship of other gods, and reduced to an external rite without inward consecration. This includes prayer that was offered inappropriately (Isa. 1:15), though there is no serious suggestion that the prophets rejected the practice of prayer.

58. Goldingay speaks about God's commitment to and renewal of the priesthood (*OT Theology*, 2:491–504), which includes bringing appropriate sacrifices (pp. 492–493).

As we have noted, the suppliant in Psalm 51 has placed himself beyond the scope of the sacrificial system, and his words in verses 16–17 might be taken not as a general statement about sacrifice but as a comment *on his own situation before God*. Because he stands outside the covenant, there is no animal sacrifice *that he can bring* to make atonement for his sin. The only sacrifice he might offer in those circumstances is true contrition. This is borne out in the narrative in 2 Samuel 12:1–14, which gives the canonical setting of Psalm 51. There David's repentance is immediately followed by absolution: *the LORD has taken away your sin* (2 Sam. 12:13), with no mention of sacrifice. There may be an element of this too in the prophetic indictment of sacrifice. Indeed it might even be possible to see Psalm 51 as providing a pattern for the repentance of the nation as a whole. As well as condemning religious formalism and syncretism, the prophets also announce the breakdown of the covenant relationship between God and his people (Isa. 24:5; Jer. 11:10; 31:32; Hos. 6:7; 8:1; Mal. 2:14; cf. Isa. 50:1; Jer. 3:8). For them, as for the psalmist, standing outside the covenant, no more sacrifices can be offered to make atonement for their sin. And comments about God not accepting or being pleased with sacrifice could be related specifically to that context, rather than taken as general statements about the continuing relevance (or otherwise) of the sacrificial system. Given the spiritual condition of the nation, *there are no sacrifices that the people can bring*,[59] all that remains, as in the case of the psalmist, is a sincere and heartfelt repentance and return to God. And also, as in the case of the psalmist, forgiveness and the possibility of restoration is based on divine *hesed*. The covenant has been broken, but God's faithful commitment to his people opens the way for the possibility of a new relationship and a new covenant, and, as in Psalm 51, for the opportunity to offer righteous sacrifices.

However, if more serious sin can be forgiven by direct appeal to God's *hesed*, surely lesser sins could be dealt with in the same way; so is there any need for sacrifice? Commenting on Psalm 51, Tate says, 'the suppliant is sure that the sacrifices of a "broken spirit" and a "contrite heart" would be acceptable to

---

59. See Mic. 6:6–8 and maybe also Jer. 6:20; Hos. 6:6; see also Eichrodt's discussion, *Theology*, 1:168. A further factor in the attitude towards sacrifice of the pre-exilic prophets may be the imminence of exile. The interior approach to God might be seen as preparing the way for an approach to God in a situation where sacrifices would be impossible. However, the exile is also viewed as a separation from God, reflecting the breakdown of the covenant relationship, and the inability to offer sacrifices (which are in any case corrupt) may be part of that (Jer. 3:6–10; Ezek. 16; Hos. 2:11–13; 3:3–4).

God . . . The worshiper who offers this sacrifice, accompanied by burnt offerings or not, can be sure of divine acceptance.'[60] This suggests that animal sacrifices are an optional extra, and that when it comes to forgiveness, penitent prayer provides a better way. From a Christian perspective, that strikes a chord; but it is not what the psalmist is saying. He appeals to God's *ḥesed* not because of a profound theological awakening as to the true nature of sacrifice but because he has no choice. He would bring burnt offerings if he could (Ps. 51:16); it is only because he cannot that he looks for a different basis of appeal. And he looks forward to a restored relationship where he may again offer *righteous sacrifices*, including *burnt offerings* (v. 19).

More generally, in the life of the nation, the prophets' condemnation of sacrifice is not presented as the result of theological enlightenment; it is a necessity occasioned by the corruption of true worship, and the people's spiritual condition. And there is no reason to suppose that if these factors were not present, and the sacrificial system was sincerely applied, such a negative view of sacrifices would be so evident. Plus, as we have noted, sacrifice and other elements of cultic worship condemned by the prophets, continue to feature in the vision of God's coming kingdom, and are still acceptable after the spiritual renewal of the nation.

Prayer and sacrifice

Focusing on the attitude to sacrifice in some of the psalms, Eichrodt points to the priority of prayer without the need for sacrifices, and refers to God's 'right to dispense with sacrifices, wherever their essential meaning, spiritual intercourse with God, has been overpoweringly experienced in prayer'.[61] This emphasizes the importance of spiritual communion with God; however, it almost certainly overstates the case, since none of the passages quoted in support need imply that sacrifices are actually dispensed with.[62] A right

---

60. Marvin E. Tate, *Psalms 51–100*, WBC 20 (Dallas: Word, 1990), p. 28; Kiuchi appears to take a similar view: 'when the symbol and what is symbolized become one in reality, there is no need for sacrifices and offerings' (*Leviticus*, p. 32).

61. Eichrodt, *Theology*, 1:168.

62. Eichrodt claims support from Pss 40:6; 51:16–17; 69:30–31. We have already noted problems with this interpretation of Ps. 51:16–17. Ps. 40:6 may envisage a similar situation to Ps. 51, where the cult is not applicable, and appeal is made to God's mercy (*raḥămîm*) and (*ḥesed*) (v. 11); or it might be, as Craigie suggests, that the king will have carried out all the cultic requirements, but knows that more is required of him; see e.g. Peter C. Craigie, *Psalms 1–50*, WBC 19 (Waco: Word, 1983),

interior approach to God need not, and may not, be separated from the appropriate offering of sacrifices. Rowley rightly emphasizes the need to maintain
the balance between spirit and ritual: 'where the ritual act was prescribed, sin-
cerity of penitence could not dispense with it. Neither could the act dispense
with the spirit, and the prophets therefore insisted that the act must be infused
with the spirit'.[63] The move from dependence on sacrifices to a direct appeal
to God's *ḥesed* is not simply the result of a development from external ritual to
a deeper communion with God. It is made necessary because the sinner is
outside the covenant and so in a place where the provisions of the cult do not
apply. Where sacrifices may be offered appropriately, the existence of true penitence and contrition does not remove the need for them. In the canonical
form of Psalm 51 these approaches to God (one from outside the provision
of the covenant, the other from inside it) exist side by side. The argument
about which approach is better is academic: they apply to different circumstances, and the worshipper does not have a choice.

As we have noted, a right interior attitude is important, and was an essential part of sacrifice from the beginning. This cannot be viewed as a mechanistic ritual: forgiveness remains God's prerogative, and though in covenant
love and faithfulness (*ḥesed*) he has committed himself to accept sacrifices
properly offered, his hand cannot be forced. But the ritual is also significant.[64]
A key emphasis of the covenant is right living, as revealed in the Law. It was
recognized that the people would fail, and that was provided for, but while
there was confession and the recognition of sin, there was not deep soul-
searching. Sacrifices were never a formality, but they were routine, with the
emphasis on sorting out the problem and getting back to the real issue of living
as the covenant people of God. This requires a delicate balance between
being aware of the seriousness of sin, on the one hand, and confidence in the

---

Footnote 62 (*continued*)

p. 315. It is not obedience and listening to God *instead of* sacrifice, but *in addition
to* it, as part of its true meaning. Again, this does not reflect a rejection of the
sacrificial system. Ps. 69:31 does imply that sincere praise and thanksgiving are
more acceptable to God than sacrifice. This is set in the context of thanksgiving
for deliverance rather than an appeal for forgiveness, but here too it does not
imply a repudiation of the cult. The passage is relative: the right attitude of the
worshipper is vital to sacrifice, and more pleasing to God than mechanistic
sacrifice alone.

63. Rowley, *Worship*, p. 246.
64. See Brueggemann, *Theology*, p. 195.

readiness of God to forgive, on the other, a balance Christians also seek to maintain – and not always with great success. Within the OT context, sacrifice and the shedding of blood play an important part in holding that balance. The sacrificial system, set in the context of relationship and of the worshippers' sincere desire to maintain that relationship, asserts God's willingness to forgive, and provides the assurance that when a worshipper offers his sacrifice in the right way, he will be forgiven and accepted by God. Also, though sacrifice may be routine, it demonstrates the nature and serious effect of sin. Bringing an unblemished animal is costly, and shows that sin cannot simply be ignored. The worshipper's full involvement in killing the animal would have been a stark reminder of the effect of the sin he confesses, and a warning not to step outside the provision of the covenant, where no ransom could be offered.[65] Its public nature also recognizes that individual sin has an effect on the life of the community.[66]

Where sacrifice is inappropriate and it is necessary to appeal directly to God's *ḥesed*, the inward reality that sacrifice points to, which includes recognition of the seriousness of sin and a proper understanding of what sin can do (and in this case has already done) to the relationship with God, needs to be, in Eichrodt's words, 'overpoweringly experienced in prayer'.[67] However, the exceptional circumstances mean that the sinner is no longer in a place where forgiveness can be routine, and calls for greater contrition. We see this in Psalm 51, where the level of soul-searching and expressions of contrition and repentance go beyond what was required within the sacrificial system.

It is tempting for Christians to favour the idea that the attitude to sacrifice developed within the OT faith from exterior ritual to interior reality, and to see the attitude to prayer and forgiveness in the NT as part of that development. As a result, discussion of the OT view of sacrifice tends to emphasize its inadequacy, rather than its ongoing theological significance. I have argued that that premise is incorrect. The sacrificial system was part of God's intention, and within the OT was not intended to be replaced. It remained in force until its fulfilment in Christ's once-for-all sacrifice. This does indeed replace the offerings for sin in the OT sacrificial system, not by driving a final nail into

---

65. There may be the idea that those who sin wilfully may share the same fate as the animal. If the animal dies in place of the sinner, the consequence of not being able to offer sacrifices is that the sinner must perish instead.

66. This may be linked to the fact that the most serious sin resulted in being cut off from the community.

67. Eichrodt, *Theology*, 1:168.

the coffin of a spiritually defunct system but by fulfilling an important OT theme.

The ongoing significance of sacrifice within the faith of the OT suggests that the principles underlying it (such as the seriousness of sin and the demands of God's holiness, the recognition that sin affects the community's as well as the individual's relationship with him, and the importance of seeking forgiveness regularly in order to maintain the relationship and go on with the primary task of living out what it means to be the people of God) remain relevant to the life of the church. On this basis, OT texts relating to sacrifice can be examined in their own right, and can be seen to set out theological principles that apply to our relationship with, and approach to, God through Christ.

Other elements of worship

Prayer[68]

Sacrifice clearly played a key part in the worship of the OT, and from the previous discussion it is clear that prayer too was an important element. We have examples of prayers offered by several OT characters (e.g. Gen. 18:23–33; Num. 14:13–19; 2 Sam. 7:18–29; 1 Kgs 8:23–53; Neh. 9:5–37; Dan. 9:4–19), and also significant insights into the content of different kinds of prayer in the Psalms. Prayer is linked with the earliest expressions of religious faith (Gen. 4:26). As communication with God, it was, for the people of Israel, rooted in the covenant, and is offered on assumption that God hears and answers prayer (e.g. Pss 17:6; 65:2; 86:7; 102:17; Prov. 15:29; Jer. 33:3),[69] though there is too the concern and frustration of prayers that appear to go unheeded (e.g. Pss 22:2; 35:22–23; Lam. 3:8, 44). Prayer might be offered as an act of private devotion, or publicly as part of corporate worship. However, because it is the expression of an intimate and personal relationship with God, prayer is affected by those things that undermine the relationship; so, for example, unconfessed sin prevents prayers from being heard (e.g. Ps. 66:18–20; Prov. 15:29; 28:9; Lam. 3:41–44; Isa. 1:15; 59:2; cf. Jer. 7:16; 11:14), and prayer, as with all other aspects of worship, may be reduced to meaningless ritual (Isa. 1:15).

---

68. See Pieter A. Verhoef, 'Prayer', in *NIDOTTE* 4:1060–1066; Rowley, *Worship*, pp. 257–264; Preuss, *OT Theology*, 2:245–250.

69. This is also implied in passages where the supplicant pleads for his prayer to be heard (e.g. Pss 4:1; 20:9; 27:7).

Because prayer is directed towards God as the object of the people's worship, it often includes adoration and praise. Many psalms have been categorized as 'hymns of praise', calling the people to worship and setting out why God deserves to be praised.[70] They include victory songs (Ps. 68); processional hymns, sung by pilgrims and worshippers as they approached the temple (Pss 24; 84; 122; 132); songs of Zion, which celebrate God's presence in the city (Pss 46; 48; 76); and enthronement psalms, which celebrate God's reign as King over the whole earth (Pss 47; 93; 96 – 99). It is impossible, though, to stand in God's glorious presence without becoming aware of sin, and prayer also includes confession, and pleas for forgiveness. We see this in some of the individual laments in the Psalms (e.g. Pss 38; 39; 51; 130), and also in Job's response to hearing God's voice (42:1–6) and Isaiah's cry of despair following the revelation of God's holiness and glory (Isa. 6:5). Daniel (9:4–19) and the Levites (9:5–37) offer prayers of confession on behalf of the nation; significantly, both also begin with praise. As we have already seen, prayers for forgiveness often include appeals to God's *ḥesed* (e.g. Pss 51:1; 130:7; Neh. 9:17; Dan. 9:4). Prayer also includes calling on God for help: thus Hannah prays for a child (1 Sam. 1:10–12) and Solomon prayed at the dedication of the temple (1 Kgs 8:23–53), though again there is a strong element of praise. In several 'psalms of lament' the psalmist prays for help, either individually or on behalf of the nation.[71] Westermann suggests that a key element of lament in Israel is complaint,[72] which includes 'accusatory questions and statements directed against God'.[73] In the face of the bitter realities of life the petitioner asks why God has turned away (e.g. Num. 11:11–15; Job 3:11–26; Pss 10:1; 22:1; 42:9; 44:23–24; Jer. 14:19; 20:18; Lam. 5:20). Such prayers also

---

70. This is usually thought to include Pss 8; 19; 29; 33; 46 – 48; 65; 66; 68; 76; 84; 87; 93; 95 – 100; 103 – 104; 111; 113 – 114; 117; 122; 134 – 136; 145 – 150. See Claus Westermann, *Praise and Lament in the Psalms* (Edinburgh: T. & T. Clark, 1981), pp. 15–162. For further discussion of types of psalms and the use of psalms in Israel's worship, see e.g. B. W. Anderson, *Living World*, pp. 540–567; John Day, *Psalms*, OTG (Sheffield: Sheffield Academic Press, 1995); LaSor, Hubbard and Bush, *OT Survey*, pp. 429–446; Artur Weiser, *The Psalms*, OTL (London: SCM, 1962; repr. Louisville: Westminster John Knox, 2000), pp. 19–91.

71. Day lists individual laments as Pss 3 – 7; 9 – 10; 13; 17; 22; 23; 25 – 28; 31; 35; 38 – 39; 40:13–17 = 70; 42 – 43; 51 – 52; 54 – 57; 59; 61; 64; 69 – 71; 77; 86; 88; 94:16–23; 102; 109; 120; 130; 131; 139 – 143; and community laments as Pss 12; 44; 60; 74; 79 – 80; 83; 85; 94:1–11; 126; 137; and maybe 58 and 90 (*Psalms*, pp. 19–38 [19, 33]).

72. Westermann, *Praise and Lament*, pp. 165–170.

73. Ibid., p. 177.

express, implicitly or explicitly, the confident hope in God's favourable response.[74] This is evident too in 'hymns of thanksgiving', which note the suffering and cry for help – and give thanks to God for his deliverance.[75]

Another important element in prayer is intercession. Abraham prayed for Sodom (Gen. 18:23–33); Moses interceded on behalf of Israel (Num. 14:13–19); Samuel interceded for the people after the capture of the Ark (1 Sam. 7:5–6);[76] an unnamed 'man of God' interceded for Jeroboam's hand to be restored (1 Kgs 13:6), and Ezra interceded for Israel (Ezra 9:6–15).

An important question here is, what is the purpose of prayer? It would appear that when people call on God, it is with the intention of changing his mind. Commenting on Abraham's prayer for Sodom, Goldingay says, 'the object of prayer is not to discover God's will in order to align oneself with it but to take part in determining God's will'.[77] There is something in this. Through prayer, the worshipper becomes a participant, with God. But the idea that God is persuaded by our prayers to do what he might otherwise not do raises questions about his sovereignty. Prayer is not a means of imposing our will on God, though some might have seen it that way. On the other hand, if it makes no difference, then why do it? This is a tension we cannot easily resolve. God is sovereign; his purposes stand for ever. But in his grace and mercy, he also responds to the prayers of his people.[78]

Music and singing[79]
Music and singing played an important part in the life and worship of Israel. The people celebrated God's mighty acts on behalf of his people in song: so,

---

74. Brueggemann claims that these 'psalms of complaint' assume God has not honoured his covenant commitment and that he is moved to action by the insistence of the petitioner (*Theology*, pp. 374–381). Ps. 44 raises the question of God's faithfulness (vv. 17–22) and even accuses him of sleeping (v. 23); however, through the apparent contradiction, the psalmist continues to call on God for help.

75. According to Day, thanksgiving psalms include Pss 30; 32; 34; 40; 41; 116; 138 (individual); and maybe Pss 66:8–12; 67; 124; 129 (communal). Brueggemann sees 'thanksgiving' (Hebrew: *tôdâ*) as a key element in Israel's normative testimony about God (*Theology*, pp. 126–130).

76. The prayers of Daniel and Nehemiah may be seen in a similar way.

77. Goldingay, *OT Theology*, 1:219; see also Brueggemann, *Theology*, pp. 321–322, 378–381.

78. For more on whether or not God changes his mind, see below, pp. 251–254.

79. See e.g. Rowley, *Worship*, pp. 176–212; Leslie C. Allen, "*nh*', in *NIDOTTE* 3:453–454; 4:99–100.

after the deliverance at the Red Sea, Moses and Miriam led the people in a song of praise (Exod. 15:1–21), accompanied by *tambourines and dancing* (v. 20).[80] Music and dancing feature prominently in worship, for example when David brought the Ark to Jerusalem (2 Sam. 6). Prophecy is sometimes accompanied by music (1 Sam. 10:5; 2 Kgs 3:15); Isaiah 30:29 indicates that songs were sung at festivals,[81] and that processions to the temple were accompanied by music. More negatively, singing and dancing also were part of the ritual surrounding the worship of the golden calf (Exod. 32:18–19), and music and singing were part of the corrupt worship condemned by Amos (5:23; cf. 8:3).

As we have seen, the psalms played an important part in Israel's worship,[82] and were often accompanied by musical instruments.[83] Worshippers probably sang *songs of ascent* (Pss 120 – 136) as they went up the hill to the temple. The expression 'according to' in some psalm titles may indicate musical directions or tune titles. Stringed instruments were to be played *according to alamoth* and *sheminith* (1 Chr. 15:20–21; Pss 6; 12; 46); these are probably instructions for playing the instruments, though we can only guess at what the terms mean. *Selah*, which occurs in many psalms, may be a musical instruction.[84] As we have noted, Levites had particular responsibility for music and singing (e.g. 1 Chr. 15:16, 19, 27; 2 Chr. 5:12–13; 7:6; 23:13; Neh. 12:8, 27). Some are associated with particular psalms, including Asaph (1 Chr. 6:39; Pss 50; 73 – 83), Heman (1 Chr. 6:33; Ps. 88) and Ethan (1 Chr. 6:44; Ps. 89). The *sons of Korah* appear to be a family of singers and musicians

---

80. Another example is the song of Deborah and Barak (Judg. 5:1–31); see also e.g. Judg. 11:34; 1 Sam. 18:6–7.

81. E.g. the Hallel (Pss 113 – 118) is traditionally associated with the Passover.

82. There is debate about the 'life-setting' of some of the psalms. Gunkel and Mowinckel link them closely with Israel's worship, though their use in worship does not preclude the possibility that some of them came from real-life situations. E.g. Ps. 18 is canonically linked with a particular historical situation (2 Sam. 22:2–51), was possibly composed by David to celebrate his deliverance by God and later included in the book of Psalms to be used in worship.

83. The terms 'psalm' and 'song' often appear in the psalm titles; a 'psalm' would usually be accompanied by music; it is not clear how a 'song' is different, though maybe it was sung without music.

84. It may signal a musical interlude, or be an instruction to sing or play louder or to repeat a passage from the beginning, or to indicate points for the congregation to bow down in worship.

descended from Levi (1 Chr. 6:37; Pss 42; 44 – 49; 84; 85; 87; 88), perhaps led by Heman.

Singing included praise and lament. It may also have been a part of teaching: reminding the people of what God has done and encouraging them to remain faithful to him.[85]

---

85. This seems to be indicated in Deut. 31:19–22.

6. GOD AND HIS PEOPLE (3): RECEIVING INSTRUCTION

A key element in the relationship between God and his people is the fact that God makes himself and his will known. We have noted already the significance of the Law,[1] and the role of the priesthood in bringing God's instruction to the people.[2] Two other important means of revelation in the OT are through prophecy and wisdom teaching.[3]

Prophets and prophecy[4]

What is a prophet?
The usual Hebrew word for 'prophet' in the OT is *nābî'*. This is probably linked

---

1. See above, pp. 173–174. For further discussion of the importance of the Law as a basis for ethics, see below, pp. 242–245.
2. See above, pp. 172, 184.
3. Jer. 18:18 suggests three ways instruction was received in Israel: teaching of the Law by priests, wisdom and the prophetic word. Other significant factors in divine revelation already noted include creation, God's action in history, and the divine name.
4. For more detailed discussion, see e.g. B. W. Anderson, *Living World*, pp. 247–253; Bright, *History*, pp. 264–266; Joseph Blenkinsopp, *A History of Prophecy in Israel*, rev.

with the verb 'to call',[5] and points to someone called by God or who called to others on God's behalf. The divine call was vital: it validated the prophet's ministry and gave authority to his message.[6] Two further Hebrew words, *rō'eh* and *hōzeh*, come from verbs meaning 'to see', and are often translated 'seer'.[7] Divine revelation enabled prophets to see what others could not. These might be

---

Footnote 4 (*continued*)

and enlarged ed. (Louisville: Westminster John Knox, 1996); Brueggemann, *Theology*, pp. 622–649; Childs, *Biblical Theology* (1992), pp. 167–180; *OT Theology*, pp. 122–144; Clements, *Prophecy and Covenant*, pp. 11–26; Drane, *Introducing the OT*, pp. 169–172; Dyrness, *Themes*, pp. 211–224; Goldingay, *OT Theology*, 1:668–691; E. W. Heaton, *A Short Introduction to the Old Testament Prophets*, rev. ed. (Oxford: Oneworld, 1996); Eichrodt, *Theology*, 1:309–391; H. L. Ellison, *Men Spake from God: Studies in the Hebrew Prophets* (London: Paternoster, 1958); Goldingay, *OT Theology*, 1:668–691; House, *OT Theology*, pp. 263–265; Jacob, *Theology*, pp. 239–246; Lindblom, *Prophecy*; J. A. Motyer and J. B. Payne, 'Prophecy, Prophets', in *IBD* 3:1276–1287 (1276–1284); Miller, *Israelite Religion*, pp. 508–525. Harry Mowvley, *Guide to Old Testament Prophecy*, new ed. (Cambridge: James Clarke, 2002); H.-P. Müller, '*nābî*', etc.', in *TDOT* 9:129–150; Preuss, *OT Theology*, 2:67–96; von Rad, *OT Theology*, 2:6–98; Rendtorff, *Hebrew Bible*, pp. 157–162, 651–662; Rowley, *Worship*, pp. 144–175; LaSor, Hubbard and Bush, *OT Survey*, pp. 221–230; Pieter A. Verhoef, 'Prophecy', in *NIDOTTE* 4:1067–1078.

5. See Motyer and Payne, 'Prophecy', in *IBD* 3:1278; Müller, '*nābî*', etc.', in *TDOT* 9:131–134; Verhoef, 'Prophecy', in *NIDOTTE* 4:1067–1068.

6. Many of the prophetic books describe the prophet's call, e.g. Isa. 6:8–9; Jer. 1:4–10; Amos 7:14–15; Jon. 1:1–2. Some, such as Isaiah, accepted God's call willingly. Others were more reluctant. Jeremiah argued with God; Jonah tried to run away. Amos was willing, but seems surprised by his call.

7. At one time there may have been a difference between a 'prophet' (*nābî*') and a 'seer' (*rō'eh, hōzeh*) (e.g. 1 Chr. 29:29; 2 Chr. 9:29; 29:25). Rowley notes that at one point scholars regarded the *nābî*' as an ecstatic prophet, while seers prophesied to order, though this, like all other simple divisions, breaks down (*Worship*, pp. 147–178). It appears that by the time of Samuel any official distinction had disappeared (e.g. 1 Sam. 9:9). Samuel is described as both a *rō'eh* (e.g. 1 Sam. 9:19; 1 Chr. 29:29) and a *nābî*' (1 Sam. 3:20; 2 Chr. 35:18); and Gad is both a *hōzeh* (2 Sam. 24:11; 1 Chr. 29:29; 2 Chr. 29:25) and a *nābî*' (1 Sam. 22:5; 2 Sam. 24:11). In these descriptions the distinction between *rō'eh* and *hōzeh* is preserved, and Nathan, mentioned alongside Samuel and Gad, is only called a *nābî*'. This suggests that there may still have been some informal difference, maybe in function, though if so we do not know what it was.

glimpses of the future, or deep spiritual truths. They might also be very practical: Saul came to Samuel because he hoped the 'seer' could help him to find his father's lost donkeys (1 Sam. 9:3–11). Two Hebrew words translated 'vision' come from the same roots:[8] seeing visions was a normal part of what was expected of a 'seer'. Another common title is 'man of God', emphasizing the prophet's close relationship with God (e.g. 1 Sam. 9:6–10; 1 Kgs 17:24; 20:28; 2 Kgs 1:9–13; 13:19).[9]

The role of the prophet

The principal role of the OT prophet was as a mediator: bringing direct communication from God to the people. A description of the prophetic office is found in Exodus 7:1–2, *the LORD said to Moses, 'See, I have made you like God to Pharaoh, and your brother Aaron will be your prophet. You are to say everything I command you, and your brother Aaron is to tell Pharaoh'* (see also Exod. 4:16).[10] The prophet received his message from God and proclaimed it to the people on God's behalf. That message was received in a variety of ways. One way, which we have already noted, is through the Spirit of God.[11] Prophets also received revelation through dreams and visions (Num. 12:6; see also e.g. Isa. 30:10; Hos. 12:10),[12] and by being

---

8. I.e. *hāzôn* (e.g. Isa. 1:1; Ezek. 12:27; Dan. 8:1; Hos. 12:10; Mic. 3:6); *mar'â* (e.g. Num. 12:6; 1 Sam. 3:15; Dan. 10:16).

9. Jacob notes that this term is reserved only for prophets, with the exception of Moses, Samuel and David, who also had other mediatoral roles (*Theology*, p. 239).

10. Eichrodt describes the *nābî'* as 'the mediator through whom the divine life made its way into a world otherwise sealed against it' (*Theology*, 1:326).

11. See above, pp. 114–115. Some suggest that a characteristic of OT prophets was ecstatic or frenzied behaviour (cf. 1 Sam. 19:23–24). However, that kind of uncontrolled or trancelike behaviour is rare in the OT. The prophet is not taken over by God. The word he receives is usually clear and intelligible; he remains conscious and in control of himself while he listens to what God is saying. Ecstatic behaviour was common in other nations, and may have been copied by false prophets in Israel. As noted above, a desire not to be identified with this may have led some pre-exilic prophets to be cautious about attributing their inspiration to the Spirit.

12. In 1 Sam. 3:1 the absence of visions is linked with the absence of the prophetic voice (see also Lam. 2:9). The young Samuel heard God speak in a vision (1 Sam. 3:15). Ezekiel (e.g. Ezek. 1:1; 8:3–4; 11:24; 40:2; 43:3), Daniel (e.g. Dan. 2:19; 7:1–2; 8:1; 10:1) and Zechariah (Zech. 1:8) also received revelation in visions. Isaiah's whole prophecy is described as a 'vision' (Isa. 1:1; 29:11; 2 Chr. 32:32); so are the prophecies of Obadiah (Obad. 1), Micah (Mic. 1:1) and Nahum (Nah. 1:1). False prophets also claimed to have visions (e.g. Jer. 14:14; 23:16; Lam. 2:14; Ezek. 13:6–9, 16; 22:28).

admitted into the divine council.[13] In many cases we are told only that *the word of the LORD came to* a particular prophet (e.g. 1 Sam. 15:10; 2 Sam. 7:4; 1 Kgs 16:1; 17:2, 8; 18:1; 19:9; 2 Kgs 20:4; Isa. 38:4; Jer. 1:2, 4, 11, 13; 2:1; 7:1; Ezek. 1:3; 3:16; 6:1; 7:1; Hos. 1:1; Joel 1:1; Jon. 1:1; Mic. 1:1; Hag. 2:10; Zech. 1:1). This suggests a close, ongoing relationship with God. Isaiah 50:4 describes how the Servant of the Lord, who has a prophetic role,[14] is wakened to listen to God morning by morning in order to receive his prophetic word. It is unclear to what extent the prophet then declared those exact words. That may have happened sometimes, though it may have been more usual to interpret the message received, and present it using whatever rhetorical techniques would allow it to make most impact.

Until the eighth century BC the main prophetic role appears to have been in national affairs. Moses, sometimes described as the 'prophet *par excellence*',[15] was a national leader; so was Samuel. Israel's first king, Saul, is also described as a prophet (e.g. 1 Sam. 10:11–12), and in the NT, Peter describes David too as a prophet (Acts 2:30) – though that is not explicitly stated in the OT (but see 2 Sam. 23:2). During the monarchy, prophets advised, and often confronted and challenged, kings. Before setting out on a military campaign, a king consulted his prophets (e.g. 1 Kgs 22:6–7; 2 Kgs 3:11). Elisha passed on military intelligence given by God to the king of Israel during his war with Syria (2 Kgs 6:8–12). A key prophetic task was to counsel and guide the leaders of the nation and to encourage them to walk in God's ways. So, as well as giving help and advice to the king, Samuel challenged Saul (e.g. 1 Sam. 13:13); Nathan rebuked David over his sin with Bathsheba (2 Sam. 12:1–14) and Elijah confronted Ahab and Jezebel (e.g. 1 Kgs 18:16–18; 21:20–24). There seems to be a change in emphasis in the eighth century BC.[16] Prophets such as Amos, Isaiah and Jeremiah still had messages from God to deliver to kings and to other national leaders, but their prophetic words were directed more towards the people and

---

13. See above, p. 121.

14. For further discussion of the Servant of the Lord, see below, pp. 291–296.

15. Ellison, *Men Spake*, p. 13. This is based on Deut. 18:15, 34:10, though Moses' experience at the burning bush (Exod. 3), where he received a message from God to proclaim to the people, also suggests a prophetic role. Albertz links the emphasis on Moses as the ideal prophet with a post-exilic development of the Deuteronomic movement, which wanted to retain an emphasis on prophecy, but also to subordinate it to Mosaic law (*History*, 2:477–480).

16. The prophets from the eighth century BC onwards are known as the 'classical' or 'writing' prophets. Though their role may differ, it is not necessary to see a significant discontinuity between them and earlier prophets; see Lindblom,

to society as a whole. The reason for this change may have been the worsening historical crisis facing Israel and Judah. The kings and leaders of the nation had failed to maintain godliness, and the result was impending judgment. A key task of the prophets was now to warn the people and call them to repentance. In this context the prophets were, essentially, preachers, proclaiming God's word to whoever would listen. And they used various rhetorical and dramatic means to attract attention and to drive their message home.[17] Another distinction, related to the more general role in society of the classical prophets is that collections of their oracles were written down.

There is some debate as to how prophets were organized.[18] There appear to have been prophetic bands or guilds, sometimes referred to as the *sons of the prophets* (e.g. 1 Kgs 20:35; 2 Kgs 2:7; 4:1, 38; 6:1; 9:1). Some of these groups may have been attached to sanctuaries,[19] though their precise role is unclear. Prophets may also have been part of the royal court (e.g. 1 Kgs 18:19;

Prophecy, pp. 216–219; Preuss, *OT Theology*, 2:70–73; von Rad, *Theology*, 2:6–32, 176–187; Rendtorff, *Hebrew Bible*, pp. 157–162.

17. So, in Amos 1 – 2 the prophet attracts the attention and support of his audience by first condemning Israel's enemies, before turning on the Israelites themselves. Sometimes prophets present their message in the form of a parable or allegory (2 Sam. 12:1–7; Isa. 5:1–7; Ezek. 16). Isaiah, Jeremiah and Ezekiel use what is sometimes called 'prophetic symbolism': acting out their message in a dramatic way. Isaiah went *stripped and barefoot* (Isa. 20:2–3) to indicate the fate of the Egyptians and Cushites at the hands of Assyria; Jeremiah buried a *linen belt*, which, by the time he recovered it, had become *ruined and completely useless* in order to demonstrate God's judgment (Jer. 13:1–11); he also smashed a clay pot as part of his message to indicate the destruction coming on the nation (Jer. 19:10–13). Ezekiel drew and laid siege to a representation of Jerusalem; he then lay on his left side for 390 days and his right for 40 days (Ezek. 4:1–6); later he gathered his belongings and dug through the wall of his house (Ezek. 12:3–7).

18. For further discussion, see e.g. Albertz, *History*, 1:150–156; Heaton, *OT Prophets*, pp. 32–41; Lindblom, *Prophecy*, pp. 69–70, 78–83, 206–210; Motyer and Payne, 'Prophecy', in *IBD* 3:1282–1284; Rowley, *Worship*, pp. 149–153.

19. Saul encountered a procession of prophets who had come down from the high place near Gibeah (1 Sam. 10:5, 10), and there were prophetic communities linked with Bethel (2 Kgs 2:3) and Gilgal (2 Kgs 4:38). Amos may have been regarded as an official prophet, making his living by prophesying at Bethel, though he makes it clear he is not linked with any official group, but was called by and is answerable only to God (Amos 7:12–15).

22:6).[20] When the classical prophets condemn the political and religious institutions, they criticize other prophets as well as priests, suggesting that prophets
too may have had official status as leaders of the nation (e.g. Isa. 28:7; Jer. 2:26;
5:31; 23:11; Ezek. 7:26; Mic. 3:11; cf. Neh. 9:32; Zech. 7:1–3).[21] Official
prophets, though, might be tempted to agree with their paymasters, or to
prophesy to please their audience, giving the potential for false prophecy (e.g.
1 Kgs 22:13; Jer. 23:16; Lam. 2:14; Ezek. 13:19; 22:28).

True and false prophets[22]

Distinguishing between true and false prophecy was (and is) very important,
but not straightforward. The main issue is the source of the prophecy. The true
prophet is called by God and receives his message from God, while false
prophets speak on their own authority or in the name of other gods.[23] There
are some indicators of whether a prophecy is from God or not.

First, if a prophet brings a message that is unfulfilled, then that message is
not from God, and the prophet is false (Deut. 18:21–22). Both Ezekiel
and Jeremiah trusted that events would prove the truth of their message and
show up the emptiness of their opponents' words (e.g. Jer. 14:14–16; 23:19–
22; 28:9; Ezek. 2:5; 33:33). But how long is a prophet given for his word to
come true? What about those who prophesy about events beyond their lifetime? And what about those occasions where true prophets give deliberately
false messages (e.g. 1 Kgs 13:18; 22:15)? In general we might expect a true
prophet to announce messages that can be tested, so establishing his creden-
tials. That might then provide the basis for accepting other words not so easily
tested.[24]

---

20. Nathan and Gad appear to have been officials in David's court (e.g. 1 Kgs 1:8;
     1 Chr. 21:9).

21. The expression 'prophets of Israel' (Ezek. 13:2) also suggests an official position.
     With the exception of Amos 7:14 there are no references to 'sons of the prophets'
     (*běnê hannĕbî'îm*; the NIV usually uses the expression 'company of the prophets')
     in the classical period. It may be that by this time all such prophetic groups had
     become 'official'.

22. See e.g. Childs, *OT Theology*, pp. 133–144; Lindblom, *Prophecy*, pp. 210–215; Motyer
     and Payne, 'Prophecy', in *IBD* 3:1281–1282; Preuss, *OT Theology*, 2:82–86.

23. This is the distinction made in Deut. 18:20. See also e.g. Jer. 23:16, 18; Ezek.
     13:1–12; 22:28.

24. The question of God giving deliberately misleading or deceitful messages will be
     considered below, pp. 250–251.

Second, a false prophet receives his inspiration from other gods (Deut. 18:20). That test can be applied in some cases, for example when Elijah confronted the prophets of Baal. But often both true and false prophecies are given in the name of Yahweh (e.g. 1 Kgs 22:11; Jer. 28:1–4). A third test is that a true prophet will not lead the people away from the worship of Yahweh and the obedience that accompanies it (Deut. 13:1–5). Part of Jeremiah's criticism of false prophets is that they themselves practise injustice, immorality and idolatry, and lead others to do the same (Jer. 23:9–14), indicating that they do not speak in Yahweh's name.[25]

The message of the prophets

As we have seen, a key role of Israel's prophets after the monarchy was to call the nation back to the ways of God, by challenging political and spiritual leaders, and by addressing the people directly. They spoke out against immorality and social injustice, particularly the oppression and exploitation of the weak by the strong.[26] They also condemned the nation's unfaithfulness in turning away from the worship of Yahweh to follow other gods, describing it as spiritual adultery. Because of the nation's sin, the prophets pronounced coming judgment; though several also point to the ultimate restoration and renewal of the nation and the coming of God's kingdom.[27] This will be discussed in more detail below.

Wisdom[28]

Wisdom and wisdom teaching

'Wisdom' in the OT is wide ranging: it includes intelligence, discernment, insight and understanding (e.g. Gen. 41:39; 1 Kgs 4:29; 2 Chr. 2:12; Prov. 5:1;

---

25. Jeremiah recognized the syncretistic source of the words of his opponents, charging them with prophesying *by Baal* (Jer. 2:8; 23:13). This should probably not be taken to imply that their inspiration had a supernatural or demonic origin. The emphasis is on the nature of the message: it led people away from worship of Yahweh.

26. See below, pp. 246–247.

27. See below, pp. 265–272.

28. See e.g. Albertz, *History*, 2:511–514; B. W. Anderson, *Living World*, pp. 568–603; *Contours*, pp. 260–274; Brueggemann, *Theology*, pp. 680–694; Childs, *Biblical Theology* (1992), pp. 187–190; *OT Theology*, pp. 210–212; John Day, Robert P. Gordon and

10:13; Dan. 5:11, 14), and also technical and artistic ability.[29] Above all, wisdom is practical. The wise man has insights into the way the world works or possesses specialist knowledge or skill, and applies his understanding and ability to become successful in what he does. Drane notes this connection and suggests that wisdom denotes 'the possession of whatever abilities were necessary for a particular individual to be successful in their own sphere of life'.[30]

Although wisdom teaching was common throughout the ANE and there seems to have been some interchange of ideas, wisdom in the OT has a clear theological dimension (e.g. Job 28:28; Ps. 111:10; Prov. 1:7; 9:10; 15:33; cf. Ps. 14:1); wisdom without God is lacking, and the wisest plans, made without reference to God, will be confounded (e.g. Isa. 10:13–16; 19:12–13). As something possessed by and proceeding from God, wisdom has too a cosmic dimension (Prov. 8:22–31); it existed before, and was instrumental in, the

---

Footnote 28 (*continued*)

Hugh G. M. Williamson (eds.), *Wisdom in Ancient Israel: Essays in Honour of J. A. Emerton* (Cambridge: Cambridge University Press, 1995); Drane, *Introducing the OT*, pp. 112–119, 279–287; Dyrness, *Themes*, pp. 188–199; Eichrodt, *Theology*, 1:80–92; John A. Emerton, 'Wisdom', in G. W. Anderson, *Tradition*, pp. 214–237; Goldingay, *OT Theology*, 2:576–631; David A. Hubbard, 'The Wisdom Movement and Israel's Covenant Faith', *TynBul* 17 (1966), pp. 3–33; D. A. Hubbard, 'Wisdom Literature', in *IBD* 3:1650–1652; House, *OT Theology*, pp. 253–255, 439–454, 470–482; Derek Kidner, *The Wisdom of Proverbs, Job and Ecclesiastes* (Leicester: IVP; Downers Grove: IVP, 1985); H.-P. Müller and M. Krause, '*ḥākam*, etc.', in *TDOT* 4:364–385; Roland E. Murphy, 'Wisdom in the OT', in *ABD* 6:920–931; Preuss, *OT Theology*, 1:184–188, 228–230; 2:126–133, 203–207; von Rad, *OT Theology*, 1:418–459; *Wisdom in Israel* (London: SCM, 1972); Rendtorff, *Hebrew Bible*, pp. 336–369, 374–383, 665–666; LaSor, Hubbard and Bush, *OT Survey*, pp. 447–459; Bruce K. Waltke and David Diewert, 'Wisdom Literature', in Baker and Arnold, *Face of OT Studies*, pp. 295–328; Gerald H. Wilson, 'Wisdom', *NIDOTTE* 4:1276–1285.

29. Wisdom includes the skill of those commissioned to make Aaron's high priestly vestments (Exod. 28:3); of women who spun yarn for the tabernacle (Exod. 35:25–26); the craftsmanship of Bezalel, working with metal, stone and wood (Exod. 31:2–5); military skill (Isa. 10:13); the ability of professional mourners (Jer. 9:17); the seamanship of men of Tyre (Ezek. 27:8–9). It also describes the political acumen of the Princes of Zoan who counselled the Egyptian king (Isa. 19:11) and of the advisors of the Persian King Xerxes, who are described as *wise men who understood the times* (Esth. 1:13).

30. Drane, *Introducing the OT*, p. 280.

creation of the world. And there is the implicit belief that, in a world which continues to be ordered and regulated by divine wisdom, there is in the moral realm, as in the physical, a law of cause and effect: the outworking of divine providence and justice means that certain actions have certain inevitable consequences. Those who are wise seek to discover, understand and explain that law, and then conduct their own lives, and instruct others to live, in accordance with it.[31]

Wisdom teaching began, probably, in the family or clan.[32] Each generation needed to be prepared: parents, elders and other wise teachers had learned from their experiences of the world and had words of wisdom and common-sense advice to pass on, including instruction about family responsibilities, farming the land, the value of hard work and the folly of laziness. This practical wisdom often took the form of short sayings easy to remember. During the monarchy, there may have been a school to train officials in wisdom, and by the time of Jeremiah there appears to have been a group of wise counsellors who worked alongside priests and prophets (Jer. 18:18). Ahithophel may have been such an adviser to David (e.g. 2 Sam. 16:23).[33] The growth of the

---

31. Though it was also acknowledged that human beings could not receive full insight into the workings of a world in which God remains in final control (e.g. Prov. 16:1, 9; 19:21; 21:30–31).

32. The relationship between teacher and student is often described in terms of the relationship between parent and child (e.g. Gen. 45:8; Judg. 5:7; 2 Kgs 2:12; Prov. 1:8; 23:19; Eccl. 12:12). This suggests that teaching was originally focused within the family. The importance of the household, both as a context for teaching and learning and as a subject for instruction, is emphasized by Ronald E. Clements, *Wisdom in Theology* (Carlisle: Paternoster 1992), pp. 126–150; see also Gerstenberger, *Theologies*, pp. 61–75. The development of more formal education in Israel is unclear. In Mesopotamia and Egypt schools were well established in the third millennium BC. In Israel formal schooling may have developed during the period of the monarchy, though this is debated; see further G. I. Davies, 'Were There Schools in Ancient Israel', in Day, Gordon and Williamson, *Wisdom*, pp. 199–211. For further discussion of education in Israel, see Gerald H. Wilson, 'Education in the OT', in *NIDOTTE* 4:559–564.

33. Official groups of 'wise men' are evident elsewhere in the ANE. We have already noted the existence of groups of wise men in Tyre (Ezek. 27:8–9; cf. Zech. 9:2), Egypt (1 Kgs 4:30; Isa. 19:11; cf. Gen. 41:8; Exod. 7:11) and Persia (Esth. 1:13). There are also references to the *wise men of Edom* (Obad. 8), of Teman (Jer. 49:7) and of Babylon (Jer. 50:35; 51:57; Dan. 2:12).

wisdom movement in Israel is closely related to the monarchy,[34] and is especially linked with Solomon. According to the writers of Kings and Chronicles,
Israel's horizons widened during this time. There were trade links as far afield
as India, and visitors from distant countries came to the royal court. Solomon's
wisdom was legendary (1 Kgs 4:29–34). While he may not have been responsible for all the writings attributed to him, he features prominently in Israel's
wisdom traditions, and is likely to have played a significant part in promoting
wisdom in Israel. Hubbard suggests that the Egyptians were the first to
commit wisdom teaching to writing, and that others followed suit.[35] The
wisdom literature of the OT comprises the books of Proverbs, Job and
Ecclesiastes (as well as some psalms).

Wisdom in the ancient Near East

Wisdom was international. In particular we have examples of this kind of
teaching among Israel's neighbours in Egypt and Mesopotamia that go back
to the third millennium BC.[36] The Egyptians associated order in the universe
with the idea of *ma'at*.[37] In order to ensure the stability of the state and individual prosperity it was necessary to live in harmony with *ma'at*, and this underlies the instructions passed on from one generation to the next. Similar kinds
of instructions are found in Mesopotamian texts. And in texts from both
Egypt and Mesopotamia there is evidence of the more speculative reflections
and discussions of some of life's difficult issues, such as the meaning of life or
the problem of suffering, that we also see in the OT.[38]

---

34. Albertz suggests that during this period, wisdom spread from the royal court to
    become the 'educational ideal of well-to-do urban circles' (*History*, 2:512). That is
    possible, especially if it is linked with the progress of formal education in Israel,
    which would mainly have benefited the wealthy and privileged.

35. Hubbard, 'Wisdom Literature', in *IBD* 3:1651.

36. Murphy points out that 'wisdom' is not a prominent term in these writings; the use
    of the term comes mainly from biblical studies. Nevertheless they contain the same
    idea of guiding principles for life that are evident in the OT and intertestamental
    literature ('Wisdom', in *ABD* 6:928).

37. This term is sometimes translated 'justice' or 'order'. It refers to the cosmic order that
    binds the universe and everything in it. Sometimes Ma'at is portrayed as a goddess.

38. See Kidner, *Wisdom*, pp. 125–141; John E. Hartley, *The Book of Job*, NICOT (Grand
    Rapids: Eerdmans, 1991), pp. 6–11; Murphy, 'Wisdom', in *ABD* 6:928–930. See also
    Arnold and Beyer, *Readings*, pp. 175–182; John A. Wilson et al., 'Didactic and
    Wisdom Literature', in *ANET*, pp. 405–452, 589–602.

The OT writers refer to the wisdom and the wise men of other nations. Sometimes this is disparaging and emphasizes the superiority of wisdom in Israel; so, for example, Solomon's wisdom is *greater than the wisdom of all the men of the East, and greater than all the wisdom of Egypt* (1 Kgs 4:30). There appears, also, to have been some sharing of ideas. People from other nations came to visit Solomon because of his wisdom (e.g. 1 Kgs 10:24), and this gives the picture of a common quest for truth, a shared pool of wisdom, a debate, and probably some competition, among the wise men of different nations. We have noted that wisdom in Israel was essentially theological, but it is also true that wisdom relates to the rules observed in everyday experience, and many of the conclusions (though not the theological understanding that underlies them) were available to those outside Israel. It was not only worshippers of God who saw the harmful consequences of laziness, arrogance or adultery, or appreciated the value of friendship. As a result, it was recognized that the wisdom of people from other nations might have value. The book of Proverbs includes wise sayings from non-Israelites: Agur (Prov. 30:1–33) and King Lemuel (Prov. 31:1–9) are probably Arabian. Another section, Proverbs 22:17 – 24:22, is widely thought to contain sayings based on an Egyptian collection, the *Wisdom of Amenemope*.[39] There are also similarities between the book of Job and writings from Mesopotamia, and between Ecclesiastes and Egyptian, Babylonian and Greek literature.[40] This does not mean the biblical material is not original. It shows that the life issues dealt with are universal: people from different religious and cultural backgrounds were asking the same questions about suffering and about the meaning of life.

Wisdom in the Old Testament

Wisdom in the Old Testament is theological

Some argue that the wisdom books are based more on human reason than on divine revelation. It is true that the OT literature comes from a variety of sources and has much in common with similar literature from Babylon and

---

39. The similarity between this section of Proverbs and the (probably) earlier Egyptian collection suggests that the Bible writer knew and used it, but also adapted it to suit his own needs and emphasis. See e.g. Kidner, *Wisdom*, pp. 44–45.

40. The most significant parallels are noted, with extracts, by Kidner, *Wisdom*, pp. 125–141. Texts addressing similar issues to Job include *A Man and his God, I will Praise the Lord of Wisdom* (see Arnold and Beyer, *Readings*, pp. 175–179) and the *Babylonian Theodicy* (c. 1000 BC). *The Dialogue of a Man with his Soul* (T. W. Thacker, 'A Dispute over Suicide', in *DOTT*, pp. 162–167) contains similar themes to Ecclesiastes.

Egypt. It is true too that the observations appear, often, to be based upon experiences of life, moral common sense and natural law, rather than on salvation history, which is notable by its absence from OT wisdom literature. However, as we have noted, wisdom in the OT is theological. True wisdom is possessed by and proceeds from God, and may only be properly discerned by those who know God.[41] This principle is set out in Proverbs 9:10:

> *The fear of the LORD is the beginning of wisdom,*
> *   and knowledge of the Holy One is understanding.*[42]

Its converse is also true: the fool, the opposite of the wise man, *says in his heart, 'There is no God'* (Pss 14:1; 53:1). God has created the moral as well as the physical order; he created the world through wisdom (Prov. 3:19) and has set in place the rules of life that the wise strive to discover. Consequently, while those who do not know God may discern something of his truth from what they see in creation, because God is the author of wisdom, wisdom points those who truly seek it to him (Prov. 2:1–5; 22:17–19), and only those who are in a relationship with him can be truly wise (e.g. Job 28; cf. Prov. 3:5–8). Even within the book of Proverbs, which sets out clear directions for how to find success in life, there is the recognition that human beings can never know all the answers (Prov. 20:24), and that the last word always lies with God.

The personification of wisdom

Within the book of Proverbs, wisdom is portrayed in personal terms. In the style of the prophets, *she calls aloud in the street, / she raises her voice in the public squares* (Prov. 1:20; see also 8:1–3), and calls the foolish to change their ways.[43] This personification reaches its height in Proverbs 8:1 – 9:6. In contrast to the

---

41. On several occasions the knowledge and ability possessed by those deemed to be wise is specifically linked with God's enabling (e.g. Gen. 41:39; Exod. 28:3; 31:3; Dan. 5:11).

42. Some claim that Prov. 1 – 9 is relatively late, and that its addition is part of a development of wisdom from something essentially secular to a theological concept; see e.g. Albertz, *History*, 2:511–513; Eichrodt, *Theology*, 2:81–92; Preuss, *OT Theology*, 2:203–207; von Rad, *OT Theology*, 1:441–453; *Wisdom*, pp. 53–73. However, it can be argued that significant theological and religious elements were present from the start; see e.g. B. W. Anderson, *Living World*, pp. 579–580; Hubbard, 'Wisdom Movement'; Murphy, 'Wisdom', in *ABD* 6:928–930.

43. See e.g. B. W. Anderson, *Contours*, pp. 269–270.

adulteress who lures the unwise to their destruction, Lady Wisdom calls to those who lack understanding (8:4–5); she builds her house with its seven pillars, and invites the simple and immature to dine with her (9:1–6).

We have already noted the link between wisdom and creation in Proverbs 8:22–31. Here Wisdom is again personified; it is described as the first of God's created works, at his side in the beginning, as a *craftsman* (NIV) or *master worker* (NRSV) while the universe was made. It is debated whether this portrayal of Wisdom is the *personification* of an idea, used here as a poetic device, or a *hypostasis*, something that has come to be regarded as almost a separate divine being. The view of Wisdom as a personification fits the OT context better.[44]

Tension within the canonical wisdom literature

As we have seen, a significant feature of wisdom is to set out maxims for a successful and prosperous life. This is particularly evident in the book of Proverbs. The divine wisdom that orders the universe leads to a view of the world that is ordered, predictable and fair. Proverbs gives (usually) clear answers: one thing leads to another. And those rules provide a good general foundation on which to build. The idea of cause and effect in the moral realm is sometimes referred to as 'the law of retribution': people reap what they sow. This principle is expressed negatively in Eliphaz' words to Job:

> *As I have observed, those who plough evil*
> *   and those who sow trouble reap it.*
> (Job 4:8; cf. Hos. 8:7; 10:12)

His conclusion is that Job's problems are of his own making. But is the world that fair? Does the law of retribution always hold good? And is it possible for

---

44. Under Hellenistic influence, The Wisdom of Solomon (c. 30 BC – AD 40) views Wisdom (Sophia) as a hypostasis (see especially 7.22b – 8.1). This builds on the portrayal of wisdom in Proverbs, and some of its terminology is reflected in the NT; see also Sirach 24.1–12. Some see Hellenistic influence in Prov. 8:22–31. Others argue for an ANE background and suggest links with the Canaanite Ishtar or the Egyptian Ma'at. Though links are tenuous, there are sufficient similarities to indicate that the personification of wisdom in Proverbs is in line with practice in the ANE long before the Greek period. See e.g. Emerton, 'Wisdom', in G. W. Anderson, *Tradition*, pp. 231–233; House, *OT Theology*, p. 445; Kidner, *Proverbs*, TOTC (London: IVP, 1964), pp. 78–79; *Wisdom*, pp. 22–24, 41–44; Murphy, 'Wisdom', in *ABD* 6:926–927.

human understanding to fathom the divinely appointed order that lies behind the universe?

We are aware from our own experience of the world that some things that happen are difficult or even impossible to explain. At times there are no easy answers, or no answers at all; what happens makes little sense and certainly seems unfair. Job and Ecclesiastes present another aspect of wisdom teaching. They recognize that traditional wisdom has its limitations. Proverbs says, seek wisdom and you will find life; work hard and you will prosper. These are good general rules, but life is often more complicated, and things do not always work that way. That is where Job and Ecclesiastes come in. According to Hubbard, 'Proverbs seems to say "Here are the rules for life; try them and find that they will work". Job and Ecclesiastes say "We did, and they don't."'[45]

That is not to say that the view of the world presented by Proverbs is mechanistic, simplistic and naive.[46] As we have noted, there is an admission that human wisdom is limited (Prov. 20:24; 30:2–9).[47] There is too the implicit recognition that things may not always work out quite the way they should, and the benefits of right living are contrasted with the lure of wealth (e.g. Prov. 15:16; 16:8, 19). The main focus of these verses is to emphasize the value and importance of wisdom, but they do indicate that in some cases the wicked may appear to prosper materially, and those who have little may be tempted to follow their course. However, this idea is not developed in Proverbs. It is in the books of Job and Ecclesiastes that the generalized application of the law of retribution and the possibility of always making sense of the world are directly questioned.

The book of Job focuses on the suffering of one who has done nothing to deserve what is happening to him, and on different responses to that suffering. Job's comforters try to explain what he is going through in accordance with the law of retribution, even though we as readers are made aware from the start that this does not address Job's situation. Job, convinced of his innocence, responds with patience and integrity, though his frustration also leads him to complain against divine justice, before finally submitting to the will and purpose of a sovereign God who does not need to explain himself. We will look more closely at Job and the problem of innocent suffering later.[48]

---

45. Hubbard, 'Wisdom Movement', p. 6; see also e.g. Goldingay, *OT Theology*, 2:615–662; Kidner, *Wisdom*, pp. 116–124; Murphy, 'Wisdom', in *ABD* 6:926; Preuss, *OT Theology*, 1:185–188; Gerald H. Wilson, 'Wisdom', in *NIDOTTE* 4:1276–1285.

46. See e.g. Fyall, *Now my Eyes*, pp. 184–185.

47. See B. W. Anderson, *Contours*, pp. 275–276.

48. Below, pp. 255–260.

Job asks why certain things happen in life. Ecclesiastes goes further and asks about the point of life itself.[49] The book starts and ends with the same conclusion: *'Meaningless! Meaningless! . . . Everything is meaningless'* (1:2; 12:8). Life is full of frustration and uncertainty (9:11; 11:6). Nothing lasts, so nothing is worth striving for. Nothing satisfies, and in the end death comes to rich and poor, wise and foolish, righteous and wicked, human beings and animals (2:15–16; 3:19–21; 7:2; 9:2–6). There is injustice (3:16): the weak are oppressed (4:1; 5:8–9) and the wicked prosper (7:15; 8:14). There is sorrow and loneliness (4:8). Ecclesiastes acknowledges God's governance of the world, but with such injustice, frustration and uncertainty that could be seen as an indictment. Even applying himself to the search for wisdom in the end proves fruitless (1:12–18; 2:21), for there seems to be no divinely appointed order that makes sense of the way the world works. Job wants to know 'Why?' Ecclesiastes does not seem to have Job's passion, and one of the overwhelming impressions given by the book is its sense of resignation. No one can understand God's ways (11:5) and so it is better to ask and say little (5:2).

It is important to read Ecclesiastes against the background of traditional wisdom teaching. The writer's concern is not simply to set out a pessimistic view of life; he wants to expose the limitations of human wisdom and understanding. Writing from the perspective of Solomon, the wisest man in history, he acknowledges that even his great wisdom cannot make sense of the world. To the human mind, God's world is not a fair and fulfilling place; God, himself, stands aloof, and acts in ways his creatures cannot understand. The message of Ecclesiastes, though, is not all negative. He points to the futility of earthly existence but encourages his readers to acknowledge and obey God (12:13), to trust God's final justice (3:17) and to seek contentment in the life God gives (2:24; 5:18; 8:15; 9:7–10). Such contentment may be possible only by recognizing that human understanding cannot fathom divine mysteries, and by accepting the world as it is, with all its apparent unfairness.

Despite the evident tensions, Job and Ecclesiastes stand alongside Proverbs in the OT canon. Proverbs offers a more positive view of wisdom and its

---

49. On Ecclesiastes, see also e.g. B. W. Anderson, *Contours*, pp. 282–284; Michael A. Eaton, *Ecclesiastes*, TOTC (Leicester: IVP, 1983); House, *OT Theology*, pp. 470–482; Derek Kidner, *A Time to Mourn and a Time to Dance: The Message of Ecclesiastes*, BST (Leicester: IVP, 1976); D. C. Fredericks, 'Ecclesiastes: Theology of', in *NIDOTTE* 4:552–555; Roland E. Murphy, *Ecclesiastes*, WBC 23a (Dallas: Word, 1992); R. N. Whybray, *Ecclesiastes*, NCB (London: Marshall, Morgan & Scott, 1989).

ability to make sense of the world, and on that basis gives general rules for living. Job and Ecclesiastes emphasize the limitations of wisdom, and particularly of the law of retribution; in the real world things do not always work out in such an ordered and predictable way. Both ways of looking at the world have value, and, as the OT writers recognized, they need to be held together.

7. GOD AND HIS PEOPLE (4): KINGSHIP IN ISRAEL[1]

In parts of the ANE the king was regarded as divine. In Egypt, Pharaoh was thought of as the offspring of Ra, and so himself an incarnate deity; in

---

1. See e.g. Albertz, *History*, 1:106–123; B. W. Anderson, *Living World*, pp. 207–220; *Contours*, pp. 211–217; John Bright, *The Kingdom of God* (Nashville: Abingdon, 1981); *History*, pp. 184–228; Brueggemann, *Theology*, pp. 234–241, 600–621; Martin Buber, *The Kingship of God* (London: Allen & Unwin, 1967); Childs, *Biblical Theology* (1992), pp. 152–156; *OT Theology*, pp. 115–119; Clements, *OT Theology*, pp. 89–91; Eichrodt, *Theology*, 1:436–456; Jacob, *Theology*, pp. 234–239; Drane, *Introducing the OT*, pp. 87–119, 301–303, 332–334; Heinz-Josef Fabry, Helmer Ringgren and K. Seybold, '*melek*, etc.', in *TDOT* 8:346–375; H. Frankfort, *Kingship and the Gods* (Chicago: University of Chicago Press, 1948); Gerstenberger, *Theologies*, pp. 180–205; Goldingay, *Theological Diversity*, pp. 64–73; *OT Theology*, 1:549–562, 656–668; 2:59–64, 216–218; B. Gray, 'Canaanite Kingship in Theory and Practice', *VT* 2 (1952), pp. 193–220; Bruce Halpern, *The Constitution of the Monarchy in Ancient Israel*, HSM 25 (Chico: Scholars Press, 1981); House, *OT Theology*, pp. 184–186, 232–239; A. R. Johnson, *Sacral Kingship in Ancient Israel* (Cardiff: Cardiff University Press, 1967); Sigmund Mowinckel, *The Psalms in Israel's Worship*, 2 vols. (Oxford: Oxford University Press, 1962; repr. Grand Rapids: Eerdmans, 2004); Philip J. Nel, '*mlk*', in *NIDOTTE* 2:956–965; Preuss, *OT Theology*, 1:152–159; 2:19–38; Hermann

Mesopotamia, the king was a man chosen and exalted by the gods and given divine status by being linked with a dying and rising god at the New Year festival. Elsewhere, for example, in Assyria, the king was seen as the representative of the ruling deity. It was this election and commissioning by the god(s) of a people or land that provided the basis for the king's authority and power. The king was the channel of the divine blessing the people needed to live. In Israel too the king was appointed by God and enjoyed a close relationship with him (though he was never viewed as divine) and was seen as a channel of God's blessings to the people, which included material prosperity.

The king in the ANE also had legislative power. Mesopotamian law codes were linked with kings; the best known is the Hammurabi law code. In Israel, God was the lawgiver, and the king had responsibility both to uphold and observe covenant law (Deut. 17:18–20; see also 2 Kgs 22 – 23; 2 Chr. 31:3; cf. 2 Sam. 12:1–6; 14:4–8; 1 Kgs 3:16–28; 7:7).

In general, kingship was hereditary, and succession was often, though not necessarily, passed to the eldest son. In Egypt, Assyria and Ugarit the king appointed an heir from among his sons. In Israel too appointment by the king was necessary (1 Kgs 1:20, 27; 2 Chr. 21:3), and he was not bound to choose the eldest of his sons (e.g. 1 Kgs 1:17, 30).

God as king

The monarchy in Israel was a relatively late development. Following the settlement, and prior to Saul's appointment as Israel's first king, the people were governed by various, usually local, leaders. From the days of the exodus onward, God was Israel's king;[2] the nation was his kingdom (Exod. 19:6) and

---

Footnote 1 (*continued*)

> Kleinknecht, Gerhard von Rad et al., '*basileus*, etc.', in *TDNT* 1:564–593 (565–571); Rendtorff, *Hebrew Bible*, pp. 560–574, 611–613; Ringgren, *Israelite Religion*, pp. 220–238; Martin J. Selman, 'The Kingdom of God in the Old Testament', *TynBul* 40 (1989), pp. 161–183; de Vaux, *Ancient Israel*, pp. 94–114.

2. Von Rad suggests that Yahweh was regarded as *melek* only after the rise of the monarchy. However, while the designation may not be common in the pre-monarchic era, Israel would have been acquainted with the concept from earliest times. Eichrodt notes that personal names compounded with *melek* go back to the ancient period (*Theology*, 1:194) and, as we have seen, suggests that the Ark was viewed as God's throne (1:108). Wenham suggests that the Israelite camp in the

sĕgullâ (Exod. 19:5; cf. Deut. 4:20), a term that denotes the personal property of a king.

The kingship of God is given particular prominence in what have been termed 'enthronement psalms'.[3] A key feature of several of these psalms is the cry *Yhwh mālāk* (Pss 93:1; 96:10; 97:1; 99:1; cf. 47:2). This may be translated *the LORD is king* (NRSV) or *the LORD reigns* (NIV), indicating an ongoing status. Mowinckel prefers the translation 'Yahweh has become king', suggesting that Yahweh has just come to the throne. In his view these psalms were composed for an annual 'Enthronement Festival', which was part of the Feast of Tabernacles. At the end of the agricultural year, before the autumn rains, when the land was devoid of crops and the forces of chaos once again threatened to engulf the earth, Yahweh appeared as the victorious king – to defeat those cosmic forces, as he did at the beginning, and to recreate the earth for the coming year. According to Mowinckel, the festival celebrated 'Yahweh's cosmic conflict, victory and enthronement'.[4] The OT, though, does not mention such a festival, indicating that, even if it existed, it did not have the prominence Mowinckel gives it.[5] There may have been some kind of cultic celebration of Yahweh's kingship in Israel, though not necessarily in the form envisaged by Mowinckel; one possibility is an event to commemorate bringing the Ark to Jerusalem.[6]

The enthronement psalms describe Yahweh as creator. He reigns over the world because he made it (Pss 93:1; 95:3–5; 96:5, 10) and the whole created order is exhorted to praise him (e.g. 96:1–4, 11–13; 98:4–9). These psalms also have an eschatological dimension, pointing forward to Yahweh's ultimate victory and the consummation of his rule over all the earth. They celebrate Yahweh's kingship, and their recital in worship, whether or not as part of an annual festival, was an occasion when God's people reviewed his mighty works, saw themselves afresh as inheritors of his salvation, acknowledged his

---

desert, with the tabernacle at the centre and tribal groups arranged around it, was modelled on the Egyptian army camp: with various companies arranged around the royal tent (*Numbers*, pp. 66–67, 175).

3. See Mowinckel, *Psalms*. This grouping includes Pss 47, 93, 95 – 99 and has links with Pss 24, 46, 48, 75, 76, 81.

4. S. Mowinckel, *He That Cometh* (Oxford: Blackwell, 1956; repr. Grand Rapids: Eerdmans, 2005), p. 140; see also B. W. Anderson, *Contours*, pp. 214–217; Brueggemann, *Theology*, p. 238; J. H. Eaton, 'The Psalms and Israel's Worship', in G. W. Anderson, *Tradition*, pp. 238–273; Preuss, *OT Theology*, 2:231–233.

5. See e.g. de Vaux, *Ancient Israel*, pp. 502–506.

6. Pss 24, 96, 105 (possibly 68) and 132 may be linked with that setting.

kingship over the whole world as a present reality one day to be confirmed by his coming in power, and renewed their allegiance to him: an occasion when the past saving acts of God and the promise of the future consummation of his reign confronted the worshipper and called for a present response.[7]

Despite Mowinckel's emphasis, the idea of Yahweh's victory over the waters of primeval chaos is not prominent in the enthronement psalms, though there is an echo of it in Psalm 93:3–4. As noted earlier, this theme (more evident in e.g. Pss 74:12–17; 89:9–13; 104:5–9) affirms Yahweh's sovereignty and lordship, not only over creation and nature but also over Israel's historical enemies. The historicizing of the creation myth is seen in the events of the exodus, where the waters of the Red Sea are likened to the primeval flood (e.g. Ps. 89:10; Isa. 51:9–10). The dividing of the waters for his people when they came out of Egypt thus signifies the creative act through which Yahweh establishes his reign over Israel (e.g. Exod. 15:18; Ps. 114). This last point highlights a fundamental element in Israel's understanding of Yahweh's kingship: that while Yahweh is acknowledged as Lord over all the nations of the earth because he is their Creator, he is King over Israel in a unique way, through divine election, and that special relationship is embodied within the covenant.

The institution of monarchy in Israel

Israel was established as a theocratic state. God was the people's suzerain, and they had his Law to guide them. This is seen in Gideon's response to those who wanted to make him king: *I will not rule over you, nor will my son rule over you. The LORD will rule over you* (Judg. 8:23). However, the settlement brought a marked decline in the moral and spiritual values of the nation. God might be king, but the people, scattered through the land, took little or no notice of him, and with no earthly representative to enforce the Law, the result was a slide into anarchy. This is summed up in the repeated complaint *in those days Israel had no king; everyone did as he saw fit* (Judg. 17:6; 21:25; see also 18:1; 19:1). Also threats from other nations made it increasingly necessary for a central authority to co-ordinate national defence. During the period of the judges, this role was fulfilled by leaders whose charismatic qualities allowed them to unite tribes to overcome a common enemy. These leaders appear to be credited too with maintaining spiritual discipline (Judg. 2:18–19), which usually ended when the judge died. This emphasizes a key issue in the book of Judges: right leadership. Under the right leader the people

---

7. See e.g. Derek Kidner, *Psalms 1–72*, TOTC (Leicester: IVP, 1973), pp. 9–15.

walked in God's ways and the land had peace. Without good leadership, the people turned away from God and, in consequence, were defeated and oppressed.[8] The last judge, Samuel, led the people well, but as he grew old and authority passed to sons who *did not walk in his ways* (1 Sam. 8:3), there might have been the fear that the painful cycle of disobedience and defeat would begin again, which led to the clamour for a new system of national government.

The institution of the monarchy represented a significant change from the traditions associated with the exodus and the Sinaitic covenant. Under the older system, government was more devolved, focusing on local communities rather on central authority. There was no standing army, and threats were met by the tribal muster. This continued even into the early days of Saul's reign (1 Sam. 11:6–8). However, as we have seen, the system was already under severe strain in the period of the judges. The lack of central direction led to spiritual and moral anarchy, and the traditional gathering of tribes to fight took place often only after the problem had already become serious. In such circumstances it is easy to see how the appointment of a king might appear to be a necessity both for the religious and political survival of the nation.[9] At the same time, there was the risk of tension between the central administration, with its standing army and growing civil service and possible loss of contact with local needs and issues, and the older traditions.[10] This tension is reflected in the OT account, which seems ambivalent about the institution of the

8. It is widely held that the books of Joshua, Judges, Samuel and Kings emphasize the contrasting consequences of obedience and disobedience reflected in the book of Deuteronomy: obedience leads to blessing, peace and prosperity in the land, while disobedience leads to defeat and eventual exile from the land. See the discussion below, pp. 261–263.

9. See e.g. Brueggemann, *Theology*, pp. 601–603; Goldingay, *Theological Diversity*, pp. 69–73; Preuss, *OT Theology*, pp. 21–22. The military threat was an important factor in the institution of the monarchy, though there may also have been significant social and environmental pressures. See e.g. Israel Finkelstein, 'The Emergence of the Monarchy in Israel: The Environmental and Socio-Economic Aspects', *JSOT* 44 (1989), pp. 43–74; Norman K. Gottwald, 'The Participation of Free Agrarians in the Introduction of Monarchy to Ancient Israel: An Application of H. A. Landsberger's Framework for the Analysis of Peasant Movements', *Semeia* 37.1 (1986), pp. 77–106; *The Politics of Ancient Israel* (Louisville: Westminster John Knox, 2001); *Hebrew Bible*, pp. 319–325.

10. Cook sees the change from tribal muster to standing army as an important part of the centralization that accompanied the monarchy, and which proponents of the Sinai tradition opposed (*Social Roots*, pp. 226–228). Von Rad notes the significance of

monarchy. It appears that 1 Samuel 8 – 12 sets contrasting viewpoints along-side one another: 1 Samuel 8:1–22, 10:17–27 and 12:1–25 are generally taken to be opposed to the appointment of a king, while 1 Samuel 9:1 – 10:16 and 11:1–11 are thought to be more positive.[11] The monarchy is also viewed posi-tively in passages that represent the covenant with David as a fulfilment of God's promises to Abraham (e.g. Ps. 72:17; 2 Sam. 7:12; cf. Gen. 15:4),[12] and those that view David's reign as a pattern for the coming Messiah.[13]

A close reading of the different accounts of Saul's appointment by Samuel reveals different nuances. In 1 Samuel 9:1 – 10:16 Saul meets Samuel, who anoints him as leader, or prince (*nāgîd*). Here Samuel does not appear negative towards Saul. Saul is God's choice (9:17), confirmed by the presence of the Spirit (10:9–11). This account avoids using the term 'king' (*melek*), indicating that Saul's role does not necessarily usurp God's place as Israel's king. In 1 Samuel 10:17–25 Saul is chosen by lot; divine involvement may be assumed, but is not mentioned by the writer. In this account Samuel accuses the people of rejecting God as king. Here Saul is described as king, suggesting that there may be conflict between the earthly and divine rulers, and Samuel wants to dis-tance himself from the decision of the people.

These readings suggest that a significant part of the problem is in the choice

---

Footnote 10 (*continued*)

> holy war in Deuteronomy, which is linked with the pre-monarchical period, and may have originated among those who, under that older system, would have been called up as part of the tribal muster. He identifies this group with 'the people of the land' (see above, p. 182, n. 14), among whom tribal traditions were preserved. These include the old style of militia, which gave way during the monarchy to a paid, standing army, but which, according to von Rad, the writers of Deuteronomy seek to reintroduce in the seventh century BC, when the loss of the professional army and continuing Assyrian strictures made it necessary to rely on the tribal levy to provide troops (*Studies in Deuteronomy*, pp. 60–66).

11. A summary of source-critical views is included in e.g. Lyle Eslinger, 'Viewpoints and Point of View in 1 Samuel 8–12', *JSOT* 26 (1983), pp. 61–76; J. Maxwell Miller, 'Saul's Rise to Power: Some Oberservations Concerning 1 Sam 9:1–10; 10:26–11:15 and 13:2–14:46', *CBQ* 36.2 (1974), pp. 157–174; see also Joyce G. Baldwin, *1 and 2 Samuel*, TOTC (Leicester: IVP, 1988), pp. 82–84.

12. For further discussion of the relationship between Abraham and David, see below, pp. 235–236.

13. For discussion of the relationship between the Messiah and David, see below, pp. 283–287.

of the term 'king', and the attitude and expectations of the people that were associated with it. From the time of the exodus there had been no problem with the delegation of God's authority to leaders, and Samuel does not appear to be against the appointment of the right kind of leader. However, the people do not simply want someone to be God's representative and to lead in his ways; their request is for Samuel to *appoint a king to lead us — such as all the other nations have* (1 Sam. 8:5; see also 8:20). They want to take their model of kingship from the practice of the nations round about them, including the royal paraphernalia that accompanies it, and part of Samuel's criticism points out the cost of such a move, particularly of the establishment of a standing army (1 Sam. 8:11–18). The people's request also denies what lies at the very heart of the Sinai tradition: their distinctiveness as God's own people. They were set apart from the nations, with God as their king, yet now they want to be like everyone else. By rejecting theocratic government they are rejecting Yahweh as king (1 Sam. 8:7; 10:19). A third factor here is the people's lack of trust in God (1 Sam. 8:20). They want a king who can be seen at the head of their armies, an impressive-looking figurehead who will inspire confidence in his own people and provoke awe in the enemy. Something of this may have been behind their disastrous decision to take the Ark of the Covenant ahead of them into battle (1 Sam. 4:3–11), and though subsequent events did demonstrate God's power, the people seem to have wanted something more visible and tangible than God's presence could provide.

The account of Saul's appointment in 1 Samuel 9:1 – 10:16 is in line with the pattern of leadership in the book of Judges. Saul's victory over the Ammonites in 1 Samuel 11 also follows that earlier pattern. This suggests the possibility of a model of kingship unlike that of the surrounding nations, which preserves Israel's distinctiveness and does not conflict with the nation's relationship with God. However, the root problem of the people's sin in making the request remains. This is addressed in 1 Samuel 12. In what appears to be an official handing over of power, Samuel calls the people to affirm the honesty and integrity of his own period of service (1 Sam. 12:1–5),[14] before going on to point out the sinfulness of the decision to ask for a king (vv. 6–17). That is followed by the people's repentance (v. 19) and a restatement of God's commitment (v. 22), thus opening the possibility of moving forward.[15]

---

14. One reason for this may have been to counter Samuel's earlier feelings of rejection.

15. This argument is developed from Dennis J. McCarthy, 'The Inauguration of the Monarchy in Israel: A Form-Critical Study of 1 Samuel 8–12', *Int* 20.4 (1973), pp. 401–412. He sees the narrative in 1 Sam. 8 – 12 as a statement and resolution

If the people continue to walk in God's ways, they and their king may still know his blessing (vv. 21–24). There may be a hint of Samuel's unease at the new situation, in that he does not suggest that the king will contribute anything positive to this; nevertheless there is, again, the implicit suggestion that there need not be conflict between the earthly ruler and the divine king. However, there is a grim alternative. If the king chooses to go his own way, king and people will face God's condemnation (v. 25). This tension is evident immediately in the disobedience and consequent rejection of Saul, and surfaces again in the relationship between the king and divinely appointed agents, such as prophets.[16]

A corrective to the abuse of royal power is the 'Law of the King' in Deuteronomy 17:14–20,[17] which emphasizes that the king is himself under the authority of the divine monarch. Because it so accurately reflects the behaviour of Israel's kings, some claim that it comes from a time when what it warns about was already an unfortunate reality.[18] However, Moses would have been familiar with the problems of institutionalized monarchy from his own experience in Egypt and from the examples of other nations, and possibly anticipated the dangers of monarchy in Israel. The words may have been

---

Footnote 15 (continued)

of the problem of leadership, and concludes that in the final scene of 1 Sam. 12, 'kingship has been integrated into the fundamental relationship between Yahweh and the people' (p. 412). See also Walter Brueggemann, *First and Second Samuel*, Interpretation (Louisville: John Knox, 1990), pp. 57–97; Eslinger, 'Viewpoints', pp. 65–69.

16. See Goldingay, *Theological Diversity*, pp. 72–73; *OT Theology*, 1:685–691.

17. According to Cook, this reflects Sinai theology, which acknowledged God as king and favoured a less centralized structure. It eventually allowed a king, though only as a concession, and sought to set limits on his action (Cook, *Social Roots*, pp. 40–44). There is little doubt that some were unhappy with the institution of the monarchy, and sought to moderate its impact, though in my view these form a more general group who held on to Israel's covenant faith and saw the possibility of conflict with the institution of monarchy, rather than being advocates of a clearly defined theological stream, preserved by a particular group within society.

18. The reference to acquiring horses from Egypt and *many wives* (vv. 16–17) suggests that it may be directed against Solomon (cf. 1 Kgs 10:26–28; 11:1–4); Bright suggests that the verses reflect the feeling that 'a king ought to be as unlike Solomon as possible' (*Kingdom*, p. 49). The decision to appoint a king *like all the nations round us* is also reminiscent of the people's request in 1 Sam. 8:5.

revived by later reformers who wanted to curb the excesses of the king and to emphasize the need for submission to covenant law.

God's covenant with David

We have noted the link between Deuteronomy 12:8, which sees the establishment of a central sanctuary as the antidote to anarchy, and Judges 17:6 and 21:25, which see the institution of the monarchy as the solution to the same problem.[19] There is a crucial connection between the presence of God among his people and the institution of an earthly king, who would reign on Yahweh's behalf as his representative. This reflects the widely held view in the ANE that the king was the earthly steward of the deity, and that there was a correspondence between the political structure of the state and the cosmic order lying behind it.[20]

God's choice of David met the need both for an earthly representative and for a central sanctuary. David reigned on Yahweh's behalf, as the shepherd of his flock (e.g. 2 Sam. 5:2; 7:7; Pss 78:52, 70–72; 79:13; 95:7; 100:3; Isa. 40:11). By installing the Ark, as the symbol of God's presence and kingship, in Jerusalem and by making plans for the construction of the temple, which would be a 'palace' for the divine king (see also 2 Sam. 7:2), David established the city as the focal point of Israel's worship and of the nation's religious traditions. As a result, the election of David was closely related to the election of Jerusalem.[21]

While the choice of Saul is similar to the selection of earlier judges, the election of David and his heirs marked a significant change from charismatic leader to dynastic monarch. This receives divine authentication in 2 Samuel 7:8–17, and though the word *běrît* does not appear, that passage is generally taken to mark the establishment of the covenant relationship between Yahweh and the house of David.[22] Through this covenant God gave David the assurance that his house and kingdom would be established for ever (e.g. 2 Sam. 7:13, 16; Ps. 89:2–4, 28–29). Like the covenant with Abraham, the Davidic covenant was unconditional: despite the failure of individual monarchs, and

---

19. Above, p. 179.
20. See e.g. B. W. Anderson, *Contours*, pp. 199–208; Dumbrell, *Covenant*, pp. 141–143; see also the discussion of the divine council, above, pp. 120–122.
21. For more on the significance of Jerusalem (Zion), see below, pp. 276–277.
22. The relationship is formally described as a covenant in 2 Sam. 23:5; Pss 89; 132:11–12; Isa. 55:3.

even of the monarchy itself, the divine promise would not be withdrawn. This covenant thus anticipates the messianic king – in whom the kingly ideal would be fulfilled, and through whom the glories of David would be restored (Isa. 9:2–7; 11:1–9).[23] Several 'royal psalms',[24] which may have been composed to celebrate the accession of a particular Davidic king, were reinterpreted in the context of Israel's worship and ultimately applied to this coming ruler (e.g. Ps. 2).

Israel's king was not divine, but did have a close relationship with God. He was God's anointed (Pss 2:2; 89:20; see also e.g. 1 Sam. 24:5–7), and as such was endowed with God's Spirit (1 Sam. 16:13). The king ruled in God's strength (Pss 18:1; 21:1) and administered justice on his behalf (Ps. 72:1); he relied on God's help and protection in times of trouble (Pss 18; 20; 28:7); he enjoyed God's presence (Pss 21:6; 61:7) and was surrounded by his *hesed* (Pss 18:50; 21:7; 63:3; 89). The election, anointing and installation of the king were viewed as an adoption, through which he became God's son (2 Sam. 7:14; Pss 2:7, 12; 89:26–27) and entered into an inheritance that included kingship over the whole world (Ps. 2:8–9; cf. 72:8–11). This universal kingship reflects the fact of God's present rule over all creation, and also points forward to the coming of God's kingdom, which, under its messianic ruler, will extend to the ends of the earth (Mic. 5:4; Zech. 9:9–10).

This intimate relationship between king and Yahweh may be seen in the king's involvement with the cult. Saul failed to unite the monarchy with the older institutions. Under David, though, the link was established, and at important times in the life of the nation, the king was seen leading the people in worship, including offering sacrifices (2 Sam 6:13; 24:25; 1 Kgs 3:3–4; 8:62–63; 12:32–33; 2 Kgs 16:1–16), and praying and pronouncing God's blessing (1 Kgs 8:14–66; 2 Kgs 19:14–19). In Psalm 110:4 the king is described as a *priest*,[25] and

---

23. For further discussion of the Messiah, see below, pp. 280–289.

24. Gunkel and Mowinckel classify Pss 2, 18, 20, 72, 89 and 110 as 'royal psalms' because they are prayers for, or addressed to, a reigning monarch.

25. This is another royal psalm, which was probably first related to a Davidic king but was later applied to the Messiah (see below, p. 286). Melchizedek was priest-king of Jerusalem (Gen. 14:8), and, because of the special relationship between David and Jerusalem, traditions associated with Melchizedek appear to have been linked with David; however, it is unnecessary to go as far as to suggest that Davidic ideology arose out of a fusion of the cult of Yahweh and the Jebusite El Elyon following the city's capture. See e.g. Day, *God's Conflict*, pp. 130–131; John A. Emerton, 'The Riddle of Genesis XIV', *VT* 21 (1971), pp. 403–439.

when the Ark was brought to Jerusalem, David offered sacrifices while wearing a priest's ephod (2 Sam. 6:12–19). Aspects of this are seen later; however, it was in the person of David that the ideal of a monarchy linked with the institution of priesthood came closer to being realized than under any of his successors.

It is widely accepted that there is a close relationship between the Davidic and Abrahamic covenants. There is speculation as to how the two traditions may have influenced one another,[26] but there seems little doubt that the golden age of Israel's history under David and Solomon came to be regarded as a fulfilment of the promises made to the patriarchs. Under David, Israel emerged on the world scene as a significant nation whose dimensions corresponded closely to the borders promised by God to Abraham (Gen. 15:18–21).[27] Like the patriarch, David was promised a great name (2 Sam. 7:9; cf. Gen. 12:2). The Davidic king also inherited the promise made to Abraham that *All nations will be blessed through him, / and they will call him blessed* (Ps. 72:17b; cf. Gen. 12:3; 18:18). Through the king, the divine blessing, the subject of the Abrahamic covenant, would be conferred upon Israel, and through him would extend to all peoples.[28] A further link is evident in the similar language with which God promises David, as he had Abraham, an offspring *who will come from your own body* (2 Sam. 7:12; cf. Gen. 15:4), suggesting that God's promise of seed to the patriarch would be fulfilled through David and his royal line. Continuity between the promises to Abraham and David is seen too in Jeremiah 33:22, where God's words *I will make the descendants of David my servant and the Levites*

---

26. Though traditions associated with the Abrahamic covenant may be ancient, they probably took the shape in which they appear in the OT after the time of David; thus while the form of the older covenant influenced the latter, the shape of the earlier tradition may have been influenced by David's achievements. See e.g. Bright, *Covenant*, p. 71; Clements, *Abraham and David*.

27. Many commentators regard the land promised to Abraham as a reading back of what the actual borders of Israel were at the height of the Davidic empire, though the correspondence is not exact.

28. This promise of universal blessing is the only Abrahamic promise not explicit in 2 Sam. 7. However, several commentators see an implicit reference in 2 Sam. 7:19 in the phrase *and this is the law of mankind* (NIV). The varied translations illustrate the difficulty of its interpretation, though it seems likely that it points to some relationship between the house of David and God's purposes for the world. See e.g. Dumbrell, *Covenant*, pp. 151–152; McComiskey, *Covenants*, pp. 22–23.

who minister before me as countless as the stars of the sky and as measureless as the sand on the seashore echo Genesis 22:17.[29]

There are tensions within the OT between the Davidic and Sinaitic covenants.[30] Nevertheless, just as the Sinaitic covenant is continuous with and represents a partial fulfilment of the Abrahamic, so too the covenant with David, as well as fulfilling elements of the Abrahamic covenant, also fulfils and seeks to maintain the Sinaitic ideal.[31] As we have seen, the establishment of a central sanctuary (Deut. 12:8) parallels the appointment of a king (Judg. 17:6; 21:25) as the antidote to anarchy. A similar link is evident between the same passage in Deuteronomy, where God promises the people *rest from all your enemies around you* (Deut. 12:10), and 2 Samuel 7:1, which refers to the Lord having given David *rest from all his enemies around him*. And, significantly, having been given rest from his enemies, David responds by expressing a desire to build a sanctuary.[32]

The king and justice

In the ANE the king was responsible for the administration of justice.[33] This was regarded as important for maintaining the harmony of the created order,

---

29. The significance of this link between Abraham and David is indicated by Matthew, who, in the genealogy of Christ, traces a line of descent from Abraham to David and then to Jesus (Matt. 1:1–17). See also the discussion below, p. 283, n. 54.

30. See below, pp. 268–269.

31. Dumbrell, for example, concludes that 'the covenant of David lies within the framework of the Sinai covenant with Israel' (*Covenant*, p. 151); Clements notes attempts within the book of Deuteronomy and the Priestly document to provide a unified doctrine of covenant (*Abraham and David*, p. 82); see also Jon D. Levenson, 'The Davidic Covenant and its Modern Interpreters', *CBQ* 41 (1979), pp. 205–219; *Sinai and Zion*, pp. 209–217.

32. See e.g. R. A. Carlson, *David the Chosen King: A Traditio-Historical Approach to the Second Book of Samuel* (Stockholm: Almqvist, 1964), pp. 99–106. Carlson suggests that building a sanctuary was the expected response of a ruler who has received divine blessing. David was prevented from doing so in order to concentrate on his primary task: making permanent the temporary rest he had secured (pp. 119–120); cf. Dumbrell, *Covenant*, pp. 148–149. See also 1 Kgs 5:3–4.

33. In the prologues to their law codes both Ur-Nammu and Hammurabi emphasize the calling to establish and maintain justice. Hammurabi's purpose is 'to make

and guaranteed not only right relationships within society but also the prosperity of the nation. The idea of the king of Israel as upholder of justice is seen in Psalm 72:1–4.

Psalm 72 points to the vital role the king played in the life of the nation. The king is dependent upon Yahweh and because his subjects belong to Yahweh (*your people*; v. 2), the king is answerable for the right use of his royal power. Administering righteousness and justice includes giving special protection to the weaker members of society, who also belong to Yahweh (*your afflicted ones*; v. 2; see also vv. 12–14).[34] This idea that the people belong to Yahweh, and the king exercises authority on Yahweh's behalf, is expressed further in the description of Israel as Yahweh's flock. The Davidic king is called to *shepherd* the people of God (2 Sam. 5:2; 7:7; Ps. 78:71): to provide for them (Jer. 3:15; Ezek. 34:2–3), to protect them (Ezek. 34:5) and to care for those in need (Ezek. 34:4). We also see a relationship between *justice* and *prosperity* (*šālôm*; Ps. 72:2–3). *Šālôm* is often translated 'peace', but refers to well-being of every kind.[35] Here it is the spiritual, moral, social and material well-being that derives from the just and righteous rule of a king who reigns on God's behalf. The righteous conduct of the king brings blessing – and even enables the corn to grow (v. 16). This follows from the link between the political and cosmic structures, and the idea that the harmony of the created order depends upon the king fulfilling his judicial responsibility. And, as we have noted, in anticipation of a worldwide kingdom, the blessing associated with the Davidic king also extends to other nations (Ps. 72:17). The cosmic dimension of justice is also seen in Psalm 82, where the failure of God's appointed representatives to uphold justice means *all the foundations of the earth are shaken* (v. 5).[36] The importance of the king's judicial function is seen too in Jeremiah 22:2–5, where the proper administration of justice is a necessary condition for the continuation of the Davidic monarchy. Significantly, a chief function of the ideal Davidic king of the future is to establish and maintain true righteousness and justice (Isa. 11:3–5; 16:5; Jer. 23:5–6).

---

justice prevail in the land, to abolish wicked and evil, to prevent the strong from oppressing the weak' (Arnold and Beyer, *Readings*, p. 112; see also pp. 104–105).

34. See e.g. B. W. Anderson, *Contours*, pp. 206–207; Brueggemann, *Theology*, pp. 611–614; Goldingay, *OT Theology*, 2:687–689; Rendtorff, *Hebrew Bible*, p. 569.

35. See Philip J. Nel, '*šlm*', in *NIDOTTE* 4:130–135; F. J. Stendebach, '*šālôm*', in *TDOT* 15:13–48.

36. See H. H. Schmid, 'Creation, Righteousness and Salvation', in B. W. Anderson, *Creation in the OT*, pp. 102–117.

8. GOD AND HIS PEOPLE (5): ETHICS AND ETHICAL QUESTIONS

Right living in the covenant community[1]

In the OT, religion and conduct are closely related: faith must be worked out in practice in individual and national life; it involves relationship with God and

---

1. See e.g. John Barton, 'Approaches to Ethics in the Old Testament', in John W. Rogerson (ed.), *Beginning Old Testament Study* (London: SPCK, 1983), pp. 113–130; *Understanding Old Testament Ethics: Approaches and Explorations* (Louisville: Westminster John Knox, 2003); *Ethics and the Old Testament* (Harrisburg: Trinity Press International, 1998); R. Bauckham, *The Bible in Politics: How to Read the Bible Politically* (London: SPCK; Louisville: Westminster John Knox, 1989); M. Daniel Carroll R. and Jacqueline E. Lapsley, *Character Ethics and the Old Testament: Moral Dimensions of Scripture* (Louisville: Westminster John Knox, 2007); Drane, *Introducing the OT*, pp. 277–305; Dyrness, *Themes*, pp. 135–141, 170–199; Eichrodt, *Theology*, 2:316–379, 483–495; Goldingay, *Approaches*, pp. 38–65; Jacob, *Theology*, pp. 173–177; Walter C. Kaiser, Jr., *Toward Old Testament Ethics* (Grand Rapids: Zondervan, 1991); Hetty Lalleman, *Celebrating the Law? Rethinking Old Testament Ethics* (Carlisle: Paternoster, 2004); Robin Parry, *Old Testament Story and Christian Ethics: The Rape of Dinah as a Case Study*, Paternoster Bible Monographs (Carlisle: Paternoster, 2004); Preuss, *OT Theology*, 2:185–208; Vriezen, *Outline*, pp. 315–342; John W. Rogerson,

so may not be reduced to a mechanistic system of appeasement or seeking divine favour through ritual. True faith in God must be accompanied by practical commitment that shows itself in right living. This is expressed in the Law, but the principle goes back to the covenant with Abraham (e.g. Gen. 18:19). The attempt to separate religion from lifestyle and to focus, instead, on external ritual, is strongly condemned by the prophets (e.g. Isa. 1:11–17; Hos. 8:12–13; Amos 5:21–24).

The true basis of ethical behaviour in the OT is the nature and character of God himself. The qualities God requires of human beings in general, and of his people in particular, are the qualities he himself displays in his relationship with them (e.g. Jer. 9:24). Jacob observes that 'if man's nature can be defined by the theme of the image of God, his function can be qualified as an imitation of God'.[2] According to Christopher Wright, 'biblical ethics . . . assumes the existence of the one living personal God and sets the whole of human life in response to him. Ethics is . . . primarily a response to God, who he is and what he has done.'[3]

Wright argues that ethics cannot be separated from world view, and, alongside their relationship with *God*, identifies two further key elements in Israel's understanding of herself and of the world: the community of *Israel* and *the land*. He then develops his discussion of ethics in the OT according to the triangular relationship between these three things:[4]

The *theological angle* emphasizes the importance of God's character in ethics. Elsewhere in the ANE there was the belief that laws were given by the gods; for example the stele inscribed with Hammurabi's famous law code depicts the king receiving it from the sun god, Shamash. Israel's ethical outlook is unique

---

Margaret Davies and M. Daniel Carroll R. (eds.), *The Bible in Ethics* (Sheffield: Sheffield Academic Press 1995); Gordon J. Wenham, *Story as Torah: Reading the Old Testament Ethically* (Edinburgh: T. & T. Clarke, 2000); Christopher J. H. Wright, *Living as the People of God: The Relevance of Old Testament Ethics* (Leicester: IVP, 1983); *Walking in the Ways of the Lord: The Ethical Authority of the Old Testament* (Leicester: Apollos, 1995); these have been revised, expanded and integrated into a single volume: *Old Testament Ethics for the People of God* (Downers Grove: IVP, 2004); *God's People in God's Land: Family, Land and Property in the Old Testament* (Grand Rapids: Eerdmans; Exeter: Paternoster, 1990); see also Christopher J. H. Wright, 'Ethics', in *NIDOTTE* 4:585–594.

2. Jacob, *Theology*, p. 173.

3. C. J. H. Wright, *Walking*, p. 117.

4. C. J. H. Wright, *OT Ethics*, pp. 17–20.

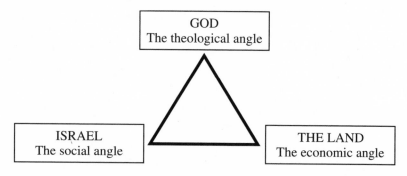

because of the unique character of Israel's God, and an important aspect of ethical conduct is the imitation of God (e.g. Lev. 19:2, *Be holy because I, the LORD your God, am holy*).

The *social angle* emphasizes that OT ethics is not concerned, primarily, with abstract principles, but with right living in the real world: relationship with God has implications for life in society (the God–Israel axis). A key part of this is Israel's distinctiveness as a nation, also tied to its mission to the world: Israel is called to be a model of a community redeemed by God, and also a means by which God's redemption may include other nations.[5] In this, Wright sees Israel as a paradigm: an example to and model for the church.[6]

The land too plays an important part in Israel's understanding of herself and her relationship with God. The God–land axis emphasizes that the land is given by God. He needs to be acknowledged as its owner, and prosperity in and continued possession of the land is closely linked with dependence upon and obedience to him. Because the economic life of Israel cannot be separated from the land, this also has social implications (the Israel–land axis), including warnings against extending property and taking land from weaker members of society, and the need to share the blessings of the land.[7] According to Wright,

---

5. See below, pp. 322–325.

6. C. J. H. Wright, *OT Ethics*, pp. 62–75; on the paradigmatic approach, see below, p. 241, n. 8.

7. Cook suggests that key aspects of Israel's Sinai tradition were concerned with the land. God was sole landlord, over against other gods who might also be linked with the land, and this led to a rejection of polytheism. As landlord, God apportioned land to family groups as an inheritance to be preserved within the family, rather than acquired by land-grabbing wealthy classes. However, occupation of the land was conditional, opening the possibility of exile (*Social Roots*, pp. 15–44).

the relationship between God and Israel in the land is a paradigm for God's relationship with the earth.[8]

Wright also discusses the significance of the land for OT ethics in his earlier book *God's People in God's Land*. He points to an organic link between land and covenant theology, and so between Israel's relationship with the land and the nation's relationship with God. An important factor in this was the family: 'the landholding household units constituted the basic social fabric through which Israel's relationship with God was "earthed" and experienced'.[9] Kinship groups were important for the administration of justice and for the proper instruction of children and the maintenance of religious traditions. Wright argues that being part of the covenant community was closely linked with being part of a landowning household, and this, in part, accounts for the opposition of the prophets to the undermining of land rights, which are not only a symptom of a general moral slide but also threaten something at the heart of

---

8. C. J. H. Wright, *OT Ethics*, pp. 182–211. By referring to Israel and the land as *paradigms*, Wright argues they are patterns that intentionally embody 'governing principles' (*OT Ethics*, p. 63), which may then be applied authoritatively to the church and to the church in the world. This goes beyond typological correspondence, which is retrospective: looking back to notice patterns, structures and common ways of working. Wright also discusses the problem of dissociating ethical principles from the OT and from the realities of the narrative, e.g. to produce an overarching principle of 'love', or of the 'greatest good': 'once you have a principle in your pocket, why keep the wrapping?' (*OT Ethics*, p. 70). To avoid such a problem we need to hold on to both principle and context; principles such as 'love' have meaning only when linked to a narrative context. And this is true also of theological principles. We have seen that an important part of OT theology is to uncover principles that may then be reapplied to the life of the church, and those principles too cannot be separated from the narrative context that gives rise to them. That said, the language of paradigm may be too rigid. To speak of Israel as a paradigm for the church suggests an exact parallel in which every aspect of Israel's relationship with God can be interrogated for principles that may be applied to the church: the class of Israel parallels the class of the church. However, the parallels are not always exact or complete. While recognizing the value of the paradigmatic approach, I would rather affirm that the OT has authority when addressing the church and then speak in more general terms about principles and typological correspondences in specific areas, rather than in terms of paradigms that govern whole classes.

9. C. J. H. Wright, *God's People*, p. 71.

Israel's relationship with God.[10] This is reflected in property rights in the OT, which are concerned not with the importance of property in itself but with what it represents as a symbol and guarantee of membership of the community of God's people. It is seen too in the responsibilities of those who own land – including the importance of maintaining the land within the family (e.g. Lev. 25:25–28).[11]

Within the OT, ethical values are revealed in several ways.[12]

Ethics and Law

As we have seen, the Law is central to the institution of the Sinaitic covenant, and so to the relationship between God and his people. It is a revelation of God's own character, and of his will for the life of the people he has called

---

10. According to C. J. H. Wright, 'the prophetic protest against these evils, therefore, must be illumined by the fact that there was an essential link between the social and economic facts of life and the theological self-understanding of Israel. That link was the family' (*God's People*, p. 109).

11. This included the responsibility of the *gō'ēl*, a close family member, to buy land from a relative who needed to sell it and so ensure it remained within the family. There is an example of this practice in the book of Ruth. If there was no *gō'ēl*, the seller had the responsibility to attempt to buy it back, and where that was also impossible, the land reverted to its original owners during the Jubilee. See Robert L. Hubbard, '*g'l*', in *NIDOTTE* 1:789–794; Helmer Ringgren, '*gā'al*, etc.', in *TDOT* 2:350–355.

12. In his paper 'Understanding Old Testament Ethics' (in *Understanding OT Ethics*, pp. 15–31), first published in 1978, Barton questions whether it is possible to speak about *OT* ethics, as this implies a unity of rationale that was, in his opinion, never in evidence. He argues that at any point in Israel's history there were diverse social groups, each with its own ethical rationale. In particular he challenges Eichrodt's view that OT ethics developed only in response to the expressed will of God. That is one model, but it is not normative for the OT writers, and as additional models he also notes natural law and (based on work by E. Otto) the 'imitation of God'. In a later paper, 'The Basis of Ethics in the Hebrew Bible' (in *Understanding OT Ethics*, pp. 45–54), first published in 1995, Barton allows that 'obedience to the declared will of God is probably the strongest model for ethical obligation in most books of the Hebrew Scriptures' (p. 47). He also gives greater prominence to the third model, the imitation of God, and suggests that 'Otto may well be right to see in it a potentially unifying theme for much that the Old Testament has to say about ethics' (p. 52).

into relationship with himself and chosen to bear his name. God's people are to be holy because he is holy (Lev. 20:26): they are to reflect in their life in community the holy character of the God who has set them apart, and, by obedience to the Law, maintain their distinctiveness as the covenant people of God.

At the heart of the Law are the *Ten Commandments* (Exod. 20:1–17). This is a summary statement, probably intended to be learned by heart and repeated by counting off the rules on the fingers. The Decalogue emphasizes the dual responsibility central to OT faith: a right attitude to God as the one, true God who alone is to be worshipped, and the outworking of that in right behaviour to others. The 'Book of the Covenant', which follows the Decalogue (Exod. 21 – 23), is generally thought to be very old, perhaps even going back to the time of Moses. It resembles other 'law codes' (e.g. of Ur-Nammu, c. 2050 BC, and of Hammurabi, c. 1700 BC) and is mainly concerned with instructions for community life. It includes *apodictic law*: rules about what should or should not be done, often beginning: *'Do not. . .'* (e.g. Exod. 22:21–22). It also includes *casuistic law*: instructions of what to do in particular cases; these usually begin *'If . . .'* (e.g. Exod. 21:2; cf. Deut. 12 – 26).

Drane breaks down non-cultic OT law codes into four main areas.[13] (1) *Criminal law* includes offences against God,[14] against human life[15] and against the family.[16] (2) *Civil law* gives guidance for more general conduct, and prescribes appropriate compensation when rights are violated (e.g. Exod. 21:18–36; Lev. 24:18–21; Deut. 25:11–12). This includes the familiar dictum *eye for eye, tooth for tooth* (Exod. 21:24), intended to limit the retribution rather than

---

13. Drane, *Introducing the OT*, pp. 291–297; see also C. J. H. Wright, *Walking*, pp. 181– 274; *OT Ethics*, pp. 281–326. It is common to separate what is sometimes described as 'moral law' from other kinds of law in the OT, as something more relevant to the life of the church. This distinction is arbitrary; it is better, as Wenham does, to talk about laws that have more general application and those that relate to a specific context (Wenham, *Leviticus*, pp. 34–35); though, as we have seen, principles underlying even specific laws may have contemporary relevance (see e.g. Wenham, *Leviticus*, pp. 32–37).

14. Including idolatry (Exod. 22:20; Lev. 20:1–5; Deut. 13:1–18), blasphemy (Lev. 24:10–16) and sorcery (Exod. 22:18; Lev. 20:27).

15. Including kidnap (Exod. 21:16; Deut. 24:7) and murder (Exod. 20:13; 21:12; Lev. 24:17).

16. Including incest, adultery, homosexuality (Lev. 20:10–14) and disrespect for parents (Exod. 21:15; Lev. 20:9; Deut. 21:18–21).

set in place a rigid system of penalties. (3) *Family law* gives instructions on relationships within the family, including the rights of the firstborn (Deut. 21:15–17), regulations governing divorce (Deut. 24:1–4) and the duty to redeem a relative who had sold himself into slavery (Lev. 25:47–49). (4) *Social law* is concerned to safeguard the well-being of disadvantaged members of society, including orphans, widows, foreigners (Exod. 22:21–22; Deut. 24:17; 27:19) and even slaves (Exod. 21:1–6, 20, 26–27; 23:12; Deut. 5:12–15; 23:15–16), and to provide for the needs of the poor (Exod. 23:11; Lev. 19:9–10; Deut. 24:19–21). We have noted that laws relating to property prevent land passing permanently out of the hands of families. Long-term damage caused by poverty is also minimized by regulations regarding loans and debts. It is forbidden to charge interest (Exod. 22:25; Lev. 25:35–37; cf. Deut. 23:19),[17] and there are restrictions on what can be given as security (Exod. 22:26–27; Deut. 24:6). Every seventh year (the sabbatical year) and every fiftieth year (the Jubilee) all debts are cancelled and all Hebrew slaves freed (Exod. 21:1–6; Lev 25:8–17; Deut. 15:1–15).

A key function of the Law was to maintain the distinctiveness of Israel and enable the nation to fulfil its mission to the world, which, as we have seen, may be seen in terms of the revelation of God's glory. This suggests that the OT law might be understood, not as a series of absolute, invariable rules that apply to God's people in every age but as a particular application of an ethical principle that views actions and behaviour in the light of whether they contribute to the distinctiveness that allows for the revelation of God's glory. Christians are also called to be distinct from the world, and in that sense the church parallels the role of Israel (e.g. 1 Pet. 1:13–16; 2:9–12), but the social, cultural and religious setting is different. This is not to say that the Law is irrelevant to Christians. But focusing on the purpose of the Law as a means of ensuring the

---

17. The prohibition against charging interest seems to have been primarily to protect those who needed to borrow money in a time of crisis and prevent the lender profiting from a fellow-Israelite's misfortune (Exod. 22:25; Lev. 25:35–37). Deut. 23:19 appears to extend the prohibition to interest on any loan made to another Israelite regardless of economic status. It is widely thought, though, that within Israelite society almost all such loans would have been charitable rather than commercial, and so Deut. 23:19 can be set in the same context as passages that specifically mention the poor; see e.g. Craigie, *Deuteronomy*, pp. 302–303; Robin Wakely, '*nšk*, pay/give/earn interest', in *NIDOTTE* 3:185–188 (186); however, cf. Edward Neufeld, 'The Prohibition against Loans at Interest in Ancient Hebrew Laws', *HUCA* 26.1 (1955), pp. 355–412.

distinctiveness of God's people and their effectiveness in revealing God's glory gives a context in which decisions about the relevance of particular OT laws and their contemporary equivalents can be taken.

Ethics and narrative

Ethical conduct in the OT also has its roots in Israel's history. We have already observed that for the OT writers, history is an important medium of divine revelation. Through his mighty acts on behalf of his people, especially in the events of the exodus, God has made himself known. This encounter with God, at what was the formative time in the nation's history, was significant for Israel's understanding of God and of herself as his people, and was also a basis for ethical conduct. This sets the ethical imperative in a narrative context. In some cases the story of what God has done in the lives of his people is used as an incentive, calling for grateful obedience (e.g. Deut. 5:15; 16:12; cf. Exod. 20:2). On other occasions there is a close link between the command and Israel's own experience.

So, for example, in Exodus 23:9 the command *do not oppress an alien* is given the explanation *you yourselves know how it feels to be aliens, because you were aliens in Egypt.* Instructions about the redemption of (Hebrew) slaves are linked with Israel's own experience, and also with the imitation of God: *remember that you were slaves in Egypt – and the LORD your God redeemed you* (Deut. 15:15a).[18] In all of this we see the significance of narrative. According to Robin Parry, 'the ethics of ancient Israel are deeply rooted in the stories of the community'.[19] Gordon Wenham notes that discussion of ethics in the OT usually focuses on Law and wisdom literature, though argues that there is a gap between what the Law requires, as a minimum, enforceable, standard, and the ethical ideal.[20] A key medium for exploring that ideal, and the hopes and aspirations of the OT writers, is narrative. Wenham focuses on narratives in Genesis, and argues that from them 'we can build up a catalogue of the virtues as they are perceived by the [implied]

---

18. The 'imitation of God' features too in the Creation narrative that accompanies the command to observe the Sabbath in Exod. 20:8–11, *for in six says the LORD made the heavens and the earth, the sea, and all that is in them, but he rested on the seventh day* (v. 11).

19. Parry, *OT Story*, p. 69. Parry reviews the three ethical models suggested by Barton and notes that 'one cannot adequately understand "natural law", the imitation of God or the commands of the torah apart from the stories recounted in the Hebrew Bible' (p. 69).

20. Gordon J. Wenham, 'The Gap Between Law and Ethics in the Bible', *JJS* 48.1 (1997), pp. 17–29.

author, an identikit picture of the righteous'.[21] This, again, allows us to establish principles of ethical behaviour that may be reapplied to the church.

Ethics and prophecy

One of the emphases of the prophets is to call people back to the ethics of the covenant faith. Though prophets before Jeremiah make relatively few specific references to the Sinaitic covenant, the relationship between God and Israel is a central concern of their preaching. Even where they do not use the term *běrît* their theology is deeply rooted in Israel's covenant traditions.[22]

The prophet Micah sums up God's requirements for his people:

> *He has showed you, O man, what is good.*
> *And what does the LORD require of you?*
> *To act justly and to love mercy*
> *and to walk humbly with your God.*
> (Mic. 6:8; cf. Hos. 12:6)

'Mercy' translates the Hebrew word *ḥesed*, which, as we have seen, refers to right conduct within a relationship. God's people have been brought together into a covenant relationship with God, and so have an obligation to one another and to society as a whole. *Ḥesed* in this context is closely related to faithfulness, loyalty and dutiful action; it is conduct in accordance with the divinely appointed order that allows society to function. Here it is also closely linked with justice. We have noted that justice is the responsibility of the king and national leaders, but is also required of all God's people in their dealings with one another. In the OT the administration of justice (and righteousness, which is closely linked with it) has a legal dimension (e.g. Exod. 23:6–7; Lev. 19:15; Deut. 16:18–20; 1 Sam.

---

21. Wenham, *Story as Torah*, p. 100. Parry notes Wenham's discussion and also N. T. Wright's view that the story of Israel is part of a single metanarrative that includes our story too and offers a helpful framework for looking at ethics in a narrative context. As already noted, a problem with this approach can be how to move from Israel's narrative to the narrative of the church. Wenham's view, that OT narrative reveals ethical ideals, is helpful here.

22. See e.g. Bright, *Covenant*, pp. 41–42, 81–94; Clements, *Prophecy and Covenant*, pp. 16–19. Cook (*Social Roots*) appears to want to limit this Sinai theology to particular circles within Israel/Judah; however, the prophets as a whole condemn injustice, greed and other excesses and encourage a return to traditional social, ethical and religious values.

8:3; Isa. 5:23; Amos 5:15), but includes all aspects of fair dealing, such as using honest measures (Amos 8:5), and not exploiting the needy (Ezek. 18:7; 22:29; Amos 2:6–7; 5:11; 8:6; Mic. 3:1–2), for example by charging interest on loans (Ezek. 18:8; cf. Lev. 25:37).[23] Within Israelite society, true justice means giving special protection to those who are least able to defend themselves (e.g. Isa. 1:17; 10:1–2; Amos 2:6–7; Zech. 7:9–10). Here again we see that the ethical imperative is the revelation of the character and will of God. Right conduct in society is the evidence of walking with God; living in covenant relationship with God results in a felt obligation towards his people, and in the practical outworking of that obligation in social duty and responsibility.

Ethics and natural law

A factor governing the social life of most communities is what Eichrodt terms 'popular morality':[24] moral and ethical norms that arise from the experience of a community, which are passed from one generation to the next to ensure the survival and well-being of that society. The OT contains rules similar to those found in the law codes of other nations, but they are distinctive in that they arise not from a concept of natural justice or community survival but from the revealed will of God. Ethical conduct in the OT is primarily theological.

There are instances, though, where the OT does seem to appeal to a more general moral law. In Amos 1:2 – 2:3 Israel's neighbours are called to account for particular sins. Though probably unaware of the specific requirements of God's Law, which is mentioned only in relation to Judah and Israel, these nations are still held accountable, presumably because their behaviour offends against a universally recognized code of moral decency, of which everyone is aware as part of being human.[25] This is *natural* law in the sense that it is available to all without

---

23. See above, p. 244, n. 17.

24. Eichrodt, *Theology*, 1:316–322.

25. John Barton, *Amos's Oracles against the Nations* (Cambridge: Cambridge University Press, 1980), suggests that the basis for judgment is infringement of moral norms that are part of the 'common moral sense of all right minded men' (p. 43). He links this with international custom rather than universal moral law; see also James L. Mays, *Amos*, OTL (London: SCM, 1969), pp. 27–28. However, all morality must, in some sense, derive from God; otherwise it becomes elevated to a higher principle to which he must conform. Hans Walter Wolff, *Joel and Amos*, Hermeneia (Philadelphia: Fortress, 1977), refers to violations against a 'universally valid law' (p. 152; see also pp. 172–173); Goldingay notes the nations' failure 'to behave in accordance with the way they are wired' (*OT Theology*, 2:812–814 [813]).

the special revelation given to Israel and Judah, though it is still from God: he is the Creator, and any laws built into the fabric of the universe, or planted within the hearts or consciences of people, have been put there by him.

The existence of a universal moral law may be linked to the idea of a 'covenant with creation' through which God has entered into a relationship with the natural order.[26] More specifically, it may be related to the unique relationship between God and humankind. Human beings are made *in the image of God* and this has several implications for ethical conduct. First, all human beings are called to reflect the character of the one in whose likeness they have been made; this has particular significance for the life of the people of God, but also has implications for the conduct and accountability of all people. Second, it emphasizes the sanctity of human life (e.g. Gen. 9:5–6; cf. Num. 35:33). Third, it stresses the equality of human beings and the importance of proper conduct towards others, who are also made in God's image. Again this is significant for the life of God's people and their concern for weaker members of society, but it also has a wider application (e.g. Ps. 82:4; Amos 1:13; 2:1b).

Ethics and wisdom

Wisdom literature contains practical advice on personal morality and relationships. It points to the importance of the family, warning against the dangers of, and damage caused by, adultery (e.g. Prov. 2:16; 5:3–4; 6:26, 32; 7:1–23) and emphasizing the blessings of good family relationships (5:18–19; 12:4; 18:22; 31:10–31). Parents are responsible for bringing up children, teaching them by word and example (Prov. 22:6; see also e.g. 1:8; 4:1–4; 6:20), and offering discipline and correction (e.g. Prov. 13:24). Wisdom emphasizes the importance of friendship (e.g. Prov. 17:17; 18:24; 27:6–10; Eccl. 4:9–12), and gives advice on social relationships in general (e.g. Prov. 3:27–29; 6:16–19; 15:1). It is generally recognized that the main emphasis of wisdom teaching in the OT is on personal morality. However, there is also a significant emphasis on social justice, including condemnation of unjust business practices (Prov. 11:1; 16:11), bribery (Prov. 15:27) and charging interest on loans (Prov. 28:8).[27] Honesty is

---

26. For more detailed discussion of this universal covenant, see below, pp. 321–325.

27. The expression *běnešek wětarbît* is translated 'exorbitant interest' by the NIV and NRSV. It is probably better to see these two terms as two different kinds of interest; see e.g. Samuel E. Loewenstamm, '*nšk* and *mtrbît*', *JBL* 88.1 (1969), pp. 78–80; Wakely, '*nšk*', in *NIDOTTE* 3:187. The second half of the verse suggests that those who have amassed wealth have done so at the expense of the poor, in violation of the instructions in Exod. 22:25 and Lev. 25:35–37.

commended (Prov. 12:19, 22; 14:5; 16:13; 24:26; 28:6); other things are more important than wealth (Prov. 3:13–15; 15:16–17; 17:1; 22:1; cf. Job 31:24–28; Eccl. 2:11); the rich are urged to share with the poor (Prov. 14:21, 31; 19:17), and those in authority are called to avoid injustice and exploitation (Prov. 31:8–9; see also e.g. Prov. 13:23; 16:10; 17:5; 18:5; 22:16; 28:3–5; 30:14). Many of these things are also found in the prophetic books. There is some debate about the relationship between sages and prophets. Hubbard suggests that they had a considerable influence on one another, and notes that a number of the prophetic books use literary techniques drawn from wisdom circles.[28]

Unlike the teaching of the prophets, OT wisdom literature does not justify right action by relating it to Israel's salvation history.[29] Canonical wisdom teaching, with its greater emphasis on personal piety,[30] is based more on a theology of creation. It draws many of its conclusions from observations of the natural world, and is directed towards human beings as human beings under God as creator, rather than as members of a chosen people. Nevertheless, while wisdom may represent a distinct stream within Israelite teaching, covenant theology is not far below the surface.[31] We have noted the importance for true wisdom of a relationship with God. The call for social responsibility also echoes the demands associated with the covenant, and Proverbs 2:21–22 links upright behaviour with continued possession of the land, echoing passages in the book of Deuteronomy.[32] While ethics found in the wisdom literature are compatible with those found in the Law, the approach is different. Both call for right behaviour, but while the Law points to the penalties for disobedience, wisdom focuses on the advantages and disadvantages of doing the right thing,[33] and so encourages serious thought about ethical issues.

---

28. Hubbard, 'Wisdom Movement', pp. 8–11.

29. Links with Israel's history are much more prominent in apocryphal wisdom books (e.g. Wisdom of Solomon 10 – 19; Sirach 44 – 50), which seem to have a more nationalistic aim.

30. Though, as we have noted, the application of this to the community should not be overlooked.

31. See Hubbard, 'Wisdom Movement'.

32. Note the discussion above, p. 220, n. 42.

33. Goldingay, *OT Theology*, 2:598–600; Kidner, *Wisdom*, p. 11; C. J. H. Wright, *Walking*, pp. 120–122. For example, the Law prohibits adultery (Exod. 20:14; Deut. 5:18) on pain of death (Lev. 20:10); whereas the wisdom teacher argues against it as gross stupidity that results in a person destroying his life (Prov. 6:32).

Questioning God's activity[34]

Will not the Judge of all the earth do right?

Abraham questioned the rightness of God's decision to destroy Sodom and Gomorrah: *far be it from you to do such a thing . . . will not the Judge of all the earth do right?* (Gen. 18:25). The idea that God could sweep away the righteous with the wicked presented the patriarch with a moral dilemma that offended his sense of justice, so he looked for an explanation. We too expect that God will do right, that his actions will be consistent with our ideas of justice and right-eousness. But we see things in the OT (as well as in the world around us) that might lead us to repeat Abraham's question.

Alongside the clear moral guidance we find in the OT are ethically ques-tionable areas. The OT writers do not condemn the practice of polygamy (though they do sometimes highlight problems that arise as a consequence). Practices we would deem unethical, such as slavery (e.g. Gen. 16:6; Lev. 25:44–46; Neh. 7:67), are condoned; some, such as the annihilation of whole peoples, including women and children, are commanded (e.g. Josh. 11:14–15; 1 Sam. 15:2–3).

Although God is described as righteous and just (e.g. Deut. 32:4; Ps. 111:7), sometimes his actions seem dubious. He sends an evil spirit to trouble Saul (1 Sam. 16:14) and a lying spirit to mislead Ahab (1 Kgs 22:19–23). He incites David to number Israel (2 Sam. 24:1), with disastrous (and intended) conse-quences. He allows Satan to afflict Job (Job 1 – 2). He hardens the heart of Pharaoh (e.g. Exod. 10:1, 20) in order to justify further plagues, thus prolong-ing the suffering not only of the Egyptians but of the Israelites too. He makes Israel unresponsive to Isaiah's message (Isa. 6:9–10), and brings judgment on them as a result.

Some things can be said by way of explanation. In the matter of slavery, Israel adopted a common practice in the ANE and in fact gave slaves a dignity and legal status greater than any of her neighbours did. The extermi-nation of certain peoples was never an act of pure hatred and hostility, but was a necessary cleansing in view of the sin of certain peoples, and the threat they posed to the fulfilment of God's redemptive purposes through his people. However, such explanations do not properly answer our concerns.

---

34. See also B. W. Anderson, *Contours*, pp. 242–249; Brueggemann, *Theology*,
    pp. 333–399; Andrew Davies, *Double Standards in Isaiah: Re-Evaluating Prophetic Ethics and Divine Justice* (Leiden: Brill, 2000).

In presenting God as ultimately responsible for evil as well as good, the OT writers emphasize his sovereignty. When they suggest that God *allows* evil, they are making a statement not about his ethical character, but about his ultimate authority in the affairs of the world. Clearly, though, there is a tension, and Brueggemann points to this as part of the conflicting testimony within the OT.[35] Another aspect of this is that sometimes God allows the evil already present to grow, and so to become 'ripe for judgment'.[36] This might be applied to the hardening of Pharaoh's heart, Saul's hostility toward David, Ahab's readiness to listen to the *lying spirit*, and the unbelieving and unresponsive hearts of the people to whom Isaiah was sent. Here, according to Eichrodt, 'God's power operates . . . within the evil which has been begun by the perversion of the creature's will':[37] God confirms people on the rebellious path they have already chosen. Goldingay argues that when God hardens (or softens) a person's heart, he does so, not by manipulation of the mind or will but by other influences. For Pharaoh, that may have been reminding him of the cost of letting Israel go. The final decision of how to respond to such divine prompting, however, still lies with Pharaoh.[38]

Does God change his mind?

This raises the question of God's reliability. Are his words and intentions subject to change in the light of changing circumstances? On the one hand, the OT writers express confidence in one who is faithful (e.g. Deut. 7:9; 11:13–15; 32:4; Pss 33:4; 57:10) and unchanging (e.g. Num. 23:19; 1 Sam. 15:29; Mal. 3:6). On the other hand, some passages refer to God changing his mind (e.g. Gen. 6:6; Exod. 32:14; Amos 7:3, 6).[39] Are we to infer from this that God is reacting to something unforeseen, and taking action not originally planned?[40]

---

35. Brueggemann, *Theology*, pp. 353–355.

36. Eichrodt, *Theology*, 2:179.

37. Ibid.

38. Goldingay, *OT Theology*, 1:353.

39. Brueggemann also notes instances where, he claims, a change in Yahweh's attitude takes place, but without an open acknowledgment of it (*Theology*, pp. 362–367), demonstrating that 'Yahweh is a conundrum of contradictions' (p. 362). However, the passages quoted do not support the claims made for them and can be readily explained in other ways. See also Michael Butterworth, '*nḥm*', in *NIDOTTE* 3:81–83.

40. The recently articulated 'open theism' position is that the future is indeterminate, and though God works towards general goals, the details of how those goals may

This raises the further issue of whether God is to be thought of as *omniscient*. Goldingay argues that though God could know everything, it is not an automatic knowledge, but comes through discovery: so, for example, he asks questions in the Garden of Eden (Gen. 3:9–13); he comes down to find out what is happening at Babel (Gen. 11:5); he tests Abraham in order to know the extent of his commitment (Gen. 22:12).[41]

Does the fact that God appears to search out information and is portrayed changing his mind in the light of new developments imply that God is not omniscient, at least in the generally accepted sense? Not necessarily.[42] As we have seen, the OT writers often use anthropomorphic terms as a way of conveying truth about God. In such cases they focus on a particular aspect of God's character or action, and do not intend the description to be interrogated too deeply. When they refer to God's 'hand', it is clear what is meant, and it is fatuous to ask why only one hand, or to enquire about the number of fingers.

Footnote 40 (*continued*)

> be achieved are contingent on interaction between God and human beings, and cannot be known, even to God; see Clark Pinnock, Richard Rice, John Sanders, William Hasker and David Basinger, *The Openness of God: A Biblical Challenge to the Traditional Understanding of God* (Carlisle: Paternoster; Downers Grove: IVP, 1994). For a defence of the more traditional view, see Steven C. Roy, *How Much Does God Foreknow? A Comprehensive Biblical Study* (Nottingham: Apollos; Downers Grove: IVP, 2006).

41. Goldingay, *OT Theology*, 1:136–139. He suggests the analogy of the relationship between a novelist and novel, though there may be a general idea how characters will develop, sometimes the characters appear to take on a life of their own, and develop in a way the writer had not originally intended; see also 2:69–71, 89–91, 132–133.

42. The reason we look for an alternative explanation for the use of this kind of language is that the theological implications of the idea that God changes his attitude or action in the light of 'new information received' are profound. I believe that God has committed himself to us, that he loves us and that, in Christ, he has opened the way for our salvation. But what if that commitment is based on only limited knowledge, with the result that, if more information comes to light, God's attitude toward us might change? How can we rely on the promise of a God who might change his mind? We do need to take account of passages that point to God's interaction with human beings, but not at the expense of God's faithfulness, reliability and unchangeableness, which are vital, if we are to have real assurance of salvation.

Why might the idea of God seeking out information or changing his mind not be understood in a similar way? In these cases the OT writers are not making statements about the sovereignty, foreknowledge or reliability of God. These things are a theological given, and to imply that the idea raises questions about them is reading too much into the language.[43] Certainly the term is theologically imprecise – but theological precision is rarely a concern of the OT writers. In my view the picture of God asking questions indicates that he is not distant, but interacts with the people in his world, and emphasizes that his action is not arbitrary, and his judgments are based on a clear understanding of the human situation he is dealing with. That is an important reassurance, particularly against a background in the ANE where gods *did* act arbitrarily with little or no regard for how their actions might affect humans beings. With regard to God changing his mind, often the change in attitude and action is in response to human sin (Gen. 6:6; 1 Sam. 15:11; Jer. 18:10). This emphasizes, first, the seriousness of sin and the fact that it impacts on God's purposes for his people, and, second, the effect of sin on God himself: he feels it, is offended by it, it affects his attitude towards human beings and it brings divine wrath. Similarly, when God is portrayed as relenting of sending, or continuing, judgment (Exod. 32:12, 14; 2 Sam. 24:16; Ps. 106:45; Jer. 18:8; 26:3; 42:10; Amos 7:3, 6; Joel 2:13; Jon. 3:9–10; 4:2), the emphasis is on his compassion and willingness to forgive and to offer the opportunity to start again.

These passages give us important insight into the heart of God: they present him not as a dispassionate observer, but as a participant, involved with

---

43. This is a major weakness in Brueggemann's approach. When God is portrayed as a character within the biblical narrative, the writers focus only on those aspects of his character and his relationship with his people and with the world that are relevant to that particular story. Consequently different sections of the narrative emphasize different characteristics. Brueggemann, and others who adopt a deconstructive approach to the text, consider the way God is described in a particular case, extend its theological significance beyond the context of the narrative (and beyond the intention of the writer) and use it as an example of dissonance within the OT canon. This approach often emphasizes tension (and even contradiction) where there is none, and points to a much more varied, and much more uncertain, understanding of God than the text justifies. Goldingay seems to acknowledge that there will be tensions between one passage's portrayal of God and another's; though, in some cases, and the discussion of God's omniscience is one of them, he also appears to use one picture of God to make general comments.

his people, who listens to their prayers and is affected by what goes on in their lives. This may bring a sense of inner turmoil and even of suffering (e.g. Hos. 11:8–9), but that comes as a result of the tension between love and wrath, and not (contra Brueggemann) because of any contradiction or inconsistency within God's interior life.[44]

Why do the wicked prosper?

As we have seen, behind much of the wisdom teaching in the OT is the belief that a law of cause and effect operates in the moral realm: certain actions and behaviour bring certain results. We see this elsewhere in the OT too. When God chose Israel and entered into a covenant with them, he set a choice before them: blessing, life and prosperity would follow obedience, and death and destruction would follow disobedience (e.g. Deut. 11:26–29; 27 – 30; esp. 30:15–18).[45] This principle is also expressed as a general rule of life (e.g. Pss 1:1, 6; 37:25).[46]

Experience of life shows, though, that this does not always appear to happen. Jeremiah asks:

> *Why does the way of the wicked prosper?*
> *Why do all the faithless live at ease?*
> (Jer. 12:1)

---

44. Goldingay suggests that God's controversial action (e.g. in putting a lying spirit in the mouths of Ahab's prophets) is portrayed as serving a higher cause: to show mercy, and he claims that 'Yhwh will do anything, even tell lies, to get people to turn back' (*OT Theology*, 1:653). We need to be aware of the tension in the way God is portrayed and avoid being overly naive. However, it seems to go too far to suggest that God may set aside righteousness in order to pursue mercy. The danger, again, is in pressing the anthropomorphism too far. For human beings the conflict cannot be resolved without compromise, but that is not so for God (cf. Hos. 11:9).

45. According to Albertz, the Deuteronomic movement in Israel was led by aristocrats influenced by wisdom traditions (*History*, 1:202). There is little evidence to support such a view; it seems better to see both as reflections of the general belief that God would, ultimately, reward the righteous and punish evildoers.

46. These psalms are often linked with wisdom teaching and have affinities with Proverbs. It is worth noting, though, with Kidner (*Psalms 1–72*, p. 47), that in Ps. 1, godliness is rooted in the Law (v. 2).

The psalmist has a similar concern:

> *This is what the wicked are like –*
> *always carefree, they increase in wealth.*
> *Surely in vain have I kept my heart pure;*
> *in vain have I washed my hands in innocence . . .*
> (Ps. 73:12–14)

One explanation, which seeks to preserve the integrity of God's character, is that this is only a temporary state of affairs. The days of the wicked are numbered, whereas the righteous will, ultimately, receive their reward (e.g. Pss 37:35–36; 73:17–19). Wealth does not bring happiness (e.g. Pss 37:16; 39:6, 11; 52:7–8; cf. Prov. 11:4), is transient and does not provide true security (e.g. Ps. 49:5–10). By contrast, God satisfies his people and gives them hope and strength through all circumstances (Ps. 73:24–28). Nevertheless the sense of injustice remains. Habakkuk also questions God's inactivity in the face of injustice (Hab. 1:2–4; cf. Mal. 2:17). In this case God's response, to use the Babylonians to punish his sinful people, only compounds the problem:

> *Your eyes are too pure to look on evil;*
> *you cannot tolerate wrong.*
> *Why then do you tolerate the treacherous?*
> *Why are you silent while the wicked*
> *swallow up those more righteous than themselves?*
> (Hab. 1:13)

As we have noted, further questions about God's justice, this time in relation to innocent suffering, are raised in the book of Job.

God and suffering in the book of Job[47]
The orthodox explanation of suffering
The implicit question Job asks is, why are these things happening to one who is innocent and upright? The speeches of his friends express the prevailing

---

47. Andersen, *Job*, pp. 64–73; B. W. Anderson, *Contours*, pp. 276–282; David Atkinson, *The Message of Job*, BST (Leicester: IVP, 1991); Brueggemann, *Theology*, pp. 386–393; Catherine Chin, 'Job and the Injustice of God: Implicit Arguments in Job 13.17–14.12', *JSOT* 64 (1994), pp. 91–101; Drane, *Introducing the OT*, pp. 116–117, 249–250; Fyall, *Now my Eyes*; Goldingay, *OT Theology*, 2:615–631; Robert Gordis, *The Book of*

theological understanding, the law of retribution. This is stated by Eliphaz: *Those who plough evil and those who sow trouble reap it* (4:8). Job has brought this misfortune upon himself, though Eliphaz notes too that God uses trouble to reprove and correct (5:17–18), and Job's suffering should prompt him to turn back to God and ask for mercy and grace. Bildad extends this principle. He appeals to traditional teaching (8:8–10) and to natural law (8:11–19). God is just and thus blesses the righteous and punishes the wicked (8:20–22). Zophar completes the picture. Because of God's unsearchable wisdom, nothing escapes him (11:5–12); his justice cannot be challenged. Job may protest his innocence, but there must be some hidden sin that has led to his condition, which must be confessed (11:13–20).

The second and third cycles of speeches build on the first. Having established that Job's suffering is a consequence of his sin, the scale of the disasters that have befallen him point to very great wickedness indeed. Zophar even begins to speculate as to what Job's crimes might be, and suggests his earlier prosperity came from exploiting the poor (20:10).

Another figure, Elihu,[48] elaborates on the theme of *disciplinary suffering* (33:14–30; 36:8–12, 15–16). Answering Job's complaint that God has left him (29:2–5), Elihu notes that God's voice is heard even in distress (33:14): through suffering, God punishes, but also disciplines and instructs (see also Prov. 3:11–12). This is an important aspect of suffering. Though, in his attempt to defend God's justice, Elihu too overstates the case.

Footnote 47 (*continued*)

> *God and Man: A Study of Job* (Chicago: University of Chicago Press, 1966); Norman C. Habel, *The Book of Job*, OTL (London: SCM, 1985); Hartley, *Job*; House, *OT Theology*, pp. 424–438; A. S. Peake, *The Problem of Suffering in the Old Testament* (London: Epworth, 1947); Preuss, *OT Theology*, 2:129–131, 141–146; Rendtorff, *Hebrew Bible*, pp. 336–357; H. H. Rowley, *Job*, NCB (London: Marshall, Morgan & Scott, 1978); Elmer B. Smick, *EBC* 4:843–1060; Tur-Sinai, *Job*; R. S. Wallace, 'Suffering', in *IBD* 3:1491–1492.

48. The place of the 'Elihu speeches' is debated. One issue is whether they are additions to the original book; another is their theological value. Some consider that these speeches have great depth and insight and that Elihu comes closest to reflecting God's voice in the debate. Others suggest that Elihu provides a lighthearted, even comic, interlude. In his opening speech, for example, he says how urgent his message is, but takes a whole chapter to get to the point! In the end he adds little to the argument. The emphasis on Elihu's youth (Job 32:6–7) suggests he is a student of wisdom, and his inability to answer Job's questions may reinforce the failure of conventional wisdom and wisdom schools.

As we have seen, what they are saying is not wrong, and similar principles are stated in other parts of Scripture. The error is in their rigid *application* of it. As a general rule, God judges sin and rewards the righteous; those who live unwisely will suffer the consequences. But that general rule should not be taken to infer that all misfortune is evidence of a wicked life, or that all prosperity is a sign of a godly life and of divine favour. Eliphaz says he has never seen it happen any other way; if that is so, as Andersen observes, he has 'not seen much!'[49]

Throughout, Job protests his innocence. He is not claiming to be sinless, but has done nothing to bring about the dramatic change in the circumstances he now faces. His friends take Job's protestations and unwillingness to humble himself under their wisdom as indications of even greater sin. However, while their principles may be sound, they do not deal with Job's situation, and still leave him asking, 'Why?'

The hiddenness of God

Job's friends base their arguments on orthodox theology and traditional understanding, but they do not have the full picture. The prologue shows us what neither Job nor his comforters see, and reveals the limitations of their arguments. Job is upright, and that, not his sin, leads to his suffering, as God allows Satan to put his piety to the test. Job's faithfulness in the face of suffering has an influence in the heavenly realm: it proves the truth of God's words and gives the lie to Satan's accusation. Because of the prologue, we know Job is looking for answers his friends cannot supply. In the end only a direct encounter with God can bring meaning to what has so far seemed meaningless.

It may be that hearing God's voice is enough for Job. Job's main concern seems to be what his suffering indicates about his relationship with God. He knows he is innocent, but does not know why God has withdrawn his blessing. Something has gone wrong with the relationship; he wants to plead his cause but God is nowhere to be found (e.g. 23:8–9). To hear God's voice at last reassures him the relationship is intact. In the midst of all he has suffered, however hard he has found it to understand the bitter experiences of his life, through the times when God has seemed to be silent, God has not left him. As Job holds firm in faithful and patient endurance, God ultimately makes himself known.

In his reply God not only reassures Job but also enlarges his vision and understanding of the world around him. The universe is much bigger than Job

---

49. Andersen, *Job*, p. 112.

realizes. There is much more going on than Job knows about; God's concern for creation does not begin and end with Job. Though God gives no direct explanation of what is happening to Job, opening his eyes to the bigger picture may help him see that his suffering can serve some wider purpose of which he, with his limited knowledge, is unaware.

God's final purpose

The book of Job challenges the principle of retribution: that trouble in life must be a person's own fault. However, it does appear to allow for the ultimate vindication of the righteous within their lifetime. Some dispute this, and argue that there is the suggestion that Job expects to be vindicated after death (14:13–17; 19:25–27).[50] That is possible, though the interpretation of those passages is unclear, and others seem to say the opposite: that once a person dies there is no return (e.g. 7:6–10; 10:20–22; 14:7–12, 18–22). It is more likely that Job was expecting to be vindicated before death, which is what we see. God speaks to him at last; his friends are finally made to realize that they misjudged him, as he had been righteous all along; the material loss Job suffered is more than made good. This is necessary in a theological context where there is no clear view of a future life of glory and blessing beyond the grave;[51] if there is to be a promise of vindication and hope beyond the struggle, it has to be expressed in terms of an earthly reward.

In the light of the greater revelation we have received through Christ, we know that our final vindication lies beyond this world. God blesses us now, but the best is yet to come. We have a better hope, and in the light of the glory to be revealed, we persevere. We cannot infer from Job's experience that all who suffer innocently will receive material recompense within their lifetime. But the

---

50. Most of the debate focuses on Job 19:25–26; for arguments in favour of post-mortem vindication, see e.g. Andersen, *Job*, pp. 193–194; Fyall, *Now my Eyes*, pp. 49–52; Habel, *Job*, p. 293; Kidner, *Wisdom*, p. 69; for the alternative view, see e.g. David J. A. Clines, *Job 1–20*, WBC 17 (Dallas: Word, 1989), pp. 455–466; Hartley, *Job*, pp. 295–297; Philip S. Johnston, *Shades of Sheol: Death and Afterlife in the Old Testament* (Leicester: Apollos; Downers Grove: IVP, 2002), pp. 209–214. Another question relates to the identity of the 'Redeemer' in Job 19:25. Fyall argues for the traditional view that this refers to God, though notes that most scholarly opinion has moved away from that view (*Now my Eyes*, pp. 47–49); see also Hartley, *Job*, pp. 293–294; cf. Clines, *Job 1–20*, pp. 459–460; Goldingay, *OT Theology*, 2:52–54; Habel, *Job*, pp. 305–306; Johnston, *Shades*, pp. 211–212.

51. For further discussion of death and afterlife, see below, pp. 302–309.

theological principle applies to us as it did to him: we believe that, ultimately, like Job, we will be vindicated and will receive our reward.

Though he denies his suffering is the consequence of sin, Job accepts the value of suffering. He acknowledges that though he cannot see it, God is at work in what he is going through, and Job looks forward to a time when God's purposes for him will become plain (23:8–10). We have already noted that, though Job has no knowledge of it, his suffering is achieving a purpose within the heavenly realms. Our belief that God is sovereign as well as loving and compassionate leads us too to believe that suffering is not purposeless. We may not understand God's action, but we trust him. Sometimes in retrospect those reasons may become clearer; sometimes they do not. Although Job is never given an explanation for what he has been through, even in the midst of agony and questioning he remains confident in God's knowledge of his situation and that God will bring good from it:

> He knows the way that I take;
>   when he has tested me, I shall come forth as gold.
> (Job 23:10)

The idea of God bringing good out of evil, not as a by-product but as a part of his intention in allowing the suffering in the first place, is clearly seen in the cross: 'in [Christ] the greatest evils, the betrayal and crucifixion of the Son of God, become, and now are, the greatest good for all mankind'.[52]

The inscrutability of God

With all of this there remain unanswered questions and we must recognize that in some cases we cannot, or may not, know the mind of God. The OT writers do not say we should never ask questions of God, and their own questions are among the most searching. But there is also a need to recognize that God is greater than us. Job's insistence on his own innocence and his desire to be vindicated lead him to question God's justice and call him to account. But that is something neither he nor any other human being has the right to do. Thus when God does break silence, it is to emphasize his own lordship over heaven and earth and to rebuke Job's presumption. Job is brought to his knees before God. The questions God asks show the difference between Creator and creature: they point to Job's smallness and his total ignorance when compared with God's infinite and all-embracing wisdom. In the light of this, Job is invited to

---

52. Andersen, *Job*, p. 69.

accept God's sovereign authority, which he is more than willing to do (42:2–6). In the face of things we do not understand and cannot explain, we are called, similarly, to submit to one whose divine wisdom and ultimate purposes we can never fully comprehend.

When Abraham expresses his concern about God's apparent injustice, God debates with him and demonstrates the justice of his case (Gen. 18:23–33).[53] That does not happen often. Usually we receive no justification or explanation. As we have seen, even when God does finally reveal himself to Job, no explanation is given for what Job has been through. Faced with difficult ethical issues (both in our reading of Scripture and in our own lives), we need to balance the approaches we find in the OT. When the usual rules do not seem to apply, or when we do not understand what God is doing, it is in order to seek an explanation (as Abraham, Job, the psalmist and Jeremiah did). But where that explanation is not forthcoming, we must also be willing to accept God's silence and trust that he knows what he is doing. In the book of Job we are made aware that God's purposes may be hidden, and that they encompass far more than any one person's life and experience; there is also a rebuke for those who presume to challenge the ultimate justice of God. Recognizing the hiddenness of God, and the limitations of human wisdom and understanding, the writer of Ecclesiastes urges us to make the most of the life he has given – with all its frustrations, uncertainties and unanswered questions. In such cases Abraham's question becomes the answer: *Will not the Judge of all the earth do right?* We can only trust that he will, and accept his decisions:

> *God is in heaven*
> *and you are on earth,*
> *so let your words be few.*
> (Eccl. 5:2b)

---

53. This section of the narrative ends with Abraham returning home, indicating that he is satisfied with the promise God has given him. God's readiness to accept Abraham's conditions may indicate he is not taking arbitrary action against Sodom, but has already taken those concerns into account. In other words this is less a negotiation and more a justification of why he has made the decision to destroy the city. The justice of God's action is emphasized in the next section of the narrative, which emphasizes the gross wickedness of the inhabitants of Sodom, and their unwillingness to listen to (righteous) Lot. At the same time, God's willingness to rescue Lot and his family shows that his judgment does discriminate between the righteous and the wicked.

9. GOD AND THE FUTURE

Crisis and hope

Israel's faith in God allowed them to hold on to the belief that one day the nation would be restored to a former greatness and would participate in the glory of God's kingdom. However, increasing sin and a corresponding unwillingness to listen to God's call to return to him led to the conclusion, among the pre-exilic prophets, that hope lay only at the far side of judgment. Those who experienced the exile and tried to make sense of it recognized that it was God's judgment on sin, but that it also opened the way to renewed blessings in the future.

Divine judgment
The Deuteronomistic History[1]
God chose the people of Israel as an act of sovereign grace, but to go on enjoying God's blessings and remain in the land he had given, they had to obey him:

---

1. The term 'Deuteronomistic History' is attributed to Martin Noth; it comprises Deuteronomy and the historical books Joshua, Judges, Samuel and Kings (the Former Prophets); see Martin Noth, *The Deuteronomistic History*, JSOTSup 15 (Sheffield: JSOT Press, 1981).

if they disobeyed, the divine blessings would cease. These 'two ways' are set before the people in the book of Deuteronomy (e.g. Deut. 30:15–18), and this principle provides a theological basis for interpreting the history of Israel and Judah. Faced with the fall of Jerusalem and the exile of the nation, the writers of Joshua, Judges, Samuel and Kings set out to explain how such a disaster could have taken place; how God, who had chosen and called the people, could apparently have turned against them. The answer was to be found in the people's continued disobedience. God was not unfaithful; rather, after years of bearing with the nation's sins, he was fulfilling his word.

The Deuteronomistic History is so called because the writers appear to interpret the events that led to the defeat and exile of Israel in 722–721 BC and of Judah in 587 BC in the light of the principle set out in Deuteronomy: obedience leads to blessing and prosperity, disobedience results in defeat and eventual exile from the land.[2] So, in the books of Joshua and Judges, victory

---

2. Noth claimed that the Deuteronomistic History was the work of a single author during the sixth century BC and was intended to give a unified history of Israel, with Deuteronomy providing a theological introduction and setting out the basis on which events were to be understood. A more recent view is that there was a major redaction of the historical material during Josiah's reign, and a further redaction following the exile; see e.g. Gottwald, *Hebrew Bible*, pp. 139–139; Richard Nelson, 'The Double Redaction of the Deuteronomistic History: The Case Is Still Compelling', *JSOT* 29.3 (2005), pp. 319–337. Thomas Römer, *The So-Called Deuteronomistic History: A Sociological, Historical, and Literary Introduction* (London: T. & T. Clark, 2006), argues for a third redaction, in the Persian period. While the compilers of the historical material in the former prophets appear to reflect the Deuteronomic principle of the 'two ways' (see e.g. Josh. 23; 1 Sam. 12:6–25; 1 Kgs 8:33–51), that is not the only influence (according to von Rad, the theme of God's promises to David is also significant – see the comment below), suggesting that the link with Deuteronomy is not quite as close as this view implies. See also Albertz, *History*, 2:387–399; *Israel in Exile*, pp. 271–302; B. W. Anderson, *Living World*, pp. 183, 359; *Contours*, pp. 165–170; Bright, *Covenant*, pp. 132–135; Brueggemann, *Theology*, pp. 434–436; Drane, *Introducing the OT*, pp. 84–86; House, *Theology*, pp. 170–171; LaSor, Hubbard and Bush, *OT Survey*, pp. 135–136; J. Gordon McConville, 'Deuteronomic/istic Theology', in *NIDOTTE* 4:528–537; Preuss, *OT Theology*, 2:263–265; Gerhard von Rad, 'The Deuteronomic Theology of History in I and II Kings', in *Problem of the Hexateuch*, pp. 205–221 (= *Genesis to Chronicles*, pp. 154–166); Walther Zimmerli, *Man and his Hope in the Old Testament* (London: SCM, 1971), pp. 70–85; note also Cook, *Social Roots*, pp. 58–59, 63–65, 141–142.

and occupation of the land depend on obedience; in the book of Kings, rulers are not judged by their achievements but by how God views their actions (e.g. 2 Kgs 13:1–3), and the eventual defeat of the northern kingdom by the Assyrians is explained as the result of Israel's failure to listen to God's warnings and obey his Law (2 Kgs 17:7–20). Von Rad makes the comment 'God's word is the key to the history of salvation. God has given his commandments, and he has threatened severe judgments as the consequence of disobedience. Those judgments have occurred.'[3]

We have noted that the promise of 'rest' (Deut. 12:10) is fulfilled under David (2 Sam. 7:1).[4] Solomon also refers to the rest God has given him and the nation, and links it with the absence of any 'adversary' (1 Kgs 5:4). Following Solomon's idolatry, we are told that God raised up an adversary, in fact there were two of them, Hadad and Rezon, who continued to trouble Solomon (1 Kgs 11:11–25). Here we see a similar principle at work: enjoyment of the rest promised in Deuteronomy is conditional upon faithful obedience, while sin causes that peace to be disrupted.

In Noth's view the Deuteronomistic History is negative: it explains the defeat and exile of the nation. Von Rad, however, notes that alongside this principle of blessings and curses is the long-suffering of God. This also plays an important part in the interpretation of salvation history, and is explained on the basis of God's promises to David. When the sin of the people deserved a much earlier and much more complete judgment, God held back (e.g. 1 Kgs 11:13; 2 Kgs 8:18–19). And, even after the fall of Jerusalem and the imprisonment of its last kings, Jehoiachin and Zedekiah, the postscript in 2 Kings 25:27–30 gives a glimmer of hope. After thirty years, Jehoiachin was released from prison and given a place of honour at the king of Babylon's table. The writer's decision to end here, rather than on a note of judgment, points to the belief that God's judgment on his people and on the monarchy was not his final word.

The prophets

Impending judgment as a result of apostasy is also a key theme of the pre-exilic prophets.[5] Amos condemned the social sin of the northern kingdom,

---

3. Gerhard von Rad, 'God's Word in History according to the Old Testament', in *God at Work in Israel* (Nashville: Abingdon, 1980), pp. 139–159 (146); see also *Studies in Deuteronomy*, pp. 74–91.

4. See above, p. 236.

5. See e.g. B. W. Anderson, *Contours*, pp. 181–192; Childs, *OT Theology*, pp. 228–230; Clements, *OT Theology*, pp. 137–140; Dyrness, *Themes*, pp. 235–237; Eichrodt,

especially the oppression of the poor and the corruption of justice (e.g. 2:6–8; 5:10–12; 6:4), and linked these with coming disaster (5:2; 6:7; 8:2). Hosea spoke against the people's religious sins, including idolatry, meaningless ritual and the failure to show Yahweh the faithfulness their covenant relationship demanded (e.g. 4:11–14, 17–19; 6:4, 6–10). And again, the consequence is judgment (chs. 7 – 10). The same message of judgment, this time for the southern kingdom, is present in the preaching of Isaiah (e.g. 3:1–5; 5:5–6; 28:14–18; 29:1–4), Jeremiah (e.g. 4; 6; 14:1– 6; 22) and Ezekiel (e.g. 4 – 7; 21).

Amos also challenged false confidence. The Israelites believed their election by God guaranteed their future, and so they had no need to repent. In his prophecy Amos first attacks the sins of Israel's traditional enemies: Syria, Philistia, Tyre, Edom, Ammon, Moab and Judah. Then, having gained his audience's attention, he turns on Israel. In God's eyes Israel is like the rest: a *sinful kingdom* (9:8), deserving to be punished. And, significantly, it is Israel's election, the very thing on which the nation has built its confidence, that is the basis of God's indictment

> *You only have I chosen*
>   *of all the families of the earth;*
> *therefore I will punish you*
>   *for all your sins.*
> (Amos 3:2; cf. 2:9–11)

Israel's false confidence is seen too in the hope associated with the Day of the Lord. The people expect a day of victory and vindication, but Amos and Joel in particular warn the people that it will be, rather, a day of defeat and judgment (Joel 1:15; 2:1–2; Amos 5:18, 20).[6]

Though the pre-exilic prophets (before Jeremiah) do not often refer to the Sinaitic covenant, the idea that the people have broken faith with God and have not lived up to the obligations of their special relationship with him is a central theme. In the desert, when God brought Israel out of Egypt, he took her as his bride (e.g. Jer. 2:2; Ezek. 16:8; Hos. 2:14–16); by worshipping other gods,

---

Footnote 5 (*continued*)

> *Theology*, 1:374–381, 457–511; Goldingay, *OT Theology*, 2:254–310; Donald E. Gowan,
> *Theology of the Prophetic Books: The Death and Resurrection of Israel* (Louisville:
> Westminster John Knox, 1998), pp. 24–142; Lindblom, *Prophecy*, pp. 346–360;
> Preuss, *OT Theology*, 2:267–271; Rendtorff, *Hebrew Bible*, pp. 163–314.

6. For further discussion of the Day of the Lord, see below.

the people have committed adultery (e.g. Jer. 2:32; 3:1; Ezek. 16:15–43; 23; Hos. 1:2; 2:2–13; 8:9–10). Israel is in breach of her covenant obligations, and several passages depict God bringing a lawsuit against the nation (see e.g. Jer. 2:4–13; Hos. 4:1–3; Mic. 6:1–5; cf. Isa. 1:2–3; 3:13–15).[7] For Jeremiah, the Sinaitic covenant is central to his message. He reasserts the message of Deuteronomy, that God's promise of blessing in the land is conditional upon obedience, and that disobedience brings God's curse (e.g. Jer. 11:3–8). The picture painted by the prophets is thus of a nation that has failed and a covenant that has been broken. That, however, is only part of the overall view.

Judgment and hope
Alongside this message of judgment, prophetic writings also contain a message of hope for the future (e.g. Isa. 2:2–4; 11:1–9; 14:1–2; 32:1–8; Jer. 31; 33; Ezek. 20:39–44; 37 – 48; Hos. 11:8–11; 14:4–7; Amos 9:11–15).[8] Some scholars argue that the real emergence of hope came only during the Babylonian exile, and the hopeful words of the pre-exilic prophets are editorial; however, there are good grounds for accepting the message of hope as part of the original prophecies.[9] The prophets give an explanation of the defeat and

---

7. The covenant lawsuit may have originated in the context of international law where a party to a treaty could be held accountable for failure to meet its covenant responsibilities. See further e.g. H. B. Huffmon, 'The Covenant Lawsuit in the Prophets', *JBL* 78 (1959), pp. 285–295; James L. Mays, *Micah*, OTL (London: SCM, 1976), pp. 128–136; Kirsten Nielsen, *Yahweh as Prosecutor and Judge*, JSOTSup 9 (Sheffield: JSOT Press, 1978).

8. See also e.g. Albertz, *Israel in Exile*, pp. 166–179; Bright, *Covenant*; Brueggemann, *Theology*, pp. 438–449; Childs, *Biblical Theology* (1992), pp. 177–190; *OT Theology*, pp. 236–247; Clements, *OT Theology*, pp. 140–149; Eichrodt, *Theology*, 1:480–501; Goldingay, *OT Theology*, 2:311–516; Gowan, *Theology*, pp. 144–200; Lindblom, *Prophecy*, pp. 360–375; Preuss, *OT Theology*, pp. 269–277; Rendtorff, *Hebrew Bible*, pp. 688–715; Claus Westermann, *Prophetic Oracles of Salvation in the Old Testament* (Edinburgh: T. & T. Clark, 1991).

9. Clements notes that there was a significant resurgence of hope during the reign of Josiah and argues 'that a message of hope entered into the mainstream of Israelite-Judean prophecy no later than the seventh century BC, and probably before this time' (*OT Theology*, p. 142). For further discussion, see e.g. David A. Hubbard, *Joel and Amos*, TOTC (Leicester: IVP, 1989), pp. 96–102, 236–245; Mays, *Amos*, pp. 163–165; Wolff, *Joel and Amos*, pp. 112–113, 350–355; Zimmerli, *Man and his Hope*, pp. 86–137.

exile of the nation. Throughout Israel's history, despite repeated calls to repent, the nation had been unfaithful. The exile was a turning point. It was God's judgment on sin, but the prophets saw it too as the means by which God would bring about a new beginning for his people. What seemed to be a national catastrophe was, in fact, a theological requirement. The nation had to die before it could be reborn; renewal could come only when all pretensions and false hopes had been swept away. The theme of the prophetic books is the death and rebirth of Israel: death, in the form of defeat and exile; rebirth in the return from exile, resettlement in the land and the recovery of Israel's status as a nation. As Clements notes:

> Israel would be judged and the covenant brought to an end. Yet beyond this judgment
> they pointed also to a new beginning when Israel would be reborn, and would
> become once again the people of the covenant. The old election traditions were used
> by the prophets to portray the re-election of Israel, and the new covenant which
> Yahweh would make with them. The ancient covenant promises were now expected
> to find their fulfilment when the judgment was passed, and a new beginning made.[10]

The remnant[11]

In the OT, words from the Hebrew root *š'r* often relate to those who survive a particular crisis. In the days of Ahab and Jezebel the nation as a whole embraced Baal worship; nevertheless (and much to Elijah's surprise) God preserved a remnant of those who remained faithful to him (1 Kgs 19:18). After the destruction of the northern kingdom, the people of Judah may have felt they were the remnant, especially when they compared what was left of the nation with the extensive kingdom David had ruled over. Following the Assyrian invasion of Judah, which resulted in the destruction of most of its cities, those shut up in Jerusalem saw themselves as the remnant (2 Kgs 19:4; cf. vv. 30–31). Later, Jews who remained in Judah after the exile, and who were

---

10. Clements, *Prophecy and Covenant*, p. 118.

11. See Gerhard F. Hasel, *The Remnant: The History and Theology of the Remnant Idea from Genesis to Isaiah*, 3rd ed. (Berrien Springs: Andrews University, 1980); see also e.g. R. E. Clements, '*šā'ar*, etc.', in *TDOT* 14:272–286; Mark W. Elliott, 'Remnant', in *NDBT*, pp. 723–726; Craig Evans, 'Isa. 6:9–13 in the Context of Isaiah's Theology', *JETS* 29.2 (1986), pp. 139–146; Goldingay, *OT Theology*, 2:214–216, 334–347; E. Jenni, 'Remnant', in *IDB* 4:32–33; Lester V. Meyer, 'Remnant', in *ABD* 5:669–671; Sang Hoon Park, '*š'r*', in *NIDOTTE* 4:11–17; Preuss, *OT Theology*, 2:271–272; Rendtorff, *Hebrew Bible*, pp. 705–713.

joined by others from the surrounding areas, are referred to as a 'remnant' (e.g. Jer. 40:11; Ezek. 9:8). In a theological context, though, '*the* Remnant' refers to a relatively small section of the population who, following the exile (which is seen as divine judgment on the faithlessness of the nation), will turn back to God and receive the blessings of his salvation.

As we have noted, the prophets saw judgment and exile as part of God's purpose for his people. Judgment, though devastating and fully deserved, would not result in total destruction. Rather, as Bright observes, it 'would serve a pedagogical function; it would serve as a purge designed to discipline and refine the people and bring forth a chastened remnant'.[12] As an example, Bright points to Isaiah 1:21–26. This laments the spiritual and moral decay of Jerusalem and threatens judgment, but it is a judgment intended to remove dross and so prepare the way for restoration. The nation as a whole has failed; nevertheless a faithful few will come through the fire of judgment to experience the blessings of God's salvation. It seems likely that the prophets who ministered before and during the exile associated this remnant with those who would return from Babylon (e.g. Isa. 11:11, 16; 28:5; Jer. 23:3; 31:7; 50:20; Mic. 2:12; 5:7–8), and the returning exiles saw themselves as the survivors of the nation (e.g. Zeph. 3:13; Hag. 1:12, 14; 2:2; Zech. 8:6, 12–13). However, the return was not as glorious as the people expected. It did not result in the establishment of God's kingdom, and, from the way old sins quickly re-emerged, it was clear that the crisis of the exile had not brought about the hoped-for inward renewal. As a result, the idea of a faithful remnant became linked with the distant future.

The prophet Isaiah introduced another important element to the idea. The (symbolic) name of Isaiah's son *Shearjashub* means 'a remnant will return' (Isa. 7:3). In the light of the crisis facing the nation, this may be interpreted as a warning: '*only* a remnant will return'; or as a promise that the coming devastation will not be total: 'a remnant *will* return'. The same twofold interpretation is given in Isaiah 10:20–23, which points to the decimation of the nation, yet promises some survivors. For Isaiah, this distinction is linked with faith in God (10:20; cf. 7:9). Thus, as well as offering hope, the idea of the remnant also calls for faith, and so confronts people with a choice. Not all will enter the blessings of the coming age, but only those who turn to God and put their trust in him.[13]

---

12. Bright, *Covenant*, p. 105.

13. Oswalt notes the significance of this theme for the book of Isaiah as a whole. Though there are relatively few specific references to the remnant, he maintains

The Sinaitic and Davidic covenants[14]

We have noted the tension between the Sinaitic and Davidic covenants. By breaking the Sinaitic covenant, the people might have expected their relationship with God and the blessings associated with it to end. The (unconditional) Davidic covenant gave a theological basis for Israel's continuation as the people of God and for future hope.[15] Bright notes the importance of both covenants for Israel's faith: 'The one stressed God's election of Israel, his purposes for her and his sure promises to her, which nothing could cancel; the other stressed the righteous commandments . . . which they were obligated to obey if the covenant bond was to be maintained.'[16] There was, though, the need to maintain a delicate balance between these two emphases, and by the time of Jeremiah that balance had been upset. Because of God's unconditional promises to David and especially his election of Zion, people in Jerusalem believed a secure future was assured. God was present in the city, and would protect it and its inhabitants.[17]

Jeremiah, rooted in the theology of the Sinaitic covenant, had a different message. The people had violated that covenant and must repent before it was too late. Later in his ministry, when it was clear there would be no repentance, Jeremiah's preaching became a stern warning of impending doom. Even after

----

Footnote 13 (*continued*)

>   that 'it is still perhaps the most apt summary of the entire book, since it captures the interwoven themes of redemption and judgment that prevail from beginning to end' (*Isaiah 1–39*, p. 269). See also Goldingay, *OT Theology*, 2:346–347; House, *OT Theology*, pp. 284–286.

14. See e.g. B. W. Anderson, *Contours*, pp. 206–207, 239–242; Bright, *Covenant*, pp. 49–77, 111–114; McCarthy, *OT Covenant*, pp. 46–52; von Rad, 'God's Word', in *God at Work*, pp. 145–147.

15. Within the Deuteronomistic History, God's promise to David is important and gives an explanation of why God held off judgment for so long; nevertheless a key theological emphasis is on the blessings and curses associated with the Sinaitic covenant. Chronicles offers a different theological assessment, focusing primarily on the promises to the house of David. See B. W. Anderson, *Contours*, pp. 218–223 (cf. pp. 165–170); Childs, *Biblical Theology* (1992), pp. 157–159; Robert P. Gordon, 'David', in *NIDOTTE* 4:505–512; LaSor, Hubbard and Bush, *OT Survey*, pp. 542–549; H. G. M. Williamson, 'Chronicles 1, 2: Theology of', in *NIDOTTE* 4:466–474.

16. Bright, *Covenant*, p. 171.

17. This appears to be the basis for Hananiah's opposition to Jeremiah (Jer. 28); see also e.g. Jer. 7:4; 8:19. For further discussion of 'Zion tradition', see below, pp. 276–277.

the deportation of many of Jerusalem's inhabitants, this popular confidence in God's protection of Zion remained. Isaiah had warned of a judgment that would produce a purified and chastened remnant (Isa. 1:21–26). Those left in the city after the fall of Jerusalem in 587 BC saw themselves as that remnant (e.g. Ezek. 11:15; 33:24), and now looked forward to the promised restoration. Jeremiah rejected that view: the city would be laid waste and its people taken into exile. But he also trusted God's promises. The coming judgment was part of God's purpose for his people and he would not intervene to prevent it, nor would he finally cast his people off. This hope for the future is expressed in the promise of a new covenant (Jer. 31). Bright comments:

> God, who has condemned his people by the terms of his covenant, will come to them again in the wilderness of exile and will make with them a new and eternal covenant. The awful chasm between the demands of covenant by which the nation was judged, and the sure promises of God which faith could not surrender, is bridged from the side of the divine grace.[18]

The new covenant[19]
Continuity with the Sinaitic (old) covenant

The new covenant is a fulfilment of the Sinaitic covenant. Jeremiah 31 contains many allusions to the exodus, indicating that the return from exile was seen as a second wilderness experience. The references to desert wanderings (Jer. 31:2, 9) and deliverance from captivity (Jer. 31:11, 16), and God's reference to Israel as *my firstborn son* (Jer. 31:9), an expression found elsewhere only in Exodus 4:22, all recall the escape from Egypt. In the past, God graciously delivered his people from Egypt and, through the covenant, took them as his own people. Now, in a parallel situation, he again promises deliverance, restoration and a new relationship based upon a new, eternal covenant.[20]

---

18. Bright, *Covenant*, p. 196.

19. See e.g. Bright, *Covenant*, pp. 194–197; Dyrness, *Themes*, pp. 122–123; Goldingay, *OT Theology*, 2:380–386, 431–433; House, *OT Theology*, pp. 317–321; Walter C. Kaiser, Jr., 'The Old Promise and the New Covenant', *JETS* 15.1 (1972), pp. 12–23; McCarthy, *OT Covenant*, p. 33; von Rad, *OT Theology*, 2:212–217; Rendtorff, *Hebrew Bible*, pp. 698–701; *Covenant Formula*, pp. 69–78; J. Skinner, *Prophecy and Religion* (Cambridge: Cambridge University Press, 1961), p. 330.

20. McCarthy comments, 'in this chapter we are never far from the covenant, an old covenant broken and the new covenant to be restored, but with new affective overtones' (*OT Covenant*, p. 33).

The reference to the husband–wife relationship between God and Israel (Jer. 31:32), as we have seen, also points back to Sinai and to the 'honeymoon' period in the desert (e.g. Jer. 2:2). Hosea too, drawing on his own unhappy domestic experience, likens the covenant at Sinai to a marriage bond between God and Israel, which Israel has broken (Hos. 2:2–13). However, though apostasy brings divine judgment, God's purpose is not to reject his wife but to bring about reconciliation. Thus he will lead Israel again into the desert (Hos. 2:14–15), to where the relationship began. And in that place of new beginnings he will make a covenant that will be markedly different from the covenant at Sinai and will result in a 'marriage' that will last for ever (Hos. 2:16–23; cf. Ezek. 16:60–63; 37:26–28). The *Valley of Achor* (trouble), which lay at the entrance to the Promised Land and which had been the scene of failure and judgment (Josh. 7:26), will be renamed the *door of hope* (Hos. 2:15), showing God's readiness to forgive and his desire to restore the blessings of the people's early relationship with him.

What made Jeremiah's covenant new?
One important difference is that while the external demands of the Law characterized the Sinaitic covenant, the new covenant is characterized by an internal law, planted in the minds and written on the hearts of the people, and bringing with it the necessary inner renewal that will make obedience possible. The inward orientation of the law was anticipated by the old covenant (Deut. 6:6, *These commandments that I give you today are to be upon your hearts*; cf. 10:16; 30:6); but, because the people's hearts were hard and unreceptive (e.g. Ps. 95:8; Zech. 7:12; cf. Lev. 26:41; Jer. 9:26), that did not happen. By contrast, the inward transformation that accompanies the new covenant will result in a new nature and a new heart able to receive God's instruction in a way impossible before (Jer. 4:4; 24:7). This change in heart will result in the realization of the covenant ideal that was the essence of the relationships established with Abraham and at Sinai:

> *I will be their God*
>   *and they will be my people.*
>   (Jer. 31:33b; cf. Gen. 17:8; Exod. 6:7; Deut. 29:13)[21]

In Jeremiah 32:38–41 this heart change is again associated with a new-covenant relationship, a covenant that, because God has done everything necessary to

---

21. See above, p. 169, n. 28.

ensure its continuance, may be described as *everlasting* (see also Isa. 55:3; 61:8; Jer. 50:5; Ezek. 16:60; 37:26). Bright notes that 'since the stipulations are inscribed on their minds and wills, the people are enabled to conform to them, and truly to be God's people'.[22] Von Rad makes a similar comment: 'What is here outlined is the picture of a new man, a man who is able to obey perfectly because of a miraculous change in his nature.'[23] This new, inward, enabling to meet God's requirements is seen too in the promise of a new heart and new spirit in Ezekiel 36:26–27. This points to the means by which God will bring about the inward renewal of his people, and so will motivate and empower them to live according to his *decrees* and *laws*: the indwelling of the Spirit (see also Ezek. 37:14; 39:29; cf. Isa. 59:21). Here, again, we see that God's purpose in renewal is to fulfil the covenant ideal: *you will be my people, and I will be your God* (Ezek. 36:28).

Another *new covenant* distinctive is that this new relationship with God will not need human mediation:

> *They will all know me,*
> *from the least of them to the greatest.*
> (Jer. 31:34b)

The old-covenant relationship with God was mediated, uniquely, by Moses (e.g. Exod. 20:19; 24:3–4; Num. 12:6–8; Deut. 5:4), but also by priests (e.g. Lev. 9:7; 2 Kgs 11:17; cf. Heb. 5:1), prophets (e.g. 1 Sam. 12:6–25) and the king (e.g. 2 Kgs 23:3). Under the new covenant, everyone will have direct access to God, and may enjoy personal, intimate fellowship with him. This correlates with the gift of the Spirit who had been poured out only on certain individuals but who, in the era of salvation, will be poured out on all people (Joel 2:28–29).

Individual knowledge of God is linked to the further provision

> *I will forgive their wickedness*
> *and will remember their sins no more.*
> (Jer. 31:34c)

The sin that has proved so damaging to the relationship between God and his people in the past will be dealt with in such a way that it may be blotted out, and so no longer create a barrier between God and humankind. This is not, in

---

22. Bright, *Covenant*, pp. 195–196.
23. Von Rad, *OT Theology*, 2:213–214.

itself, new. As we have seen, there was elaborate (though limited) provision for the forgiveness of sins under the old covenant within the cult. And even apart from the sacrificial system God's people knew that they could rely on his mercy and faithful love to forgive and restore the fellowship broken by sin (e.g. Pss 51:12; 103:12; 130:3–4; Isa. 43:25). Jeremiah's words would first have been understood against this background of God's continued willingness to forgive. So this is not, in the first place, offering a new and more effective means of securing divine forgiveness; rather it is the promise of a new beginning. A faithful and merciful God will forgive past failure and rebellion; he will forget the way they have repeatedly broken their covenant vows and ignored his constant calling to them to return to him; no matter what may have gone before, God will come to his people again, to renew and so bring about a restored relationship with them (see also e.g. Isa. 44:22; Jer. 33:8; 50:20; Mic. 7:18).[24]

Old Testament eschatology[25]

What is 'eschatology'?

In Jewish apocalyptic writings and in the NT, eschatology relates to the final consummation that will bring history, the cosmos and the present world order to an end, and usher in an eternal era of salvation. This is the view taken by Mowinckel. He defines eschatology as

> a doctrine or a complex of ideas about 'the last things' . . . Every eschatology includes in some form or other a dualistic conception of the course of history, and implies

---

24. Though the means by which that forgiveness and new start are to be achieved is not the main emphasis here, the NT makes it clear that the promise of the new covenant does anticipate a radically new provision – the sacrifice of Christ. Thus on the eve of his crucifixion, as he shared a last meal with his disciples, he took a cup of wine and announced, *This cup is the new covenant in my blood, which is poured out for you* (Luke 22:20).

25. See e.g. Clements, *Prophecy and Covenant*, pp. 103–118; Eichrodt, *Theology*, 1:385–387, 424–433; Goldingay, *OT Theology*, 2:350–516; Donald E. Gowan, *Eschatology in the Old Testament* (Philadelphia: Fortress, 1986); Jacob, *Theology*, pp. 317–357; E. Jenni, 'Eschatology of the OT', in *IDB* 2:126–133; Lindblom, *Prophecy*, pp. 360–375; Mowinckel, *He that Cometh*; Preuss, *OT Theology*, 2:253–283; von Rad, *OT Theology*, 2:99–125; Th. C. Vriezen, 'Prophecy and Eschatology', *Congress Volume, Copenhagen 1953*, VTSup 1 (Leiden: Brill, 1953), pp. 199–229.

that the present state of things and the present world order will suddenly come to an end and be superseded by another of an essentially different kind.[26]

Understood in that way, there is little eschatology in the OT.[27] Clements notes that a key aspect of this view of eschatology is that the coming consummation lies 'on the other side of history',[28] and though the OT does envisage a coming age when God's purposes for his people and the world will be fulfilled, this is expected *within history* and so does not fit within the formal definition. For this reason it makes sense to use a wider definition of eschatology in relation to the OT hope. A characteristic feature of eschatology is the idea of two ages: the present age and the age to come. This idea is developed in later apocalyptic writings, but is also present in the OT. The prophets look forward to God's decisive intervention in human history to bring about a transformation of the present world order so profound and far-reaching that it may properly be thought of as a new age. This provides the basis for a broader definition of OT eschatology as *everything that pertains to that new world order.*[29]

Eschatological hope in the Old Testament

The growth of eschatology

As we have seen, the prophets look forward to a time, beyond judgment, when God will deliver and restore his people and usher in a new age, an era of salvation and peace, where his reign will be established over the whole earth. This hope receives its clearest expression in prophetic writings from the eighth century BC onwards, but its roots go deep into Israel's covenant faith.[30]

---

26. Mowinckel, *He that Cometh*, p. 125.

27. Vriezen, for example, notes that this definition would exclude 'not only all pre-exilic prophetic ideas *a priori*, but also all post-exilic prophetic ideas, except possibly a few apocalyptic pieces within the writings of the prophets' ('Prophecy and Eschatology', p. 202).

28. Clements, *Prophecy and Covenant*, p. 104.

29. See e.g. Bright, *Covenant*, p. 19; Clements, *Prophecy and Covenant*, p. 105; Jenni, 'Eschatology', in *IDB* 2:126; Lindblom, *Prophecy*, p. 361; von Rad, *OT Theology*, 2:114–116; Vriezen, 'Prophecy and Eschatology', pp. 201–202.

30. The view that Israel's eschatological hope had a foreign origin has little support, not least because it appears to have been unique in the ANE. For further discussion, see e.g. Bright, *Covenant*, p. 21; Ladislav Cerny, *The Day of Yahweh and Some Relevant Problems* (Prague: University Karlovy, 1948), pp. 35–38; Eichrodt, *Theology*, 1:495–496; Mowinckel, *He that Cometh*, pp. 127–128; von Rad, *OT Theology*, 2:113–114.

Three key (overlapping) themes may have influenced the development of OT eschatology: the Day of the Lord, the motif of God's battle with chaos (*Chaoskampf*) and the traditions surrounding David and especially the city of Zion.

The Day of the Lord (*yôm yhwh*)

The first mention of the *yôm yhwh* is in Amos 5:18.[31] This tells us little about the day itself, but the prophet is clearly referring to an idea well established by the eighth century BC. Other passages suggest it is a day of battle, when Yahweh will finally defeat all those powers that oppose him and will establish his reign.[32]

Mowinckel links the Day of the Lord with the annual enthronement festival, which celebrated God's renewed victory over the forces of chaos, and gave assurance that he would not fail his people. He argues that this theme was later taken up by Deutero-Isaiah after the fall of Jerusalem, though by then its fulfilment focused on the distant future.[33] As we have noted, there is a question about whether the kind of enthronement festival envisaged by Mowinckel ever took place. There may have been an annual celebration of Yahweh's reign, possibly commemorating bringing the Ark to Jerusalem,[34] which looked back

---

31. The expression *yôm yhwh* occurs also in Isa. 13:6, 9; Ezek. 13:5; Joel 1:15; 2:1, 11, 31; 3:14; Amos 5:20; Obad. 15; Zeph. 1:7, 14; Mal. 4:5; and in an equivalent form in Isa. 2:12; Ezek. 30:3; Zech. 14:1. It is referred to as *the day of the LORD's wrath* (Ezek. 7:19; Zeph. 2:2; cf. Zeph. 1:15, 18), the Lord's *day of vengeance* (Isa. 34:8; Jer. 46:10; cf. Isa. 61:2; 63:4), and *of trampling and tumult* (Isa. 22:5). Sometimes it is referred to simply as *the day* (Lam. 1:21; Ezek. 7:7) or *that day* (Isa. 2:11; cf. 24:21; 27:1). For more detailed analysis, see Cerny, *Day of Yahweh*, pp. 17–21.

32. E.g. Isa. 13:4–5; 34:1–6; 63:1–6; Jer. 46:10; Ezek. 13:5; 30:3–4; Joel 2:11; Obad. 1; Zeph. 1:16; Zech. 14:3. Eichrodt describes it as a day when 'the nations as far as the ends of the earth would be crushed before his onslaught, and with them their gods would topple from their thrones, that Israel's God might ascend the throne of the universe alone' (*Theology*, 1:459–462 [460]); see also Dyrness, *Themes*, pp. 227–228; Goldingay, *OT Theology*, 2:775–777, 807–818; Paul R. House, 'The Day of the Lord', in Hafemann and House, *Central Themes*, pp. 179–224; Preuss, *OT Theology*, 2:272–274; von Rad, *OT Theology*, 2:119–125; Rendtorff, *Hebrew Bible*, pp. 701–705.

33. Mowinckel, *He that Cometh*, pp. 132–133, 138–143; see also Eichrodt, *Theology*, 1:127–128.

34. See above, p. 227.

at his mighty works on behalf of his people and anticipated his future victory and coming in glory and power,[35] and that would have helped to keep hope alive during times of national crisis. It is likely that such an event would have recalled traditions associated with the exodus as the time when God took Israel as his own people,[36] and that the *yôm yhwh* is to be linked with the battles associated with the exodus and conquest, when God fought on behalf of his people (e.g. Exod. 15:2–3; Judg. 5:4–5). The Day of the Lord is closely linked too with the description of divine theophany, where God appears in awesome power, often accompanied by earthquake, storm and upheaval in the natural order (e.g. Ps. 18:7–19; Hab. 3:2–15).

At first these elements were probably associated with the hope of deliverance from a particular threat. The people trusted that God, who had fought for them in the past, would continue to fight on their behalf. The theophany in Judges 5:4–5 is associated with a particular battle; the believer who cries to God in Psalm 18 is expecting help in an immediate crisis; Habbakuk, in the face of a Babylonian invasion of Judah, is praying for God to intervene soon (Hab. 3:2). In time, the hope that God would deliver his people from a particular threat developed into the eschatological belief that God would intervene, finally, to remove every threat and establish a new age of peace and prosperity. It is unclear when this hope took on an eschatological character, though by the eighth century it was probably clear that only dramatic divine intervention could safeguard Israel's future as a nation.

Chaoskampf

Also closely linked with Yahweh's theophany are allusions to his victory over the monsters of primeval chaos.[37] As we have seen, this was first brought into history and applied to God's victory over Israel's political enemies; it was then reapplied to a cosmic future battle, when God would, again, defeat all that opposed him and bring about a new creation. The primordial battle that resulted in creation and the defeat of rebellious and chaotic elements will be

---

35. The idea that Amos 5:18 refers to a particular festival is supported by e.g. Clements (*Prophecy and Covenant*, pp. 107–109), Lindblom (*Prophecy*, pp. 317–318) and Vriezen ('Prophecy and Eschatology', p. 204); cf. Preuss, *OT Theology*, 2:273.

36. Focus on the Ark suggests links with the Davidic covenant, and the idea of a future king like David had an important place in Israel's future hope (see the discussion below of the Messiah). Probably more significantly, in this context, the Ark recalls God's presence with his people during the exodus and conquest.

37. See above, pp. 127–130.

repeated in the final overthrow of evil and the promise of God's new world order.

Zion tradition[38]

The ideology surrounding the city of Jerusalem was a basis for national hope. The presence of the Ark and the building of the temple as God's dwelling place emphasized his presence among his people. When the temple was dedicated, God's glory filled it, as it had filled the tabernacle at Sinai, and other traditions formerly associated with Sinai were also connected with Zion.[39] The city's special place in the purposes of God is expressed in the 'hymns of Zion' (Pss 46; 48; 76), and its importance gave rise to what is known as *Zion tradition*. This has three main elements: (1) Zion (as the successor to Sinai) is the dwelling place of God, (2) Zion is the place from which God reigns, together with his chosen king, and (3) Zion can therefore expect to receive special help and protection from God. An important aspect of this is the description of God's conflict with nations that attack Jerusalem, and their defeat at the gates of the city. So, for example, in Isaiah 29:4–8 God comes with the power of the storm, with earthquake, wind and fire, to defeat the enemies that surround Jerusalem and drive them away like chaff.

---

38. See e.g. B. W. Anderson, *Contours*, pp. 195–199, 224–236; Bright, *Covenant*, pp. 49–77; Brueggemann, *Theology*, pp. 654–662; Ronald E. Clements, *Isaiah and the Deliverance of Jerusalem*, JSOTSup 13 (Sheffield: JSOT Press, 1984), pp. 28–51, 72–90; B. S. Childs, *Isaiah and the Assyrian Crisis*, SBT 2.3 (London: SCM, 1967); Goldingay, *OT Theology*, 2:449–476; John H. Hayes, 'The Tradition of Zion's Inviolability', *JBL* 82 (1963), pp. 419–426; Peter J. Leithart, 'Where Was Ancient Zion?', *TynBul* 53.3 (1992), pp. 161–175; Levenson, *Sinai and Zion*, pp. 89–184; Gowan, *Eschatology*, pp. 4–20; J. Gordon McConville, 'Jerusalem in the Old Testament', in P. W. L. Walker (ed.), *Jerusalem Past and Present in the Purposes of God* (Cambridge: Tyndale House, 1992), pp. 21–51; Ben C. Ollenburger, *Zion, the City of the Great King: A Theological Symbol of the Jerusalem Cult*, JSOTSup 41 (Sheffield: Sheffield Academic Press, 1987), pp. 15–22, 107–129; Preuss, *OT Theology*, 2:39–51; von Rad, *OT Theology*, 1:46–48; Rendtorff, *Hebrew Bible*, pp. 575–585; Robin L. Routledge, 'The Siege and Deliverance of the City of David in Isaiah 29:1–8', *TynBul* 43.1 (1992), pp. 181–190; John T. Strong, 'Zion: Theology of', in *NIDOTTE* 4:1314–1321.

39. McConville concludes that 'Jerusalem succeeds Sinai as the symbol of Israel's status as the special people of God' ('Jerusalem in the OT', in Walker, *Jerusalem*, p. 25); see also Levenson, *Sinai and Zion*.

Zion tradition sometimes uses mythological imagery (e.g. Ps. 46; Isa. 17:12–14). References to wind and storm are also reminiscent of the Ugaritic myth where victory over the chaos monsters is won by the storm god, Baal. As we have seen, it is also linked with the election of the Davidic king who reigned on God's behalf and who, as God's adopted son, entered into an inheritance that included kingship over the whole world (Ps. 2:8–9; cf. 72:8). Like the Day of the Lord, it may also be rooted in exodus and conquest traditions (e.g. Exod. 15:17–18).

The 'conflict with the nations' motif gave confidence in the face of particular crises. Isaiah appears to base hope for the deliverance of Jerusalem from the Assyrians on the special relationship between God and David (e.g. Isa. 37:35). Clements argues that Zion Tradition was based on a development of Isaiah's message by Josianic redactors in the light of the events of 701 BC;[40] however, while it is likely that Isaiah's preaching and the deliverance of the city in 701 BC helped to shape the doctrine, it is less likely that it originated with those who interpreted Isaiah's message.[41]

Zion tradition is also applied to the eschatological future. The prophecy against Gog (Ezek. 38 – 39) describes hordes of nations gathering against God's people. God's coming to fight for his people will be accompanied by earthquake, plague and storm. In Zechariah 14:1–15 we also have a description of Yahweh as he comes to fight against the nations that surround Jerusalem. His coming will be accompanied by plague (14:12–15; cf. Ezek. 38:22; Hab. 3:5) and upheaval in the natural order (14:4, 6–7). In this passage Zion tradition is also linked with the Day of the Lord (14:1).

The era of salvation
Spiritual rebirth
As we have seen, the prophets regarded the exile as a necessity for the future of the nation. There was a need to sweep away all false hopes. The exile was the death from which the true nation of Israel could be reborn; it was a refining that would bring forth a chastened, faithful remnant. While it is likely

---

40. Clements argues that the account of the deliverance of Jerusalem was a reflection on earlier events, rather than an accurate account of what took place (*Deliverance of Jerusalem*, pp. 84–85); for a defence of the historicity of the biblical narrative, see Routledge, 'Siege'; see also Richard S. Hess, 'Hezekiah and Sennacherib in 2 Kings 18–20', in Hess and Wenham, *Zion*, pp. 23–41.

41. Zion tradition appears to be applied to the defeat of Assyria in Isa. 8:9–10; 10:28–34; 14:24–27; 17:12–14; 31:4–5.

that all the exiles wanted was to go home, the prophets announced that God would do more, and would bring about the spiritual as well as political renewal of the nation (e.g. Ezek. 40 – 48; Jer. 31). Thus the exile and the promised return became a springboard for hope. The message of Deutero-Isaiah had a particular relevance to the exiles in Babylon. It expresses confidence in God as the Lord of history (e.g. Isa. 45:21; 46:10); he is exalted above the worthless gods of the nations (e.g. Isa. 44:9–20; 46:1–7); and his power will be demonstrated in the coming deliverance and vindication of his people (e.g. Isa. 41:21–29; 43:8–13; 46:9–11). This deliverance is described as a second exodus (e.g. Isa. 43:16–17; 48:20–21), which like the first would mark the beginning of a new era in the life of the nation and in its relationship with God and with the world. The 'new thing' God is doing includes the creation of *new heavens and a new earth* (Isa. 65:17) and the inauguration of a kingdom of righteousness and peace (Isa. 65:20–25; cf. 11:6–9), in which a renewed and restored Jerusalem will reflect God's glory to the rest of the world (Isa. 60:1–3).

The kingdom of God[42]

The coming age will be characterized by the establishment of God's reign over the whole earth. It will include God's victory over his enemies. It will include too the restoration of Israel, and particularly Jerusalem. God will gather the scattered exiles (e.g. Isa. 11:11–12; Jer. 3:14–18; Ezek. 11:16–17; 28:25). Jerusalem will be rebuilt and, following the spiritual renewal of the people (e.g. Isa. 1:25–26; 33:5; Ezek. 11:17–20; Hos. 2:16–17), will be given prominence among the nations as the centre of God's kingdom (e.g. Isa. 2:2–4; 24:21–23; 25:6–8; Zech. 8:1–8; 14:9–21). Closely linked with the reign of God is the restoration of the throne of David and the expectation of a kingdom of righteousness and peace under the Davidic Messiah (e.g. Isa. 9:6–7; 11:1–9; Jer. 30:9; Ezek. 34:23–24; Amos 9:11). This peaceful kingdom is portrayed as a return to Eden (e.g. Isa. 51:3), evident in passages that describe the harmony within nature that will accompany the new age (e.g. Isa. 11:6–9; 65:20–25; Hos. 2:18) and the overflowing fruitfulness of the land (e.g. Isa. 35; 41:18; Ezek. 47:7–12; Joel 3:18). It may be implicit too in passages that liken Israel's restoration to a new creation (e.g. Isa. 40:26–31; 41:18–20).

---

42. See e.g. George R. Beasley-Murray, *Jesus and the Kingdom of God* (Grand Rapids: Eerdmans; Carlisle: Paternoster, 1986), pp. 3–25; Bright, *Kingdom*; Vriezen, *Outline*, pp. 350–352.

Interpreting Israel's future hope

The main concern of the OT is to emphasize the certainty of God's kingdom, rather than give a detailed description of it. The description is given in earthly terms. God's kingdom will come by direct divine intervention, and will mark the end of the present age and the start of a new era. In that sense it is eschatological. But the new age is viewed in similar terms to what has gone before. Politically and militarily Israel can never recover the greatness of David's empire, so God must intervene, but the result of that intervention is political restoration. The people will be renewed spiritually, but the result will be to worship God, as before, through festivals and sacrifices (e.g. Isa. 19:21; 33:20; 56:6–7; 66:23; Zech. 14:16. The overflowing blessings associated with the new age are described in terms of the fruitfulness of the land and material prosperity (Joel 2:19–32; Amos 9:13–15; Mic. 4:4; Zech. 8:12–13). The physical character of this kingdom is clearly seen in passages such as Isaiah 11:6–9 and 65:17–25.

But how far are these to be taken as literal descriptions of the age to come, and how far are they to be interpreted figuratively or symbolically? Some link the OT pictures of an earthly kingdom with Christ's millennial reign (see also Rev. 20:2–6).[43] This is often linked too with the idea of a final battle with the nations outside Jerusalem, and of a restored and rebuilt Jerusalem standing at the centre of Christ's world kingdom. The belief in a preliminary messianic kingdom was common in first-century Judaism,[44] but it is not found in the OT. There is no suggestion there of a two-phase salvation. According to the OT writers, God will establish his kingdom, and that kingdom will last for ever. The kingdom is described in earthly terms, and elements within it may seem to fall short of the eternal state described in the NT, but there is no sense that this is a temporary earthly kingdom that will be replaced by an eternal, heavenly one.

The OT points to the glorious future God has prepared for his people, using language and imagery appropriate to those who first announced and received the message. The world view of much of the OT focuses on the physical world, and so future hope is also portrayed in those terms. To describe the overflowing blessings of the coming age to a largely agricultural community, the prophets talk in terms of an abundant harvest. To give assurance to those

---

43. E.g. Wayne Grudem, *Systematic Theology: An Introduction to Biblical Doctrine* (Leicester: IVP; Grand Rapids, 1994), pp. 1127–1130.
44. See e.g. D. S. Russell, *The Method and Message of Jewish Apocalyptic*, OTL (London: SCM, 1964), pp. 291–297, 334.

who for most of their lives have experienced oppression and injustice, they emphasize God's victory over attacking nations, and future freedom and security. To describe restoration, they talk about the reversal of the tragedies the people have suffered, such as the return of exiles and the rebuilding and future exaltation of Jerusalem. To describe the spiritual renewal of the nation, they again use familiar ideas, and talk about a purified and restored temple, about sacrifices offered sincerely and the meaningful celebration of festivals. This principle applies too to the idea of a final battle against the nations. This eschatological motif draws on existing images and traditions, such as the Day of the Lord, *Chaoskampf* and Zion tradition. For people born in the midst of conflict with the nations, whose greatest days had come through victories over the nations, and who, through dark days of defeat and oppression by the nations, looked for those days of victory to come again, God's battle with and defeat of the nations was an obvious and appropriate way to express their hope of final vindication.

The view of the future is different, though, for those whose world view is shaped by the additional revelation of the NT: who see Christ's death and resurrection as the basis of victory over the power of evil and who view salvation and God's eternal kingdom as spiritual rather than earthly realities. As we interpret the OT hope from a NT perspective, we need to look at the underlying, rather than the literal, meaning of these images. The principles underlying the OT description of future hope include God's final victory over the powers of evil, the establishment of his reign and authority over the whole of creation, the salvation and vindication of his people, and the inauguration of a new age of peace and prosperity. To be meaningful to people in OT times, that vision took a particular form. To say that things may not look quite like that when the time comes is not to say that the OT writers were mistaken, or that their hopes have failed. The divine promise will be fulfilled – but in ways that go far beyond what the people then could have expected or expressed.

Messianic expectation

The Messiah[45]

The term 'Messiah' as an official title is not found in the OT.[46] It may be moving towards its later, more technical, sense in Daniel 9:25–26, where

---

45. See also e.g. B. W. Anderson, *Living World*, pp. 230–234; J. Becker, *Messianic Expectation in the Old Testament* (Edinburgh: T. & T. Clark, 1980); Bright, *Covenant*,

'Anointed One' is generally taken to refer to some future historical figure, though, who that is or whether the verses refer to one messianic figure or two, is unclear. Elsewhere the term refers to historical individuals (e.g. 1 Sam. 2:10, 35; 24:6, 10; 26:9, 11; Ps. 2:2; Isa. 45:1). The word is not used in the OT to refer to an eschatological figure associated with the kingdom of God.

Mowinckel maintains that the Messiah is a truly eschatological figure.[47] With the fall of the monarchy and of the state it became clear that Israel's fortunes could not be restored within the present world order, and this led to the eschatological hope of a new order, presided over by the messianic king. However, according to Bright, there is the beginning of messianic hope in the eighth-century prophecy of Isaiah, in whose 'royal redeemer figure . . . we have the first appearance of what was later to become the figure of the hoped

---

Brueggemann, *Theology*, pp. 616–621; Childs, *Biblical Theology* (1992), pp. 453–456; *OT Theology*, pp. 119–120; Ronald E. Clements, 'The Messianic Hope in the Old Testament', *JSOT* 43 (1989), pp. 3–19; Dyrness, *Themes*, pp. 233–234; Eichrodt, *Theology*, 1:482–486; Joseph A. Fitzmyer, *The One Who Is to Come* (Grand Rapids: Eerdmans, 2007); Goldingay, *OT Theology*, 2:476–504; Gowan, *Eschatology*, pp. 32–42; House, *OT Theology*, pp. 242–243, 388–390 (and *passim*); Jacob, *Theology*, pp. 327–344; Walter C. Kaiser, Jr., *The Messiah in the Old Testament*, Studies in Old Testament Biblical Theology (Grand Rapids: Zondervan, 1995); J. A. Motyer and R. T. France, 'Messiah', in *IBD* 2:987–995 (987–994); Mowinckel, *He that Cometh*; Clements, *OT Theology*, pp. 149–154; Stanley E. Porter (ed.), *The Messiah in the Old and New Testaments*, McMaster New Testament Studies (Grand Rapids: Eerdmans, 2007); Preuss, *OT Theology*, 2:34–38; Rendtorff, *Hebrew Bible*, pp. 691–696; Helmer Ringgren, *The Messiah in the Old Testament*, SBT 18 (London: SCM, 1956); Satterthwaite, Hess and Wenham, *Lord's Anointed*; LaSor, Hubbard and Bush, *OT Survey*, pp. 688–694; H. G. M. Williamson, *Variations on a Theme: King, Messiah and Servant in the Book of Isaiah*, Didsbury Lectures (Carlisle: Paternoster, 1998).

46. See e.g. J. Gordon McConville, 'Messianic Interpretation of the Old Testament in Modern Context', in Satterthwaite, Hess and Wenham, *Lord's Anointed*, pp. 1–17; he notes that 'common to all modern treatments of the idea of Messiah in the Old Testament is the recognition that it cannot be tied to the occurrence of the term *māšîaḥ* ("anointed one"), which is not used in its later technical sense in the Old Testament' (p. 2); see also Fitzmyer, *The One*, pp. 1–25; Martin J. Selman, 'Messianic Mysteries', in Satterthwaite, Hess and Wenham, *Lord's Anointed*, pp. 281–302 (284–285).

47. Mowinckel, *He that Cometh*, p. 3.

for Messiah'.[48] Motyer points out that it did not require the fall of the monarchy for people to be aware of its shortcomings and to hope for something better.[49] Even David fell short of the ideal of kingship, and no king after him met the expectations his reign raised. Mowinckel too notes that from early in the monarchy there was the hope that one day the ideal king would come to the throne, and this provided the basis for messianic faith. But while ever a historical king might fulfil the expectation, this hope was not eschatological and so, in his view, not messianic in the strict sense. There is little doubt that the growth of eschatology and messianic expectation was significantly influenced by the fall of the political establishment; however, we do not need to assume that it all dates from after that time.

The lack of direct references to the Messiah in the OT and the lack of consensus about which texts are messianic make any study of the idea subjective. Some adopt a very broad definition: a passage is messianic if it can be interpreted as pointing forward to Jesus.[50] This might, however, result in imposing a messianic interpretation on OT texts not meant to be taken that way. It also presents a one-dimensional picture of Israel's future hope. Jesus fulfils the eschatological expectations of the OT, but not all of those expectations are linked with his role as Messiah, who is to be seen, primarily, as a Davidic ruler, associated with the era of salvation.[51] At the other extreme, Mowinckel regards a passage as truly messianic only if its original outlook and intention were eschatological. Using Mowinckel's definition of eschatology, there are very few of these and all are, necessarily, post-exilic.[52] This approach is more acceptable

---

48. Bright, *Covenant*, p. 107.

49. Motyer and France, 'Messiah', in *IBD* 2:989.

50. This view is represented by e.g. G. van Groningen, *Messianic Revelation in the Old Testament* (Grand Rapids: Baker, 1990).

51. As noted above, Bright describes the Messiah as a 'royal redeemer figure' (*Covenant*, p. 107); similarly Richard Schultz, 'The King in the Book of Isaiah', in Satterthwaite, Hess and Wenham, *Lord's Anointed*, pp. 141–165, refers to a 'royal Saviour figure' (pp. 146–147); see also Wolter H. Rose, *Zemah and Zerubbabel: Messianic Expectations in the Early Post-Exilic Period*, JSOTSup 304 (Sheffield: Sheffield Academic Press, 2000), p. 23.

52. Mowinckel, *He that Cometh*, pp. 15–20. Fitzmyer takes a similar view, arguing that though the concept of a Messiah emerged out of the OT, it was not developed until the second century BC (*The One*). He rightly questions the too broad understanding of what is messianic and the tendency to impose a messianic reading on OT texts not intended to be read that way. However, he goes too far

if we adopt the wider definition of eschatology and include passages that refer to the coming era of salvation, though we must also allow that some originally non-messianic passages may be open to a messianic interpretation.

In addition, when we come to look at messianic expectation, we need to recognize that while the NT writers see Jesus as the fulfilment of the messianic hopes of the OT, that view is different from that of their Jewish contemporaries, who rejected Jesus in part because he did not conform to their ideas of what the expected Messiah should be. This suggests that the OT picture of the Messiah is, at best, ambiguous.[53]

The Messiah and David

Israel's messianic expectation is most closely associated with David, and the hope of a future Davidic king through whom the glory associated with David's reign would be restored. This was also related to the hope of the protection, deliverance and future exaltation of Jerusalem. God's promise to David in 2 Samuel 7:11b–16 is widely thought to be the foundation of Israel's messianic hope. That promise relates to David and, in connection with the building of the temple, to his immediate successor, Solomon; but it also anticipates an eternal dynastic succession.[54] We have noted already that the failure of the historical monarchy points to the need for a future, ideal ruler. The release of Jehoiachin from prison (2 Kgs 25:27–30) indicates that God has not

---

in insisting that the OT contains no strictly messianic texts (with the possible, arbitrary, exception of Dan. 12:25), and his arguments dismiss key texts too summarily.

53. See Selman, 'Messianic Mysteries', in Satterthwaite, Hess and Wenham, *Lord's Anointed*, pp. 281–302.

54. As we have seen, the promise to David of an offspring (*zera'*) from his own body (2 Sam. 7:12) echoes the promise to Abraham (Gen. 15:4; see also 22:18; 26:24; cf. Ps. 72:17). Alexander notes the significance of the term *zera'* in the book of Genesis, and identifies a line of seed from Adam, through Seth, Abraham and Judah, forming part of the ancestry of David and so of the Davidic Messiah ('Abraham Re-Assessed', in Hess, Satterthwaite and Wenham, *He Swore an Oath*, p. 25; 'Messianic Ideology', in Satterthwaite, Hess and Wenham, *Lord's Anointed*). He argues that the promise of an 'offspring' in Genesis 3:15, which has traditionally been regarded as a messianic text (see above, p. 149, n. 61), also needs to be set in this context ('Messianic Ideology', in Satterthwaite, Hess and Wenham, *Lord's Anointed*, pp. 27–32); he includes too the blessing of Judah (Gen. 49:8–12) in this discussion (pp. 32–37).

abandoned his promise to David.[55] However, the instruction to regard Jehoiachin *as if childless* (Jer. 22:30) might point to a deliberate discontinuity between the earthly line of David and the coming Davidic ruler.

The Davidic Messiah in Isaiah

The hope of an ideal future king descended from David is clearly expressed in the prophecy of Isaiah.[56] An important passage is Isaiah 9:2–7. Some see this as an accession oracle for a Davidic king (maybe Hezekiah or Josiah). However, the extravagant language and great claims made for this coming ruler suggest that the prophet is looking beyond the immediate context to one greater than Hezekiah or Josiah, in whom all the promises contained within the oracle will be fulfilled in a way they could never be through any historical monarch. In particular, the titles *mighty god* and *everlasting father* suggest divinity,[57] though this idea is not developed further. We should probably understand this passage against the background of the Assyrian invasions of 734–732 BC, which resulted in the annexation of a large part of Israel's territory, including Zebulun and Naphtali. Into that gloom the light of the coming Ruler shines, with the hope that, ultimately, all foreign domination will be brought to an end.

A second passage is Isaiah 11:1–9. This is frequently regarded as post-exilic, after the Davidic monarchy has been judged by God and deposed. However, the passage may also be seen against the background of Assyrian invasion that foreshadowed the more devastating judgment to come. That judgment, though, is not God's last word. Out of the 'stump' that remains of the royal house a new ruler will emerge; one anointed by God who will bring peace, righteousness and justice to the whole earth. The fact that this deliverer will

---

55. E.g. Carlson, *Chosen King*, pp. 263–264; cf. Isa. 9:7; 11:1; 16:5; Jer. 33:15, 20–22; Amos 9:11.

56. See e.g. Bright, *Covenant*, pp. 94–110; Goldingay, *OT Theology*, 2:478–484; Rendtorff, *Hebrew Bible*, pp. 175–178; Williamson, *Variations*, pp. 30–72.

57. Kaiser suggests that the title 'mighty god' (*'ēl gibbôr*) 'describes the king as the legitimate representative of God on earth' (*Isaiah 1–12*, p. 129; see also Smith, *Origins*, p. 159), and explains the only other occasion where the king is described as 'god' (Ps. 45:6) in the same way. However, *'ēl gibbôr* clearly refers to God in Isa. 10:21 (see also e.g. Neh. 9:32; Jer. 32:18). The title 'everlasting father' may also point to divine qualities: 'everlasting' can only properly be applied to God. See also John Goldingay, 'The Compound Name in Isaiah 9:5 (6)', *CBQ* 61.2 (1999), pp. 239–244; Selman, 'Messianic Mysteries', in Satterthwaite, Hess and Wenham, *Lord's Anointed*, pp. 292–293.

come from *the stump of Jesse* (v. 1), rather than from the line of David, suggests that Isaiah is looking forward to a second David, who will restore the glories of the original Davidic empire.

Some also see a link between the Davidic Messiah and the Immanuel prophecy (Isa. 7:14).[58] Two things have contributed most to this: first, the description of the young mother in the verse as a 'virgin', and second, its application by Matthew to the virgin birth of Jesus (Matt. 1:23). There is, though, doubt about whether 'virgin' is an accurate translation of the Hebrew word *'almâ*;[59] at the very least, the term is ambiguous, suggesting that a virgin birth is not the main issue for Isaiah.[60] The text itself does not require us to look beyond the immediate situation for its fulfilment. The sign of Immanuel had a contemporary relevance; it related to the crisis Ahaz and Judah were facing, and so is not strictly messianic. It has been suggested that Immanuel might be a royal child, indicating a direct link with the Davidic monarchy, though there are problems with that interpretation.[61] The name Immanuel does, though,

---

58. For further discussion, see e.g. R. E. Clements, 'The Immanuel Prophecy of Isaiah 7:10–17 and its Messianic Interpretation', in *Old Testament Prophecy: From Oracles to Canon* (Louisville: Westminster John Knox, 1996), pp. 65–77; E. Hammershaimb, 'The Immanuel Sign', *ST* 3 (1949), pp. 124–142; W. McKane, 'The Interpretation of Isaiah VII 14–25', *VT* 17 (1967), pp. 208–219; Motyer, *The Prophecy of Isaiah*, pp. 84–85; Jan Bergman, Helmer Ringgren and M. Tsevat et al., '*bĕtûlâ*, etc.', in *TDOT* 2:338–343; John H. Walton, '*bĕtûlâ*', '*alûmîm*', in *NIDOTTE* 1:781–784; 3:415–419; Gordon J. Wenham, 'Betulah: "A Girl of Marriageable Age"', *VT* 22 (1972), pp. 326–348; Williamson, *Variations*, pp. 73–112; Herbert Martin Wolf, 'A Solution to the Immanuel Prophecy in Isaiah 7:14–8:22', *JBL* 91 (1972), pp. 449–456; E. J. Young, 'Immanuel', in *IBD* 2:685–686.

59. This refers more generally to a young woman (maybe one who has not borne children); some argue that Isaiah would have used the word *bĕtûlâ*, which can specifically denote a 'virgin' if that was what he wanted to say.

60. Isaiah could have made the matter unambiguous, as in e.g. Gen. 19:8, 24:16 and Judg. 21:12, which note that the young women in question have not slept with a man. Though probably not the main emphasis in Isa. 7:14, the ambiguity does leave open the deeper significance attached to the verse in Matt. 1:23.

61. Hezekiah is the most likely candidate; see e.g. Christopher R. Seitz, *Isaiah 1–39*, Interpretation (Louisville: John Knox, 1993), pp. 60–75, though this has chronological difficulties. Another possibility is to identify Immanuel with Isaiah's son, *Maher-Shalal-Hash-Baz* (Isa. 8:3), especially in the light of the similar theological significance attached to the children (Isa. 7:16; cf. 8:4).

recall the refrain of Psalm 46, which is significant in the Zion tradition and so is closely related to God's promises to David.

Royal psalms

Psalms 2 and 110 (and maybe also Pss 72 and 101) are thought to have been composed for a particular king's coronation. Again, though, their extravagant language has led to their also being interpreted messianically. The expectations are, at best, only partly fulfilled by the kings of Israel and Judah, and even David himself does not match up to them. The people soon recognized the shortcomings of the monarchy, and these coronation hymns contain an implicit longing for the ideal ruler who would be all David had been, and more. After the fall of the monarchy, their focus shifted entirely to the future, and the term 'Messiah' (anointed), previously applied to the Davidic king, took on an eschatological dimension.[62] The extent of the king's reign, *from sea to sea / and from the River to the ends of the earth* (Ps. 72:8), is taken up in Zechariah's description of the coming king (Zech. 9:9–10), which is generally taken to refer to the Messiah.

The Branch

In Isaiah 11:1 the messianic king is referred to as *a Branch* (*nēṣer*) from the roots of Jesse.[63] The idea is of life emerging from something that seemed to have no future, in this case the Davidic monarchy, though the same picture is also applied to the nation as a whole. The Messiah will bring life and hope to a people familiar with death and despair. Another Hebrew word, *ṣemaḥ* (again translated *Branch*), is also used to describe the coming king (Jer. 23:5; 33:15; Zech. 3:8; 6:12; and probably also Isa. 4:2). Jeremiah links this title directly with David, and there is an indirect link in Zechariah 6:12–13, where the *ṣemaḥ* is associated with rebuilding the temple. There may be a further indi-

---

62. Some see the dissonance between expectation and reality in the royal psalms as a key factor in the development of Israel's messianic hope; see further e.g. Craigie, *Psalms 1–50*, p. 68; J. Day, *Psalms*, OTG (Sheffield: Sheffield Academic Press, 1992), p. 97; John I. Durham, 'The King as "Messiah" in the Psalms', *RevExp* 81.3 (1984), pp. 425–435; Tremper Longman III, 'The Messiah: Explorations in the Law and Writings', in Porter, *Messiah*, pp. 13–34 (17–20); Mowinckel, *He that Cometh*, pp. 96–102; Preuss, *OT Theology*, 2:31–36; Ringgren, *Messiah*, pp. 11–24.

63. Some see a link between *nēṣer* and Matthew's comment that Jesus *fulfilled what was said through the prophets: 'He will be called a Nazarene'* (Matt. 2:23).

cation of the divinity of this figure in the designation *the LORD Our Righteousness* (Jer. 23:6).[64]

The *ṣemaḥ* is also linked with the priesthood. Priests, as well as kings, were anointed leaders, and also feature (though less prominently) in Israel's messianic expectation. In Jeremiah 33:14–22 the promise of the Messiah is seen as the fulfilment both of the covenant with David and the covenant with the Levites (v. 21). In Zechariah 3:8–9 the Branch is associated with the (priestly) work of taking away sin (see also Isa. 4:2–4). In Zechariah 6:12–13 the link is even clearer: *the Branch . . . will be a priest on his throne*, thus unifying the offices of king and priest (see also Ps. 110:4).[65] As we have seen, there was a link between king and cult going back to David. David brought the two offices closer together than any of his successors; in the Messiah they will be united.

Another David

As we have noted, the reference to the *stump of Jesse* (Isa. 11:1) suggests that the Messiah will be a second David; this is implied too by Micah 5:2, which indicates that Bethlehem, David's birthplace, will also be the place of origin of the coming king. Other passages refer to a 'David of the future' (Jer. 30:9; Ezek. 34:23–24; 37:24; Hos. 3:5). They point to the reunification of God's people under a future Davidic king, and emphasize the close relationship between the coming king and God. This is especially clear in Ezekiel 34, where God says that he will be the shepherd of his people (vv. 11–22) and will appoint his servant David to be shepherd over them (v. 23; Ezek. 37:24). This indicates that the coming king will reign and care for the people on behalf of Yahweh as his earthly representative. David was taken from shepherding his father's flock to be the shepherd of God's flock (Ps. 78:71; 2 Sam. 5:2). Subsequent rulers had failed in their responsibility (Ezek. 34:1–10), but in the coming days another David will be appointed to fulfil that calling. There is a further reference to God's shepherd in Zechariah 13:7 (see also Zech. 11:4–17), though the writer appears to have chosen not to link this directly with David.

The Messiah and the kingdom

Our understanding of the Messiah in the OT is as a descendant of David who will preside over the coming era of salvation. However, several passages refer

---

64. See Selman, 'Messianic Mysteries', in Satterthwaite, Hess and Wenham, *Lord's Anointed*, pp. 293–294.

65. See e.g. Goldingay, *OT Theology*, 2:491–504; Selman, 'Messianic Mysteries', in Satterthwaite, Hess and Wenham, *Lord's Anointed*, pp. 295–297.

to God's rule in the coming kingdom – but without mentioning the Messiah (e.g. Isa. 2:2–4; 24:23; 33:22; 65:17–25; Zech. 14:1–9). Mowinckel suggests that Israel's future hope had two aspects: one religious, which focused primarily on God's rule; the other political, which included the restoration of the Davidic monarchy. Early messianic expectation grew out of this political aspect, and where the emphasis is on political restoration, the Messiah is prominent. Where the emphasis is, instead, on the religious and otherworldly aspect of Israel's future hope, the focus is on Yahweh.[66] We can agree that the context is important. Thus the portrayal of the kingdom in Isaiah 11:1–9, set against the background of a political crisis, focuses on the Davidic king; while the similar portrayal in Isaiah 65:17–25, which quotes from the earlier passage, focuses on new creation – and there is no reference to the Messiah.[67] The way older traditions are used may also influence the way the kingdom is depicted. Thus the language and imagery of Zechariah 14:1–9 recall earlier traditions of Yahweh coming to deliver his people. Where Zion in the future kingdom is seen as the successor of Sinai (e.g. Isa. 2:2–4; 24:23), again it is more appropriate to focus on Yahweh. The difference, though, is one of emphasis; there is no fundamental distinction between the rule of Yahweh and the reign of his chosen king.

The Messiah will fulfil the kingly ideal, and to that extent will be different from all other kings of Israel or Judah. His role, though, will be similar. Even after the inception of the monarchy it was recognized that God was the true king of his people. Israel's kings exercised authority on his behalf; through them his kingship was worked out in the everyday life of the nation. In the coming age, when God establishes his rule over the whole earth, the Messiah will reign on his behalf and preside over the administration of judgment and salvation in the new age.[68] Thus both God, and the Messiah as his representative, can properly be described as kings. The fact that it is possible to describe

---

66. In such circumstances, according to Mowinckel, 'the ideal, earthly king of David's line recedes into the background behind Yahweh himself' (*He that Cometh*, p. 172); see also Lindblom, *Prophecy*, pp. 393–397. Mowinckel suggests that the Messiah re-emerges, with a different character, in later Judaism and the apocalyptic writings.

67. The king in this section of the book is Yahweh (e.g. Isa. 66:1). See Schultz, 'The King', in Satterthwaite, Hess and Wenham, *Lord's Anointed*, pp. 160–165.

68. In the OT the Messiah is not primarily a military figure. Yahweh will come to establish the kingdom; the Messiah will administer justice and righteousness within it. See e.g. Schultz, 'The King', in Satterthwaite, Hess and Wenham, *Lord's Anointed*, p. 152; Beasley-Murray, *Jesus*, p. 22; Mowinckel, *He that Cometh*, pp. 155, 173. There appears to have been a major shift in emphasis between the testaments, maybe

the coming era of salvation without mention of the Messiah does indicate, however, that his role is not as prominent in the future hope of the OT as is sometimes thought. There, the main focus is on the coming of God to save and reign over his people.

The Son of Man[69]

Another figure associated with Israel's eschatological hope is the *one like a Son of Man* (Dan. 7:13). The expression means 'one like a human being', and contrasts with the portrayal of successive world empires, and particularly the last, as beasts (Dan. 7:3–7). The imagery in this passage is probably drawn from ANE mythology. The picture of beasts coming up out of the sea recalls the chaotic waters defeated at creation, and points to God's final overthrow of the powers of evil and the establishment of his new world order. There are some parallels with the Canaanite myth 'Baal and the Sea'.[70] In this myth the sea god, Yam, challenges the gods, presided over by El, who is described in terms similar to Daniel's Ancient of Days.[71] In the divine assembly Baal, the 'rider on the clouds', is promised an eternal kingdom, which, after defeating Yam, he duly receives.[72]

---

related to a worsening political crisis and renewed emphasis on the Messiah reigning over an earthly kingdom, so that by the NT period there was considerable focus on the Messiah as a military leader.

69. See Joyce G. Baldwin, *Daniel*, TOTC (Leicester: IVP, 1978), pp. 148–154; Beasley-Murray, *Jesus*, pp. 26–35; Eichrodt, *Theology*, 1:487–488; John Goldingay, *Daniel*, WBC 30 (Milton Keynes: Word, 1987); House, *OT Theology*, pp. 504–511; Ernest Lucas, *Daniel*, AOTC (Leicester: IVP, 2002); Motyer, 'Messiah', in *IBD* 2:993; Mowinckel, *He that Cometh*, pp. 346–450; Norman Porteous, *Daniel*, OTL (London: SCM, 1965), pp. 95–117; Russell, *Method and Message*, pp. 324–352.

70. Arnold and Beyer, *Readings*, pp. 50–62; Ginsberg, 'Ugaritic Myths', in *ANET*, pp. 129–155; Gray, 'Texts from Ras Shamra', in *DOTT*, pp. 129–133. There may also be points of contact with the Babylonian *Enuma Elish*, though the Ugaritic parallels are more direct. It needs to be stressed, however, that mythological elements have been transformed and pressed into the service of Yahwistic monotheism. See also Lucas, *Daniel*, pp. 167–176; Tremper Longman III, *Daniel*, NIVAC (Grand Rapids: Zondervan, 1999), pp. 179–186.

71. E.g. El is described as grey haired and grey bearded, and is given the title 'father of years'.

72. In other OT allusions to Ugaritic myths Yahweh combines attributes of El and Baal; here, though, the writer keeps them separate, and uses the myth to point

In Daniel's vision the 'son of man' is a heavenly being. He has the appearance of being human, and may exhibit human characteristics,[73] but the reference to his *riding on the clouds* links him closely with Yahweh.[74] He is thus Yahweh's representative. It is unclear from the passage whether this figure is responsible for defeating the monster from the sea; though, from the mythological parallels and the fact that in other OT passages when Yahweh comes with the clouds it is to bring judgment and/or deliverance, it seems likely.[75]

In the interpretation of the vision, *the one like a son of man* (7:13) is replaced with *the saints of the Most High* (7:18).[76] This might suggest that the 'son of man' symbolizes the people of God in the same way the beasts symbolize world empires,[77] or, perhaps more likely, that he is the heavenly representative of God's people, whose victory and exaltation secures their release from oppressive rule and their participation in the kingdom of God.

As a heavenly being, the *one like a son of man* is different from the Davidic Messiah, who is generally portrayed as having an earthly origin. However, there are also important points of contact. Both figures represent God, are linked with the inauguration of God's kingdom, and are given eternal and universal dominion. Thus, though they may have different origins and represent different aspects of Israel's eschatological hope, we may reasonably conclude

---

Footnote 72 (*continued*)

> to a heavenly figure, alongside Yahweh, who will play a part in the final overthrow of evil and the establishment of his kingdom.

73. As noted, this is in contrast to the beastlike character of the earthly kingdoms; see e.g. Goldingay, *OT Theology*, 2:776; Preuss, *OT Theology*, 2:281.

74. Elsewhere a similar description is applied to Yahweh (e.g. Deut. 33:26; Pss 18:9–11; 68:4; 104:3). In these cases it points to God coming from heaven to effect judgment or deliverance, and though the general view is that the *one like a son of man* ascends into the presence of the Ancient of Days, it is perhaps better to see him too coming from heaven; see Beasley-Murray, *Jesus*, pp. 28–29; Goldingay, *Daniel*, p. 167; Preuss, *OT Theology*, 2:281.

75. See e.g. Beasley-Murray, *Jesus*, pp. 27–29; however, see Goldingay, *Daniel*, p. 153.

76. For further discussion of the identity of the 'saints' (literally 'holy ones'), see e.g. Baldwin, *Daniel*, pp. 150–152; Beasley-Murray, *Jesus*, pp. 29–33; Goldingay, *Daniel*, pp. 176–178; Lucas, *Daniel*, pp. 191–192; Porteous, *Daniel*, pp. 115–116.

77. However, while the text makes it clear that *the four great beasts are four kingdoms*, it does not state a similar equivalence between the *one like a son of man* and the *saints of the Most High*.

that there is a correspondence between them,[78] and both are fulfilled in Jesus Christ.[79]

The Servant of the Lord[80]

Another important figure linked with Israel's future hope is the *Servant of the*

---

78. According to von Rad, 'the Son of Man . . . is initially presented as a Messianic figure in the wider sense of the term' (*OT Theology*, 2:312); see also e.g. Beasley-Murray, *Jesus*, pp. 33, 35; House, *OT Theology*, pp. 505–507, 508–509.

79. There is debate about whether 'Son of Man' was recognized as a messianic title at the time of Jesus, and so about the significance of Jesus' use of the expression to refer to himself (see e.g. D. A. Carson, *EBC*, 8:209–213; O. Michel et al., 'Son, Son of God, Son of Man, etc.', in *DNTT* 3:607–668 (613–634). Karl A. Kuhn, 'The "One Like a Son of Man" Becomes the "Son of God"', *CBQ* 69.1 (2007), pp. 22–42, notes similarities between a figure in the Qumran text 4Q246 (the *Aramaic Apocalypse*) who is designated 'son of the Most High' and 'Son of God', and is probably to be understood as the Davidic Messiah, with the 'Son of Man' in Daniel 7. This recasting of Daniel's vision indicates that the Son of Man was viewed as a messianic figure before the NT period – though maybe only in limited circles; see also Mowinckel, *He that Cometh*, pp. 333–336, 360–370; Russell, *Method and Message*, pp. 331–340. Where the expression did not have an eschatological significance it might emphasize humanity. Carson suggests that this ambiguity made it a useful expression for Jesus to use – pointing to his humanity and his messiahship, though without the misunderstanding that surrounded the latter term.

80. See e.g. B. W. Anderson, *Living World*, pp. 488–502; Stephen G. Dempster, 'The Servant of the Lord', in Hafemann and House, *Central Themes*, pp. 128–178; John Goldingay, *God's Prophet, God's Servant* (Exeter: Paternoster, 1984); *OT Theology*, 2:221–228, 410–415, 744–746; House, *OT Theology*, pp. 286–293; Gordon P. Hugenberger, 'The Servant of the Lord in the "Servant Songs" of Isaiah: A Second Moses Figure', in Satterthwaite, Hess and Wenham, *Lord's Anointed*, pp. 105–140; Lindblom, *Prophecy*, pp. 267–270; McComiskey, *Covenants*, pp. 31–33; Christopher R. North, *The Suffering Servant in Deutero-Isaiah* (Oxford: Oxford University Press, 1948); H. M. Orlinsky, 'The So-Called "Servant of the Lord" and "Suffering Servant" in Second Isaiah', in H. M. Orlinsky and N. H. Snaith, *Studies in the Second Part of the Book of Isaiah*, VTSup 14 (Leiden: Brill, 1967), p. 157; Rendtorff, *Hebrew Bible*, pp. 189–192; Ringgren, *Messiah*, pp. 39–53; H. H. Rowley, *The Servant of the Lord and Other Essays on the Old Testament* (Oxford: Blackwell, 1965), pp. 3–88; N. H. Snaith, 'The Servant of the Lord in Deutero-Isaiah', in H. H. Rowley (ed.), *Studies in Old Testament Prophecy: Presented to Professor Theodore H. Robinson* (Edinburgh: T. & T. Clark, 1950), pp. 187–200; 'Isaiah

LORD who appears in Isaiah 40 – 55, primarily in four passages known as 'Servant Songs' (Isa. 42:1–9; 49:1–9; 50:4–11; 52:13 – 53:12).[81]

The identity of the Servant

The identity of the Servant in these passages is the subject of much debate.[82] Some take the term to refer, collectively, to Israel.[83] Both are called by God, have a mission to the world and will suffer and be restored. In some passages Israel is clearly identified as God's servant (e.g. Isa. 41:8; 49:3), though it is equally clear that the nation has failed to be all that God's servant should be (e.g. Isa. 42:19–20; 43:7–8). In the Servant Songs, though, the Servant appears to be an individual. The relationship between the Servant and the nation may be indicated by different uses of the term 'Israel' in Isaiah 49:1–6. In verse 3 the Servant is identified *as* Israel; however, in verses 5–6 the Servant also has a mission *to* Israel. This is best explained by taking verse 3 to indicate that the Servant is the embodiment of what Israel was intended to be.[84] God called the nation to be his servant: he took the people as his own and made a covenant with them in order that they, as a kingdom of priests, should minister to the world. The nation as a whole failed; the people were called to be witnesses, but are deaf and blind to what God has done among them (Isa. 42:18–19; 43:8). Nevertheless God's purposes are kept alive through another Servant, who is all that Israel should be, and through whom Israel will be restored.

Footnote 80 (*continued*)

40–66: A Study of the Teaching of the Second Isaiah and its Consequences', in Orlinsky and Snaith, *Studies*, pp. 3–134; Williamson, *Variations*, pp. 113–116.

81. Duhm, who first drew attention to these passages, listed them as 42:1–4; 49:1–6; 50:4–9; 52:13 – 53:12; and there is debate about whether some or all of the additional verses should be included. The Servant Songs form a distinct unit, with a distinct theological emphasis (see e.g. North, *Suffering Servant*, pp. 178–188). According to Duhm, they have a different author, though many recent commentators accept Deutero-Isaianic authorship and note that the 'Songs' should be interpreted within their immediate context. There may be further references to the ministry of the Servant in Isa. 48:16b; 51:16; 61:1–4.

82. See e.g. Hugenberger, 'Servant', in Satterthwaite, Hess and Wenham, *Lord's Anointed*, pp. 106–119; North, *Suffering Servant*, pp. 6–103; Rowley, *Servant*, pp. 3–59.

83. E.g. Albertz, who takes the Servant Songs to refer to 'Israel under various guises' (*Israel in Exile*, p. 408).

84. See Childs, *Isaiah*, pp. 383–385; Goldingay, *Isaiah*, pp. 281–282; Oswalt, *Isaiah 40–66*, p. 291.

A view that goes back at least to the NT is that the Servant is the prophet himself (Acts 8:34). Elsewhere in Isaiah, prophets are referred to as God's 'servants' (e.g. Isa. 20:3; 44:26), and the Servant often speaks in the first person (e.g. Isa. 49:1–6; 50:4–9). Links have also been suggested between the Servant and other prophetic figures, such as Jeremiah.[85] Indications within the Servant Songs that the Servant is a royal figure have led to his being associated with Moses – who has the functions of both prophet and ruler. This may also be suggested by the second-exodus imagery in Isaiah 40 – 55.[86]

In the NT writers the Servant is identified with Jesus Christ (e.g. Matt. 12:18–21; Luke 2:32; Acts 8:35). Rowley finds little evidence within Judaism that the Servant was linked with the Messiah before the time of Christ.[87] Nevertheless there are links within the OT. There are close similarities, for example, between the description of the Servant in Isaiah 42:1–6 and the description of the messianic king in Isaiah 11:1–5. Both are endowed with the Spirit (Isa. 11:2; 42:1), and with righteousness (Isa. 11:4–5; 42:6), and both have the task of establishing justice (Isa. 11:3–4; 42:1, 4). As we have noted, the Servant may also display royal characteristics.[88] Schultz concludes that 'there is reason enough to view the King and the Servant not as two completely separate figures but as one messianic royal figure carrying out various tasks on Israel's behalf'.[89] Another significant passage is Isaiah 55:3–4. Here David is described as a *witness to the peoples*, an expression that reflects Israel's (failed) calling, which will finally be realized in the era of salvation. As we have seen, this is embodied in the ministry of the Servant. In these verses, however, it is

---

85. Westermann lists correspondences between the description of the Servant in Isa. 50:4–11 and Jeremiah; see Claus Westermann, *Isaiah 40–66*, OTL (London: SCM, 1969), pp. 227–228.

86. Hugenburger identifies the Servant as the prophet like Moses promised in Deut. 18:15, 18; cf. 34:10–12 ('Servant', in Satterthwaite, Hess and Wenham, *Lord's Anointed*, pp. 119–140). Some interpret this promise as messianic (e.g. Motyer, 'Messiah', in *IBD* 2:987–994), giving a further possible link between Servant and Messiah. Klaus Balzer, *Deutero-Isaiah: A Commentary on Isaiah 40–55*, Hermeneia (Philadelphia: Fortress, 2001), suggests that Deutero-Isaiah is a liturgical drama, based on the feast of Passover/Unleavened Bread (hence the exodus traditions) and identifies the Servant as Moses.

87. Rowley, *Servant*, pp. 61–88; see also Russell, *Method and Message*, pp. 334–340.

88. See e.g. Eichrodt, *Theology*, 1:483–484; Goldingay, *OT Theology*, 2:744; Williamson, *Variations*, pp. 132–135.

89. Schultz, 'The King', in Satterthwaite, Hess and Wenham, *Lord's Anointed*, p. 162.

also linked with the fulfilment of the Davidic covenant, through the community of God's people.[90] According to Childs, this 'is a strong indication that already within Second Isaiah a link between the imagery of the servant and the messianic Davidic rule has been formed'.[91] Commentators also note points of contact between Isaiah 61:1–3 and the Servant passages,[92] and the opening statement *the LORD has anointed me* (v. 1) suggests a further link between Servant and Messiah ('anointed one').

Goldingay suggests a relationship between the messianic view and the identification of the Servant with Israel or with the prophet, and notes the significance for the church:

> The servant calling belongs first to Israel as the people of God. She cannot fulfil it, however, and God calls the prophet to be his servant. But the prophet realises that in its ultimate dimensions the role of servant embodies a vision which goes beyond his calling. The Christian finds it fulfilled in Jesus, but also sees it as passed on by him to those who follow him and those who claim to represent him.[93]

North expresses a similar idea in a diagram (below), illustrating how God's purposes through his people began with Israel, found their focus in the Servant Messiah, Jesus Christ, and continue to be fulfilled through the church.[94]

ISRAEL

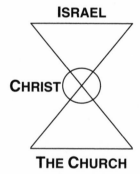

CHRIST

THE CHURCH

90. For further discussion of the 'democratization' of the traditions associated with David, see e.g. Childs, *Isaiah*, pp. 435–437; Goldingay, *Isaiah*, pp. 313–314.

91. Childs, *Isaiah*, pp. 435–437 (437); see also Oswalt, *Isaiah 40–66*, pp. 439–440.

92. E.g. Oswalt, *Isaiah 40–66*, pp. 562–563; Westermann, *Isaiah 40–66*, pp. 365–367; R. N. Whybray, *Isaiah 40–66*, NCB (London: Marshall, Morgan & Scott, 1975), pp. 239–240; see also Mowinckel, *He that Cometh*, p. 254.

93. Goldingay, *God's Prophet*, p. 80.

94. Christopher R. North, *Isaiah 40–55*, TBC (London: SCM, 1956).

The Servant Songs in Isaiah 40 – 55 point ultimately for their fulfilment to Christ. In part, though, the description may be autobiographical. The writer draws on his own experience of God's call, his rejection by an unbelieving people, his dismay, his continued faithfulness in the face of suffering and perhaps the eventual recognition of his ministry by a faithful minority. He sees himself as partially fulfilling the role of God's Servant, though he also looks beyond the present situation to the coming of one whose suffering and achievements far exceed his own. He may also draw on descriptions of other characters such as Jeremiah and Moses, and may reflect too on the suffering and hoped for future vindication of the nation. The description of the Servant may, thus, be a composite.

The role of the Servant

In the discussion of a possible narrative substructure of Isaiah, we noted that God had appointed the Servant to bring to Israel the restoration and renewal that would enable the nation to fulfil her divine calling to reveal God's glory to the nations of the world. This emphasis on role, rather than identity, means that our interpretation of the Servant passages is not bound up with our ability to say who the Servant is. Also, while recognizing that the Servant's role is ultimately fulfilled in Christ, we may again think in terms of a composite figure, incorporating all who assist Israel in her task.

The suffering Servant

A significant element within the Servant Songs is the idea that the Servant will accomplish his mission through suffering. The Servant faces opposition to his ministry by those to whom he is sent. This includes indifference to his message, hostility and persecution (Isa. 49:4; 50:5–7; 52:14; 53). Nevertheless he remains faithful to his calling: he sets his face like flint, and trusts in God for his vindication (Isa. 50:6–9). The fourth Servant Song (Isa. 52:13 – 53:12) begins and ends with the exaltation of the Servant – but only after rejection, humiliation and eventual death.[95] At first it was thought this was punishment for his own sin (v. 4b); later it was recognized that he suffered unjustly, in the place of

---

95. R. N. Whybray, *Thanksgiving for a Liberated Prophet: An Interpretation of Isaiah Chapter 53*, JSOTSup 4 (Sheffield: JSOT Press, 1978), pp. 79–105, argues that the Servant's death is not explicit in the text, and that he came only close to death; see also Goldingay, *OT Theology*, 2:414–415; cf. Oswalt, *Isaiah 40–66*, p. 393. The most natural reading of Isa. 53:8–9 is that the Servant does die.

others (vv. 4a, 5–6),[96] giving himself as a ransom, to turn away God's anger and so make available the forgiveness and renewal necessary for Israel to fulfil her role as God's servant.[97]

The idea of a suffering Messiah may also be present in Zechariah's description of the good shepherd who is struck, causing the sheep to scatter (13:7).[98] Shepherd imagery is often used to refer to the leaders of Israel, and God's condemnation of false shepherds in Ezekiel 34 is accompanied by the promise of another shepherd, *my servant, David* (v. 23). Though he does not make a direct link, it is reasonable to identify the shepherd in Zechariah's prophecy with this David of the future. However, there is a significant new element: in order to bring about a renewed covenant relationship between God and the people,[99] this future leader will face rejection and affliction. Zechariah also describes the people mourning over *the one they have pierced* (12:10). The identity of this figure is uncertain, though the indirect links with David suggest that this too is a reference to the Davidic Messiah, whose death in some way brings cleansing from sin (Zech. 13:1).[100]

Divergent messianic views

The picture of the Messiah in the OT is multifaceted. The link with the Davidic monarchy emphasizes his human origin: he is chosen and equipped by God, with divine qualities, but is not generally portrayed as a supernatural being. However, some passages do appear to suggest divinity (e.g. Ps. 45:6; Isa. 9:6; Jer. 23:6), and the description of the 'Son of Man' in Daniel 7:13–14 also

---

96. In Isa. 53:1–6 the writer appears to be speaking on behalf of a group within Israel who (along with the rest of the world) do not at first recognize that God is at work through the Servant, but who, finally, see the light.

97. The Servant is described as a 'reparation offering' (Isa. 53:10). For further discussion, see above, pp. 193–195; see also e.g. Goldingay, *OT Theology*, 2:410–415; Thielman, 'Atonement', in Hafemann and House, *Biblical Themes*, pp. 106–108; Wenham, *Leviticus*, pp. 111–112.

98. See e.g. Iain Duguid, 'Messianic Themes in Zechariah 9–14', in Satterthwaite, Hess and Wenham, *Lord's Anointed*, pp. 269–276.

99. Refining and renewal is followed by a restatement of the covenant formula *I will say, 'They are my people,' and they will say, 'The LORD is our God'* (Zech. 13:9; see also e.g. Exod. 6:7; Jer. 24:7; 32:38; Ezek. 11:20; 37:27).

100. Some see a mythological background to these verses, though the reference to Megiddo may allude to the death of Josiah (2 Kgs 23:29); see e.g. Joyce G. Baldwin, *Haggai, Zechariah, Malachi*, TOTC (Leicester: IVP, 1972), pp. 192–195.

points more towards a heavenly figure. There is also the idea of suffering – though this is absent from the later development of the theme.

Mowinckel notes that in later Judaism the tension already present between the earthly and heavenly aspects of God's kingdom gave rise to two views of the future, each associated with its own messianic figure developed from the OT.[101] On the one hand, there was the this-worldly hope of national and political restoration under an ideal Davidic king; on the other, there was the hope of God's new world order, which incorporated new heavens and a new earth – linked with a pre-existent, transcendent figure, similar to the OT description of the Son of Man.[102] In time there was a fusion of these ideas; according to Mowinckel, 'there emerged a Messianic figure both eternal and transcendental, and also historical and human, in an eschatology both historical and supra-historical and absolute'.[103] The combination of this- and other-worldly elements led to the idea of a temporary (earthly) messianic kingdom.[104] So, for example, in 2 Esdras (dated around AD 100) the Messiah is a mortal king who will reign for 400 years and then, when the earthly kingdom is brought to an end, will die (7.28–29). Later, in a passage that recalls the imagery of Daniel 7, the Messiah is mentioned as the deliverer of the remnant of God's people (12.32), and in a further passage, which also alludes to Daniel 7, the deliverer is portrayed as a pre-existent figure (described as God's 'Son'), who will come from the sea and save creation (13.25–32).[105]

It is possible, though, that this linking of ideas took place only in fairly narrow apocalyptic circles, and that outside those circles the two aspects of future hope existed side by side. At a difficult time in the life of the nation it was the promise of national recovery that would have appealed most to the general population, which may explain the view, predominant at the time of Jesus, that the Messiah would be a human deliverer. The idea of a mortal Messiah, who will die and be succeeded by his son, is part of the

---

101. Though in the intertestamental period, as in the OT, some writings describe the coming golden age without referring to the Messiah.

102. Mowinckel, *He that Cometh*, pp. 280–284; see also e.g. Russell, *Method and Message*, pp. 308–310.

103. Mowinckel, *He that Cometh*, p. 436.

104. See e.g. Russell, *Method and Message*, pp. 291–297.

105. For further discussion, see e.g. Loren T. Stuckenbruck, 'Messianic Ideas in the Apocalyptic and Related Literature of Early Judaism', in Porter, *Messiah*, pp. 90–113.

traditional Jewish teaching systematized by Maimonides in the twelfth century AD.[106] Rabbinic writings look for the coming of a king to restore the nation, gather scattered Jews, and deliver Israel from her enemies. Rabbi Aqiba, for example (as mentioned earlier), believed Bar Kochba, the leader of a revolt against the Romans, was the Messiah. With the restoration of Israel under the Hasmoneans, Simon, the brother of Judas Maccabaeus, is described in messianic terms (1 Maccabees 14.8–15). Because Simon was from the tribe of Levi, not Judah, this may have led to a development of the Messiah's priestly role into the idea of a Levitical Messiah.[107] Texts from Qumran also point to two Messiahs, from Aaron and from Israel, and also to a prophetic figure, probably identified with the 'prophet like Moses' (Deut. 18:18).[108]

The Messiah in the OT and between the testaments is one who is human and divine, mortal and transcendent, as well as king, priest and maybe prophet, bringing political and spiritual renewal. At the time of Jesus the main emphasis seems to have been on a human deliverer, and it was as this kind of Messiah that the crowds welcomed Jesus. But Jesus, uniquely, also fulfils the other aspects of messianic expectation, including the role of the Servant, who would suffer for the sin of others.

---

106. Within traditional Judaism, looking forward to the messianic age is a key part of the weekly Shabbat service. It is believed, though, that this will be established within history, and that messianic redemption is physical rather than spiritual, so making it possible to work towards that hope in the present. At Passover, participants pour wine into Elijah's cup as an expression of their commitment to speed the Messiah's coming. R. Irving Greenberg, *The Jewish Way* (New York: Simon & Schuster, 1988), writes, 'The concept of a personal Messiah should not represent . . . some divine intervention that will relieve humanity of its responsibility or of the consequences of its folly. Rather it is meant to underscore that, in the final analysis, humans must take responsibility for their own fate: the final liberator will be a human redeemer. Then all our limited strides forward will become part of the way to the realisation of the grand design' (p. 242).

107. See e.g. *He that Cometh*, pp. 286–291; Russell, *Method and Message*, pp. 310–316.

108. For a more detailed survey of Qumran texts, see e.g. Fitzmyer, *The One*, pp. 88–111; Russell, *Method and Message*, pp. 319–323; Al Wolters, 'The Messiah in the Qumran Documents', in Porter, *Messiah*, pp. 75–89.

Old Testament apocalyptic[109]

Features of apocalyptic literature

Israel's prophets looked forward to the rebirth, restoration and renewal of the nation after the exile. However, the return was not all that had been hoped for, leading to disappointment and frustration. Israel's problems continued, the promised salvation did not come, and instead of the establishment of God's kingdom, the people suffered under a succession of pagan rulers, culminating in Antiochus Epiphanes and his opposition to the Jewish faith and way of life. In the normal course of historical and political events, there was little hope for the nation, but, not wanting to abandon the promises of the prophets, apocalyptic writers looked forward to a day, beyond the events of history, when God would defeat the powers of darkness and evil and bring the present age to an end.

'Apocalypse' means 'unveiling, disclosure', and apocalyptic writings claim to receive their revelation directly from God, through visions or as a direct encounter with the heavenly order. During the difficult national and political circumstances from 200 to 100 BC, and the continuing absence of the prophetic word, many such writings appeared. Apocalyptic was, thus, a response to a particular historical situation. It also has many affinities with the earlier prophetic literature. An important influence was the book of Ezekiel. This stresses the transcendence of God and humankind's individual accountability; it contains imagery and symbolism that were a feature of later apocalyptic; there is too a reference to a final battle and the triumph of good over evil, a familiar theme among apocalyptists. In Zechariah, the prophet receives revelation in the form of visions, and future hope is expressed in terms of a coming Golden Age, the appearance of God's chosen messianic leader and the final destruction of evil. Other prophets refer to the *Day of the LORD* when God will bring to an end the pride and power of the nations and establish his own kingdom. These OT passages provide the ground out of which apocalyptic grew.

---

109. See e.g. Albertz, *History*, 2:563–597; *Israel in Exile*, pp. 38–44; B. W. Anderson, *Living World*, pp. 618–622; *Contours*, pp. 302–311; Baldwin, *Daniel*; R. J. Bauckham, 'Apocalyptic', in *IBD* 1:73–75; Drane, *Introducing the OT*, pp. 216–224; Goldingay, *Daniel*; W. J. Dumbrell, 'Apocalyptic Literature', in *NIDOTTE* 4:394–399; Gowan, *Theology*, pp. 193–195; E. W. Nicholson, 'Apocalyptic', in G. W. Anderson, *Tradition*, pp. 189–213; Porteous, *Daniel*; Preuss, *OT Theology*, 2:277–283; D. S. Russell, *The Jews from Alexander to Herod* (Oxford: Oxford University Press, 1967), pp. 218–249; *Apocalyptic Ancient and Modern* (London: SCM, 1978); *Method and Message*; *Daniel*, Daily Study Bible (Edinburgh: St Andrew Press, 1981).

There are also differences between apocalyptic and prophecy. Prophets were preachers with a contemporary message. They wanted to influence and shape the nation's history according to God's will. They also express a strong moral and ethical interest. When they looked to the future, it was often to stress God's judgment on sin and to call the people to repent before it was too late. Apocalyptic writers were less concerned with the present; they were pessimistic about this world, and instead, focused on the new world order God would soon establish – not as a vague future hope, but as an imminent reality.

In this we see a *dualism* between the present age, ruled by evil powers, and in which world empires oppose God and oppress his people, and God's future reign of righteousness. And because human beings could do nothing to avert or hasten that consummation, this also led to a *deterministic* view of world events. There is emphasis too on God's *transcendence*: a widening of the divide between God and humankind, with the relationship usually mediated by angels. Apocalyptic is also generally *pseudonymous*, often bearing the name of an important figure from Israel's past.

The view of history presented in apocalyptic literature is significant. The apocalyptists despaired of the present world order, but continued to believe, even in the face of fierce persecution and seemingly impossible odds, that God was in control of their affairs; 'tyrants might rule, but it was only by the permissive will of God. The rise and fall of empires were in the control of one in whose hands lay the final victory and in whose kingdom they would have a glorious part'.[110] They saw history as a unity ruled over by God, who was guiding it inexorably towards its goal, according to a purpose that would ultimately be revealed, and in the light of which the whole of history would finally make sense. This is sometimes demonstrated by reviewing world history, to show how it had taken place according to God's plan. Such reviews are usually *pseudo-predictive*, rewriting history between the time of the pseudonymous author and the actual writer as though it were prophecy.

The book of Daniel

Daniel is the only true apocalypse in the OT. The book is widely thought to be pseudonymous and pseudo-predictive, and many scholars date it around 165 BC. This is partly because the language seems closer to that of the second than the sixth century BC, and also because the content of chapter 11 appears to become more detailed, and more accurate as it moves from the Persian period (when the book purports to have been written) to the time of Antiochus. The

---

110. Russell, *Apocalyptic*, p. 29.

absence of accurate detail about the ruler's death (in 164 BC) is taken to indicate that it was written not long before this time.[111]

A key theme of Daniel is God's authority in human affairs: *that the living may know that the Most High is sovereign over the kingdoms of men* (4:17; see also 4:25, 32; 5:21). This is evident in the earlier part of the book (chs. 1 – 6) in the way God preserves his servants at court and also in his dealings with Nebuchadnezzar and Belshazzar. It is seen too in the detailed historical accounts contained in Daniel's visions in the second part of the book. Thus the vision of four beasts in chapter 7, representing four powerful empires, concludes with a view of the throne room of heaven and asserts God's ultimate control and his final victory on behalf of his people – even in the face of formidable opposition. The second vision (ch. 8) describes the defeat of the Medo-Persian kingdom by the Greeks under Alexander, the subsequent division of Alexander's empire into four,[112] and the emergence of Antiochus Epiphanes, the main enemy of God's people in these later chapters, and his persecution of the Jews. Daniel's third vision concerns the restoration of Jerusalem, and refers to the coming of *the Anointed One, the ruler* (9:25). The passage is obscure; but, again, it emphasizes God's control over historical events. Chapter 11 gives more precise historical detail about the kings of the North (the Ptolemies) and the South (the Seleucids), and includes another description of the career, blasphemous claims, and eventual demise of Antiochus Epiphanes. Whether the writer is concerned with events only up until Antiochus' death, or looks beyond it to the final overthrow of the anti-God figure he foreshadows, is a matter for speculation. But the principle of God's control over history, and his ultimate victory over every power that rises up against him, is made clear.

---

111. Porteous, for example, seems to assume a second-century date (*Daniel*, pp. 13–21). While not dismissing the possibility of predicting second-century events from the sixth century, Goldingay aligns Daniel with other apocalyptic texts and takes it as pseudonymous and pseudo-prophetic (*Daniel*, pp. 321–322). Ernest Lucas notes that both possibilities can be argued, and both are consistent with a view of divine authority and inspiration – though he too appears to favour a later date (*Daniel*, pp. 306–315). By contrast, Baldwin considers arguments for a sixth/fifth and a second-century date, and concludes that the evidence best fits the former (*Daniel*, pp. 17–46); Tremper Longman III also argues for an earlier date (*Daniel*, pp. 21–24). Problems of dating the book, however, do not impact significantly on its theology.

112. After Alexander's death, his generals divided his empire among themselves. Two are particularly significant for the Jews: Ptolemy, who took control in Egypt, and Seleucus, who was based in Syria.

In the book of Daniel we are introduced to a God who minutely ordains the events of history. The writer looks toward the inbreaking of God's kingdom and depicts the events of history as steps along the way to that goal. Implicit in the way the course of world events is set out in the form of prophecy is the understanding that no decree can be altered. The delay of the heavenly messenger sent to Daniel (10:13) suggests a measure of contingency in human history, influenced by conflict in the heavenly realm, but that too is under divine control. Just as the world empires fulfil only their allotted span, so also will interference from their heavenly representatives be limited.

Death and afterlife[113]

Death

Death is the consequence of sin (e.g. Gen. 2:17; 6:3; Deut. 24:16; 2 Sam. 12:13; Ps. 90:7–9; Jer. 31:30; Ezek. 3:18–20; 18:20). As we noted when discussing the consequences of Adam and Eve's disobedience to God's command, the principal effect of sin is to bring separation from God and spiritual death; but God's judgment on the first pair indicates that it also includes mortality (Gen. 3:19, 22–24).[114] As such the OT attitude towards death is generally negative

---

113. See e.g. B. W. Anderson, *Contours*, pp. 312–324; James Barr, *The Garden of Eden and the Hope of Immortality: The Read-Tuckwell Lectures for 1990* (London: SCM, 1992); Stephen L. Cook, 'Funerary Practices and Afterlife Expectations in Ancient Israel', *Religion Compass* 1.6 (2007), pp. 660–683; Drane, *Introducing the OT*, pp. 273–276; Dyrness, *Themes*, pp. 237–242; Eichrodt, *Theology*, 2:210–216, 496–529; Wendell W. Frerichs, 'Death and Resurrection in the Old Testament', *WW* 11.1 (1991), pp. 14–22; Goldingay, *OT Theology*, 2:631–644; Jacob, *Theology*, pp. 299–316; Philip S. Johnston, '"Left in Hell"? Psalm 16, Sheol and the Holy One', in Satterthwaite, Hess and Wenham, *Lord's Anointed*, pp. 213–222; *Shades*; Köhler, *OT Theology*, pp. 149–150; Jon D. Levenson, *Resurrection and the Restoration of Israel: The Ultimate Victory of the God of Life* (New Haven: Yale University Press, 2006); Robert Martin-Achard, *From Death to Life: A Study of the Development of the Doctrine of the Resurrection in the Old Testament* (Edinburgh: Oliver & Boyd, 1960); Preuss, *OT Theology*, 2:105–107, 147–153; Rendtorff, *Hebrew Bible*, pp. 430–431; Ringgren, *Israelite Religion*, pp. 239–247, 322–323; Klaas Spronk, *Beatific Afterlife in Ancient Israel and in the Ancient Near East*, AOAT 219 (Neukirchen-Vluyn: Neukirchener, 1986); Wheeler Robinson, *Religious Ideas*, pp. 91–101; N. T. Wright, *The Resurrection of the Son of God* (London: SPCK, 2003), pp. 85–128.

114. Above, pp. 151–152.

(e.g. Pss 6:5; 55:4; Eccl. 9:4; Ezek. 18:32). Death is portrayed as a frequently hostile, and an almost always unwelcome, reality.[115] Nevertheless, in common with the beliefs of other cultures, it is also seen as inevitable and natural. At the end of their lives both Joshua and David announce, *I am about to go the way of all the earth* (Josh. 23:14; 1 Kgs 2:2; cf. 2 Sam. 14:14; Job 7:9; Eccl. 3:1–2).[116] Because of its inevitability, death was accepted when it came at the end of a long and fulfilled life. Abraham (Gen. 15:15; 25:8), Gideon (Judg. 8:32) and David (1 Chr. 29:28) died at a *good old age*. By contrast, premature or violent death was unnatural and unwelcome. Those involved in Korah's rebellion were denied a natural death because of their sin (Num. 16:29–30); David did not want Joab to die naturally because of his violence (1 Kgs 2:6); Hezekiah prayed to be spared an early death (2 Kgs 20:1–3).

Although undeveloped, even from earliest times there was the view that the dead survived in some way after death. Eichrodt points to the importance attached to burial rites, especially being buried close to other members of the family (e.g. Gen. 47:30; 2 Sam. 17:23).[117] This suggests the belief that some kind of fellowship continued beyond the grave. Belief in a life after death is evident in Egypt, Babylon and Ugarit. Because it was believed that the dead could influence the world of the living, in Egypt and Ugarit, for example, elaborate provisions were made for the comfort and sustenance of the deceased.[118] Some of these superstitions appear to have been shared by Israelites. The practice of providing food for the deceased may be in view in Deuteronomy 26:14. Saul went to a medium to contact Samuel (1 Sam. 28:3–19), and the fact that it was necessary to forbid such consultations and to expel mediums from Israel (e.g. Lev. 19:31; 20:6, 27; Deut. 18:11; Isa. 8:19; 19:3) suggests the practice was common.

---

115. Job presents a more positive aspect of death as a place where the weary are at rest and slaves are free (Job 3:11–19). However, this needs to be seen against the background of his own situation: death is a release from suffering.

116. The inevitability of death is seen too in the Gilgamesh Epic: 'When the gods created mankind, death for mankind they set aside, life in their own hands retaining' (Speiser and Grayson, 'Akkadian Myths', in *ANET*, p. 90).

117. Eichrodt, *Theology*, 2:213. See also e.g. Elizabeth Bloch-Smith, *Judahite Burial Practices and Beliefs about the Dead*, JSOTS 123 (Sheffield: Sheffield Academic Press, 1992); Saul M. Olyan, 'Some Neglected Aspects of Israelite Interment Ideology', *JBL* 124.4 (2005), pp. 601–616.

118. See e.g. Drane, *Introducing the OT*, pp. 274–275.

Sheol[119]

It is a common view among scholars that the OT depicts individual survival beyond death as a vague, shadowy existence in *šĕ'ôl*. As we have noted, Sheol was thought to be in the lowest parts of the earth.[120] There are frequent references to going *down* to Sheol (e.g. Gen. 37:35; Job 7:9; Isa. 14:15); it is described as being in the *depths* (Ps. 86:13; Prov. 9:18; Jon. 2:2), and is presented as the antithesis to heaven (Job 11:8; Ps. 139:8; Isa. 7:11; Amos 9:2). References to decay (Ps. 16:10), worms and maggots (Job 24:19–20; Isa. 14:11) suggest a link with the grave,[121] though the term more generally indicates the underworld.[122]

The OT does not point to the separation of soul and body at death. As we have seen, *nepeš* refers to the whole person as a living being.[123] In texts that refer to the *nepeš* going into Sheol or being delivered from Sheol (Pss 16:10; 30:3; 49:15; 86:13; 88:3; 89:48; Prov. 23:14) again it stands for the whole person. In Psalm 88:3, for example, 'my *nepeš*' parallels 'my *life*', and to have one's *nepeš* delivered from Sheol means to be delivered from death. The inhabitants of Sheol are described as 'shades' (*rĕpā'îm*; e.g. Isa. 14:9) rather than 'souls'. Death comes when God withdraws the breath of life (*rûaḥ*); the body, then, returns

---

119. See also e.g. Eugene H. Merrill, '*šĕ'ôl*', in *NIDOTTE* 4:6–7; L. Wächter, '*šĕ'ôl*', in *TDOT* 14:239–248.

120. Above, pp. 130–131.

121. The NIV translates *šĕ'ôl* as 'grave' in fifty-seven of its sixty-six occurrences.

122. R. Laird Harris, 'The Meaning of the Word Sheol as Shown by Parallels in Poetic Texts', *Bulletin of the Evangelical Theological Society* 4.4 (1961), pp. 129–135, claims that *šĕ'ôl* means only 'grave'. His arguments, though, are not always convincing, particularly in relation to *šĕ'ôl* as a cosmological extremity (Deut. 32:22; Job 11:8; Ps. 139:8; Amos 9:2); see Johnston, *Shades*, pp. 73–75. According to Merrill, *šĕ'ôl* 'designates both the grave and the netherworld, particularly the latter' ('*šĕ'ôl*', in *NIDOTTE* 4:6); see also Wächter, '*šĕ'ôl*', in *TDOT* 14:241–242.

123. See the discussion of the make-up of human personality above, pp. 143–144. Fredericks suggests that *nepeš* initially meant 'breath' and so was linked with 'life' and thus came to refer to the whole person ('*nepeš*', in *NIDOTTE* 3:133). Some take passages that refer to the *nepeš* leaving (Gen. 35:18; Jer. 15:9) or returning (1 Kgs 17:21–22) to the body to suggest a meaning closer to 'soul' (see e.g. Cook, 'Funerary Practices', p. 668; Barr, *Garden of Eden*, pp. 36–47). However, these passages refer to death and resuscitation, not afterlife, and *nepeš* may be understood in the sense of 'breath' or 'life'. There is no direct indication that it refers to a disembodied immortal soul.

to the dust (e.g. Job 34:14–15; Ps. 104:29), and the *nepeš*, the whole person, ceases to exist. What survives is a shadowy representation of the person. According to Eichrodt, 'a shadowy image of the dead person detached itself from him and continued to eke out a bare existence, and we only confuse the idea if we mix it up with our own idea of the soul . . . What survives . . . is not part of the living man, but a shadowy image of the whole man.'[124]

The dead in Sheol lack vitality; they are separated from God and unable to worship him (e.g. Ps. 6:5; Isa. 38:18). One of the clearest pictures of Sheol is Isaiah 14:9–11, which describes the entry of the fallen king of Babylon into the world of the dead. In Sheol there is a semblance of the earthly order; kings sit on thrones, but there is emphasis on their weakness: the Babylonian king is greeted with the words *you also have become weak, as we are* (v. 10b). Elsewhere, Sheol is characterized as a place of no reward, knowledge or wisdom (Eccl. 9:10), and from which there is no return (Job 7:9; cf. 2 Sam. 12:23; Isa. 26:13–14).[125]

---

124. Eichrodt, *Theology*, 2:214.

125. Levenson qualifies this. He argues that those facing severe illness or under serious threat may see themselves as being in Sheol (e.g. Ps. 88:2–10; Jon. 2:2), while still hoping that God will reverse their condition; however, he distinguishes these from the 'permanent residents of Sheol' (*Resurrection*, pp. 36–46 [39]). While Levenson may be right in pointing to a degree of continuity, in Hebrew thought, between serious illness or some other desperate situation, and death, there is also a clear discontinuity. So, for example, David fasted and prayed for the son born to him by Bathsheba while the child was still alive, hoping that God would heal him; but once the child was dead, David held no hope of any kind of return (2 Sam. 12:16–23). Similarly, in the case of those facing a serious threat, who feel they are already in Sheol and look to God as their only hope of rescue, such a possibility exists only while they are still alive and so able to call out for help. It seems better to take this language as figurative; see Johnston, *Shades*, pp. 86–97. There is no such hope of rescue and return for those who have actually died and so are permanently resident in Sheol. The appearance of Samuel to Saul at Endor (1 Sam. 28:3–19) may be seen as an exception. When Saul asks the medium to call up the dead prophet, Samuel is depicted *coming up out of the ground* (v. 13), which may suggest he returned from Sheol. However, the term *šě'ōl* does not appear, and the expression may point only to Samuel coming out of the grave. The story does suggest that the dead were thought to continue to exist in some form; it may even point to an alternative to Sheol (see the discussion below), but there is no explanation of the nature or quality of that existence.

Philip Johnston questions whether the traditional understanding of Sheol as the place of all the dead is correct. He notes that Sheol 'is almost exclusively reserved for those under divine judgment, whether the afflicted righteous, or all sinners. It seldom occurs of all humanity and only in contexts which portray mankind's sinfulness and life's absurdity.'[126] He suggests that Psalm 16:10 points to a belief in some form of continued fellowship with God that the godly may enjoy after death. A similar idea seems to be expressed in Psalm 49:15. This indicates that there may be an alternative to Sheol for the righteous dead, but what that alternative may be is not clearly stated.[127] Levenson also argues against Sheol as a universal destination. He sees it as 'a prolongation of the unfulfilled life';[128] the alternative, though, is not another location, but to die fulfilled – as a result of seeing descendants.

Afterlife

There are several texts in the OT that refer to the dead being raised to life. Sometimes those who have recently died are resuscitated (1 Kgs 17:22; 2 Kgs 4:32–35; 13:21), but this is not a general picture of resurrection and we assume they will eventually die again. In Ezekiel 37:1–10 the prophet speaks to dry bones, and the dead come to life, though this refers to the revival and restoration of the nation (Ezek. 37:11–14) and, again, there is no indication of personal resurrection to new life beyond the grave.[129] This national perspective is important. As the OT writers look forward to the coming of God's kingdom and to future vindication, their main concern appears to be with what will happen to the community. Individuals may not survive to participate personally in Israel's future glory; however, because they see themselves as being vitally linked to the community, the hope of the resurrection and continued survival of the nation becomes their hope.[130]

---

126. Johnston, *Shades*, p. 83.

127. The translations of Enoch (Gen. 5:24) and Elijah (2 Kgs 2:11–12) may also be taken to indicate another destination: they did not die and so are not in Sheol, so where are they? However, the OT writers make no attempt to answer that question. Neither is mentioned in any OT texts in relation to the afterlife. Enoch's translation is given no theological significance in the OT. There is the view that Elijah will return to herald the Day of the Lord, but this is not linked with the future destination of the righteous.

128. Levenson, *Resurrection*, pp. 71–81 (78), 108–122.

129. Isa. 26:19 and Hos. 6:1–2 are also frequently taken in the same way.

130. This may once have been explained as an example of 'corporate responsibility': the view that Israelites saw themselves not as individuals but as part of a psychical

The one clear OT reference to personal resurrection is Daniel 12:2, *multitudes who sleep in the dust of the earth will awake: some to everlasting life, others to shame and everlasting contempt.* Since Daniel is usually dated in the second century BC, this is taken to support the general view that this idea of resurrection and afterlife was a relatively late development. If the book of Daniel was written in the sixth century BC, this would be uncharacteristic of the theological understanding of the time, and it would appear that his insight into the future state of the righteous and the wicked was not immediately incorporated into mainstream OT theology. The question of the destination of the righteous dead did, though, become more significant at times of persecution, such as those Daniel envisaged and reflection on, or anticipation of, such times may have led to a more concentrated focus on these issues.[131]

---

whole with the community, put forward by H. Wheeler Robinson, *The Christian Doctrine of Man* (Edinburgh: T. & T. Clark, 1911). In the form suggested by Robinson this has little support today; see e.g. John W. Rogerson, 'The Hebrew Conception of Corporate Personality: A Re-Examination', *JTS* 21 (1970), pp. 1–16. It is important, though, to recognize the importance of community in Israel's faith. Individual Israelites saw themselves, not in isolation, but as part of a community, which embraced not only contemporaries but also past generations (e.g. in the celebration of the Passover). This identification with the community results in seeking its well-being above personal interests – and that includes rejoicing in its future vindication and blessing; see e.g. Goldingay, *OT Theology*, 2:527–537; Preuss, *OT Theology*, 1:60–64. Levenson maintains that in Jewish expectation 'resurrection of the dead is always and inextricably associated with the restoration of the people Israel; it is not, in the first instance, focused on individual destiny' (*Resurrection*, pp. 156–165 [165]). This lays the foundation for the (later) view that the righteous dead experience vindication personally, and not only through the fulfilment of God's promises to their descendants (p. 213).

131. A common view is that the doctrine of personal resurrection arose from the theological problem posed by the martyrdom of the righteous. Several scholars note the importance of Canaanite and Persian influences (see e.g. Day, *Yahweh*, pp. 116–126; Martin-Achard, *Death to Life*, pp. 186–205; Spronk, *Beatific Afterlife*, pp. 45–54); particularly, Zoroastrianism (however, see Eichrodt, *Theology*, 2:516; Johnston, *Shades*, pp. 234–236; Levenson, *Resurrection*, pp. 157–158; Spronk, *Beatific Afterlife*, pp. 57–59). Day sees a predominantly Canaanite influence. He argues that imagery echoing the dying and rising of Baal is, in Hos. 13:14. applied to the exile and restoration of Israel; this in turn influenced Isa. 26:19, which is reinterpreted

Several OT passages prepare for the later, more developed, view. Isaiah 26:19 is set in the context of national restoration;[132] however, it appears to indicate that God's victory on behalf of his people includes victory over death and the hope of personal resurrection.[133] Psalm 49:15a expresses the hope *God will redeem my life from šĕ ʾōl*. Similar expressions refer to deliverance from an immediate deadly threat (e.g. Pss 30:3; 86:13; cf. Job 33:28); however, Psalm 49:15 does not refer to a particular threat, but to a general state of affairs. Wealthy oppressors cannot escape death (v. 14); however, unlike his persecutors, the psalmist, who will also die, will be ransomed from Sheol by God. Again, the alternative destination is not made clear; however, while Sheol is characterized by separation from God, the psalmist has a better hope: *he will surely take me to himself.*[134]

Commenting on Isaiah 26:19, Oswalt warns against trying to impose too neat a theory of development on a theology that ultimately depends on revelation.[135]

Footnote 131 (*continued*)

in Dan. 12:2 in the context of literal resurrection from the dead. However, while this may have helped supply the *language* and *imagery* of death and resurrection, the theological content and application are original. Thus, when the belief in resurrection emerged, it was, as Johnston describes it: 'distinctively Israelite' (*Shades*, p. 237). Levenson also points to key biblical antecendents that prepare the way for the later view – particularly, Isa. 26:19; 52:13 – 53:12; Hos. 13:14 (*Resurrection*, pp. 181–216).

132. See Clements, *Isaiah 1–39*, p. 216; J. Goldingay, *Isaiah*, NIBCOT (Carlisle: Paternoster, 2001), p. 146.

133. Childs notes that the 'promise of v. 19 transcends all the promises of Second Isaiah . . . The hope for those living between the times is projected beyond the grave to a resurrection of life, a final victory over death itself' (*Isaiah*, p. 191); see also Johnston, *Shades*, pp. 224–225; Levenson, *Resurrection*, pp. 198–200; Oswalt, *Isaiah 1–39*, pp. 485–488. Kaiser also takes the verse (along with Isa. 25:8) to refer to personal resurrection, but regards it as a later addition; see O. Kaiser, *Isaiah 13–39*, OTL (London: SCM, 1974), pp. 215–220.

134. Kidner links *take me to himself* with Gen. 5:24, *Enoch was no more because God took him* (*Psalms 1–72*, p. 185). Note the interpretation given by Craigie, *Psalms 1–50*, p. 360; cf. Johnston, *Shades*, p. 204; Levenson, *Resurrection*, pp. 103–105. See also David C. Mitchell, '"God Will Redeem my Soul from Sheol": The Psalms of the Sons of Korah', *JSOT* 30.3 (2006), pp. 365–384. Mitchell links references to Sheol in these psalms with the judgment on Korah and his followers, who *went down alive into Sheol* (Num. 16:38), and suggests that the sons of Korah, who were spared (Num. 26:11), may have perpetuated some idea of resurrection.

135. Oswalt, *Isaiah 1–39*, p. 485.

Clearly there is a development of ideas in the long period covered by the OT, and this is true when it comes to life after death. But we must still allow that ideas that may only have become widespread and more fully understood at a relatively late date might still have been introduced, or at least prepared for, much earlier. The idea of resurrection and life beyond the grave is not clearly developed through most of the OT period. Nevertheless there are suggestions of it.[136] The idea is not something new that emerged in the second century BC, but grew out of a faith that recognized God as the source of life, and relied on him for protection from death and for ultimate vindication.

We have already noted that hope in the OT is viewed in physical terms. Because of the emphasis on the unity of the whole person, resurrection too must include the resurrection of the body. Where the OT points to the hope of resurrection it envisages the reversal of physical death and the renewal of life as it was before. This is not simply resuscitation; nor is it the hope of a life to come that is qualitatively different from life in this world. The view of death and resurrection as a gateway to something new and better is consistent with the OT faith, and finds echoes in later Judaism, but is based ultimately on the resurrection of Jesus.

Resurrection between the testaments[137]

With the rise of apocalyptic literature, there was an increased focus on eschatology, the Day of Judgment and the establishment of God's kingdom on earth. An important part of this view of the future is the vindication of the righteous and the judgment of the wicked. This may be anticipated by some OT passages, but comes into much sharper focus in the intertestamental literature. It seems probable that in the light of the eschatological hope some would ask about the righteous who have already died.[138] The idea that they might miss out on the future kingdom might seem unjust, especially if they had suffered martyrdom. It may be that increased persecution and the death of believers led to greater consideration of these issues and to a more detailed and developed statement

---

136. Job 19:25–27 is also sometimes taken to indicate resurrection (see the discussion above, p. 258, n. 50). Some take the expression *when I awake* in Ps. 17:15 to refer to waking from the sleep of death (cf. Dan. 12:2); see e.g. Kidner, *Psalms 1–72*, pp. 89–90. It seems more likely, though, that the psalmist is contemplating these things at night (v. 3), and trusts that things will be different in the morning; see e.g. Craigie, *Psalms 1–50*, pp. 164–165; Johnston, *Shades*, pp. 206–207.

137. See Russell, *The Jews*, pp. 148–154; *Method and Message*, pp. 353–390; for a more recent overview, see N. T. Wright, *Resurrection*, pp. 129–206.

138. This is similar to the question addressed by Paul in 1 Thess. 4:13–18.

of the doctrine. There was, though, still a lack of consistency of belief. The Sadducees did not believe in it. In some literature, as in some OT passages, the hope of resurrection is related to the rebirth of the nation; in others, the focus is more on the individual. Some continue to think in terms of Sheol; others take over the Greek idea of the immortality of the soul. There is, though, a core belief that the righteous will be raised to enjoy life in the kingdom of God, and that the wicked will also be raised – to face judgment and punishment.

The *Psalms of Solomon* talk about the righteous rising to eternal life. *1 Enoch* 83 – 90 describes them taking their place within the kingdom, and also talks about the wicked being thrown into the fires of Gehenna. *1 Enoch* 37 – 71 refers to the righteous sharing a meal with the Messiah. Other literature speaks of the resurrection of all men: some to glory, some to shame. *1 Enoch* 22 (from the first half of the second century AD) describes Sheol with four compartments representing different degrees of reward or punishment. The first, for the spirits of the righteous dead, contains a spring of water. In the second and third, the righteous and wicked who have not yet been rewarded wait for the Day of Judgment. The fourth is a place of punishment. According to Russell, 'we have the very first allusion, in this literature, to the pains of Hell. The spirits of sinners, we are told, are "set apart in great pain . . . scourgings and torments of the accursed forever".'[139]

Elsewhere the division is into two: Gehenna, the ever-burning rubbish tip outside Jerusalem, which became, in this literature, the place of eternal fire, and Paradise, the eternal home of the righteous, 'where there is no toil, neither grief nor mourning; but peace and exultation and life everlasting'.[140] In some literature this is linked with a 'third heaven' (see also 2 Cor. 12:2).

Jesus' parable of the rich man and Lazarus (Luke 16:19–26) reflects some of the views expressed by this literature, and indicates how far the idea had developed by the first century AD. The parable points to separation between the righteous and the wicked, and the fact that their eternal destinies involve reward and punishment for things done on earth. Lazarus went to *Abraham's side*. This may be a reference to Paradise, and the rich man's request for water may suggest the picture of Paradise given in *1 Enoch* 22; it may also refer to fellowship with Abraham at the messianic banquet (see also Matt. 8:11; Luke 13:29). The rich man found himself in Hades. This may be an intermediate destination as he waits for final judgment, though the flames suggest it may have been hell. The gulf that separates the two also reflects the division in *1 Enoch* 22.

---

139. Russell, *The Jews*, p. 153.

140. *Testament of Abraham* 20; quoted by Russell, *The Jews*, p. 153.

10. GOD AND THE NATIONS

God and history[1]

The divine purpose in history

Several passages in the OT suggest the idea of God's providence ordering and overruling in human affairs. A classic expression of this is in Genesis 50:20, where Joseph, now a ruler in Egypt, tells the brothers who had earlier

---

1. Bertil Albrektson, *History and the Gods* (Lund: CWK Gleerup, 1967); Denis Baly, *God and History in the Old Testament: The Encounter with the Absolutely Other in Ancient Israel* (New York: Harper & Row, 1976); Ronald E. Clements, *Prophecy and Tradition* (Oxford: Blackwell, 1975); Eichrodt, *Theology*, 2:167–194; Goldingay, *OT Theology*, 1:606–612; 2:692–709; Norman K. Gottwald, *All the Kingdoms of the Earth: Israelite Prophecy and International Relations* (New York: Harper & Row, 1964); H. H. Guthrie, *God and History in the Old Testament* (London: SPCK, 1961); Köhler, *OT Theology*, pp. 78–82, 92–95; Elmer A. Martens, *Plot and Purpose in the Old Testament* (Leicester: IVP, 1981); Mays, *Amos*; Preuss, *OT Theology*, 1:208–219; 2:285–295; Gerhard von Rad, 'The Beginnings of Historical Writing in Ancient Israel', in *Problem of the Hexateuch*, pp. 166–204 (= *Genesis to Chronicles*, pp. 125–153); 'God's Word', in *God at Work*; Rendtorff, *Hebrew Bible*, pp. 678–687; Vogels, *Universal Covenant*.

sold him into slavery, *You intended to harm me, but God intended it for good to accomplish what is now being done, the saving of many lives* (see also Gen. 45:5–8). This indicates a belief that God is active in history, that he controls and directs events, and works through, and even in spite of, human agents to fulfil his purposes.

In his discussion of the OT idea of providence, which he describes as 'God's guiding of human destinies',[2] Eichrodt notes that Israel's confidence that God was directing her history was based upon her experience as a nation, especially the events associated with the exodus. Through these God showed both his power and his concern for his people and, in the light of them, 'all later historical developments acquired their meaning as acts of Yahweh'.[3] In his discussion Eichrodt speaks of 'the goal of history'.[4] Köhler too describes history as 'movement towards a goal, not a mere purposeless and endless series of events', and stresses that God directs and controls that movement: 'history is under God's management . . . all history has its source in God and takes place for God'.[5] To illustrate this he points to Joshua's address to the people in Joshua 24:1–28, where the covenant renewal at Shechem is presented as the climax to a series of events that began with the call of Abraham (v. 3). Köhler comments, 'the covenant is concluded, God has his people, the people its inheritance; the goal has been reached'.[6]

This raises the question of what is meant by 'the divine purpose in history'. Lindblom considers that the OT prophets saw the history of Israel 'as the realisation of a fixed divine plan from its beginning to its end'.[7] Albrektson, on the other hand, argues that while God does act purposefully in history, we may speak of a divine 'plan' only in a very limited sense: 'it concerns a definite chain of events and a limited goal'.[8] Goldingay also questions the idea of a detailed outworking of God's plan through human history.[9] God sets constraints, and his purpose is ultimately fulfilled; nevertheless 'most events happen independently of Yhwh's actual will'.[10]

---

2. Eichrodt, *Theology*, 2:168.

3. Ibid.

4. Ibid., 2:170.

5. Köhler, *OT Theology*, p. 93.

6. Ibid.

7. Lindblom, *Prophecy*, p. 325; cf. Gottwald, *Kingdoms*, p. 349.

8. Albrektson, *History*, p. 87.

9. Goldingay, *OT Theology*, 1:59–61; 2:700–701.

10. Ibid., 2:701; see also Brueggemann, *Theology*, pp. 355–357.

Several OT passages make specific reference to a divine 'plan'.[11] Half of these are in Isaiah 1 – 39, indicating the importance of the idea for this prophet.[12] At his call Isaiah received an overwhelming revelation of the holiness and glory of God (6:3). This had a powerful impact on his preaching, and is reflected in the view of God presented through the book, and in its favourite designation of God as *the Holy One*. It is also seen in the understanding of God's purpose for his people and the world. Underlying the specific references to God's plan in the prophecy it is possible to discern a single divine purpose: to reveal God's holiness and glory throughout the earth so that it is acknowledged by all peoples.[13] In Isaiah 5:19, for example, *the plan of the Holy One of Israel* is to reveal his holiness through acts of righteous judgment (see also 5:16). In 14:24–27 God's immediate intention is to bring judgment on the king of Assyria because of his pride in exalting himself against God. But this is part of a wider purpose: a *plan determined for the whole world* (v. 26). Assyria here represents a world power in opposition to God, attempting to usurp the glory that belongs to God alone. It is God's plan to bring down all who exalt themselves in that way. We see the same thing in relation to Tyre:

> *The LORD Almighty planned it,*
>   *to bring low the pride of all glory*
>   *and to humble all who are renowned on the earth.*
> (Isa. 23:9)

In 25:1–5 this purpose has an eschatological setting. The proud city again represents human power in opposition to God. It appears strong and unassailable, but will ultimately fall. In Isaiah's vision of the future, God alone will be glorified, for his glory will fill the earth. This ultimate goal can be seen in other OT passages that make specific mention of a divine plan (e.g. Isa. 46:10–13; Jer.

---

11. The most common Hebrew terms are the noun *'ēṣâ* and the verb *yā'aṣ*; these refer to the divine plan in Pss 33:11; 106:13; Isa. 5:19; 14:24, 26–27; 19:12, 17; 23:8–9; 25:1; 46:10; Jer. 49:20; 50:45; Mic. 4:12. Other terms include *maḥăšābâ* (Jer. 29:11; 51:29; cf. Gen. 50:20; Isa. 55:8–9) and *mĕzimmâ* (Jer. 23:20; 30:24; 51:11).

12. For a classic discussion, see J. Fichtner, 'Jahwes Plan in der Botschaft des Jesajas', *ZAW* 63 (1951), pp. 16–33; see also e.g. Joseph Jensen, 'Yahweh's Plan in Isaiah and in the Rest of the Old Testament', *CBQ* 48.3 (1986), pp. 443–445; von Rad, *OT Theology*, 2:161–165.

13. This is in line with the narrative substructure identified in the book of Isaiah; see Routledge, 'Narrative Substructure', and the discussion above, pp. 47–50.

29:11–14; 49:20; 50:45; Mic. 4:12–13). Though emphases vary, the two main themes that emerge are salvation and judgment. These are different sides of the same divine purpose: namely the vindication of Yahweh and of his righteousness and holiness. His power, authority and glory will be revealed either through those who submit to his righteous rule (Isa. 46:10–13; Jer. 29:11–14) or in the divine judgment of those who do not (Mic. 4:12–13; Jer. 49:20; 50:45).

There are also passages where the idea of a divine plan is implicit. Albrektson suggests that J, written from a standpoint in the days of the Solomonic empire, describes, after the event, how God had guided the nation's history: 'at a summit of Israelite prosperity the Yahwist looks back and sees the past as a series of divine actions, where even the corruption and disobedience of men have been forced to serve God's aims'.[14] Von Rad notes ways in which God affects the course of history. One is to intervene directly, though miracles; but God also acts to influence the course of history without direct intervention. The story of Joseph is an example of this:

> Only at the very end, when God has resolved everything for good, does one learn that God has held the reins in his hand all along and has directed everything . . . But how? No miracle ever occurred. Rather, God's leading has worked in secret, in the plans and thoughts of men's hearts, who have savagely gone about their own business. Thus the field for the divine providence is the human heart. One would ask in vain how God intervened here. The immanently causal connection of the events was as tight as possible; there was no gap, no hollow spot set aside for human intervention. God did his work in the decisions of men.[15]

Another example is the incident recorded in 1 Kings 12:15, where Rehoboam, following bad advice, stirred up the anger of the northern tribes and so precipitated the division of the kingdom. According to the writer, *this turn of events was from the LORD, to fulfil the word the LORD had spoken to Jeroboam son of Nebat through Ahijah the Shilonite*. God's control over history is also seen in the Deuteronomistic history. Here, though, the emphasis is not on direct intervention, or on God working secretly in human hearts (though both elements may be present), but on God's word and its fulfilment – bringing either judgment or salvation (see e.g. 1 Kgs 2:27; 12:15; 2 Kgs 15:12). Finally, in relation

---

14. Albrektson, *History*, p. 81. See also B. W. Anderson's discussion of the Priestly view of history (*Living World*, pp. 454–466).

15. Von Rad, 'God's Word', in *God at Work*, pp. 143–144; see also 'Beginnings', in *Problem of the Hexateuch*, pp. 201–204 (= *Genesis to Chronicles*, pp. 151–153).

to the divine purpose in history, we can point again to the book of Daniel and its portrayal of God as Lord, both of the powerful empires of the world and also of the detailed events of human history.

God and the non-Israelite nations

It is sometimes argued that in the OT, foreign nations are only of interest in so far as their activities impinge upon the life of God's people.[16] Eichrodt notes that Israel

> did not at once extend to their consideration of the fortunes of other nations that which they had experienced in their own destiny, and draw the logical conclusion of God's unified government of the world . . . Yahweh's guidance of the destinies of these other peoples only entered the sphere of faith in proportion to Israel's direct contact with them.[17]

However, he also maintains that there was, from the first, the idea that God would bless the nations (e.g. Gen. 12:2–3; 49:10), and the belief 'that they too at any rate in the end-event of their history would be seen to be equally the objects of divine Providence'.[18]

Eichrodt goes on to note that in the prophecy of Isaiah God's providential care for all nations is clearly seen. At a time of Assyrian expansion, the prophet glimpsed 'the far-seeing and constructive plan of God, who willed to lead the nations not into the house of bondage of the Assyrian overseer but into the Father's house of the divine world-ruler'.[19] A significant passage is the vision of the world kingdom of righteousness and peace in Isaiah 2:2–4. This represents the climax of Isaiah's prophecy. As we have suggested, Isaiah's preaching was influenced by the revelation of divine holiness and glory that he received at his call. He recognized that the purpose of the holy king, whose glory filled the whole earth, was to establish his holiness and glory throughout the world, and it is in the world kingdom depicted in Isaiah 2:2–4 that that divine purpose will ultimately be fulfilled.

---

16. See e.g. Friedrich Huber, *Jahwe, Juda und die anderen Völker beim Propheten Jesaja*, BZAW 137 (Berlin: de Gruyter, 1976). Huber argues that for Isaiah, God's dealings with the nations are entirely subordinated to his relationship with Israel.

17. Eichrodt, *Theology*, 2:169.

18. Ibid., 2:171.

19. Ibid., 2:172; see also Gottwald, *Kingdoms*, p. 204.

Condemnation of national pride

An important element in God's dealings with the nations is condemnation of pride. This is clearly expressed in the prophecies against Assyria. In Isaiah 10:5–15 the king of Assyria, described as the instrument of God's wrath, himself comes under divine judgment because he does not recognize God's hand in his victories and glories (v. 13). As we have seen, this is God's intention for all peoples who, like Assyria, seek to usurp his glory (Isa. 14:26; 23:9), and national pride is given among the reasons for God's judgment also on Babylon (Isa. 13:11; 14:11–15), Moab (Isa. 16:6) and Tyre (Isa. 23:8–9; see also Ezek. 28).

Isaiah 14:13–14 reveals the nature of pride as an attempt to exalt oneself:

> *You said in your heart,*
> *'I will ascend to heaven;*
> *I will raise my throne*
> *above the stars of God;*
> *I will sit enthroned on the mount of assembly,*
> *on the utmost heights of the sacred mountain.*
> *I will ascend above the tops of the clouds;*
> *I will make myself like the Most High.'*

Such presumption can result only in the usurper being cast down. Honour and deference in the world is due to Yahweh alone: he will not share his glory with another (Isa. 42:8; 48:11), and so opposes and condemns the pride of nations.

Oracles against the nations

God's interest in the non-Israelite nations, though still in a negative sense, is seen too in the oracles against the nations, prominent in several prophetic books of the OT.[20] In these oracles, offences against Israel do not feature as highly as might be expected among the reasons given for God's judgment. As

---

20. Notable passages are Isa. 13 – 23; Jer. 46 – 51; Ezek. 25 – 32; Amos 1 – 2. It is suggested that this kind of oracle may derive from the practice of issuing threats against an enemy (e.g. Num. 22 – 24), or possibly within the cult and especially the autumn festival where Yahweh's victory over his enemies was asserted. However, there is nothing to connect oracles against the nations directly with either of these settings; see further e.g. Albertz, *Israel in Exile*, pp. 179–196; Duane L. Christensen, *Transformations of the War Oracle in Old Testament Prophecy* (Missoula: Scholars Press, 1975); John H. Hayes, 'The Usage of Oracles against Foreign Nations in Ancient Israel', *JBL* 87 (1968), pp. 81–92; cf. Wolff, *Joel and Amos*, pp. 144–148.

we have seen, one of the things frequently condemned is human pride in opposition to God. So, in Ezekiel's prophecy against Tyre (Ezek. 26 – 28), little is said about the historical relationship between Tyre and Israel. God's indictment is, *In the pride of your heart you say 'I am a god'* (Ezek. 28:2). Similarly, though Israel is mentioned, the chief charge that Jeremiah brings against Moab is that *she has defied the LORD* (Jer. 48:26).[21]

In Amos' oracles against the nations (1:2 – 2:16) condemnation of neighbouring peoples culminates in the indictment of Israel (2:6–16).[22] The reason for the condemnation of these nations is not primarily because they are enemies of, or have committed crimes against, Israel. Rather they are guilty of offending against a universal divine law that derives from Yahweh's dominion over his creation.[23] Yahweh, as Lord of the whole earth, makes demands on all humankind, not just on his chosen people. Israel has a clearer understanding of God's will, but there is a certain level of morality that can be discerned by other nations too, and that makes them answerable to him.

Divine guidance of national destinies
The basis for Israel's accountability to God is her election (Amos 3:2). An important verse in considering the basis of the responsibility of other nations is Amos 9:7:

> *'Are not you Israelites*
> *the same to me as the Cushites?' declares the LORD.*
> *'Did I not bring Israel up from Egypt,*
> *the Philistines from Caphtor*
> *and the Arameans from Kir?'*

Here Amos makes a comparison between God's election of Israel and his relationship with other nations and draws a parallel between the central event in

---

21. Commenting on Isa. 13 – 14, Preuss notes that the Babylonians are 'the symbol of the enemy of God, and thereby the enemy of Israel' (*OT Theology*, 2:288).

22. There is debate about why Amos chose those particular nations, though it has been noted that all the states mentioned were at one time linked with the Davidic empire: either annexed by David (Moab, Syria, Ammon and Edom) or related through a treaty (Tyre); see Christensen, *Transformations*; J. Mauchline, 'Implicit Signs of an Implicit Belief in the Davidic Empire', *VT* 20 (1972), pp. 287–303; J. Priest, 'The Covenant of Brothers', *JBL* 84 (1965), pp. 400–406.

23. See above, pp. 247–248.

the history of God's dealings with Israel, the exodus, and the national migra-
tions of the Philistines and the Syrians.[24] The prophet's aim is to challenge
Israel's false security. They consider themselves *notable men of the foremost nation*
(Amos 6:1), but are likened to the *Cushites*, a people from a remote corner of
the world. They think they are a special case because God has guided their
history, but God has also guided the movements of their enemies. At one level,
then, Israel is just the same as other peoples and, like other nations, must
answer to God for her actions.[25]

This verse points to a link between God's sovereignty in directing events in
the history of the nations, and their responsibility to him. The comparison
with the exodus, rather than any other event in Israel's history, and with it the
associated ideas of election and covenant, suggests that Amos saw, in the
similar experiences of the other nations, a sense in which they too had been
brought into a relationship of belonging to God, a relationship that brings corresponding blessing and responsibility. That is not to suggest a parallel
covenant with those nations.[26] The level of belonging is not the same. Israel
has been called into a closer relationship with God (e.g. Amos 3:2), and the
demands of that relationship are greater. Nevertheless, on the basis of
Yahweh's sovereignty and the fact that he is at work within their history, all
nations are, to some extent, held accountable to him.

There are other instances of God guiding the history of non-Israelite
nations. Assyria was used to bring divine punishment (Isa. 7:18–20; 10:5–6);
Cyrus was used by God as an instrument of blessing (Isa. 44:28); God gave
victory to Syria through Naaman (2 Kgs 5:1). Some texts develop the theme,
touched on by Amos, of God giving land to the nations, including the

---

24. See Goldingay, *OT Theology*, 2:201–202, 286; Preuss, *OT Theology*, 2:285.

25. Part of Amos' argument may be that the *event* of the exodus alone, separated from
     a right relationship with God, does not set Israel apart from the nations. However,
     the verse also points to God's activity at key points in the history of other peoples;
     see e.g. Mays, *Amos*, pp. 157–159; Wolff, *Joel and Amos*, pp. 347–348. Fretheim notes
     that though God's activity is focused on Israel, this 'occurs within God's more
     comprehensive ways of acting in the larger world and are shaped by God's
     overarching purposes for the world' (*God and World*, p. 24); divine activity in the
     world preceded the call of Israel and continues independently of it, and Amos 9:7
     is one example of that. See also James Chukwuma Okoye, *Israel and the Nations: A
     Mission Theology of the Old Testament* (Maryknoll: Orbis, 2006), pp. 75–77; C. J. H.
     Wright, *Mission*, pp. 96–98, 465–467.

26. See Vogels, *Universal Covenant*, pp. 71–113; C. J. H. Wright, *Mission*, pp. 466–467.

Edomites (Deut. 2:4–5), Moabites (Deut. 2:9) and Ammonites (Deut. 2:19). God's concern for all nations is seen too in Deuteronomy 32:8:

> *When the Most High gave the nations their inheritance,*
>   *when he divided all mankind,*
> *he set up boundaries for the peoples*
>   *according to the number of the sons of God.*[27]

As we have seen, the 'sons of God' referred to here are probably heavenly beings appointed by God to supervise the nations and to be responsible for the proper administration of justice (e.g. Ps. 82). This emphasizes the special relationship between Yahweh and Israel, but also indicates that other nations are not outside his jurisdiction: they belong to him, he has fixed their boundaries and has appointed divine guardians for them.

It is against this background, not just of God's sovereignty over the nations but also of his intervention in their history, that oracles against the nations are set. Like Israel, the nations are included in the divine purpose and are subject to his requirements. In his judgment on those who flout his authority (including Israel) we see the vindication both of Yahweh's righteousness and of the glory to which only he has any right.

Salvation for all nations

Mission in the Old Testament[28]
A proper consideration of mission in the OT cannot limit discussion to its root

---

27. Following the LXX and Dead Sea Scrolls (see above, pp. 120–121).

28. Texts looking at mission in the OT include R. Bauckham, *The Bible and Mission: Christian Witness in a Postmodern World* (Carlisle: Paternoster, 2003; Grand Rapids: Baker, 2004); Arthur Glasser, *Announcing the Kingdom: The Story of God's Mission in the Bible* (Grand Rapids: Baker, 2003); Walter C. Kaiser, Jr., *Mission in the Old Testament: Israel as a Light to the Nations* (Grand Rapids: Baker, 2000); Andreas J. Köstenberger and Peter T. O'Brien, *Salvation to the Ends of the Earth: A Biblical Theology of Mission*, NSBT 11 (Leicester: Apollos; Downers Grove: IVP, 2001); R. Martin-Achard, *A Light to the Nations: A Study of the Old Testament Conception of Israel's Mission to the World* (Edinburgh: Oliver & Boyd, 1962); Okoye, *Israel*; H. H. Rowley, *Israel's Mission to the World* (London: SPCK, 1939); *The Missionary Message of the Old Testament* (London: Carey, 1944); Charles H. H. Scobie, 'Israel and the Nations: An Essay in Biblical

meaning of 'sending' or 'being sent'.[29] Mission for God's people, particularly in the OT, is participation in God's mission,[30] which, as we have seen, has as its goal the revelation of his holiness and glory throughout the whole created order.[31]

In his complaint against God's decision to spare Nineveh, Jonah prayed, *I knew that you are a gracious and compassionate God, slow to anger and abounding in love* [ḥesed] (Jon. 4:2). The formula *gracious and compassionate, slow to anger, abounding in love* is, as we have seen, an orthodox creedal confession of the attributes of God.[32] The expression occurs several times in the OT (Exod. 34:6; Neh. 9:17; Pss 86:15; 103:8; 145:8; Joel 2:13; Jon. 4:2), and is generally associated with God's gracious dealings with Israel. It appears in its fullest form in Exodus 34:6–7, where it is linked with God's forgiveness and continued commitment to Israel, following her idolatry with the golden calf (see also Neh. 9:17), and is closely related to the covenantal statement in Exodus 20:5b–6.[33] The centrality of the term *ḥesed* also links this formula to the covenant between God and Israel. In

---

Footnote 127 (*continued*)

Theology', *TynBul* 43.2 (1992), pp. 282–305; Carroll Stuhlmueller, 'The Foundations for Mission in the Old Testament', in Carroll Stuhlmueller and Donald Senior, *The Biblical Foundations for Mission* (Maryknoll: Orbis, 1983), pp. 9–140; C. J. H. Wright, *Mission*. See also Brueggemann, *Theology*, pp. 430–434, 495–502; Goldingay, *OT Theology*, 2:205–209, 818–833; Preuss, *OT Theology*, 2:301–307; Rendtorff, *Hebrew Bible*, pp. 673–675.

29. See Okoye, *Israel*, p. 10; C. J. H. Wright, *Mission*, pp. 22–23. For a discussion of this aspect of mission in the OT, see F. L. McDaniel, 'Mission in the Old Testament', in W. J. Larkin and J. F. Williams (eds.), *Mission in the New Testament: An Evangelical Approach* (Maryknoll: Orbis, 1998), pp. 11–20.

30. C. J. H. Wright, *Mission*, pp. 22–24, 61–68. Goldingay suggests that, rather than having a mission of its own, Israel 'is more the vehicle of God's mission' (*OT Theology*, 2:205).

31. Okoye notes the Orthodox confession that the goal of mission is 'that the glory of God may fill the universe' (*Israel*, p. 102); Wright quotes the Westminster Confession that 'the chief end of man is to glorify God and to enjoy him forever' and maintains that this could be equally related to the purpose of Creation (*Mission*, pp. 404–407); he notes that 'God's mission is to restore Creation to its full original purpose of bringing all glory to God' (p. 188).

32. See above, p. 108.

33. See e.g. R. W. L. Moberly, *At the Mountain of God: Story and Theology in Exodus 32–34*, JSOTSup 22 (Sheffield: JSOT Press, 1983), pp. 87–88; Brevard S. Childs, *Exodus*, OTL (London: SCM, 1974); pp. 604–609.

Jonah 4:2b the prophet takes this central affirmation of Israel's faith, reflecting the special nature of her covenant relationship with God, and uses it to describe his dealings with the Ninevites. Thus we see God's interest extending beyond the borders of Israel – to one of Israel's archetypal enemies. Psalm 145:8–9 extends the scope of the formula and of God's *ḥesed* further, to include all that he has made. This raises the question 'What is the (covenant) relationship between God and the created order that allows the operation of divine *ḥesed*?'

God's universal covenant[34]

The relationship between God and creation is expressed in terms of a covenant in Genesis 9:1–17. This covenant embraces Noah, his descendants and *all living creatures of every kind* (v. 16). The *everlasting covenant* broken by the people of the earth (Isa. 24:5)[35] and God's *covenant with day and night* (Jer. 33:20, 25)[36] probably also relate to the Noahic covenant. Whether or not the relationship between God and the created order can be viewed as a covenant from the start, the covenant with Noah does set it within a covenantal context, and expresses God's ongoing commitment to all he has made,[37] which may be seen as the basis for a wider application of divine *ḥesed*.[38]

---

34. See e.g. B. W. Anderson, *Contours*, pp. 95–97; Dumbrell, *Covenant*, pp. 11–43; Goldingay, *OT Theology*, 2:801–804; Vogels, *Universal Covenant*.

35. Covenants with Abraham (Ps. 105:10) and with David (2 Sam. 23:5) are also described as 'everlasting', though the universal aspect of the covenant in Isa. 24:5 and the reference to worldwide devastation link it particularly with Noah. Oswalt recognizes a specific reference to the Noahic covenant, but also suggests a wider reference to 'the implicit covenant between Creator and creature' (*Isaiah 1–39*, p. 446); see also Childs, *Isaiah*, p. 179; Goldingay, *Isaiah*, pp. 137–140; *OT Theology*, 2:801–803; Seitz, *Isaiah 1–39*, pp. 179–184.

36. The reference to this *covenant with the day and . . . with the night* alongside *the fixed laws of heaven and earth* (Jer. 33:25) probably alludes to God's promise in Gen. 8:22 to maintain the regular order of creation, again in the context of the Noahic covenant, though this too may be taken more widely and linked to the relationship between God as the Creator and the world (Gen. 1:5).

37. See e.g. B. W. Anderson, *Creation to New Creation*, pp. 151–164; Fretheim, *God and World*, pp. 85–87.

38. According to Eichrodt, 'divine lovingkindness . . . came to be regarded as the most profound meaning of the relationship between Creator and creature; or to put it another way, the Creation was included among those relationships based on the idea of community' (*Theology*, 1:239).

We have noted that the *Chaoskampf* motif links creation and redemption.[39] Just as the flood demonstrates that judgment on sin may be depicted as a return to a state of chaos, God's act of primordial redemption from chaos, reflected in the covenant with Noah, may be seen as the pattern for God's redemptive dealings with his world.[40] This includes the exodus and return from exile, and anticipates the last act of redemption: the final defeat of chaos and the creation of new heavens and a new earth.

Beginning with the call of Abraham in Genesis 12:1–3, Israel features prominently in God's purposes to redeem the world after the fall and subsequent decline into sin. However, Israel's call and redemption need to be set in the context of God's purpose for all creation: his commitment to the redemption of the world precedes his commitment to the redemption of Israel. God's activity at the exodus, which was both creative and redemptive for Israel, mirrors his redemptive activity at creation,[41] and points to his commitment to and redemptive purpose for the whole of the created order.[42] Thus Israel's life in relation to God may be seen as a microcosm of what God intends for the whole earth.[43]

A further example of how Israel's life models God's redemptive purpose for the world is in the idea of 'rest'. After his creative activity, God rested, and it is

---

39. See above, pp. 136–138.

40. In his discussion of the exodus Fretheim notes that 'God's work in creation provides the basis, categories and interpretative clues for what happens in redemption and related divine activity' (*God and World*, p. 110), and he goes on to argue that Israel's deliverance is part of God's purpose for all creation (pp. 109–112, 123–126).

41. Okoye argues that Creation is a redemptive act, and that Gen. 1 points to God's care for, and the equality of, all peoples (*Israel*, p. 34).

42. C. J. H. Wright views the exodus as the first act of divine redemption in the OT (*Mission*, p. 275). He describes it as 'God's Model of Redemption' (pp. 265–288), and considers it paradigmatic of God's redemptive purposes for the world by writers of both testaments (p. 275). However, this underplays the redemptive significance of the deliverance from the waters of chaos at the flood (and maybe the act of creation itself). While the exodus is of central importance as a symbol of redemption, its significance for the whole created order can best be explained by viewing it as an expression of God's prior redemptive commitment to creation, expressed in the covenant with Noah.

43. Goldingay describes Israel as 'a microcosm of humanity' (*OT Theology*, 2:517); see also Okoye, *Israel*, pp. 31–32.

reasonable to assume that this was a rest intended to be shared by all creation.[44] That was marred by the fall (e.g. Gen. 3:17–19); however, in the institution of the Sabbath, closely associated with the Sinaitic covenant (Exod. 31:12–18; Ezek. 20:10–12), Israel is invited to share in the divine rest and so to anticipate, in their national life and worship, the divine purpose for the whole world. This may be evident too in the 'rest' associated with Israel's life in the Promised Land (Exod. 33:14; Deut. 12:10; 25:19; Josh. 1:13; 21:43–44; 2 Sam. 7:1; Ps. 95:10–11). Sabbath regulations are also closely linked with instructions for building the tabernacle,[45] pointing to an important relationship between them,[46] and language describing the completion of the tabernacle echoes the description of the completion of creation.[47] This suggests that the tabernacle/temple too was intended to reflect the divine order in creation:[48] it was 'a microcosm of creation . . . the world order as God intended, writ small in Israel'.[49] This, again, points to the religious life of Israel as providing an example, on a lesser scale,

---

44. According to Dumbrell, 'the Sabbath was understood to prefigure the rest which the completion of creation had foreshadowed for mankind' (*Covenant*, p. 123). Something of the universal application is already present in that the rest associated with the Sabbath includes all foreigners within Israel, animals (Deut. 5:14) and even the land (Lev. 25:4). Fretheim further links the Sabbath with the temporal framework of creation, which is modelled by Israel (*God and World*, pp. 61–64). Goldingay takes a different view, arguing that God's rest opens the way for human beings to continue his work of subduing the earth (*OT Theology*, 2:523–524).

45. Sabbath regulations immediately follow the first set of instructions for building the tabernacle (Exod. 31:12–17) and immediately precede the second set (Exod. 35:1–3).

46. Childs argues that observing the Sabbath and building the tabernacle 'are two sides of the same reality' and 'both testify to God's rule over his creation' (*Exodus*, pp. 541–542); see also Dumbrell, *Faith*, pp. 39–40.

47. Fretheim, *God and World*, pp. 128–129; Levenson, *Creation*, pp. 85–86; Okoye, *Israel*, pp. 31–32.

48. According to Beale, the threefold division of the tabernacle/temple (outer court, inner sanctuary and holy of holies) corresponds to the earth, the heavens (with the heavenly lights) and the invisible dwelling place of God (*Temple*, pp. 32–36).

49. Fretheim, *God and World*, p. 128; see also B. W. Anderson, *Creation versus Chaos*, pp. 64–65; *Contours*, pp. 199–208; Brueggemann, *Theology*, pp. 533–534; Clements, *Temple*, pp. 65–69; Goldingay, *OT Theology*, 1:396–398.

of God's purpose for the world.[50] And that in turn implies that the Sinaitic covenant (and also the Abrahamic and Davidic covenants) can be seen as a more detailed outworking of universal principles already present in God's (covenant) relationship with the whole of creation.

We have noted that God's concern for the nations plays an important part in other divine covenants.[51] God called Abraham so that through him *all peoples on earth will be blessed* (Gen. 12:3). The Sinaitic covenant is a partial fulfilment of the Abrahamic. In order to bless and minister to the nations, God has called Israel to exercise a priestly function in the world (Exod. 19:5–6).[52] And here, again, we see Israel, served by its priests, as a microcosm of the world, served by Israel, and the relationship established with Israel as a pattern of God's intended relationship with all humanity. The covenant with David too has an outward dimension: the Davidic king inherited the promise made to Abraham that *all nations will be blessed through him* (Ps. 72:17b).

Richard Baukham also focuses on Abraham, Israel and David. These stories demonstrate a general narrative movement from the particular to the universal,[53] and each contributes to the biblical understanding of mission. Baukham notes three 'trajectories' that emphasize God's universal concern.[54] In God's choice of Abraham we see the 'trajectory of blessing', which unfolds in the book of Genesis. Israel's call, as God's special possession to be a witness to the nations, demonstrates the 'trajectory of God's revelation of himself to the world', and the choice of David as king, and Jerusalem as the centre of a kingdom that will finally extend over the whole earth points to the 'trajectory of rule, of God's kingdom coming in all creation'. Though Baukham does not mention covenant in his discussion, I would argue that these three narratives

---

50. In Okoye's view 'Israel bears within itself the vocation of the whole earth to be the home of God' (*Israel*, p. 32), and he goes on, 'Israel enshrined in her religious tradition the awareness that the purpose of God enfolds the entire creation and that somehow Israel holds brief for humanity' (p. 34).

51. The significance of divine covenants is also noted, for example, by Kaiser, *Mission*, pp. 15–28 (though Kaiser does not discuss the covenant with Noah); Köstenberger and O'Brien, *Salvation*, pp. 28–44; C. J. H. Wright, *Mission*, pp. 324–356.

52. The NIV translates Exod. 19:5 as *although the whole earth is mine*; 'although' is the Hebrew *kî*, which is more usually rendered 'because' or 'for', suggesting that the purpose of Israel's election is not to separate her from the nations, but to fulfil a role in relation to the nations, who also belong to God.

53. Bauckham, *Bible and Mission*, pp. 27–54.

54. Ibid., p. 27.

and their trajectories are significant because they are associated with divine covenants, and the narrative movement is also not very different from the revelation of God's glory to all the nations of the world – which also embraces God's promise of universal blessing, witness and sovereign authority.[55]

Mission: at the heart of a narrative substructure of the Old Testament

When we looked at the application of Greimas's structural model to the book of Isaiah,[56] we asked if there might be a similar structural pattern in the OT as a whole. We have noted that God's purpose to reveal his glory is evident throughout the OT. The divine covenants in the OT also demonstrate God's interest in and commitment to the non-Israelite nations. And we have seen too the role of God's people as the agent of God's mission: beginning with Abraham and his family and extending to the nation redeemed from Egypt. Other prophets also note Israel's present failure, and promise future restoration and renewal. In Isaiah the agent of that renewal is *the Servant*, Ezekiel associates renewal with the work of *the Spirit* (Ezek. 36:26–27; cf. Joel 2:28), while Jeremiah points to the work of *the Messiah* (Jer. 33:14–22; cf. Zech. 3:8–9; 6:12–13), though there is also considerable overlap. The message is essentially the same. God's people cannot fulfil their calling to be a nation of priests, to bring God's blessing to the nations, unless they are renewed, and God has provided the means by which that renewal may take place.

This model emphasizes the centrality of mission in the purposes of God, and invites us to set other theological themes in the OT against that primary objective. Israel has been brought into a relationship with God and been guided and blessed through her history, in order to draw others into that same relationship so that they too may submit themselves to God's authority and share the blessings of his kingdom.

Universalism

The term 'universalism', in the context of OT theology, is generally taken to mean that God's purpose is not limited to Israel, but includes all peoples, and

---

55. Bauckham also notes a fourth narrative movement, which characterizes the other three: 'to all by way of the least' (ibid., pp. 49–54). This picks up on some important aspects of the way God works through those who are outwardly of no account, and though most of the discussion focuses on the NT, the idea is certainly found in the OT – though it is not as closely related to the other narratives as Bauckham suggests.

56. See above, pp. 47–50.

that he will bring all nations to share in the relationship and blessings at first enjoyed by Israel. As we have seen, this was God's intention from the start, and is to be achieved through the witness of a restored and renewed Israel. This raises two further questions. How was Israel's mission to the nations to be accomplished, and, will the nations share in the blessings of salvation as equal partners with Israel?

Israel as a witness to the nations

The OT points to two ways in which Israel's mission to the world will be achieved. First, by showing the reality of God's presence in their community life, Israel will become a light to which the nations are drawn. Second, members of the believing community will go out to the nations. Vogels describes these respectively as *centripetal universalism* (movement towards the centre) and *centrifugal universalism* (movement outwards from the centre).[57]

Centripetal universalism

The idea of foreigners coming to worship in Jerusalem is expressed in Solomon's prayer at the dedication of the temple (1 Kgs 8:41–43). Another significant passage describing the flowing of the nations to Zion is Isaiah 2:2–4. In the era of salvation God will establish Jerusalem at the centre of the world's stage and the nations will stream to it. They recognize that God is there, and come to receive his word: to be taught by him and submit to his judgment. Isaiah 60:1–3 also describes the nations being drawn to a renewed and restored Zion (cf. vv. 7, 10–14). God's glory will be reflected from his people, enabling them to shine with a light that stands in sharp contrast to the darkness of the world round about, and this light will attract the nations. In stark contrast to the apostasy that led to God's name being *profaned among the nations* (Ezek. 36:20–21), Israel's restoration and renewal will result in God's holiness being revealed (Ezek. 36:23), and through this renewed and obedient people God's promise to Abraham of universal blessing will be fulfilled (Jer. 4:2). The pilgrimage to Zion is also described in Zechariah 8:20–23. Earlier the prophet had announced that *many nations will be joined with the LORD in that day and will become my people* (Zech. 2:11). Now that is taken up and expanded: Jerusalem will be the rallying point for peoples from many cities who come to find Yahweh and to receive his grace. The special position of Israel as mediator between God and the nations is made clear in 8:23, *This is what the LORD Almighty says: 'In those days ten men from all languages and nations will take firm hold of one Jew by the*

---

57. Vogels, *Universal Covenant*.

hem of his robe and say, "Let us go with you, because we have heard that God is with you."' The recognition of the reality of God's presence among his people will draw the nations to him. This witness to the nations is achieved primarily through Israel's national life and religious institutions, emphasizing that ethical conduct, worship and right living within the covenant community play an integral part in mission.

Centrifugal universalism

In addition to passages that refer to the nations coming to Jerusalem/Zion, some texts also speak of the nations worshipping God in their own lands. Isaiah 19:19–22 points to a day when an altar will be set up and worship and sacrifices will be offered in Egypt (see also Zeph. 2:11; Mal. 1:11). This suggests that God's revelation will reach the nations, though passages that speak about God's people going to the nations in mission are very few.

The book of Jonah is sometimes regarded as a true 'missionary' text. The announcement of coming judgment on Nineveh could be compared with other oracles against the nations, with the important difference that here Jonah is sent to speak directly to the Ninevites in their own land. However, he is not sent to call Nineveh to repentance, and the purpose of the book has more to do with the (negative) attitude to God's willingness to forgive than with mission.[58] The role of the Servant as a *light for the Gentiles* (Isa. 42:6; 49:6) who will bring God's *salvation to the ends of the earth* (Isa. 49:6), and in whose instruction the *islands will put their trust* (Isa. 42:4) also appears to indicate movement to the nations.[59]

The theme of the nations turning to God begins and ends the final section of the book of Isaiah (chs. 56 – 66). Along with the exiles of Israel, God will gather from other nations those who commit themselves to serving him (56:3–8). They will be drawn to the divine glory that shines from his renewed and restored people (60:1–3). But Israel's role in the winning of the nations here is

---

58. For discussion of the purpose of Jonah, see e.g. Leslie C. Allen, *Joel, Obadiah, Jonah and Micah*, NICOT (Grand Rapids: Eerdmans, 1976), pp. 189–191; T. Desmond Alexander, 'Jonah', in David W. Baker, T. Desmond Alexander and Bruce K. Waltke, *Obadiah, Jonah and Micah*, TOTC (Leicester: IVP, 1988), pp. 45–131 (81–91); Ronald E. Clements, 'The Purpose of the Book of Jonah', *Congress Volume, Edinburgh 1974*, VTSup 28 (Leiden: Brill, 1975), pp. 16–28; Kaiser, *Mission*, pp. 65–74; G. M. Landes, 'The Kerygma of the Book of Jonah', *Int* 21 (1967), pp. 3–31.

59. For further discussion of the role of the Servant in relation to the nations, see below, pp. 330–331.

not merely passive, and in the closing verses of the book we see God's people performing the somewhat unfamiliar task of going to the nations in order to bring them back to worship God in Jerusalem (66:18–21).[60]

God's people are also called to *declare his glory among the nations, his marvellous deeds among all peoples* (Ps. 96:3). Even though scattered among the nations God's people continue to praise him (see also Ps. 57:9–11). In these passages we see a desire to make known to the nations the glory of God. This seems to be motivated more by gratitude and wonder than from a desire to share with others, but it does, nevertheless, indicate a movement to the nations with the proclamation of God's salvation.

Israel and the nations: equal partners in salvation?
Zion
As we have seen, Zion plays a central role in the era of salvation. Does this imply that Israel will continue to enjoy a privileged position in the kingdom of God? According to Köhler, the centrality of Zion in Isaiah 2:2–4 indicates that the nations do not participate equally with Israel. In these verses,

> all nations enjoy God's leadership. But Zion remains the mountain of the Lord . . .
> Mankind is within the scope of God's providence, in his power, enjoying his peace and
> with access to his teaching: but Israel alone has been admitted to the sphere of grace.[61]

It is clear that Zion stands at the centre of God's new world order. However, the city is not given political significance. It is the place where God is to be found, and thus signifies his presence, and the hope to be found in him. This is the theme of Isaiah 28:16:

> *I lay a stone in Zion,*
>   *a tested stone,*

---

60. The 'survivors' (Isa. 66:19) are most likely Israelites who have come through God's judgment on the nation; see e.g. Oswalt, *Isaiah 40–66*, p. 688; Goldingay, *Isaiah*, p. 373; Joseph Blenkinsopp, 'Second Isaiah – Prophet of Universalism', *JSOT* 41 (1988), p. 98. Another possibility is that they are the survivors of divine judgment on the world – but then who are they sent to?

61. Köhler, *OT Theology*, pp. 230–231; see also Preuss, *OT Theology*, 2:301–303. By contrast, Eichrodt maintains that 'in this vision Israelite belief in Providence is filled with universal content' (*Theology*, 1:172); see also Goldingay, *OT Theology*, 2:821–825.

a precious cornerstone for a sure foundation;
  the one who trusts will never be dismayed.

Those who find refuge in Zion are those who have faith in God, and Zion is a symbol of the security to be found in God himself (see also Ps. 46:1). It is not the nation of Israel as a whole, but the faithful remnant who will enjoy the blessings of the age to come, and Isaiah's vision of the peoples of the world streaming to Zion indicates that the hope to be found in the city is for all who enter on the same terms (see also Isa. 26:2). When people from other nations acknowledge God's sovereignty and submit to his judgments, when they stop trusting in their own resources, symbolized here by abandoning their weapons of war, and depend, instead, on Yahweh alone, then they too may have a share in the blessings of the coming kingdom and may also be admitted to the sphere of grace.

An important aspect of this is the view of Zion as the successor of Sinai.[62] The picture of the nations gathering for a feast on Mount Zion (Isa. 25:6–8) recalls the covenant meal Israel's elders shared on Mount Sinai (Exod. 24:11).[63] God will again reveal his glory and establish a relationship no longer limited to Israel, as it was at Sinai, but that now includes all peoples, and Zion is a symbol of that universal participation. Isaiah 2:2–4 may be viewed in a similar way. Israel travelled to Sinai to receive the Law; now the nations stream to Mount Zion to receive and submit to God's word. What Israel received at Sinai, the nations will receive at Zion, and here, again, we see God's intention for the world focused, for the time being, on Israel.

The centrifugal mission in Isaiah 66:18–21 also focuses on Zion and on the temple. This is set, though, against God's declaration *Heaven is my throne, / and the earth my footstool. / Where is the house you will build for me?* (Isa. 66:1), which echoes Solomon's recognition, at the dedication of the temple, that God could not be limited to a particular place (1 Kgs 8:27). This would also tend to rule out geopolitical interpretations of the future role of Zion, and points, instead, to its significance as the centre of God's rule over all the earth.[64]

---

62. See above, p. 276.

63. It is likely that Isa. 25:6–8 follows on from Isa. 24:21–23, and the reference to 'elders' before whom God will reign 'gloriously' (v. 23) recalls the theophany in Exod. 24:9–11, which also included what was probably a covenant meal: *they saw God and they ate and drank* (Exod. 24:11).

64. See also Okoye's discussion, *Israel*, pp. 102–117.

Universalism in Isaiah 40 – 55[65]

Isaiah 40 – 55 points to the future deliverance and exaltation of Israel. The attitude to the nations, though, appears ambiguous. Some passages indicate that the nations will be saved,[66] while others suggest their subordination to Israel.[67] As a result there is a divergence among commentators: some continue to emphasize Deutero-Isaiah's universalistic message; others regard him as a nationalistic writer, offering salvation only to Israel.[68]

Van Winkle argues for a middle course: the prophet envisages the salvation of the nations, but only in submission to Israel.[69] However, these two themes are treated separately in Isaiah 40 – 55, and any attempt at synthesis does not do full justice to the text. Isaiah 45:22 does not indicate that the salvation available to the nations is different from that experienced by Israel, or that it requires the nations' submission to Israel; the condition is to turn to Yahweh. The Servant Songs also suggest the inclusion of the nations, again without the

65. See e.g. Albertz, *History*, 2:419–424; B. W. Anderson, *Living World*, pp. 485–488; Blenkinsopp, 'Second Isaiah', pp. 162–170; Clements, *OT Theology*, pp. 95–96; R. Davidson, 'Universalism in Second Isaiah', *SJT* 16 (1963), pp. 166–185; A. Gelston, 'The Missionary Message of Second Isaiah', *SJT* 18 (1965), pp. 308–318; Michael A. Grisanti, 'Israel's Mission to the Nations in Isaiah 40–55: An Update', *MSJ* 9.1 (1998), pp. 39–61; D. E. Hollenberg, 'Nationalism and the Nations in Isa. 40–55', *VT* 19 (1969), pp. 23–36; Elmer A. Martens, 'Impulses to Global Missions in Isaiah', *Direction* 35.1 (2006), pp. 59–69; David F. Payne, 'The Meaning of Mission in Isaiah 40–55', in Anthony Billington, Tony Lane and Max Turner (eds.), *Mission and Meaning: Essays Presented to Peter Cotterell* (Carlisle: Paternoster, 1995), pp. 3–11; Rikk E. Watts, 'Echoes from the Past: Israel's Ancient Traditions and the Destiny of the Nations in Isaiah 40–55', *JSOT* 28.4 (2004), pp. 481–508; D. W. van Winkle, 'The Relationship of the Nations to Yahweh and to Israel in Isaiah XL–LV', *VT* 35.4 (1985), pp. 446–458; 'Proselytes in Isaiah XL–LV? A Study of Isaiah XLIV 1–5', *VT* 47.3 (1997), pp. 341–359.

66. E.g. Isa. 45:22, *turn to me and be saved all you ends of the earth.*

67. E.g. Isa. 45:14, *they will trudge behind you, coming over to you in chains;* Isa. 49:23, *they will bow down before you with their faces to the ground; they will lick the dust at your feet.*

68. For a survey of opinion, see e.g. Grisanti, 'Israel's Mission'; van Winkle, 'Proselytes'. For a nationalistic interpretation of some of the texts given a universalistic interpretation below, see e.g. Snaith, 'Servant', in Rowley, *Studies*; 'Isaiah 40–66', in Orlinsky and Snaith, *Studies*; Whybray, *Isaiah 40–66*; see also Brueggemann, *Theology*, pp. 433–434.

69. Van Winkle, 'Relationship'; see also Watts, 'Echoes', pp. 505–508.

need to submit to Israel. Davidson identifies three key expressions that point to the universal nature of the Servant's ministry.[70] First, he will bring *justice to the nations* (42:1). In the coming age Israel looks forward to the establishment of justice (*mišpāṭ*) through the messianic king; here that is extended to include the nations. Second, the Servant will be *a light for the Gentiles* (42:6; 49:6). This may include the revelation of God's truth to the nations, but is also closely linked with bringing salvation (49:6; 51:4–5). A third, parallel, expression is *covenant for the people* (42:6; 49:8).[71] According to Childs, this implies that the Servant 'embodies a covenant relationship with the nations',[72] and Goldingay suggests that the expression points to Israel's commission to 'provide a working model of what it means to be in covenant with Yhwh and a promise of what Yhwh intends for all peoples'.[73]

Passages that appear to envisage Israel's hegemony over the nations have a different focus. Against the background of helplessness and oppression at the hands of more powerful nations, they emphasize the completeness of Israel's salvation. The nation will experience a total reversal of what has been its experience so far. These passages emphasize, in political language, the spiritual truth that Israel's redemption and restoration by God will be full and glorious. Isaiah 45:14 portrays the nations as prisoners of war; however, Childs and Goldingay see them not as Israel's captives but as those who, like Israel, have been freed by Cyrus. They recognize Israel's God as the true source of their liberation, and so submit themselves to him.[74] Here, again, we see Israel's role as witness: the nations pay willing homage to Israel, because they want to know Israel's God: *surely God is with you, and there is no other* (Isa. 45:14). In this we see that universalism and particularism both play a part in mission; acknowledging Yahweh's people and what he is doing among them must be part of acknowledging Yahweh.[75] Again, though, the emphasis is on the nations' approach to God rather than their subordination to Israel.

---

70. Davidson, 'Universalism'.

71. See also e.g. Childs, *Isaiah*, pp. 325–327; Goldingay, *Isaiah*, pp. 241–242; *OT Theology*, 2:225–226, 821–822; Oswalt, *Isaiah 40–66*, pp. 117–119; van Winkle, 'Relationship', pp. 452–457; G. E. Wright, *Mission*, p. 352.

72. Childs, *Isaiah*, p. 326.

73. Goldingay, *OT Theology*, 2:226.

74. Childs, *Isaiah*, pp. 354–355; Goldingay, *OT Theology*, 2:746–748; cf. Oswalt, *Isaiah 40–66*, pp. 214–215.

75. See e.g. Davidson, 'Universalism' p. 176; Goldingay, *OT Theology*, 2:740–758, 818–833; C. J. H. Wright, *Mission*, pp. 222–264.

Another important theme in Isaiah 40 – 55 is monotheism. Addressing exiles who were possibly interpreting the exile as a victory for the gods of Babylon, the prophet emphasizes Yahweh's supremacy and portrays other gods as worthless idols: they are not just off limits for Israel; they do not exist. The corollary of this is that as the only God, Yahweh must also be the God of the whole earth.[76] This is linked too with the idea of creative redemption in Deutero-Isaiah. Bringing together exodus and creation traditions points to a close relationship between God's creative and redemptive activity in the life of Israel: the one who created them as his people would also act to redeem, renew and restore them. With a growing recognition that God is the Creator of the whole world, it follows that the whole world needs also to experience his redemptive power. This has significant implications for Israel's mission.[77]

The community of nations

God's purpose for other nations to participate equally with Israel in the blessings of his salvation is seen very clearly in Isaiah 19:16–25.[78] This follows a passage describing divine judgment on Egypt, which echoes Israel's deliverance at the time of the exodus (19:1–15). On this occasion, though, God's action will result in the Egyptians turning to him (vv. 18–22). In verse 23 Assyria too is included in the hope of salvation, as these two enemies are united in their worship of Israel's God. In the final section (vv. 24–25) the universal scope of divine grace reaches its height, with the picture of Israel, Egypt and Assyria as joint heirs of the blessings of God: *the LORD Almighty will bless them, saying, 'Blessed be Egypt my people, Assyria my handiwork, and Israel my inheritance'* (v. 25). This points to Israel's restoration: the nation will take its place on the world stage alongside its former oppressors.[79] But those nations also take their place alongside Israel as the objects of divine grace, and their description, in terms previously reserved for Israel,[80] points

---

76. See e.g. Rowley, *Israel's Mission*, pp. 7–8; Gelston, 'Missionary Message',
    pp. 308–318.

77. C. J. H. Wright discusses the significance of monotheism for mission at length
    (*Mission*, pp. 71–188).

78. See e.g. Goldingay, *OT Theology*, 2:827–830.

79. Egypt was Israel's first, and archetypal, oppressor; Assyria is probably mentioned
    as the current oppressor.

80. The expression *my people* features in the covenant formula *they will be my people and
    I will be their God* (e.g. Lev. 26:12; Jer. 11:4; 24:7; 31:1, 33; Ezek. 11:20; 34:30; 37:23,
    27); Israel is referred to as *my handiwork* in Isa. 29:23; 60:21; 64:8.

to their acceptance into the same kind of covenant relationship. It is likely that Egypt and Assyria represent all Israel's enemies. This indicates that God's final purpose for all nations (even Israel's enemies) is not to destroy them before Israel but to save them, and to form them, together with Israel, into a new community of those faithful to him. It is significant that, as well as having echoes of the exodus, the reference to all three nations being *blessed* by God also represents the fulfilment of the promise made to Abraham.

Isaiah 56:3, 6–8 also points to the inclusion of foreigners within the people of God and their full participation in worship in the temple, which will be designated *a house of prayer for all nations*. Zechariah 14:9 (*on that day there will be one LORD [yhwh 'eḥād]*) repeats the words of Deuteronomy 6:4 (*the LORD is one*), and again universalizes a central affirmation of Israel's covenant relationship with Yahweh.[81]

Thus we see that God's commitment to his world (confirmed in the covenant with Noah and which leads to the divine promise that through Abraham all nations will be blessed) will be fulfilled through the mediation of Israel. God called this people to himself so that through their witness all the nations of the world might acknowledge his holiness and glory – and share as equal partners in the blessings of salvation Israel has received.

Postscript

This book began by emphasizing the need to treat the OT as authoritative and normative for the faith of the church. That is not always straightforward, since it includes religious ideas and practices that do not form part of the church's worship. This final section, though, helps us to recognize that the OT applies not only to Israel. From the first, God's purpose was to bring all peoples into a relationship with himself. His choice of Israel and his words to and through Israel were part of that wider universalistic purpose. From the covenant with creation, through to the covenants with Abraham, Moses and David, God expresses his concern for the whole world. The OT anticipates the birth of the church; it anticipates the coming of God's Servant-Messiah, who will bring light to the nations, and through whose death the new covenant is inaugurated; it anticipates all peoples having an equal share in the blessings of God's salvation.

---

81. See C. J. H. Wright, *Mission*, p. 527.

The inclusion of the nations is not an addendum to God's dealings with Israel: it is implicit from the start of the OT, and is fulfilled through the coming of Christ. Thus Christians may rightly regard the OT as our book too. It is a part of our heritage, and, what is more important, it is God's word to us. Because of that we should value it, read it, study it and seek to understand it.

SELECT BIBLIOGRAPHY

Albertz, Rainer, *A History of Israelite Religion in the Old Testament Period*, 2 vols. (London: SCM; Louisville: Westminster John Knox, 1994).

Anderson, Bernard W., *Contours of Old Testament Theology* (Minneapolis: Fortress, 1999).

—— *The Living World of the Old Testament*, 4th ed. (Harlow: Longman, 1988).

Arnold, Bill T., and Bryan E. Beyer, *Readings from the Ancient Near East: Primary Sources for Old Testament Study* (Grand Rapids: Baker, 2002).

Baker, David L., *Two Testaments, One Bible: A Study of the Theological Relationship between the Old and New Testaments*, 2nd ed. (Leicester: Apollos, 1991).

Baker, David W., and Bill T. Arnold (eds.), *The Face of Old Testament Studies: A Survey of Contemporary Approaches* (Leicester: Apollos; Grand Rapids: Baker, 1999).

Barr, James, *The Concept of Biblical Theology: An Old Testament Perspective* (London: SCM, 1999).

My policy with the bibliography is to include every book with two or more references. That is for two reasons: (1) two or more references suggest it is reasonably important for my research; (2) for ease of reference. The first reference includes bibliographical detail, so the information is clear enough. Subsequent references are shortened, and it helps if the reader can find full details in the bibliography rather than try to find the first reference in earlier footnotes.

Barton, John, *Reading the Old Testament: Method in Biblical Study*, 2nd ed. (Louisville: Westminster John Knox, 1996).

Bright, John, *The Authority of the Old Testament* (London: SCM, 1967; repr. Biblical and Theological Classics Library; Carlisle: Paternoster, 1998).

—— *A History of Israel*, 4th ed. (Louisville: Westminster John Knox, 2000).

Brueggemann, Walter, *Theology of the Old Testament: Testimony, Dispute, Advocacy* (Minneapolis: Fortress, 1997).

Childs, Brevard S., *Biblical Theology of the Old and New Testaments: Theological Reflection on the Christian Bible* (London: SCM, 1992).

—— *Old Testament Theology in a Canonical Context* (London: SCM, 1985).

Clements, Ronald E., *A Century of Old Testament Study* (London: Lutterworth, 1976).

—— *Old Testament Theology: A Fresh Approach* (London: Marshall, Morgan & Scott, 1978).

Collins, John J., *Encounters with Biblical Theology* (Minneapolis: Fortress, 2005).

Cook, Stephen L., *The Social Roots of Biblical Yahwism*, Studies in Biblical Literature 8 (Leiden: Brill, 2004).

Davies, Philip R., and John W. Rogerson, *The Old Testament World*, 2nd ed. (London: T. & T. Clarke; Louisville: Westminster John Knox, 2005).

Drane, John, *Introducing the Old Testament*, 2nd rev. ed. (Oxford: Lion, 2000; Minneapolis: Fortress, 2001).

Dumbrell, William J., *The Faith of Israel: A Theological Survey of the Old Testament*, 2nd ed. (Grand Rapids: Baker; Leicester: Apollos, 2002).

Dyrness, William, *Themes in Old Testament Theology* (Downers Grove: IVP; Carlisle: Paternoster, 1977).

Eichrodt, Walter, *Theology of the Old Testament*, 2 vols. (London: SCM, 1961–7).

Enns, Peter, *Inspiration and Incarnation: Evangelicals and the Problem of the Old Testament* (Grand Rapids: Baker, 2005).

Gerstenberger, Erhard S., *Theologies in the Old Testament* (London: T. & T. Clark, 2002).

Goldingay, John, *Approaches to Old Testament Interpretation* (Leicester: Apollos, 1990).

—— *Old Testament Theology*, 2 vols. (Downers Grove: IVP; Milton Keynes: Paternoster, 2003–6).

Gottwald, Norman K., *The Hebrew Bible: A Socio-Literary Introduction* (Philadelphia: Fortress, 1985; paperback with CD-ROM, 2002).

Hafemann, Scott J., and Paul R. House (eds.), *Central Themes in Biblical Theology: Mapping Unity in Diversity* (Leicester: Apollos; Grand Rapids: Baker, 2007).

Harrison, R. K., *Introduction to the Old Testament* (London: IVP, 1977).

Hasel, Gerhard F., *Old Testament Theology: Basic Issues in the Current Debate*, 4th ed. (Grand Rapids: Eerdmans, 1991).

House, Paul R., *Old Testament Theology* (Downers Grove: IVP, 1998).

Jacob, Edmond, *Theology of the Old Testament* (London: Hodder & Stoughton, 1958).

Kaiser, Walter C., Jr., *Toward an Old Testament Theology* (Grand Rapids: Zondervan, 1978; repr. 1999).

Köhler, Ludwig, *Old Testament Theology* (London: Lutterworth, 1957; repr. Cambridge: James Clarke, 2003).

LaSor, William Sanford, David Allan Hubbard and Frederick William Bush (eds.), *Old Testament Survey: The Message, Form, and Background of the Old Testament*, 2nd ed. (Grand Rapids: Eerdmans, 1996).

Merrill, Eugene H., *Everlasting Dominion: A Theology of the Old Testament* (Nashville: Broadman & Holman, 2006).

Ollenburger, Ben C. (ed.), *Old Testament Theology: Flowering and Future*, SBTS 1 (Winona Lake: Eisenbrauns, 2004).

Perdue, Leo G., *The Collapse of History: Reconstructing Old Testament Theology*, OBT (Minneapolis: Fortress, 1994).

—— *Reconstructing Old Testament Theology: After the Collapse of History*, OBT (Minneapolis: Fortress, 2005).

Preuss, Horst Dietrich, *Old Testament Theology*, 2 vols., OTL (Louisville: Westminster John Knox, 1995–6).

Provan, Iain, V. Philips Long, Tremper Longman III, *A Biblical History of Israel* (Louisville: Westminster John Knox, 2003).

Rad, Gerhard von, *Old Testament Theology*, 2 vols. (Edinburgh: Oliver & Boyd, 1962–5).

Rendtorff, Rolf, *The Canonical Hebrew Bible: A Theology of the Old Testament* (Leiden: Deo, 2005).

Ringgren, Helmer, *Israelite Religion* (London: SPCK, 1966).

Sailhamer, John H., *Introduction to Old Testament Theology: A Canonical Approach* (Grand Rapids: Zondervan, 1995).

Scobie, Charles H. H., *The Ways of Our God: An Approach to Biblical Theology* (Grand Rapids: Eerdmans, 2003).

Vaux, Roland de, *Ancient Israel: Its Life and Institutions* (London: Darton, Longman & Todd, 1961; repr. Grand Rapids: Eerdmans; Livonia: Dove, 1997).

Vriezen, Th. C., *An Outline of Old Testament Theology* (Oxford: Blackwell, 1958).

Waltke, Bruce K., with C. Yu, *An Old Testament Theology: A Canonical and Thematic Approach* (Grand Rapids: Zondervan, 2006).

Wright, Christopher J. H., *The Mission of God: Unlocking the Bible's Grand Narrative* (Downers Grove: IVP; Leicester: IVP, 2006).

—— *Old Testament Ethics for the People of God* (Leicester: IVP; Downers Grove: IVP, 2004).

SUPPLEMENTARY BIBLIOGRAPHY

Albertz, Rainer, *Israel in Exile: The History and Literature of the Sixth Century B.C.E.*, Studies in Biblical Literature 3 (Atlanta: SBL, 2003).

Albrektson, Bertil, *History and the Gods* (Lund: CWK Gleerup, 1967).

Alter, Robert, *The Art of Biblical Narrative* (New York: Basic; London: Allen & Unwin, 1981).

Andersen, Francis I., *Job*, TOTC (Leicester: IVP, 1976).

Anderson, Bernard W., *Creation versus Chaos: The Re-Interpretation of Mythical Symbolism in the Bible* (New York: Association Press, 1967).

—— 'The Crisis in Biblical Theology', *ThTo* 28.3 (1971), pp. 321–327.

—— *From Creation to New Creation: Old Testament Perspectives*, OBT (Minneapolis: Fortress, 1994).

—— (ed.), *Creation in the Old Testament*, IRT 6 (London: SPCK, 1984).

Anderson, G. W. (ed.), *Tradition and Interpretation: Essays by Members of the Society for Old Testament Study* (Oxford: Oxford University Press, 1979).

Baker, David L., 'Typology and the Christian Use of the Old Testament', *SJT* 29 (1976), pp. 137–157.

Baldwin, Joyce G., *Daniel*, TOTC (Leicester: IVP, 1978).

Barr, James, *The Garden of Eden and the Hope of Immortality: The Read-Tuckwell Lectures for 1990* (London: SCM, 1992).

Barton, John, *Amos's Oracles against the Nations* (Cambridge: Cambridge University Press, 1980).

Barton, John, *Understanding Old Testament Ethics: Approaches and Explorations* (Louisville: Westminster John Knox, 2003).

Bauckham, R., *The Bible and Mission: Christian Witness in a Postmodern World* (Carlisle: Paternoster, 2003; Grand Rapids: Baker, 2004).

Beale, G. K., *The Temple and the Church's Mission: A Biblical Theology of the Dwelling Place of God*, NSBT 17 (Leicester: Apollos; Downers Grove: IVP, 2004).

Beasley-Murray, George R., *Jesus and the Kingdom of God* (Grand Rapids: Eerdmans; Carlisle: Paternoster, 1986).

Berlin, Adele, *Poetics and Interpretation of Biblical Narrative* (Sheffield: Almond, 1983; Winona Lake: Eisenbrauns, 1994).

Bray, Gerald, *Biblical Interpretation Past and Present* (Leicester: Apollos; Downers Grove: IVP, 1996).

Bright, John, *Covenant and Promise* (London: SCM, 1977).

—— *The Kingdom of God* (Nashville: Abingdon, 1981).

Brooks, Roger, and John J. Collins (eds.), *Hebrew Bible or Old Testament: Studying the Bible in Judaism and Christianity*, Christianity and Judaism in Antiquity 5 (Notre Dame: University of Notre Dame Press, 1990).

Broyles, Craig C. (ed.), *Interpreting the Old Testament: A Guide for Exegesis* (Grand Rapids: Baker, 2001).

Carlson, R. A., *David the Chosen King, A Traditio-Historical Approach to the Second Book of Samuel* (Stockholm: Almqvist, 1964).

Carson, D. A., and John D. Woodbridge (eds.), *Scripture and Truth* (Leicester: IVP, 1983).

Cerny, Ladislav, *The Day of Yahweh and Some Relevant Problems* (Prague: University Karlovy, 1948).

Childs, Brevard S., *Biblical Theology in Crisis* (Philadelphia: Westminster, 1970).

—— *Exodus*, OTL (London: SCM, 1974).

—— *Isaiah*, OTL (Louisville: Westminster John Knox, 2001).

—— *Myth and Reality in the Old Testament* (London: SCM, 1960).

Christensen, Duane L., *Transformations of the War Oracle in Old Testament Prophecy* (Missoula: Scholars Press, 1975).

Clements, Ronald E., *Abraham and David*, SBT 2.5 (London: SCM, 1967).

—— *God and Temple* (Oxford: Blackwell, 1965).

—— *Isaiah 1–39*, NCB (London: Marshall, Morgan & Scott, 1980).

—— *Isaiah and the Deliverance of Jerusalem*, JSOTSup 13 (Sheffield: JSOT Press, 1984).

—— *Prophecy and Covenant*, SBT 43 (London: SCM, 1965).

Clines, David J. A., *Job 1–20*, WBC 17 (Dallas: Word, 1989).

—— *The Theme of the Pentateuch*, JSOTSup 10 (Sheffield: JSOT Press, 1978).

Collins, John J., *Introduction to the Hebrew Bible* (Minneapolis: Augsburg Fortress, 2004).

Cook, Stephen L. 'Funerary Practices and Afterlife Expectations in Ancient Israel', *Religion Compass* 1.6 (2007), pp. 660–683.

Craigie, Peter C., *The Book of Deuteronomy*, NICOT (Grand Rapids: Eerdmans; London: Hodder & Stoughton, 1976).

—— *Psalms 1–50*, WBC 19 (Waco: Word, 1983).

Cross, Frank M., *Canaanite Myth and Hebrew Epic: Essays in the History and the Religion of Israel* (Cambridge, Mass.: Harvard University Press, 1973; repr., 1997).

Davidson, R., 'Universalism in Second Isaiah', *SJT* 16 (1963), pp. 166–185.

Day, John, *God's Conflict with the Dragon and the Sea: Echoes of a Canaanite Myth* (Cambridge: Cambridge University Press, 1985).

—— *Yahweh and the Gods and Goddesses of Canaan*, JSOTSup 265 (Sheffield: Sheffield Academic Press, 2000).

Day, John, Robert P. Gordon and Hugh G. M. Williamson (eds.), *Wisdom in Ancient Israel: Essays in honour of J. A. Emerton* (Cambridge: Cambridge University Press, 1995).

Dumbrell, William J., *Covenant and Creation: A Theology of the Old Testament Covenants* (Exeter: Paternoster, 1984; repr. Biblical and Theological Classics Library; Carlisle, Paternoster, 1997).

Ellison, H. L., *Men Spake from God: Studies in the Hebrew Prophets* (London: Paternoster, 1958).

Eslinger, Lyle, 'Viewpoints and Point of View in 1 Samuel 8–12', *JSOT* 26 (1983), pp. 61–76.

Exum, J. Cheryl, and David J. A. Clines (eds.), *The New Literary Criticism and the Hebrew Bible*, JSOTSup 143; Sheffield: JSOT Press, 1993).

Fitzmyer, Joseph A., *The One Who Is to Come* (Grand Rapids: Eerdmans, 2007).

Forsyth, Neil, *The Old Enemy* (Princeton: Princeton University Press, 1987).

Fretheim, Terence E., *God and World in the Old Testament: A Relational Theology of Creation* (Nashville: Abingdon, 2005).

Fyall, Robert S., *Now my Eyes Have Seen you: Images of Creation in the Book of Job*, NSBT 12 (Leicester: Apollos; Downers Grove: IVP, 2002).

Gelston, A., 'The Missionary Message of Second Isaiah', *SJT* 18 (1965), pp. 308–318.

Gnuse, Robert K., *No Other Gods: Emergent Monotheism in Israel*, JSOTSup 241 (Sheffield: Sheffield Academic Press, 1997).

Goldingay, John, *Daniel*, WBC 30 (Milton Keynes: Word, 1987).

—— *God's Prophet, God's Servant* (Exeter: Paternoster, 1984).

—— *Theological Diversity and the Authority of the Old Testament* (Grand Rapids: Eerdmans, 1987; repr. Biblical and Theological Classics Library; Carlisle: Paternoster, 1995).

Goppelt, L., *Typos: The Typological Interpretation of the Old Testament in the New* (Grand Rapids: Eerdmans, 1982).

Gottwald, Norman, K., *All the Kingdoms of the Earth: Israelite Prophecy and International Relations* (New York: Harper & Row, 1964).

Gowan, Donald E., *Eschatology in the Old Testament* (Philadelphia: Fortress, 1986).

—— *Theology of the Prophetic Books: The Death and Resurrection of Israel* (Louisville; London: Westminster John Knox, 1998).

Grams, Rollin G., 'Narrative Dynamics in Isaiah's and Matthew's Mission Theology', *Transformation* 21.4 (2004), pp. 238–255.

Green, Michael, *I Believe in the Holy Spirit* (London: Hodder & Stoughton, 1975).

Grisanti, Michael A., 'Israel's Mission to the Nations in Isaiah 40–55: An Update', *MSJ* 9.1 (1998), pp. 39–61.

Gunkel, Hermann, *Schöpfung und Chaos in Urzeit und Endzeit* (Göttingen: Vandenhoeck & Ruprecht, 1895), trans. K. William Whitney, Jr., as *Creation and Chaos in the Primeval Era and the Eschaton: A Religio-Historical Study of Genesis 1 and Revelation 12* (Grand Rapids: Eerdmans, 2006).

Gunn, David M., and Danna N. Fewell, *Narrative in the Hebrew Bible*, Oxford Bible Series (Oxford: Oxford University Press, 1993).

Habel, Norman C., *The Book of Job*, OTL (London: SCM, 1985).

Hafemann, Scott J. (ed.), *Biblical Theology: Retrospect and Prospect* (Leicester: Apollos; Downers Grove: IVP, 2002).

Hamilton, Victor P., *Genesis 1–17*, NICOT (Grand Rapids: Eerdmans, 1990).

Hanson, Paul D., 'Rebellion in Heaven, Azazel and Euhemeristic Heroes in 1 Enoch 6–11', *JBL* 96 (1977), pp. 195–233.

Hartley, John E., *The Book of Job*, NICOT (Grand Rapids: Eerdmans, 1991).

—— *Leviticus 1–27*, WBC 4 (Dallas: Word, 1992).

Hayes, John H., and Frederick Prussner, *Old Testament Theology: Its History and Development* (Atlanta: John Knox, 1985).

Heaton, E. W., *A Short Introduction to the Old Testament Prophets*, rev. ed. (Oxford: Oneworld, 1996).

Hess, Richard S., Philip E. Satterthwaite and Gordon J. Wenham (eds.), *He Swore an Oath* (Cambridge: Tyndale House, 1993).

Hess, Richard S., and David T. Tsumara (eds.), *I Studied Inscriptions From Before the Flood*, SBTS 4 (Winona Lake: Eisenbrauns, 1994).

Hess, Richard S., and Gordon J. Wenham (eds.), *Zion, City of our God* (Grand Rapids: Eerdmans, 1999).

Hubbard, David A., 'The Wisdom Movement and Israel's Covenant Faith', *TynBul* 17 (1966), pp. 3–33.

Johnston, Philip S., *Shades of Sheol: Death and Afterlife in the Old Testament* (Leicester: Apollos; Downers Grove: IVP, 2002).

Kaiser, Walter C., Jr., *The Messiah in the Old Testament*, Studies in Old Testament Biblical Theology (Grand Rapids: Zondervan, 1995).

—— *Mission in the Old Testament: Israel as a Light to the Nations* (Grand Rapids: Baker, 2000).

Kidner, Derek, *Genesis*, TOTC (Leicester: IVP, 1967).

—— *Psalms 1–72*, TOTC (Leicester: IVP, 1973).

—— *The Wisdom of Proverbs, Job and Ecclesiastes* (Leicester: IVP; Downers Grove: IVP, 1985).

Kitchen, Kenneth A., *Ancient Orient and Old Testament* (Downers Grove: IVP, 1966).

—— *On the Reliability of the Old Testament* (Grand Rapids; Cambridge: Eerdmans, 2003).

Kiuchi, Nobuyoshi, *Leviticus*, AOTC (Nottingham: Apollos; Downers Grove: IVP, 2007).

Knierim, Rolf P., *The Task of Old Testament Theology: Methods and Cases* (Grand Rapids: Eerdmans, 1995).

Knight, George A. F., *Theology in Pictures* (Edinburgh: Handsel, 1981).

Köstenberger, Andreas J., and Peter T. O'Brien, *Salvation to the Ends of the Earth: A Biblical Theology of Mission*, NSBT 11 (Leicester: Apollos; Downers Grove: IVP, 2001).

Levenson, Jon D., *Creation and the Persistence of Evil: The Jewish Drama of Divine Omnipotence* (Princeton: Princeton University Press, 1994).

—— *The Hebrew Bible, the Old Testament and Historical Criticism: Jews and Christians in Biblical Studies* (Louisville: Westminster John Knox, 1993).

—— *Resurrection and the Restoration of Israel: The Ultimate Victory of the God of Life* (New Haven: Yale University Press, 2006).

—— *Sinai and Zion: An Entry into the Jewish Bible*, New Voices in Biblical Studies (Minneapolis: Winston, 1985).

Lindblom, Johannes, *Prophecy in Ancient Israel* (Oxford: Blackwell, 1962).

Long, V. Philips, David W. Baker and Gordon J. Wenham (eds.), *Windows into Old Testament History* (Grand Rapids: Eerdmans, 2002).

Longenecker, Richard, *Biblical Exegesis in the Apostolic Period*, 2nd ed. (Grand Rapids: Eerdmans, 1999).

Longman III, Tremper, *Daniel*, NIVAC (Grand Rapids: Zondervan, 1999).

Lucas, Ernest C., *Daniel*, AOTC (Leicester: IVP, 2002).

McCarthy, Dennis J., *Old Testament Covenant* (Oxford: Blackwell, 1972).

McComiskey, Thomas Edward, *The Covenants of Promise* (Nottingham: IVP, 1985).

McKane, William, *Studies in the Patriarchal Narratives* (Edinburgh: Handsel, 1979).

Martens, Elmer A., *Old Testament Theology* (Grand Rapids: Baker, 1997).

Martin-Achard, Robert, *From Death to Life: A Study of the Development of the Doctrine of the Resurrection in the Old Testament* (Edinburgh: Oliver & Boyd, 1960).

Mays, James L., *Amos*, OTL (London: SCM, 1969).

Milgrom, Jacob, *Leviticus 1–16*, AB 3 (New York: Doubleday, 1991).

Millard, Alan R., 'A New Babylonian "Genesis" Story', *TynBul* 18 (1967), pp. 3–18.

Millard, Alan R., and Donald J. Wiseman (eds.), *Essays on the Patriarchal Narratives* (Leicester: IVP, 1980).

Miller, Patrick D., *Israelite Religion and Biblical Theology: Collected Essays*, JSOTSup 267 (Sheffield: Sheffield Academic Press, 2000).

Miscall, David, *The Workings of Old Testament Narrative*, SBL Semeia Studies (Philadelphia: Fortress; Chico: Scholars Press, 1983).

Moberley, R. W. L., *The Old Testament of the Old Testament: Patriarchal Narratives and Mosaic Yahwism*, OBT (Minneapolis: Fortress, 1992).

Mowinckel, Sigmund, *He That Cometh* (Oxford: Blackwell, 1956; repr. Grand Rapids: Eerdmans, 2005).

—— *The Psalms in Israel's Worship*, 2 vols. (Oxford: Oxford University Press, 1962; repr. Grand Rapids: Eerdmans, 2004).

Murray, Robert, *The Cosmic Covenant: Biblical Themes of Justice and Peace and the Integrity of Creation* (London: Sheed & Ward, 1992).

Nickelsburg, George W. E., 'Apocalyptic and Myth in 1 Enoch 6–11', *JBL* 96 (1977), pp. 383–405.

North, Christopher R., *The Suffering Servant in Deutero-Isaiah* (Oxford: Oxford University Press, 1948).

Okoye, James Chukwuma, *Israel and the Nations: A Mission Theology of the Old Testament* (Maryknoll: Orbis, 2006).

Orlinsky, H. M., and N. H. Snaith, *Studies in the Second Part of the Book of Isaiah*, VTSup 14 (Leiden: Brill, 1967).

Osborne, Grant R., *The Hermeneutical Spiral: A Comprehensive Introduction to Biblical Interpretation*, 2nd ed. (Downers Grove: IVP, 2006).

Oswalt, John N., *The Book of Isaiah, 1–39*, NICOT (Grand Rapids: Eerdmans, 1986).

—— *The Book of Isaiah 40–66*, NICOT (Grand Rapids: Eerdmans, 1997).

Parry, Robin, *Old Testament Story and Christian Ethics: The Rape of Dinah as a Case Study*, Paternoster Bible Monographs (Carlisle: Paternoster, 2004).

Porteous, Norman, *Daniel*, OTL (London: SCM, 1965).

Porter, Stanley, E. (ed.), *The Messiah in the Old and New Testaments*, McMaster New Testament Studies (Grand Rapids: Eerdmans, 2007).

Rad, Gerhard von, *From Genesis to Chronicles: Explorations in Old Testament Theology*, Fortress Classics in Biblical Studies (Philadelphia: Augsburg Fortress, 2005).

—— *God at Work in Israel* (Nashville: Abingdon, 1980).

—— *The Problem of the Hexateuch and Other Essays* (Edinburgh: Oliver & Boyd, 1966).

—— *Studies in Deuteronomy*, SBT 9 (London: SCM, 1953).

—— *Wisdom in Israel* (London: SCM, 1972).

Rea, John, *The Holy Spirit in the Bible* (London: Marshall Pickering, 1992).

Ringgren, Helmer, *Israelite Religion* (London: SPCK, 1966).

—— *The Messiah in the Old Testament*, SBT 18 (London: SCM, 1956).

Robertson, O. Palmer, *Christ of the Covenants* (Phillipsburg: P. & R., 1980).

Robinson, H. Wheeler, *Religious Ideas of the Old Testament*, Studies in Theology (London: Duckworth, 1913).

Routledge, Robin L., 'Guest or Gatecrasher: Questioning Assumptions in a Narrative Approach to the Old Testament', *JEBS* 3.3 (2003), pp. 17–28.

—— '*Hesed* as Obligation: A Re-Examination', *TynBul* 46.1 (1995), pp. 188–191.

Routledge, Robin L., 'Is There a Narrative Substructure Underlying the Book of Isaiah?', *TynBul* 55.2 (2004), pp. 183–204.

—— 'The Siege and Deliverance of the City of David in Isaiah 29:1–8', *TynBul* 43.1 (1992), pp. 181–190.

Rowley, H. H., *Israel's Mission to the World* (London: SPCK, 1939).

—— *The Servant of the Lord and Other Essays on the Old Testament* (Oxford: Blackwell, 1965).

—— *Worship in Ancient Israel* (London: SPCK, 1967).

—— (ed.), *Studies in Old Testament Prophecy: Presented to Professor Theodore H. Robinson* (Edinburgh: T. & T. Clark, 1950).

Russell, D. S., *Apocalyptic Ancient and Modern* (London: SCM, 1978).

—— *The Jews from Alexander to Herod* (Oxford: Oxford University Press, 1967).

—— *The Method and Message of Jewish Apocalyptic*, OTL (London: SCM, 1964).

Satterthwaite, Philip E., Richard S. Hess and Gordon J. Wenham (eds.), *The Lord's Anointed: Interpretation of Old Testament Messianic Texts* (Carlisle: Paternoster, 1995).

Sawyer, John F., *The Fifth Gospel: Isaiah in the History of Christianity* (Cambridge: Cambridge University Press, 1996).

Schauss, Hayyim, *The Jewish Festivals* (London: Jewish Chronicle Publications, 1986).

Seitz, Christopher R., *Figured Out: Typology and Providence in Christian Scripture* (Louisville: Westminster John Knox, 2001).

—— *Isaiah 1–39*, Interpretation (Louisville: John Knox, 1993).

Smith, Mark S., *The Early History of God: Yahweh and the Other Deities in Ancient Israel*, 2nd ed. (Grand Rapids: Eerdmans, 2002).

—— *The Origins of Biblical Monotheism: Israel's Polytheistic Background and the Ugaritic Texts* (Oxford: Oxford University Press, 2001).

Snaith, Norman H., *Distinctive Ideas of the Old Testament* (London: Epworth, 1953).

Spronk, Klaas, *Beatific Afterlife in Ancient Israel and in the Ancient Near East*, AOAT 219 (Neukirchen-Vluyn: Neukirchener, 1986).

Stuhlmueller, Carroll, *Creative Redemption in Deutero-Isaiah*, AnBib 43 (Rome: Biblical Institute, 1970).

Thompson, John A., *Deuteronomy*, TOTC (Leicester: IVP, 1974).

Trible, Phyllis, *God and the Rhetoric of Sexuality*, OBT 2 (Philadelphia: Fortress, 1978).

Tsumura, David T., *Creation and Destruction: A Reappraisal of the Chaoskampf Theory in the Old Testament* (Winona Lake: Eisenbrauns, 2005).

Turner, Lawrence A., *Announcements of Plot in Genesis*, JSOTSup 96 (Sheffield: Sheffield Academic Press, 1990).

Tur-Sinai, Naftali H., *The Book of Job* (Jerusalem: Kiryath-Sepher, 1957).

Vanhoozer, Kevin J., *Is There a Meaning in this Text? The Bible, the Reader and the Morality of Literary Knowledge* (Leicester: Apollos, 1998).

Vogels, Walter F., *God's Universal Covenant* (Ottawa: University of Ottawa Press, 1979).

Vriezen, Th. C., 'Prophecy and Eschatology', *Congress Volume, Copenhagen 1953*, VTSup 1 (Leiden: Brill, 1953), pp. 199–229.

Walker, P. W. L. (ed.), *Jerusalem Past and Present in the Purposes of God* (Cambridge: Tyndale House, 1992).

Walton, John H., *Ancient Near Eastern Thought and the Old Testament: Introducing the Conceptual World of the Hebrew Bible* (Grand Rapids: Baker, 2006; Leicester: Apollos, 2007).

Watts, Rikk E., 'Echoes from the Past: Israel's Ancient Traditions and the Destiny of the Nations in Isaiah 40–55', *JSOT* 28.4 (2004), pp. 481–508.

Weinfeld, Moshe, 'The Covenant of Grant in the Ancient Near East', *JAOS* 90 (1970), pp. 184–203.

Wenham, Gordon, J., *Genesis 1–15*, WBC 1 (Milton Keynes: Word, 1991).

—— *Genesis 16–50*, WBC 2 (Dallas: Word, 1994).

—— *Leviticus*, NICOT (London: Hodder & Stoughton, 1979).

—— *Numbers*, TOTC (Leicester: IVP, 1981).

—— *Story as Torah: Reading the Old Testament Ethically* (Edinburgh: T. & T. Clarke, 2000).

Westermann, Claus, *Creation* (London: SPCK, 1974).

—— *Isaiah 40–66*, OTL (London: SCM, 1969).

—— *Praise and Lament in the Psalms* (Edinburgh: T. & T. Clark, 1981).

—— (ed.), *Essays on Old Testament Interpretation* (London: SCM, 1963).

Whybray, R. N., *Isaiah 40–66*, NCB (London: Marshall, Morgan & Scott, 1975).

Wilkinson, David, *The Message of Creation: Encountering the Lord of the Universe*, BST (Leicester: IVP, 2002).

Williamson, H. G. M., *Variations on a Theme: King, Messiah and Servant in the Book of Isaiah*, Didsbury Lectures (Carlisle: Paternoster, 1998).

Winkle, D. W. van, 'Proselytes in Isaiah XL–LV? A Study of Isaiah XLIV 1–5', *VT* 47.3 (1997), pp. 341–359.

—— 'The Relationship of the Nations to Yahweh and to Israel in Isaiah XL–LV', *VT* 35.4 (1985), pp. 446–458.

Wolff, Hans Walter, *Joel and Amos*, Hermeneia (Philadelphia: Fortress, 1977).

Wright, Christopher J. H., *God's People in God's Land: Family, Land and Property in the Old Testament* (Grand Rapids: Eerdmans; Exeter: Paternoster, 1990).

—— *Walking in the Ways of the Lord: The Ethical Authority of the Old Testament* (Leicester: Apollos, 1995).

Wright, George E., *God who Acts: Biblical Theology as Recital* (London: SCM, 1952).

Wright, N. T., *The New Testament and the People of God* (Minneapolis: Fortress, 1992).

—— *The Resurrection of the Son of God* (London: SPCK, 2003).

Zimmerli, Walther, *Man and his Hope in the Old Testament* (London: SCM, 1971).

INDEX OF SCRIPTURE REFERENCES

INDEX OF NAMES

Includes scholars who are quoted or whose views are specifically noted.

INDEX OF SUBJECTS